AUGUSTINE

and the Bible

THE BIBLE
THROUGH THE AGES

Volume 2

SERIES DIRECTORS

Charles Kannengiesser & Pamela Bright

The University of Notre Dame Press
gratefully acknowledges the generous support of
THE ESTATE OF NANCY R. DREUX
in the publication of this Great Work in Translation.

AUGUSTINE

and the Bible

EDITED AND TRANSLATED BY

Pamela Bright

Based on BIBLE DE TOUS LES TEMPS, volume 3,
Saint Augustin et la Bible, edited by Anne-Marie La Bonnardière

UNIVERSITY OF NOTRE DAME PRESS / NOTRE DAME, INDIANA

Translation and new edition published 1999 by
UNIVERSITY OF NOTRE DAME PRESS
NOTRE DAME, INDIANA 46556
ALL RIGHTS RESERVED

Book design by
DESIGNER'S INK

SET 10 ON 13 PALATINO

Production manager
DON J. BEVILLE

Manufactured in the United States of America by the
AMERICAN BOOK COMPANY, INC.

a division of BEVILLE PUBLISHING

LIBRARY OF CONGRESS CATALOGING-IN-PUBLICATION DATA

AUGUSTINE AND THE BIBLE

Edited [and translated] by
PAMELA BRIGHT

P. CM.

BASED ON: SAINT AUGUSTIN ET LA BIBLE, ©1986

INCLUDES BIBLIOGRAPHICAL REFERENCES AND INDEXES.
ISBN 0-268-00654-7 (CLOTH: ALK. PAPER).
ISBN 0-268-00655-5 (PBK. : ALK. PAPER)
1. AUGUSTINE, SAINT, BISHOP OF HIPPO—
CONTRIBUTIONS IN BIBLICAL INTERPRETATION.
2. BIBLE—CRITICISM, INTERPRETATION, ETC.—
HISTORY—EARLY CHURCH, CA. 30-600.
I. BRIGHT, PAMELA, 1937- .
II. SAINT AUGUSTIN ET LA BIBLE.
BS500.A84 1997
220'.092—dc21
CIP 97-20807

To Mary Rose MacGinley
whose scholarly and spiritual presence has enriched my life.

Contents

Foreword

The series *Bible de Tous les Temps* (Paris: Beauchesne Éditeur) consists of eight volumes:

1. *Le monde grec ancien et la Bible*, ed. C. Mondésert (1984);
2. *Le monde latin antique et la Bible*, eds. J. Fontaine and C. Pietri (1985);
3. *Saint Augustin et la Bible*, ed. A.-M. La Bonnardière (1986);
4. *Le Moyen-Age et la Bible*, eds. P. Riché and G. Lobrichon (1984);
5. *Le temps des Réformes et la Bible*, eds. G. Bedouelle and B. Roussel (1989);
6. *Le Grand Siècle et la Bible*, ed. J.-R. Armogathe (1989);
7. *Le siècle des Lumières et la Bible*, eds. Y. Belaval and D. Bourel (1986);
8. *Le monde contemporain et la Bible*, eds. C. Savard and J.-N. Aletti (1985).

After almost ten years of preparation under the direction of the best experts available, the project developed into a collaboration of two hundred and fifty European and American scholars, the authors of approximately 5,000 pages of text. Highly praised by a chorus of critics on the international scene, *Bible de Tous les Temps* represents a substantial contribution to the current retrieval of ancient Christian traditions by historians and other specialists.

With the kind agreement of the publishing house Beauchesne and the enthusiastic support of Jim Langford, director of the University of Notre Dame Press, two American shoots have grown out of the mighty tree planted in Paris: one due to the editorial care of Paul Blowers (Emmanuel School of Religion, Johnson City, TN), *The Bible in Greek Christian Antiquity;* and a second, *Augustine and the Bible*, secured by Pamela Bright (Concordia University, Montreal). Other volumes are in planning.

Each editor of the new volumes endeavors to retain the riches of the French edition by selecting contributions of the original edition, translated from French into English, while adding new contributions directly written in English and reflecting a broad spectrum of present scholarship.

CHARLES KANNENGIESSER
C. F. Huisking Professor Emeritus of Theology
University of Notre Dame, Indiana

PAMELA BRIGHT
Concordia University, Montreal

Easter Sunday, 1997

Acknowledgments

The volume, *Augustine and the Bible*, is the result of persevering efforts by a number of people since 1992 when I arrived in Montreal. First, I wish to acknowledge the financial assistance of Concordia University without whose grant monies this project would have been impossible. Then I wish to thank the translation and editorial team that worked with me in the Department of Theological Studies at Concordia University at key points in the production of the book. First in the translating team I wish to acknowledge the work of Constance McLeese who contributed so much to this volume as she worked on her own doctoral project on gender issues in Augustine's biblical canon. Linden Rogers generously contributed her computer and "scanning" know-how at a critical moment. A special thanks to Cher Jacek who has proved herself a true partner in this enterprise from beginning to end.

To Jim Langford and his staff at Notre Dame Press my sincere gratitude, not only for their professionalism, but for the constant encouragement and support in the face of obstacles and difficulties. That the volume has reached completion on Easter Sunday is something that Augustine would have appreciated.

Introduction

The very title of the volume, *Augustine and the Bible*, immediately calls for a flurry of explanations. Such a title should announce a series in itself, rather than a single, rather slim volume within a series. This volume was never intended as an exhaustive treatment of such a vast topic, nor was it even meant to be representative of contemporary scholarship on Augustine and the Bible. Charles Kannengiesser's selected bibliography of the scholarship of the past fifty years is a telling indication of what would be the scope of such a task. Rather, the intention is that it be a forum for a conversation about Augustine and the Bible. Certainly, it is our hope that this will be an open-ended conversation in which the present volume will have a lively contribution.

The present work is derived from the beautifully wrought volume *Saint Augustin et la Bible*, under the direction of Anne-Marie La Bonnardière, the third volume of the series *Bible de Tous les Temps* (Beauchesne, Paris: 1986, general editor, Charles Kannengiesser.) The French edition was acclaimed as a monument to the scholarly research of Anne-Marie la Bonnardière and her colleagues. It was organized around eight themes: Augustine's biblical initiation, the Bible and liturgy, the Bible and prayer, the Bible in Augustine's letters, in his preaching, and in polemics, the Bible in the *City of God* and finally as a mirror of Christian ethics. The English volume takes up a number of these themes and structures them into four sections: Augustine's biblical initiation, his encounter with the hermeneutics of his native province, Augustine and polemics, and finally his ministry of the Word. In its structure the present volume stresses a chronological, rather than a thematic treatment of the subject. Part I examines various aspects of Augustine's biblical initiation, Part II his early (but continuing) encounters with Tyconius's thought, Part III, Augustine's earliest and the latest involvement in polemical disputes, and finally Part IV introduces instances of his mature ministry of the Word. The limitations of space imposed severe restrictions on the selection of articles for translation from the French edition. As well, there was a need to be more inclusive of English-speaking scholars. In this respect, *Augustine and the Bible* is a complement to the French volume, and as such would hope to raise awareness among English-speaking readers of the rich specialization to be found in *Saint Augustin et la Bible*.

In Part I, "Encountering the Word," Anne-Marie la Bonnardière is the guide to Augustine's biblical initiation as she poses a series of questions to the reader. What can be known of the stages of Augustine's encounter with the biblical text? In what circumstances? Who were his teachers? Which biblical texts were formative for Augustine before he assumed his ministry of the Word? Even more basically, what canon of scripture was authoritative? What versions did he use? Then Mark Vessey allows the reader to enter into the "literary-colloquial mode" of biblical exegesis found in Augustine's correspondence with fellow exegetes. This study is a reminder of the interpersonal—essentially social—dimension of Augustine's biblical initiation. Finally, Michael Cameron studies the stages of development of the christological core of Augustine's biblical reflection, wherein the Word of God / Word Incarnate hold time and eternity together.

Part II is devoted to a very different kind of encounter— Augustine's grappling with an idiosyncratic hermeneutical method originating in the Province of Africa. Roman Africa saw some of the earliest Latin versions of the Bible. Here the local Christian communities were enriched by the brilliant (and controversial) writings of Tertullian, of Cyprian, and later the writings of Parmenian, the successor to Donatus, and of Optatus of Milevis who opposed Parmenian's ecclesiology and exegesis. This complex legacy lies behind the *Book of Rules* of the Donatist theologian and exegete, Tyconius. The "conflict of hermeneutics" between Augustine and Tyconius explored by Pamela Bright, Robert Kugler and Charles Kannengiesser, was kept separate from the following section on the bible and polemics because it demonstrated Augustine's gradual "inculturization" into his own African milieu. It underlines the fact that Augustine's biblical initiation was outside his own African christianity— first in heterodox circles in Carthage, and then in the intellectual ferment of the Milanese church. At first glance this distinctively African hermeneutics may have seemed alien and even fossilized to the new convert on his return to his homeland. But it was through this encounter that the young priest, soon to be bishop, was plunged into the heart of the ecclesial questions—pastoral and theological at once—as Tyconius challenged him to find his way through the "immense forest of prophecy." This very image from the prologue of the *Book of Rules* is still playing in Augustine's mind as he writes the *Confessions* ten years after his return to Africa: "Grant thereof space for our meditation amongst the hidden things of Thy law, nor close it against those who knock. For not in vain hast thou willed that the obscure secret of so many pages should be written. Nor is it that those forests should not have their harts, betaking themselves therein, and ranging, and walking..." (*Confessions* XI, 3; *NPNF* 1, 164).

Part III, "The Sword of the Word," leads straight into the heat of battle, with Augustine wielding the broadsword of the Word of God. Anne-Marie la Bonnardière offers a panoramic overview, while Roland Teske explores Augustine's first foray into the field of biblical polemics when he opposes the Manichees, the very group who had first introduced him to a study of the "obscurities" of the biblical text. Gerald Bonner rounds up the section with a reflection on Augustine's final polemic encounter with the formidable Pelagius and the sophisticated and articulate group around him.

In Part IV is heard the most familiar voice of Augustine—at least familiar to his own congregation—that of the tireless preacher of the Word. Here is his home and his place, his preferred environment. One hears Augustine nourishing, admonishing, and delighting his congregation, weaving before their eyes a variegated tapestry of biblical citations and allusions as he leads them in a celebration of the goodness of God, throughout the cosmos and throughout history. The introductory essay by Anne-Marie la Bonnardière is followed by Joseph Wolinski's study of Augustine's meditation of a phrase in Psalm 18 (LXX), "He pitched his tent in the sun." The riches of thought evoked by this single phrase give an indication of the difficulties of selecting representative material for an adequate appreciation of Augustine's ministry of the Word! Michel Albaric's study of Sermon 227 emphasizes the importance of the "liturgical Bible" in Augustine's teaching. Such a sermon reminds us of the source of Augustine's magisterial ease with the biblical text—the interplay of his constant personal prayer and his daily praying of the liturgy. Constance McLeese brings a needed focus to the thorny question of how Augustine's interpretation of the Bible, and indeed his very selection of biblical texts, has left an ambiguous legacy for gender issues. Finally, in selecting Sermon 43, Albert Verwilghen leads us to the paradox of exaltation and lowliness that lies at the heart of Augustine's encounter with Christ, the Word of God. It was the paradox that Augustine encountered in the trauma of his conversion, but it was also the paradox that continued to fuel his imagination and leave his mark on his life-long appropriation and service of the scriptures.

In the closing books of the *Confessions*, Augustine welcomes the views of his "conloquitors," other interpreters of the Bible, *cum his enim volo coram te aliquid conloqui, deus meus*. He, himself, was such a lover of conversation that it seemed imperative to invite him into the circle of discussion initiated by the present volume, especially on a topic so dear to his heart. Besides the extracts from his sermons in each of the four sections, Augustine's is the first voice to be heard at the beginning of Part I in an extract from Book XI of the *Confessions,* and his is the final comment on the relationship between faith and understanding in Part IV: "Understand, in order to believe my word; believe, in order to understand the Word of God." His voice challenges what can be a tendency to abstractness of scholarly deliberations, and perhaps provides an ironic comment on the best efforts to engage such a multi-faceted mind with whom one would prefer to spend an afternoon in the garden of Cassiciacum, rather than pore over manuscripts that hold the embers of his glowing words.

PAMELA BRIGHT

PART I

Encountering the Word:
Augustine's Biblical Initiation

1

Augustine, Confessions XI, 3–4

O Lord my God, hear my prayer, and let Thy mercy regard my longing, since it burns not for myself alone, but because it desires to benefit brotherly charity; and Thou seest my heart, that so it is. I would sacrifice to Thee the service of my thought and tongue; and do Thou give what I may offer unto thee. For "I am poor and needy," (Ps. 86:1) "Thou rich unto all that call upon thee." (Rom 10:12), who free from care carest for us. Circumcise from all rashness and from all lying my inward and outward lips. (Ex 6:12) Let Thy Scriptures be my chaste delights. Neither let me be deceived in them, nor deceive out of them. Lord, hear and pity, O Lord my God, light of the blind and strength of the weak; even also light of those who see, and strength of the strong, hearken unto my soul, and hear it crying "out of the depths." (Ps. 130:1) For unless thine ears be present in the depths also, whither shall we go? whither shall we cry? "The day is Thine, and the night also is Thine." (Ps. 74:16) At Thy nod the moments flee away. Grant thereof space for our meditations among the hidden things of Thy law, not close it against us who knock. For not in vain hast Thou willed that the obscure secret of so many pages should be written. Not is it that those forests have not their harts, (Ps. 29:9) betaking themselves therein, and ranging, and walking, and feeding, lying down, and ruminating. Behold Thy voice is my joy, Thy voice surpasses the abundance of pleasures. Give that I may love, for I do love; and this Thou has given. Abandon not Thine own gifts, not despise Thy grass that thirsts. Let me confess unto Thee whatever I shall have found in Thy books, and let me hear the voice of praise, and let me imbibe Thee, and reflect on the wonderful things of Thy law; (Ps. 26:7) and from the beginning, wherein Thou madest the heaven and the earth, unto the everlasting kingdom of Thy holy city that is with Thee.

Lord, have mercy on me and hear my desire, for I think that it is not of the earth, nor of gold and silver, and precious stones, nor gorgeous apparel, nor honours and powers, nor the pleasures of the flesh, nor necessaries for the body, and this life of our pilgrimage; all which are added to those who seek Thy kingdom and Thy righteousness. (Mat 6:33) Behold, O Lord my God, whence is my desire. The unrighteous have told me of delights, but not such as Thy law, O Lord. (Ps. 99:85) Behold whence is my desire. Behold, Father, look and see and approve; and let it be pleasing in the sight of Thy mercy, that I may find grace before Thee, that the secret things of Thy Word may be opened unto me when I knock. I beseech by our Lord Jesus Christ, Thy Son, "the Man of Thy right hand, the Son of man, whom Thou made strong for Thyself" (Ps. 80:17) as Thy mediator and ours, through whom Thou hast sought us, although not seeking Thee, but did seek us that we might seek Thee, – Thy Word through whom Thou hast made all things (John 1:3) and amongst them me also, – Thy Only–begotten, through whom Thou hast called to adoption the believing people, and therein me also. I beseech Thee through Him who sitteth at Thy right hand, and "maketh intercession for us," (Rom 8:34) "in whom is hid all treasures of wisdom and knowledge." (Col 2:6) Him do I seek in Thy books. Of Him did Moses write; (John 5:4–6) this saith Himself; this saith the Truth.

2

Augustine's Biblical Initiation

ANNE-MARIE LA BONNARDIÈRE

At the age of nineteen, after reading Cicero's *Hortensius*, which at first had filled him with exaltation, Augustine experienced a pang of disappointment. He wrote:

> ...in my ardor, the only thing I found lacking was that the name of Christ was not there. For with my mother's milk my infant heart had drunk in, and still held that name deep down in it, according to Your mercy, O Lord, the name of Your Son, my Saviour, and whatsoever lacked that name, no matter how learned and excellently written and true, could not win me wholly (*Confessions* 3.4.8).

When Augustine decided to abandon the Manichean sect a decade later and was tempted for a while by the skepticism of the academics, he described his anguished doubt in these terms:

> So in what I thought to be the manner of the Academics — that is to say, doubting of all things and wavering between one and another — I decided that I must leave the Manichees; for in that time of doubt, I did not think I could remain in a sect to which I now preferred certain of the philosophers. Yet I absolutely refused to entrust the care of my sick soul to the philosophers, because they were without the saving name of Christ. I determined, then, to go on as a catechumen in the Catholic Church — the church of my parents — and to remain in that state until some certain light should appear by which I might steer my course (*Confessions* 5.14.25).

After his revelation caused by a sermon of Ambrose's concerning the meaning of man created in God's image in Genesis 1:26, Augustine exclaimed:

> So I was first confounded and then enlightened. And I rejoiced, O my God, that Your only church, the Body of Your only Son, in which the name of Christ had been put upon me while I was still an infant, had no taste for such puerile nonsense (*Confessions* 6.4.5.).

In light of these secrets, he called to mind how on the threshold of his first childhood, Monica had exercised a determining influence by teaching her small children the gestures of prayer and the invocation of Jesus's name. Despite numerous obstacles, for thirty years the search for Christ's name became the absolute criteria for truth and the interior light which guided Augustine's path.

Between the ages of seven and sixteen, at Thagaste and later Madaura, Augustine pursued his elementary and secondary studies under the vigilant supervision of his father. This provided him with the liberal culture foundational for a professional life. His *Confessions* vehemently underline the imbalance which such an education provided young children, based as it was on false and immoral fables written by pagan authors (albeit illustrious pagans such as Virgil and Homer) and a Christian formation wherein the sacred writings appeared to have little solid foundation. In 409 when Augustine wrote to the pagan Nectarius of Calama (modern Guelma) concerning the grave troubles which existed between the Christians and the pagans, he commented:

> Personally I don't ever remember reading that a life of indigence makes one forever unhappy; I read it neither in our sacred books, to the study of which I admit with regret that I applied myself too late, nor in your books which I had in my hands since my childhood (*Confessions* 3.4.8).

This letter echoes the earlier testimony of the *Confessions* wherein Augustine regrets that the rudiments of reading and writing, the obvious base of all higher study, cannot be taught from the Bible. He deplores once having been obligated to compose and deliver a speech, supposedly by Juno, in Virgilian style:

> What could all this mean to me, O My true Life, My God? Why was there more applause for the performance I gave than for so many classmates of my own age? Was not the whole business so much smoke and wind? Surely some other matter could have been found to exercise mind and tongue. Thy praises, Lord, might have upheld the fresh young shoot of my heart, so that it might not have been whirled away by empty trifles, defiled, a shameful prey to birds (*Confessions* 1.17.27).

Augustine took up this theme at a much later date during a sermon delivered at Utica, in the month of August 417. The bishop of Hippo, received by his colleagues in the Basilica dedicated to the martyrs of Massa Candida, commented that day on Psalm 144 which glorifies God. After his usual fashion, Augustine picked out verses of the psalm and commented upon them one after the other. Verse 4 states: "...and they will announce your force." This can also be translated as "...and they will proclaim your power." Augustine took advantage of the occasion to remind his listeners of a current pedagogical custom practiced by the grammarians. In order to teach children the art of composing adulatory praise they were asked to write hymns to the sun, the sky, the earth, the rose, or the laurel. All these objects of praise are the works of God, insisted Augustine, however while the creations are glorified the Creator is ignored.[1]

Deficient as Augustine's Christian education was during his youth, it was not nonexistent. Aside from the daily example of his mother, Augustine alludes to the influence of men of prayer but remains silent about their names and their positions. Are they members of the clergy from Thagaste? He writes:

> Yet, Lord, I observed men praying to You: and I learnt to do likewise, thinking of You (to the best of my understanding) as some great being who, though unseen, could hear and help me. As a boy I fell into the way of calling upon You, my Help and my Refuge; and in those prayers I broke the strings of my tongue — praying to You, small as I was but with no small energy, that I might not be beaten at school (*Confessions* 1.9.14).

As a young child Augustine had received the first rites of the initiation leading to Baptism. He wrote: "Even as a boy, of course, I had heard of an eternal life promised because the Lord our God had come down in His humility upon our pride. And I was signed with the sign of His Cross and seasoned with His salt as I came new from the womb of my mother, who had great trust in You" (*Confessions* 1.11.17). This knowledge was enough to persuade the young Augustine to ask for the baptism of Christ when he was gravely ill and close to death. After he was restored to health, the baptism was put off. However in Augustine's judgment, on the whole, there was an imbalance between what he learned in school and his Christian background. It is not surprising to read Augustine's comment in the beginning of his anti–Manichean treatise *The Two Souls* that "there are many things that I should have done to avoid having ripped from my heart so easily and quickly either by the error or trickery, of misguided or deceitful men, the seeds of true religion which had been happily sowed in me from my childhood."[2] Augustine reproached the education provided to schoolchildren considering it to inculcate good words rather than good works. The focus was upon knowing how to speak well rather than to live well. Augustine alludes to himself in his interpretation of the prodigal son:

> For to be darkened in heart is to be far from Your face. It is not on our feet or by movement in space that we go from You or return to You: The prodigal son did not charter horses or chariots or ships, or fly with wings or journey on his two feet to that far country where he wasted in luxurious living what You as a loving father had given him on his departure — loving when You didst give, more loving still to Your son when he returned, all poor and stripped. To be lustful, that is darkened, in heart, is to be far from Your face (*Confessions* 1.18.3).

In this adaptation of the parable, Augustine locates the separation from the Father to the end of his second childhood and secondary studies. The Father whom Augustine addresses right from the start of the *Confessions* remains the self same to whose mercy he celebrates until the very last pages.

Augustine turned sixteen near the end of 369. It was the beginning of his adolescence and he traces its lively evolution in Books 2 to 6 of the *Confessions*. Two statements, forming an inclusion, are characteristic of Augustine's harsh judgment upon his life from age sixteen to twenty–nine. Book 3 opens with the declaration: "I came to Carthage, where a cauldron of illicit loves leapt and boiled about me" (*Confessions* 3.1.1). Augustine introduces Book 7: "Now my evil sinful youth was over and I had come on into young manhood..." (*Confessions* 7.1.1) This period of Augustine's life has provoked a plethora of literature. We have a single focus: What was Augustine's biblical initiation between 370 and 385?

Difficulties forced Augustine's father Patricius, to interrupt his son's education. Augustine had to return from Madaura to Thagaste and spend his sixteenth year in idleness, the account of which makes up Book 2 of the *Confessions*. A new inclusion, inspired by the parable of the prodigal son frames the narrative: "I departed further from You and You left me to myself" (*Confessions* 2.2.2). The section concludes: "I slid away from You and I went astray, O my God, deviating from Your stability in the days of my youth, and I became to myself a land of want *et factus sum mihi regio egestatis*" (*Confessions* 2.10.18).

Meanwhile Romanianus, a rich friend of Patricius, aware that Augustine was wasting his intellectual gifts in pursuit of leisure, covered the tuition for Augustine to study at Carthage to follow the studies which would enable him to become a rhetor. The youth studied at Carthage between 370 and 373. Several fateful events occurred in quick succession.

Eagerly plunging into tumultuous city life with its many licentious pleasures, Augustine quickly met the woman who would remain his concubine for fourteen years. "If the dates are precise," wrote H.–I. Marrou, "it establishes that he is bound to his companion from the age of seventeen, in a state of concubinage, which the morals of the time and the law, if not Christian morality, considered quite normal. For fourteen years he remained faithful to the woman who gave birth to their son Adeodatus during the first year of their relationship."[3] It was in fact a monogamous relationship of Roman concubinage the morality of which was admitted in 400 at the First Council of Toledo. It was a kind of morganatic marriage, meaning that it was contracted between two persons of different social status.

In 373, Augustine discovered Cicero's philosophical work, the *Hortensius*. It galvanized him and sparked a genuine quest for wisdom:

> Suddenly all the vanity I had hoped in I saw as worthless, and with an incredible intensity of desire I longed after immortal wisdom. I had begun that journey upwards by which I was to return to You (*Confessions* 3.4.7).

This allusion to the parable of the prodigal son marks the decisive moment which was the beginning of a long and painful return to the Father. We have already pointed out that the outburst of emotion which Augustine experienced while reading the *Hortensius* was dashed when he discovered that the Saviour's name was not there.

Augustine's immediate reaction was to apply himself to the study of Scripture. He had spontaneously desired to understand what the Scriptures were. This was followed by disenchantment, the disenchantment of a purist. Some fourteen years later, in the *Confessions*, Augustine analyzed this first encounter with the Bible:

> But what I came upon was something not grasped by the proud, not revealed either to children, something utterly humble in the hearing but sublime in the doing, and shrouded deep in mystery. And I was not of the nature to enter into it or bend my neck to follow it. (Augustine is writing in 397.) When I first read those Scriptures, I did not feel in the least what I have just said; they seemed to me unworthy to be compared with the majesty of Cicero. My conceit was repelled by their simplicity, and I had not the mind to penetrate into their depths. They were indeed of a nature to grow in Your little ones. But I could not bear to be a little one; I was only swollen with pride, but to myself I seemed a very big man (*Confessions* 3.5.9).

One wonders which portions of the Old or New Testament Augustine the aesthetic humanist, even more enraptured by beautiful language than philo-

9

sophical ideas, touched upon such that his sensibilities were so affronted. There was no immediate follow–up after this initial foray. One notes only that Augustine's Christian milk received from the bosom of the Church (*Catholica*) had been too insubstantial to allow him to surmount the shock in the difference in literary style between Cicero and the Bible.

Goaded by his desire for wisdom and disillusioned with the Bible, Augustine, attempting to return to the Father, errs by embarking upon the wrong road. Ill–equipped to grasp at the intellectual and the more profound spiritual level of the "hidden mysteries" of Scripture, August-ine was easy prey to the enterprising and subtle propaganda of the Manicheans. During the period when his contemporaries in the Eastern Churches, such as John Chrysostom, were receiving their scriptural ini-tiation in the fervor of eremitic or monastic life, Augustine and August-ine alone, experiences more than nine years of heretical exegesis.

> I fell in with a sect of men talking high–sounding nonsense, carnal and worldly men. The snares of the devil were in their mouths, to trap souls with an arrangement of the syllables of the names of God the Father and of the Lord Jesus Christ and of the Paraclete, the Holy Ghost, our Com-forter. Their names were always on their lips, but only as sounds and tongue noises; for their heart was empty of the true meaning (*Confes-sions* 3.6.10).

It is significant that in the *Confessions*, Augustine begins his denunciation of Manichean errors with an allusion to the Trinity. In 373, the hope of having finally found the name of Christ seduced him. In 397, nearly a quarter of a century later, his understanding had been secured. This Trinitarian text from the *Confessions* becomes highly significant when com-pared to Faustus's profession of Manichean faith which Augustine has included in the *Against Faustus*:

> God the all–powerful Father, Christ his Son from the Holy Spirit, we wor-ship the one identical deity which has these three names. But we believe that the Father lives in that supreme and original light which Paul called inaccessible (1 Tim. 6:10) that the Son exists in created light, which is vis-ible and derived, and because the Son is a double entity, the Apostle has knowledge of him when he said that Christ is the Power and the Wisdom of God. (1 Cor. 1:24) We believe that his Power resides in the Sun and his Wisdom in the Moon. As for the Holy Spirit, which is the majesty of the third level, we confess that this region entirely of air is his seat and recep-tacle. It is from his powers and from his spiritual profusion that the earth was conceived and begat the suffering Jesus who is the life and salvation of mankind, suspended upon wood. Such are our beliefs.[4]

10

The Faustus text alludes to the myth of *Jesus patibilis* which, according to F. Decret,[5] was possibly native to Africa. Decret writes however: "It is true that the only statement of it is found from the pen of Faustus of Milevus." In this case the whole of nature is nothing other than an immense cross to which is affixed *Jesus patibilis*. In other words the divine substance is imprisoned far from its original kingdom.

To the *Against Faustus* text, we must join another document addressed to the Manichees which Augustine conserved in *Against the Epistle of Manichæus called Fundamental.*

> Frequently, during the period that I was catechumen with you, I asked you why the Easter of the Saviour was so often celebrated in such a lukewarm fashion and by such a small number of people, without vigils, without even light fasts imposed upon the catechumen, simply without the accouterments of the most solemn holidays, when you distinguished with great honour your Bêma, the day when Mani had been killed? On that day you raised a five–level platform adorned with expensive cloth and readily visible to the worshipers. When I asked this question, they answered that one must celebrate the passion of the one who had really suffered, but that Christ was not truly born and had merely shown himself to men in simulated flesh which did not suffer and only pretended to suffer the Passion.[6]

The Manicheans professed one of the most radical forms of docetism. They denied that Christ had a real body. They denied his incarnation in the Virgin Mary, his real death on the cross, and his resurrection. Here we put our finger on the crux of the issue which distanced historical Christianity from mythic Manicheism. The Manichean Christ with his borrowed body had been crucified in appearance only and had not resuscitated.[7] Concerning the Holy Spirit, the Manicheans taught that their founder Mani was its visible and real manifestation.[8] Hence they refused to accept the Acts of the Apostles.

Augustine's anti–Manichean works which date from 389 to 405 contain many extracts from the writings of Mani which Augustine analyzes and criticizes. In Book 3 of the *Confessions* Augustine takes another approach. Twenty years later (373–397) he attempts to call to mind the teachings he received during his Manichean initiation. Rather than describing his youthful enthusiasm, he dwells upon his later disillusionment. He compares it to the painful situation of the Prodigal Son who is reduced to wishing for pig slops in a foreign land. Augustine writes:

> "Where then were You and how far from me? I had indeed straggled far from You, not even being allowed to eat the husks of the swine whom I

was feeding with husks *et longe peregrinabar abs te, exclusus et a siliquis porcorum, quos de siliquis pascebam.* How much better were the sheer fables of the poets and literary men than all the traps... (*Confessions* 3.6.11, an allusion to Lk. 15:16).

In the same paragraph Augustine penned one of his thoughts which has crossed the centuries: "It was You I sought...Yet all the time You were more inward than the most inward place of my heart and loftier than the highest. *Tu autem eras interior intimo meo et superior summo meo*" (*Confessions* 3.6.11, an allusion to Lk. 15:16).

In initiating their converts to the *Books of Mani*, the Manicheans did not hesitate to criticize books of the Old Testament or of the New Testament. Consequently, Augustine began to study certain biblical texts which he had barely known before if at all. His teachers drew strongly upon the Books of Moses and in particular Genesis. Augustine writes:

> I let myself be taken in by fools, who deceived me with such questions as: Whence comes evil? And is God bounded by a bodily shape and has he hair and nails? And are those patriarchs to be esteemed righteous who had many wives at the same time and slew men and offered sacrifices of living animals?

Such questions troubled Augustine in his ignorance:

> I did not even know that God is spirit, having no parts extended in length and breadth, to whose being bulk (*moles*) does not belong, for bulk...could not be wholly itself in every place, as a spirit is, as God is. And I was further ignorant what is the principle in us by which we are; and what Scripture meant by saying that we are made to the image of God (*Confessions* 3.7.12; Gen.1:26).

Combined with this aberrant presentation of God and man was a persistent criticism of the Old Testament because of its "scandals." These included the shameful morality of the Patriarchs and the Kings presented in the Bible as having multiple marriages; Moses' murder of the Egyptian overseer, and animal sacrifice which had long been prescribed by Levitic law. Consequently, the Old Testament was no longer valid and Christians were wrong to recognize it as prophetic of the New. In order to be used to the advantage of Mani's converts, the New Testament was attacked and truncated. The childhood narratives about Christ in Matthew and Luke were excluded. Docetist explanations of the chapters concerning the Passion and the Resurrection of Jesus Christ were applied. The Acts of the Apostles which contained the passages concerning the Holy Spirit of Pentecost were categorically denounced. If Paul's work received favorable treatment, one had to read it with prudent reserve, because of the falsifications to which the epistles had been subjected. This, in brief, is the Bible as it was presented to Augustine, the twenty-year-old Manichean convert. It was this version which Augustine was to hear, read and comment upon.

It is surprising that he accepted this situation without reacting for such a long time. Augustine explains the reason in a passage of a treatise which he dedicated in 392 to his friend Honoratus who was still a Manichee. Augustine reminds Honoratus of their passion and dedication in studying Virgil together. He continues:

> Now what time did we spend thus with these authors through whom ancient traditions assured us that the Holy Spirit had spoken. With all our youthful intelligence and our surprising need for rational inquiry we judged that there was nothing worth believing in them, without even skimming the books, without seeking out the masters, without questioning our possible slowness of spirit, without crediting the common good sense of those who wished that these writings be read over the generations? We allowed ourselves to be impressed by the words of their worst enemies who by their false promises of rational explanations lead us to believe and venerate thousands of their own outrageous fables.[9]

Augustine, in Book 4 of the *Confessions,* describes the ardor of his pursuit of the liberal arts *(artes liberales)* while he studied at Carthage. He had read and understood Aristotle's *Categories* (*Confessions* 4.16.28). Although this work opened his eyes to the significance of the ten treatises dealing with "substance", he was disappointed. What was the meaning and purpose of the wisdom of the liberal arts? The term *substantia* brought to mind again the parable of the Prodigal Son. He wrote:

> What ever was written either of the art of rhetoric or of logic, of the dimensions of figures or music or arithmetic I understood with no great difficulty and no need of an instructor: this You know, Lord my God, because swiftness of understanding and keenness of perceiving are Your gift. But none of this did I offer in sacrifice to You. Therefore it was not for my profit but rather for my harm, that I laboured so to have so great a part of my substance in my own power *quia tam bonam partem substantiae meae sategi habere in potestate,* and preserved my strength, but not for You, going from You into a far country *profectus sum abs te in longinquam regionem* to waste my substance upon loves that were only harlots. For what did it profit me to have good ability since I did not use it well? *nam quid mihi proderat bona res non utenti bene* (*Confessions* 4.16.30).

Therefore, for nine years Augustine was seduced by Manichean exegesis which considered itself to be rational. He was progressively taken over by the study, undoubtedly valuable in itself, of profane sciences. He was not tempted to a deeper personal understanding of the Scriptures. However, is it fair to assume that on the whole Augustine's biblical initiation during the Manichean years was a dead loss? Such a conclusion would be in error.

Even given the insidious and deformed nature of the critique, Augustine had acquired a textual knowledge of one portion of the Bible. He had read, at least partially, the Torah during his Manichean years. He had learned some Pauline writings. It was controversial reading no doubt, but a reading nonetheless.

In a concrete and personal way, Augustine knew the objections, the difficulties, the rejections, and the derision by which his Manichean masters opposed Christian and Jewish scriptures. That experience sensitized the future bishop to the multiple heterodox interpretations of scripture which he encountered during his ecclesiastic ministry. It is worth noting that Augustine would devote much attention, study and time to the examination of Donatist, Gnostic, Arian, Pelagian, and Priscillian texts sent to him for his response and elucidation. He could be severe in his judgments but he would never neglect the men who, while in the grip of heresy, had written the works. Augustine considered his dialogue with non-believers as an important pastoral duty. He had personally known the difficult experience of searching sincerely and anxiously, devoid of a master which one might consult. The immense polemical work of Augustine is rooted in this experience. It produced in him a vocation for exegetical precision and the desire to convince his adversaries by the Word of God.

If Augustine experienced the difficulties with the Bible met by the Manicheans, he became very conscious of the real difficulties which every uninstructed reader encounters, particularly vis–à–vis the Old Testament. Genesis had long proved enigmatic for him. Today with our diversified research into linguistics, history, archeology, philosophy and theology etc., we know the need for a nuanced hermeneutic of the Pentateuch. How are the first eleven chapters of Genesis to be interpreted? Where do the patriarchal traditions come from? The four source theory has been the object of intense scrutiny. What are the dates of the various documents and so forth? One should not be surprised that the great eastern and western bishops of the fourth and fifth centuries found themselves puzzled by and questioning in their reading of Scripture. The texts appeared contradictory and scandalous. They incited the reprobation of the heretics. It

14

was a difficult text, addressed by Basil, John Chrysostome, Ambrose, Jerome, and Augustine. Each, in their own period, under the guidance of the Holy Spirit attempted to actualize the Word of God.

After an initial period of enthusiasm, Augustine felt a growing disillusionment with Manicheism. At the same time his professional career was becoming more and more promising. Claude Lepelley traces the steps precisely: Augustine studied at Carthage between 370 and 372. He was a professor between 374 and 383. He taught as a municipal rhetor, not as a private teacher; he left his position in 383 to teach in Rome because he was exasperated by the rowdies and troublemakers who had free reign when he taught in public. In Rome Augustine taught at home as a private professor (*Confessions* 5.12.22) but the Roman students disappeared when it came time to pay their fees to their masters. In 384 he applied for a new position in Milan. While in Rome, he participated in a type of contest before the prefect of the city, Symmachus. This time it was for a municipal post in the imperial city to the north (*Confessions* 5.13.23).[10]

Named as Milan's city rhetor around October 384, Augustine made an official visit to Ambrose the Bishop of Milan. He wrote:

> So I came to Milan, to the bishop and devout servant of God, Ambrose, famed among the best men of the whole world, whose eloquence did him most powerfully minister to "thy people the fatness of Thy wheat and the joy of Thy oil and the sober intoxication of Thy wine".[11] For all unknowing I was brought by God to him, that knowing I should be brought by him to God (*Confessions* 5.13.23).

Attracted by Ambrose's eloquence, little by little Augustine became interested in the meaning of the words he so admired. "With his words to which I listened with the greatest care; the realities which I still held quite unworthy of attention penetrated altogether into my mind" (*Confessions* 5.13.24). For Augustine the step from the words to the realities they expressed was a decisive moment.

> I began to see that the Catholic faith, for which I had thought nothing could be said in the face of the Manichean objections, could be maintained on reasonable grounds: this especially after I had heard explained figuratively several passages of the Old Testament which had been a cause of death for me when taken literally. Many passages of these books were expounded in a spiritual sense and I came to blame my own hopeless folly in believing that the Law and the Prophets could not stand against those who hated and mocked at them (*Confessions* 5.14.24).

15

Monica arrived in Milan during the spring of 385 with her other son Navigius. She followed closely the preaching of Ambrose and each Sunday Augustine accompanied her.

> Still I heard him every Sunday preaching the word of truth to his congregation; and I became more and more certain that all those knots of cunning and calumny, which those who deceived me had tangled up against the holy books, could be untangled. I learned that the phrase "created by You in Your own image" was not taken by Your spiritual children — whom of our Catholic Church–mother You have made to be born anew by grace — to mean that You are bounded within the shape of a human body. And although I had not the vaguest or most shadowy notion how a spiritual substance could be, yet I was filled with shame — but joyful too — that I had been barking all these years not against the Catholic faith but against mere figments of carnal imaginations. I had been rash and impious in that I had spoken in condemnation of things which I should have learned more truly of by inquiry. For You, O highest and nearest, most hidden and most present, have not parts greater and smaller; You are wholly everywhere, yet nowhere limited within space, nor are You of any bodily form (*Confessions* 6.3.4).

While listening to Ambrose, Augustine began to understand the errors of the Manicheans who in interpreting the Genesis verses about the human creation in God's image incorrectly had concluded that God was a corporeal being like us. Ambrose's sermons also laid to rest Augustine's prejudices against the Old Testament. Augustine wrote:

> I was glad also that the old Scriptures of the Law and the Prophets were set before me now, no longer in that light in which they had formerly seemed absurd, when I criticized Your holy ones for thinking this or that which in plain fact they did not think. And it was a joy to hear Ambrose who often repeated to his congregation, as if it were a rule he was most strongly urging upon them, the text; *the letter killeth but the spirit giveth life* (2 Cor. 3:6).
> He would go on to draw aside the veil of mystery and lay open the spiritual meaning of things which taken literally would have seemed to teach falsehood. Nothing of what he said struck me as false, although I did not as yet know whether what he said was true. I held back my heart from accepting anything, fearing that I might fall once more, whereas in fact the hanging in suspense was more deadly (*Confessions* 6.4.6.).

Despite the painful fear of making yet another error, Augustine slowly changed his interior attitude regarding the sacred writings of the Jews and Christians and recognized in them a certain authority.

Thus, since men had not the strength to discover the truth by pure reason and therefore we needed the authority of Holy Writ, I was coming to believe that You would certainly not have bestowed such eminent authority upon those Scriptures throughout the world, unless it had been Your will that by them we should believe in You and in them seek You (*Confessions* 6.5.9).

Augustine rejoiced that sacred Scripture was accessible to all, while at the same time reserving the dignity of her mysteries for more profound interpretation. During this period Augustine was still anxious. He turned thirty in 384 and from his perspective his quest for wisdom from the age of nineteen had made little progress. Granted he now looked more favorably upon the Scriptures of the church, but how was one to find truth? He wrote:

But where shall I search? When shall I search? Ambrose is busy. I am myself too busy to read. And in any event where can I find the books? Who has them, or when can I procure them? Can I borrow them from anyone?...My pupils occupy the morning hours, but what do I do with the rest? Why not do this? But if I do, when shall I have time to visit the powerful friends of whose influence I stand in need, or when prepare the lessons I sell to my pupils, or when refresh myself by realizing my mind from too close pre–occupation with my heavy concerns? (*Confessions* 6.11.18).

The distinguished thirty-year-old rhetor of Milan, on the threshold of a brilliant literary career did not have the leisure to study the Bible nor access to its manuscripts. According to the conventions of the time, Augustine was a year beyond his adolescence and into the age of maturity. Curiously, until 384 Augustine's biblical knowledge had been acquired more by listening to either the Manicheans or Ambrose than reading the Scriptures. However, this is less surprising when one considers the values of the period and the importance attached to oral instruction.

Meanwhile Augustine struggled with the issues of the origin of evil, astrology, and what one was to think of God (*Confessions* 7.1.1–8,12). While writing the *Confessions* in 397, Augustine describes this period of his life:

At first You willed to show me how You resist the proud and give grace to the humble (1 Pet. 5:5), and with how great mercy You have shown men the way of humility in that the Word was made flesh and dwelt among men (Jn. 1:14). Therefore You brought in my way by means of a certain man — an incredibly conceited man — some books of the Platonists translated from Greek into Latin (*Confessions* 7.9.13).

This sentence is the key to the whole second half of Book 7 of the *Confessions*. In 386 while desperately searching for the path to the Father, Augustine discovers and is seduced by certain Neo–platonic writings. Contemporary scholarship has established that Augustine in all probability must have read the works of Plotinus and Porphyry. In 397–398 Augustine makes his point in an interesting manner. He repeats the word *via* ten times (*Confessions* 7.7.11, 9.13, 18.24, 20.26, 21.27; 8.1.1) in the course of his comparison between the platonic path and the Christian path as presented in Ambrose's preaching. It is presented as a comparison between pride and humility. Augustine writes:

> So I set about finding a way to gain the strength that was necessary for enjoying You. And I could not find it until I embraced the Mediator between God and man, the man Christ Jesus, who is over all things, God blessed forever (1 Tim. 2:5), who was calling unto me and saying: "I am the Way, the Truth, and the Life" (John 14:6); and who brought into union with our nature that Food which I lacked the strength to take: for the word was made flesh that Your Wisdom, by which You created all things, might give suck to our souls' infancy. For I was not yet lowly enough to hold the lowly Jesus as my God, nor did I know what lesson His embracing of our weakness was to teach (*Confessions* 7.18.24).

Nevertheless it was no small benefit that Augustine acquired out of reading Neo–platonists during this period. In his own words:

> I had read the books of the Platonists and had been set by them towards the search for a truth that is incorporeal, I came to see Your invisible things which are understood by the things that are made (Rom. 1:20). I was at a standstill, yet I felt what through the darkness of my mind I was not able actually to see; I was certain that You are and that You are infinite, but not as being diffused through space whether finite or infinite; that You truly are and are ever the same, not in any part or by any motion different or otherwise; and I knew that all other things are from You from the simple fact that they are at all. Of these things I was utterly certain, yet I had not the strength to enjoy You (*Confessions* 7.20.26).

Through Neo–platonism Augustine discovered the existence of the spiritual world, the formlessness of God, and the nonphysicality of evil. He thanked the Father who had permitted him these readings before he tackled the Scriptures:

> Where was that charity which builds us up upon the foundation of humility, which is Christ Jesus? Or when would those books have taught me that? Yet I think it was Your will that I should come upon these books before I had made study of the Scriptures, that it might be impressed on

my memory how they had affected me: so that, when later I should have become responsive to You through Your Books with my wounds healed by the care of Your fingers, I might be able to discern the difference that there is between presumption and confession, between those who see what the goal is but do not see the way, and those who see the Way which leads to that country of blessedness, which we are meant not only to know but to dwell in" (*Confessions* 7.20.26).

Finally, Augustine read for himself the writings of Saint Paul. He transcribes his burning memory at the end of Book 7 of the *Confessions*:

So now I seized greedily upon the adorable writings of Your Spirit, and especially upon the apostle Paul. And I found that those difficulties, in which it had once seemed to me that he contradicted himself and that the text of his discourse did not agree with the testimonies of the Law and the Prophets, vanished away. In that pure eloquence I saw One Face, and I learned to rejoice with trembling (Ps. 2:11). I found that whatever truth I had read in the Platonists was said here with praise of Your grace: that he who sees should not so glory as if he had not received — and received, indeed, not only what he sees but even the power to see, for what has he that he has not received (Ps. 101:28)? And further, that he who sees is not only taught to see You who are always the same...

Further on Augustine concludes: "Marvelously these truths graved themselves in my heart when I read that latest of Your apostles and looked upon Your works and trembled" (*Confessions* 7.21.27).

This study of Paul had considerable consequences for Augustine. From this time forward, the Apostle Paul was the master and final court of appeal for the future Bishop of Hippo, concerning obscurities or scandals in Scripture. At once, Augustine found in the Pauline Epistles the answer to two questions. Contrary to the Manichean version there was no disagreement between the Old and the New Testaments. Furthermore, the salvation sought by the Platonists was found in the humility of Jesus Christ.

Again it was in Paul's writings that Augustine would quickly find the answer which lead him to the intimate and definitive decision of conversion. Augustine had broken with the Manicheans. He had progressively learned that the truth of faith was not to be acquired by rational studies. Later he frequently repeated Isaiah's words: "Unless you do not believe, you will not understand" (Isaiah 7:9). However, he still had to renounce the prospect of a brilliant career which promised him glory, the dream of every Roman. He needed to break with his carnal desires even to the point of his eventual conjugal relationship in marriage. During the year 386, the Christian community in Milan provided a happy influence and some admirable examples. These obviously included Monica and Ambrose. Others such as Simplicianus, who related to Augustine the remarkable conversion of the rhetor Victorinus and Ponticianus, who described to Augustine the monastic communities in the Near East and the suburbs of Milan, also need to be considered. Book 8 of the *Confessions* describes these encounters and provides an almost hour-by-hour update of Augustine's last struggle. It is reminiscent of Paul's when he writes in the Epistle to the Galatians: "For what the flesh desires is opposed to the Spirit, and what the Spirit desires is opposed to the flesh" (Gal. 5:17, NRSV). The decisive moment occurred when Augustine opened the Apostle's book. He writes: "I snatched it up, opened it and in silence read the passage upon which my eyes first fell: 'Not in reveling and drunkenness, not in debauchery and licentiousness, not in quarreling and jealousy. Instead, put on the Lord Jesus Christ, and make no provision for the flesh to gratify its desires' (Romans 13:13 NRSV). I had no wish to read further, and no need. For in that instant, with the very ending of the sentence, it was as though a light of utter confidence shone in all my heart, and all the darkness of uncertainty vanished away" (*Confessions* 8.12.29).

Augustine clothed himself finally and forever in Jesus Christ. He became His disciple, His *servus Dei*. It was his entering into an ascetic lifestyle. All obstacles to baptism had been thrown aside forever. Augustine announced his conversion to Ambrose. He resigned as rhetor in October 386. While awaiting his official enrollment as a catechumen which would be during Lent 387, Augustine and several close friends retired to Cassiciacum on the outskirts of Milan. Verecundus had placed a country home at their disposal. We know a great deal about Augustine's time at Cassiciacum thanks to the *Dialogues* which he wrote there and his recollections in Book 9 of the *Confessions*.

What progress in his biblical knowledge did Augustine make while at Cassiciacum? Writing to Ambrose, Augustine had asked which book he should read first:

> And in a letter I told Your bishop, the holy Ambrose, of my past errors and my present purpose, that he might advise me which of Your Scriptures I should especially read to prepare me and make me more fit to receive so great a grace. He told me to read Isaiah the prophet, I imagine because he more clearly foretells the gospel and the calling of the gentiles than the other Old Testament writers; but I did not understand the first part of his book, and thinking that it would be all of the same kind,

put it aside meaning to return to it when I should be more practised in the Lord's way of speech (*Confessions* 9.5.13).

Evidently, when Augustine was writing the *Confessions*, he knew enough about Isaiah to realize that he prophesied about the call to the Gentiles. But it is also clear that when he opened Isaiah for the first time it was on Ambrose's advice. Therefore, during his entire Manichean period he had not heard about, nor at the very least paid attention to, this book and Ambrose's preaching had not awakened Augustine's interest in it. Whatever the situation, we do know that, disappointed by his first reading of Isaiah, Augustine closed the book. The record of *The Immortality of the Soul*, written in 387 bears witness to his ignorance of Isaiah. The *Revisions* confirm this. He writes:

> I reiterate my words: 'the soul cannot be separated from eternal reason because they are not joined spatially.' I would never have spoken in this manner if I had been more familiar with sacred literature *si iam tunc essem litteris sacris ita eruditus* which would have reminded me that 'Your sins create the separation between God and you' (Is. 59:2) *Peccata vestra separant inter vos et Deum*. Where is it given to think that we can speak of separation even of those things which are not only joined spatially but spiritually.[12]

Augustine's Italian works from 387 to 388 include only two citations of Isaiah. They were both Is. 7:9 *Nisi credideritis, non intellegetis* found in *On Free Will* 1. 2 and 2. 2. This was the first appearance of a fragment which promised to become a leitmotiv.[13] In fact, the text is never found in the *Confessions*. Augustine's knowledge of Isaiah, which would remain limited to certain texts, would result from his pastoral work as priest and bishop, and mainly from his discussions with the heterodox.

Augustine's great biblical revelation during the Cassiciacum period were the Psalms of David. He later described the experience: "What cries did I utter to You in those Psalms and how was I inflamed towards You by them, and on fire to set them sounding through all the world, if I could, against the pride of man! But in truth they are already sung throughout the world and there is none who can hide himself from Thy heat" (*Confessions* 9.4.8). Augustine continues, evoking the mystical exaltation he felt while meditating on the following words of Psalm 4: "When I called upon Thee, Thou, God of my justice, didst hear me; when I was in distress, Thou hast enlarged me: have mercy on me, O Lord, and hear my prayer." (Ps. 4:2) This psalm expressed not only Augustine's indignation with the Manicheans, but the thought that their ignorance excused them, and the fear of remaining short of the bewildering acknowledgment of God's mercy (*Confessions* 9.4.8–11). Thus we learn that during his Manichean years Augustine had learned nothing of the Psalms.[14] Certainly Augustine mentions several times that the elect of the cult in their private meetings gave themselves to prayers and psalms.[15] Augustine, however, as a simple auditor never took part.[16] We will not leave aside the question of Augustine's potential knowledge of properly Manichean psalms. (These were found in the twentieth century during the excavations by Medinet Madi of Fayoum.) We will simply note the total absence of allusions to these works in the *Commentaries on the Psalms* and Augustine's pastoral writings.

While the *Dialogues* and the Cassiciacum writings are poor in biblical citations, the *Soliloquies* contain a wealth of gospel allusions. The Pauline Epistles remained a privileged area of study for Augustine. The 1 Cor. 1:24 citation: "Christ the power and the knowledge of God" appears even in the very early writings from this period. This sentence from Paul would echo in all the work of the pastor of Hippo.

In the spring of 387, Augustine returned to Milan and finally gave his name to be enrolled as *competens*. It was the final stage for the catechumenate before receiving baptism coinciding with the duration of Lent. Alypius and Adeodatus joined Augustine. It became for them a period of intense biblical instruction. The Lenten period was for the *competentes* one of initiation into the ethical aspects of Christian life and a time for the study of the sources of the Christian faith. Augustine dedicated himself entirely to all these tests. He was later to call this time his first penitence. Augustine indirectly provides a witness to the experience of the catechumen in preparation for baptism, when he describes in the *Confessions*, the initiation of the rhetor Victorinus. Concerning this subject Augustine evokes the three Lukan parables about mercy. He writes:

> It is with special joy that we hear how the lost sheep is brought home upon the exultant shoulders of the shepherd and how the coin is put back into Your treasury while the neighbors rejoice with the woman who found it. And the joy we feel at the solemn feasts in Your church brings tears as we hear of that younger son who was dead and made alive again, who had been lost and was found (*Confessions* 8.3.6).

Augustine does not directly discuss in the *Confessions* what he learned about the Bible during the Lenten period and the Holy Week of his catechumenate, in his days as an *infans* in the faith. He did not have to explain this to Paulinus of Nola for whom he wrote the *Confessions*. The preparation of the *competentes* was well known. The numerous catechisms from the period describe the steps and the instruction. Augustine probably received his instruction from Ambrose.[17] This is attested to in *On the Mysteries*. The reading in the course of the liturgy of the great prophetic works of the Old Testament would have resolved any lingering Manichean prejudices which Augustine held. The harmony between the two testaments became absolute fact for Augustine. Augustine became progressively more immersed in the reading of the New Testament. He found therein the meaning of the words of Paul: "Cloth yourself in Jesus Christ", which he had read in the garden during his conversion. On the first page of the last book of the *Confessions* addressed again to the Father, Augustine exclaims:

> Do Thou not abandon me now when I call upon Thee, for it was by Thy aid going before me that I called upon Thee; and Thou hadst urged me over and over in a great variety of ways, to hear Thee from afar off and be converted and call upon Thee who wert calling me (*Confessions* 13.1.1).

In conclusion, is it possible to attempt an evaluation of Augustine's biblical background when he left Italy definitively in 388 to return to Africa? His Christian biblical formation was very new and, according to Augustine himself in his later writings, quite limited. He confides this in letters to Januarius, Jerome and Nectarius of Calama.[18] He bears witness to it several times in his *Revisions* [19] written in 426. However incomplete, Augustine's scriptural knowledge as of 388 was solid and well grounded. He had been aided perhaps by Simplicianus in 387 and his year spent studying in Rome (387–388). The proof of this is found in *On the Morals of the Catholic Church* written for the most part in Rome in 388. It reveals in Augustine's reminiscences, a biblical richness and the specific biblical reading of the authors. Here, in particular, we find the first citations from Wisdom literature, such as Ecclesiastes, Ecclesiasticus, and Proverbs. These were recommended reading for the catechumens.

It is not solely by the breadth of biblical citations that one should judge Augustine's biblical culture in 388. The primordial gain made by Augustine during the years in Milan was an insight into exegesis and interpretation of Scripture. He learned how to read the Bible. He was initiated into certain rules which were necessary for understanding the Old Testament and its relationship with the New. He discovered that it was the liturgy of the Church, which provided its initiates with the sense of the Word of God and that this word could never be fully understood outside the perspective of faith. It is not surprising that after his return to

Africa Augustine dedicated *On the Usefulness of Belief* to his Manichean friend Honoratus. At the same time Augustine, the former Manichean, made Ambrose's method of Manichean refutation his own. He took as his principle the adage, "The letter kills, but the Spirit brings to life." (2 Cor 3:6) The *On Genesis Against the Manichees* was the first application of this well learned lesson. Although it is difficult to prove, one suspects that aside from the writings of Ambrose, Augustine was familiar with other works such as those of Jerome or Hilary of Poitiers and Greek sources translated into Latin.

One can well imagine why, on his return to Africa, that Augustine spent three years in solitude at Thagaste.[20]

NOTES

1. *Commentaries on the Psalms* 144.7: Ps. 144:4b: *Et virtutem tuam annuntiabunt;* cf. H.I. Marrou, *Histoire de l'éducation dans l'antiquité,* Paris.

2. *On Two Souls, Against the Manichæans* 1.1.

3. H.I. Marrou, *Saint Augustin et l'augustinisme,* p. 24. See *Confessions* 6.2.2 and 9.6.14.

4. *Against Faustus,* 20.2.

5. F. Decret, *Aspects du Manichéism,* Paris: Et. Aug., 1970, pp. 12–13, 226, 269 and following.

6. *Against the Epistle of Manichæus called Fundamental* 8, 9.

7. See BA 13, footnote 19: "La christologie manichéenne": Here P. Solignac analyzes the different aspects of the Manichean conception of Christ insofar as they can be determined from known texts and authors. He cites the following text from Augustine which illustrates finally that the Manicheans taught three Christs not one. *"aliusne est quem de spiritu sancto concipiens terra patibilem gignit, omni non solum suspensus in ligno, sed etiam iacens in herba; et alius quem Iudaei crucifixerunt sub Pontio Pilato; et tertius ille per solem lunanque istentus"* (see *Reply to Fautus* 20.2).

8. *The Profit of Believing* 3.7; *De Agone Christiano* 23.30: *Against Faustus* 12.14, 30; 13.17; 15.4; 19.22; 22.6,12,15,87.

9. *The Profit of Believing* 6.13.7 (17–18). Also see *On Two Souls* 1.1; 8.10.

10. C. Lepelley, *Les Cités de l'Afrique Romaine au Bas–Empire,* II. Notices d'histoire municipale, pp. 31–32: Karthago, la cité et l'enseignement supérieur: Augustin rhéteur municipal.

11. Allusion to Psalm 1:8: *"A tempore frumenti, vini et olei sue multiplicati sunt"* (Augustine's version found in *Commentaries on the Psalms* 4.9). See *Hymn of Ambrose* 1.7 (23–24).

12. *Revisions* 1.5.2. Augustine cites Is. 50:2 for the first time in *Letter to the Romans.* "Expositio Inchoata 8" written during 394–395. We find the verse quoted by Parmenianus (*Against the Letter of Parmenianus* 2.3.6). This is

followed by nine citations in dossiers against the Pelagians dating from 411: *On the Merits and Remission of Sins* 1.19.25, 24.34, 28.56; 2.28.56; *On the Spirit and the Letter* 24.42; *Sermo Mai* 126.10; *Sermon* 71.12.19; *Homilies on the Gospel of John* 41.5; *Against Two Letters of the Pelagians* 4.4.8.

13. The citations of Is. 7:9 until Augustine's episcopacy : *On Free Will* 1.2 and 2.2.

14. *Against Faustus* 21.3: Augustine says to Faustus: "*Et a corde et ab ore vestro longe est psalterium nostrum ubi dicitur; Misericordiam et iudicium cantabo tibi, domine* (Ps. 100:1)." It must be noted that in the Manichean writings transcribed in Augustine's works there are no references to the Psalms except for the isolated citation of Ps. 127: 3.6.4 in *Against Adimantus* 23.

15. *On the Morals of the Manicheans* 2.15.36; 2.17.55; *Commentaries on the Psalms* 140.12.

16. *Against Fortunatus the Manichean* 1.3.

17. Ambrose of Milan. *On the Mysteries, On the Sacraments, SC* 25 bis. Also see *Sacramentum Futuri* by Jean Daniélou.

18. *Letters* 55.38 (to Januarius); 73.5 (to Jerome); 104 (to Nectarius of Calama).

19. *Revisions* 1.3.2; 1.5.2., 1.7.2, 1.18.

20. English translations of material from the Confessions are taken from Augustine, *The Confessions of St. Augustine*, translated by F.J. Shead (New York: Sheed and Ward, 1943).

3

The Canon of Sacred Scripture

ANNE-MARIE LA BONNARDIÈRE

At the beginning of Book 11 of *City of God*, alluding to the Epistle to the Hebrews, Augustine wrote:

> God spoke therefore through the prophets and through himself and finally through the apostles as He judged fit. He also instituted the canon of scripture, invested with the highest authority *quae canonica nominatur, eminentissimae auctoritatis* by which we have believed in all that is useful to know and would be incapable of knowing by ourselves (*City of God* 11.3).

This statement, made in 417, echoes numerous earlier affirmations. Around 406, in response to Cresconius who had cited a text of Cyprian, Augustine wrote:

> We are not repudiating Cyprian when we differentiate between his writings, such as they are, and the canonical authority of sacred Scripture *a canonica divinarum Scripturarum auctoritate*. It was not without reason that great vigilance established the ecclesiastic canon *est canon ecclesiasticus constitutus* and that it determined the books of the prophets and the apostles which are part of it and which we dare not judge. On the contrary, it is by these writings, that we freely judge all other writings of the faithful or unfaithful (*Against Cresconius* 2.31.19).

Augustine further stipulated that the Pauline Epistles particularly enjoyed this canonical authority. Somewhat earlier, Book 11 of *Against Faustus* included the following statement:

> Now you see the strength of the authority of the Catholic Church which is solidly supported by a succession of bishops from the foundation provided by the Apostles until the present time *fodatissimis sedibus*

Apostolorum, and by the consensus of the people *et tot popularum consensione firmatur.* Also, if the faith in certain merited texts was doubted, which has been the case upon occasion, for these variations are not numerous and are well known to those versed in scripture, one would refer to the manuscripts of the area from which the doctrine came to clarify these inconsistencies. And if the manuscripts were not in agreement upon a variant *incerta varietas* one would accord greater authority to the version which had greater support, and prefer the older to the newer. And if uncertainty remained concerning some variation, one would consult the text in its original language. This is how those, who seek to clarify something which affronts them in scripture which is the solid base for authority, proceed. They proceed in this manner not for the purpose of argument but rather to learn (*Against Faustus* 11.2).

Further on in the same book Augustine continues:

> ...A distinction has been made between the books written after the apostles and the authentic canon of the Old and New Testament. Sacred Scripture, having been confirmed during the time of the apostles by the succession of bishops and by the propagation of the Churches is placed high on a throne where it receives the submission of all pious and faithful intelligence. There, if one finds something absurd, it is not permissible to say 'The author of this book has strayed from the truth' but rather 'This manuscript is false' or 'The translator has made an error' or finally that 'You do not grasp what is said'(*Against Faustus* 11.5; we can also cite *On the Holy Trinity* 3.2.22).

These three texts are faithful echoes of the advice found in *On Christian Doctrine* 2.8.12 given by Augustine in 396. To those who sought to be initiated into the science of sacred Scripture or, in other words, canonical writings *(quae appellantur canonicae)* Augustine wrote:

> For the canonical books (are), moreover, invested with authority by so many catholic churches, among which one finds without a doubt churches who were privileged to be apostolic sees and receive their writing from the apostles. This is the rule which will be followed in the inventory of these books. Those which are accepted by the whole of catholic churches will be placed before those writings which some (churches) do not accept. Concerning the issue of books which are not universally accepted, those which are admitted by the largest number of churches and the most important churches will be placed before those which are admitted by fewer churches and churches of less authority. Finally there are certain books which are accepted by the majority of churches and some others which are accepted by important churches, in these cases I deem that both must be given the same authority (*On Christian Doctrine* 2.8.12).

From 396 to 417 we find that Augustine affirms the same basic principles. Only the canonical books of scripture require of Christians an entire adhesion and submission. Their guarantee of canonicity and authenticity comes from their apostolic origin and their tradition transmitted to the churches founded by the apostles from which succeeded the bishops. However Augustine indicates an awareness of some difficulty in this area. Not all the churches of his time are perfectly in agreement over the canonicity of all the inspired books. The list could vary from church to church. Therefore, what is constitutive of canon for Augustine? In 396 he writes:

> Now the entire canon of scripture which we will examine includes the following books: the five books of Moses, or in other words, Genesis, Exodus, Leviticus, Numbers, and Deuteronomy; the book of Jesus of Nave (Joshua), Judges, a little book entitled Ruth which seems to belong to the beginning of Kingdoms; followed by the four books of Kingdoms (1&2 Samuel and 1&2 Kings) and the two books of Paralipomenon (1&2 Chronicles) which are not a continuation but paired with them, which is to say on an equal footing with them. We have here the historical books which contain the sequence of the ages and the order of the events. There are other books of another sort, in other words, which do not belong to this order and have no link between them. They are the books of Job, Tobit, Esther and Judith; which is followed by the two books of Maccabees and the two books of Esdras (Greek version of Ezra and Nehemiah) which appear to continue the historical account that had stopped with Kingdoms and Paralipomenon. This is followed by the Prophets, in whose number we find David's Psalms, and the three books of Solomon, Proverbs, the Song of Songs and Ecclesiastes. Wisdom and Ecclesiasticus are attributed to Solomon because of a certain similarity with the preceding works, but according to an uninterrupted tradition they were written by Jesus Sirach. We must include them among the prophetic works since their prestige merited this title. The rest of these writings, properly called Prophets, form twelve books when taken separately but they have never been separated and we take them as one book. Here are the names of the prophets: Hosea, Joel, Amos, Obadiah, Jonah, Micah, Nahum, Habakkuk, Zephaniah, Haggai, Zechariah and Malachi. There follow four books of the major prophets, Isaiah, Jeremiah, Daniel and Ezekiel. That makes forty four books and brings to an end the authentic canon of the Old Testament. As for the New Testament, it includes the four gospels: Matthew, Mark ,Luke and John; the fourteen letters of Paul, one to the Romans, two to the Corinthians, one to the Galatians, one to the Ephesians, one to the Phillippians, two to the Thessalonians, one to the Colossians, two to Timothy, one to Titus, one to Philemon, and one to the Hebrews; the two epistles of Peter; the three epistles of John; the Epistle of Jude; the Epistle of James; the book of the Acts of the Apostles; and the book of the Apocalypse of John (*On Christian Doctrine*).

This text by Augustine, in the manner in which it is presented and by the brief notes which introduce it, escapes the dryness of a simple official canonical list. It is a canon which attempts to be precise and annotated. The plan is clear. The two portions of the list are the forty–four books of the Old Testament and the twenty–eight of the New Testament. If the second portion is nearly classic (we will return to the case of the Epistle to the Hebrews), the first series must be more closely examined. Augustine distinguishes between the books of the Old Testament which belong to the literary genre of history *historia* and those which he classifies under the term prophetic *prophetia*. The list of the historical books includes three different groups: 1) historical accounts containing the sequence of the ages and the order of events *historia quae sibimet annexa tempora continet atque ordinem rerum* which include the five books of Moses, Joshua, Judges, Ruth, the four books of the Kingdoms and the two books of Chronicles (Paralipomenon); 2) four books which are not related to each other or to the preceding series: Job, Tobit, Esther, and Judith; 3) the continuation of the normal historical account: Maccabees and Esdras.

Regarding the prophetic collection, Augustine makes two divisions. The first division includes the Psalms of David, and the books of Solomon (Proverbs, The Song of Songs and Ecclesiastes). In the same category are placed the two wisdom books, Wisdom and Ecclesiasticus, which, even though they resemble the works of Solomon, are not a product of the king and are attributed to Jesus Sirach *nam Jesus Sirach eos conscripsisse constantissime perhibetur* must be included in the prophetic works. The second division of the prophetic collection includes one book for the twelve minor prophets and the four books of the major prophets. Augustine concludes the list by noting that the Old Testament is comprised of forty–four books.

This ordering of the biblical canon indicates a certain theological intention even while attempting to successfully classify the books of the Bible. One can also discern a real hesitation at two points in the exposition. How are Tobit, Esther, Judith and Job related to the historical form? Given their incontestable canonicity, what is the precise origin of Wisdom and Ecclesiasticus? It is worth noting that in both these cases Augustine (whether or not he was aware of it in 396) was confronting concerns which existed in other churches concerning Tobit, Esther, Judith, Wisdom and Jesus Sirach. Since we now have the good fortune to avail ourselves of the work of a team of competent experts in the field of Old Testament canon,[1] it is feasible to compare the biblical canon of Augustine with analogous non-African documents. By way of introduction, we can state that in *On Christian Doctrine*, Augustine appears to ignore the fact that the Hebrew canon contains twenty–two books as does the alphabet.[2] He also ignores the fact that the Hebrew canon is divided into four parts: The Torah, The Early Prophets (Joshua, Judges and Kings), the Later Prophets (the 16 prophets minus Daniel), and the Writings (Psalms, Job, Proverbs; the five books of Ruth, Song of Songs, Ecclesiastes, Lamentations, Esther; and finally Daniel, Esdras, Nehemiah and Chronicles). He could have known about the Hebrew canon from Jerome. It seems that in 396 Augustine did not have on hand Jerome's *Prologue to the Book of Samuel and Kings* (389–392). It remains true that in 396, while writing *On Christian Doctrine*, Augustine does not stipulate that the Jews do not inscribe in their canon such works as Tobit, Judith, Maccabees, Wisdom, Sirach, the Greek versions of Esther and Daniel, etc. We will see further on whether or not the period subsequent to 396 indicates a new awareness or an evolution in Augustine's thinking.

It is now necessary to compare Augustine's canon with that of the Council of Carthage dated August 28, 397. Thanks to C. Munier's definitive study of subsequent traditions which were still accessible it is possible to reconstitute the canon of sacred books of the African church which were approved in Carthage August 28, 397 and conserved in the archives of that church.[3]

> Outside of canonical writing nothing was read at church under the name of sacred scripture. Here is the scriptural canon: Genesis, Exodus, Leviticus, Numbers, Deuteronomy, Jesus Nave, Judges, Ruth, the four books of the Kingdoms, the two books of Paralipomenon, Job, the Psalter of David, the five books of Solomon, the twelve books of the prophets, Isaiah, Jeremiah, Ezekiel, Daniel, Tobit, Judith, Esther, the two books of Esdras, and the two books of Maccabees. Belonging to the New Testament are the four gospels, the Acts of the Apostles, the thirteen epistles of the apostle Paul, an epistle by the same author to the Hebrews, two epistles of Peter, three of John, one of Jude, one of James and the Apocalypse of John. There are therefore twenty–seven books. In order to confirm this canon one should consult the church overseas. It was also permissible to read the Passions of the martyrs while celebrating their feast days.[4]

Compared to Augustine's text, the text from Carthage is a dry list without explanatory notes. Nothing remains of Augustine's wisely ordered plan. There are undoubtedly forty–four books in the Old Testament and twenty–seven in the New. There are some other secondary differences. Job is placed before the Psalter and is separated from Tobit, Judith and Esther.

The twelve books of the minor prophets are not indicated as being in one volume. The Pauline epistles are numbered fourteen plus one. The Davidic psalms are stripped of the adjective 'prophetic'. (Perhaps the name David included such a notion.) The most important difference concerns the five books of Solomon, wherein the Augustinian distinction between the three works of Solomon and the exceptional situation of the Wisdom books is not made.[5] One wonders why Augustine, who participated in the Council of Carthage on August 28, 397, did not react during this vote upon the canon of scripture. We need to consider the antecedents of the Council of 397 in order to understand its decisions and to the antecedents of the Augustinian canon in order to discover its sources.

The Council of Carthage that August 397 took place in two sessions. The first, starting on August 13th, was made up of Aurelius, the Bishop of Carthage and the bishops of Byzacena (one of the six imperial divisions of Roman Africa), who had arrived early for the council and were led by their primate, Mizonius. This first group worked together editing an abridged version of the canon which had been voted upon four years earlier, on October 8, 393, at the Council of Hippo. As it happened Hippo was the pastoral charge of the priest Augustine under Bishop Valerius. This breviary of Hippo *Breviarium Hipponense* included a version of the canon of sacred literature. It was this canon, edited by Aurelius and the Byzacene delegation, which was ratified on August 13, as was the entire breviary on August 28, without discussion by the Proconsular bishops and the Numidian and Mauritanian bishops.

It would seem, as C. Munier points out, that the text provided by Mizonius should had been the same one which had been deposited in Aurelius's chancellery in Carthage. However Munier has pointed out that the *Brevarium of Hippo* was subject to a subsequent tradition, vestiges of which can be discerned, which did not precisely agree with the tradition of Carthage upon certain points:

> Do the differences which appear between the witnesses to this tradition and those who reproduced the official canon received by the Carthage church on August 28, 397 stem from the fact that the local churches in Africa, Italy and Gaul freely composed their own *liber canonum*? On the other hand do they stem from the Council of Hippo on October 8, 393 and were subsequently faithfully transmitted by the Byzacene bishops on August 13, 397 and eventually found their way into the breviary?[6]

The second hypothesis suggested by Munier is interesting, although he hesitates for solid reasons to accept it. Recognizing its hypothetical nature, I shall compare the Augustinian version found in *On Christian Doctrine* and the variations from the Byzacene tradition. Firstly, the books attributed to Solomon are reduced to three (Augustine, Collection C by Corbie, Collection V of the Vatican). Secondly, the twelve minor prophets constitute one book (Augustine, Collection V of the Vatican). Thirdly, the Pauline epistles are numbered at fourteen (Augustine and the following four collections: Corbie, Vatican, Saint–Maur and Toulouse–Albi). Fourthly, the two letters of Peter, the three letters of John and the letters of James and Jude are all canonical (Augustine and the four aforementioned collections). Does this agreement between Augustine and the collections from the Byzacene tradition suggest the existence of a primitive text produced at the Council of Hippo in 393, to which these two versions attest? Munier cautiously continues:

> If Byzacene tradition does not represent the vestiges of a primitive African canon established at Hippo in 393 and later corrected either in 397 or 419 in order to harmonize with those of the Roman churches which the priests from Hippo and Carthage had decided to consult; it is at the very least a precious witness to the long and difficult formation of scriptural canon in the Occident.[7]

Add to this the fact that Augustine was an eyewitness to the Council of Hippo on October 8, 393 and one wonders whether his canon found in *On Christian Doctrine* 2. 8. 13 is not a reflection of this.

Whatever has been discovered regarding the Council of Hippo does not explain sufficiently the sources which Augustine obviously used while formulating his canon in *On Christian Doctrine*. This is particularly true concerning the books of Wisdom and Ecclesiasticus which Augustine attributes based upon unbroken tradition to Jesus Sirach. Where did he get his information?[8] It is necessary to determine what Augustine knew about Ecclesiasticus prior to writing *On Christian Doctrine*. We count, prior to 396, thirty–three citations from Ecclesiasticus. Most of these include an introduction which explains the name and the author of the book. The name of Solomon is never mentioned. Let us attend to the precious information provided by these citations. The word "Ecclesiasticus" appears twice. The first time occurs in the *Expositions on the Psalms* 7.19 written around 394. We read, *"In Ecclesiastico dicitur: Confitemini Domino in omnibus operibus eius; et haec dicetis in confessione: opera Domini universa quoniam bona valde* (Eccl. 39: 14d,15d,16d according to the Septuagint)" which translated says "Praise the Lord in all his works; Speak thusly in thanksgiving;

The works of the Lord are all perfect in goodness."[9] The same word, "Ecclesiasticus", is found in the text of *To Simplicianus* 1.2.20 written between 395–96. We will return to this.

Several times, in absence of the word "Ecclesiasticus" the citation for Ecclesiasticus is introduced by a description of its prophetic genre. In *On the Morals of the Church* 1.24.45 written in Rome in 388, Augustine cites Ecclesiasticus 19:1 (according to Septuagint numeration) as being the words of the prophet *quod a Propheta dictum est*. He then quotes Sir. 19:1: "He who despises small things will fail little by little *Qui spernit modica, paulatim decidet.* (*On the Morals of the Church* 1.24.45) While writing *On Genesis Against the Manichees* 2.5.6 at Thagaste in 389, Augustine again applies the words *verba prophetica* to the following citation of Sir. 10:9 (according to Septuagint numeration): "How can he who is dust and ashes be proud for even in life his bowels decay? *Quid superbit terra et cinis? Quoniam in vita sua proiecit intima sua*" In 394 the Sirach 5:5 (according to the Septuagint text), "Son, do not pile sin upon sin" is introduced in *On the Sermon on the Mount* 2.14.48 with the words, "as the prophet says."

The most important passage, written slightly before *On Christian Doctrine*, is the one we read in *To Simplicianus* 1, quaestio 2.20. It is found at the heart of Augustine's exegesis of Romans 9 which had been requested by Simplicianus. Augustine underlines the correspondence which exists between Romans 9:29 and another scriptural passage. He writes:

> There exists in scripture a certain passage which is very closely related to the one in question here and which confirms in an admirable witness the same ideas which have just been discussed. It is found in the book called Jesus the son of Sirach by some and Ecclesiasticus by others and where it is written...(*in eo libro qui ab aliis Jesus Sirah, ab aliis Ecclesiasticus dicitur in quo ita scriptum est*) (*To Simplicianus* 1, qu. 2.20).

The citation which follows is the integral passage of Sir. 33:10–17 as found in the Septuagint. It is commented upon verse by verse.

Consequently, prior to the *On Christian Doctrine*, Augustine knew of the tradition which attributed this Old Testament book of Wisdom to Jesus Sirach and was also known as Ecclesiasticus. This book belonged to the prophetic literary genre and was undoubtedly canonical. It bore a certain resemblance to the works of Solomon but owed nothing to this author. From this book, which he had on hand from 388, Augustine cites sentences which conform to a Latin version of Ecclesiasticus based upon the Septuagint and otherwise known as Greek I. How did Augustine come by this information?

African that he was, Augustine probably had enough familiarity with the works of Cyprian to know that he frequently cited a book called Ecclesiasticus which he considered canonical. But Cyprian attributes this book to Solomon.[10] It is not an African source which provides Augustine with the name of Jesus Sirach. Augustine was perfectly justified in citing a continuous *constantissime* tradition which attributed Ecclesiasticus to Sirach. Thanks to important documentation brought together by researchers who were responsible for the works cited above,[11] it is possible to find the citations pertaining to the Wisdom of Sirach or the son of Sirach throughout the writings of eastern and western church fathers[12] who listed the books of scriptural canon. Obviously Augustine did not know all of these texts since some were produced after 396. The tradition into which he tapped came to him without a doubt when he was in Milan while he occupied himself with the readings especially reserved for the catechumens. While many of the Fathers mentioned the book of Sirach, they did not recognize it as canonical, preferring the twenty-two books of the Hebrew canon. They did recommend however to their catechumens the following collection: Wisdom, Sirach, Tobit, the Greek version of Esther, Judith, Second Maccabees and the Greek version of Daniel.[13] These came to be known later as 'deuterocanonical'. Therefore, it is highly probable that Augustine while at Milan or during his second stay in Rome (387–388) learned of the name of Sirach. It seems that the canonicity of the book was not a problem in Milan. An in–depth analysis of the works of Ambrose concerning this issue seems so necessary! In any case, Augustine's first book, *On the Morals of the Church* 1 written in Rome and so rich in biblical citations reveals that he had discovered the books of Ecclesiasticus, Wisdom and Maccabees. He cites them without listing them and considers them to be inspired.

One last problem remains. From 396 to 430, during his episcopate, did Augustine acquire new information about biblical canon or did he change his opinion on certain issues?

1. Imagine, if you will, the case surrounding the books of the Old Testament which subsequently came to be known as deuterocanonical. They had throughout the history of the formation of canon raised numerous questions for theologians in all the churches. What was the status of Judith, Tobit, First and Second Maccabees, Wisdom, Sirach and the Greek fragments of Esther and Daniel?

What was Augustine's position at the beginning of the fifth century? Without a doubt, Augustine maintained the canonicity of these books. Making his own the first sentence of canon 47 of the *Breviarium Hipponense,* he professed: "Outside of the scriptural canon nothing should be read in church under the name of sacred scripture." The fact is that the Canon, in enumerating the books of Scripture does not leave out any of the "deuterocanonical", even if, despite Augustine's disagreement, Wisdom and Sirach are attributed to Solomon. It is liturgical usage which distinguishes canonical books. This fact seems to be operative in Africa from the time of Cyprian. In Augustine's time, the Song of the Three Children in the Furnace (Dan.3) was a prophecy proclaimed during the Easter Vigil. Chapter seven of Second Maccabees (the martyrdom of the seven brothers and their mother) was read as a 'Passion' on the first of August. Wisdom is explicitly recognized by Augustine as a liturgical book.[14] The book of Tobit was invoked on the feast of Pentecost.[15] Several passages from Ecclesiasticus were the basis of sermons preached by the Bishop of Hippo.[16] Only Judith and Esther seem not to have been read liturgically.

Even though Augustine appears ignorant of the Jewish position in *On Christian Doctrine* 2.8.13, he learns little by little the interdictions of Hebrew canon concerning certain books if not the entire content. His information appears to be arrived at late and is consigned to the *City of God* 17.20.1 regarding Wisdom and Sirach, 18.26 for Judith and 18.36 for Maccabees. This last book is already cited as not being included by Hebrew canon in *Against Gaudentius* 1.31.38. The Hebrew rejection of Ecclesiasticus, Tobit and Wisdom is repeated in *Speculum Quis Ignorat.*[17] With one stroke, the recording of the Hebrew interdictions and the opposing of them to the pastoral custom of the Church served to confirm the canonicity of the deuterocanonical writings.

Despite the rarity of reference to the books of Esther, Tobit, Judith and Maccabees in his writings, Augustine maintained their historicity. They recounted events which had occurred in the past, even though in the case of the first three books the stories were difficult to integrate into the overall history of Israel.[18] Contrary to Jerome, Augustine experienced no difficulty in allowing into canon the Greek portions of Daniel and Esther.

Yet the fact that he knew of the Hebrew interdictions lead Augustine, at the end of his episcopate, to modify the order of his canon. Consequently, in Book 17 of the *City of God* (ca. 424–425), Wisdom and Sirach are still on the list of prophetic books of the Old Testament[19] but there are changes in *Speculum Quis Ignorat.* Instead of following the books of Solomon, Wisdom and Sirach are sent with Tobit to the end of the list of the Old Testament. These three books are considered as Wisdom literature.[20] It is true that the purpose of the *Speculum* was to set forth only those biblical passages having ethical value.

Augustine steadfastly maintains Jesus Sirach's authorship of Ecclesiasticus. We found four proofs of this in the following later writings: *On the Care to be had for the Dead* 15,18; *On the Eight Questions of Dulcitius* (question 6.5); *Revisions* 2.4.2; and *Speculum Quis Ignorat* (before the account devoted to Wisdom).

If we have made an issue of the Augustinian position concerning Ecclesiasticus, it is because throughout church history (until the Council of Trent) the canonicity of this particular book has been a stumbling block for those aware of its problematic nature. Granted certain reservations, one sees here that Augustine increasingly opts for the positive solution dictated by his pastoral work.

> 2.
> The City of God follows its temporal course, David reigned in the earthly Jerusalem, a shadow of the future. He was an expert in the art of singing *in canticis eruditus*; he loved the harmony of music not for its vulgar attraction but for its religious feeling; by it he celebrated the cult of his God, who is the true God under the mysterious face of a great reality. Because the equitable and precise agreement of the various notes brought to mind by their variety the corresponding unity which was assembled in the well ordered City. In brief almost all his prophecies are found in the psalms *omnis fere prophetia euis in psalmis est* and these are found, one hundred and fifty in all, in the book which we call the Psalms (*City of God* 17.14).

With these words Augustine introduces Book 17 of the *City of God*. It is the section dedicated to David as musician, prophet and author of Psalms, found at the heart of a work reserved for the study of the time of the prophets, the fourth age in the history of the City of God.

Since writing *On Christian Doctrine*, Augustine had not changed his opinion concerning the book of Psalms. It was prophetic, canonical and written by David. During the interval between the two works (between 396 and 424–26), Augustine had commented upon all one hundred and fifty psalms either orally or in writing. Ceaselessly, like a Hilary of Poitiers or an Ambrose to name only two of the Latin Fathers, he used the word *propheta* with considerable abandon to introduce his psalmic citations. The liturgical *responsorial* which we find throughout the sermons resonates similarly. Even in the anti–Donatist writings Augustine uses psalmic texts prophetically to illustrate the universalism of the Church. The claim of Davidic origin for all the psalms provides the basis for Augustine's position. This is similar for the other Church Fathers although the discussion of which is outside of the confines of this paper.

3. There exists a section in the historic books of the Old Testament, which Hebrew canon calls the early prophets. These are Joshua, Judges, and the four books of Kings (Samuel and Kings). Augustine ignores this particular grouping. For Augustine, they are "history" (*On Christian Doctrine* 2.8.13.). However, we must make three comments about this. In Book 17 of the *City of God*, Augustine ascribes to prophecy several texts from the book of Kings, which he cites nowhere else. These include the Song of Hannah, the mother of Samuel (1 Kings 7:2–12; 1 Sam. 2:1–10 in modern versions),[21] the prophecy of the high priest Eli concerning the changing of the priesthood (I Kings 2:27-36), Samuel's reproach to Saul (1 Kings 13:13–14), Samuel's prophecy about the division of the kingdom of Israel (1 Kings 15:23, 26–29) and the prophecy of Nathan (2 Kings 7:8–16; 7:5–16 in modern versions) (*City of God* 17.4.13). It should be noted that aside from a short account of Joshua, the historic books are absent in *Speculum Quis Ignorat*. It is as if Augustine found nothing in these books which was edifying for Christian ethical reflection. On the whole Augustine does not seem very interested in the detail of historical events which is the essence of the 'historical' books. Nevertheless, Augustine devotes his energies to difficulties with Joshua and Judges in *Questions on the Heptateuch* books 6 and 7. This leads one to believe that Augustine would have undertaken a similar project with regards to the books of Kings had time allowed. It is worth noting that he had for some time amassed literature which would aid in this. These included Book 2 of the *To Simplicianus*, the numerous allusions which the Psalms allowed him to make in *Commentaries on the Psalms*, the objections brought to the forefront by the Manicheans and the Donatists, and the data brought together in the *City of God*. All of this documentation is dispersed but it does attest to the growing recognition by Augustine of the prophetic value of these books, the narratives of which were promises in and of themselves.

4. The question of the twelve minor and four major prophets remains. Augustine always taught that they were canonical. Daniel also, including the Greek portions (the Song of the Three Young Men, Bel and the Dragon and Susanna) was canonical. On this point, Augustine was completely at odds with Jerome, even though he was aware of Jerome's commentary on the book.

5. Because of its importance we must look at the following page from Book 18 of the *City of God*, which is devoted to Job:

> I don't believe that the Jews themselves dare to pretend that aside from the Israelites, no one is a child of the true God from the time that Israel

began as a nation whereas their older brother was rejected. It is true, there is nowhere found another people worthy of being strictly called the people of God *populus enim re vera qui proprie Dei populus diceretur, nullus alius fuit*, but there were even in those other nations men who belonged not because of their earthly affiliation but rather a heavenly *sed caelesti societate* affiliation to the true Israelites, citizens of the eternal kingdom *supernae cives patriae*. They cannot deny it and if they would, they should be simply proved wrong by the example of this admirable and saintly man, Job, who was neither Jew nor proselyte and therefore a stranger to the nation of Israel, a member of the Edomites. In Edom he was born and there he died. Even so the divine word makes of him such a grand elegy that for justice and piety, none of his contemporaries can be compared to him. In Chronicles without a doubt, we find no precise details about his period, but from his book which is admitted to the Hebrew canon *quem pro sui merito Israelitae in auctoritatem canonicam receperunt*), because of its value we can deduce that he belonged to the third generation after Jacob (*City of God* 18.47).

The book of Job is canonical, a canonicity recognized by the Hebrews. The book of Job is a historical book from the age of the Old Testament, from people who were strangers to the Israelites, which proves its membership in the true City of God. Nonetheless Augustine is perplexed in his attempt to date the author and the work.[22] Such a book obviously merits attention in *Speculum* where it is found between discussions of Solomon and the Prophets.

6. Augustine never questions the canonicity of the following Old Testament books which he rarely cites: Ruth, Esdras, Nehemiah, Chronicles 1 and 2, and Esther.

7. All of the New Testament is obviously canonical for Augustine, however, his insistence upon this for certain books, seems to indicate, when looked at from another perspective, that these works were disputed. Augustine knew early on that the Manicheans rejected the book of Acts. He is therefore careful to remind his readers frequently that this book belongs to the canon of the Catholic Church. It is in Acts that we learn about the descent of the Holy Spirit upon the apostles at Pentecost. This book directly contradicts the pretension of Mani to be the incarnation of the Holy Spirit. Each year the book of Acts was read between Easter and Pentecost reminding Christians all the 'pentecosts' of the Spirit.

Augustine did not ignore that two short pastoral epistles, Jude and Peter 2, were not recognized by all the churches. We find affirmation of Jude's place in canon not only in *On Christian Doctrine* 2.8.13 and canon 47 of *Breviarium Hipponense*; but also in the *City of God* 4.23 and 18.38; and

Homily 76.1 on the gospel of John. In this last case Augustine notes while commenting upon Jude's question to Christ after the Last Supper (John 14:22 "Lord, how is it that you will manifest yourself to us, and not to the world?") that this Jude also wrote one of the canonical epistles. The second epistle of Peter is listed as part of canon in *On the Literal Interpretation of Genesis* 3.2.2. It is called sacred writing *scriptura divina* in the *City of God* 4.3 where Augustine writes, "Sacred scripture states: 'For whatever overcomes a man, to that is he enslaved' (2 Peter 2:19)."

Finally, we have already had occasion to study the case of Hebrews.[23] Following Rottmanner, we think that around 409–411, while recognizing the canonicity of Hebrews, Augustine no longer attributes it to Paul. He provides no hypothesis concerning its authorship.

One can conclude that the biblical canon of Augustine, such as it is found in *On Christian Doctrine* 2.8.13 was slightly modified between 396 and 430 while its early structure remained unchanged. Most noticeably the distinction between *historia–prophetia* which is constitutive of Augustine's listing of the Old Testament results from a theological vision of the Bishop of Hippo. This vision is manifest in his canon.

NOTES

1. J. Daniel Kaestli and O. Wermelinger, *Le Canon de l'Ancien Testament, sa formation et son histoire*, (Geneva: Labor & Fides, 1984).

2. It is curious to note, with the help of Eindhoven's *Catalogi Verborum Augustini*, that Augustine, who generally is greatly interested in numbers, never cites the number 22. It is not found in *Commentaries on the Psalms*, nor in *Homilies on John*, nor in the *Confessions*, nor in the *City of God*, nor in *On the Trinity*, nor in his first fifty sermons.

3. Kaestli and Wermelinger, *Le canon de l'Ancien Testament*, p. 203, text 6. This text of Jerome is subsequent to Augustine's stay in Rome in 387–388.

4. C. Munier, "La tradition manuscrite de l'Abrégé d'Hippone et le Canon des Ecriture des Eglises africaines", *Sacris Erudiri*, vol. XXI 1972–1973, p. 48.

5. O. Wermelinger, "Le Canon des Latins au temps de Jérôme et d'Augustin", *Le Canon de l'Ancien Testament*, (Geneva, 1984) p.198. Text 2: *Breviarium Hipponense*, Canon 47, according to the *Collectio Hispana* ed. C. Munier CCL 449, (Turnhout, 1974) p.340.

6. C. Munier, "La tradition manuscrite de l'Abrégé d'Hippone...", p. 52.

7. Ibid., p. 53.

8. A.M. la Bonnardière, "Le Livre de la Sagesse", Biblia Augustiniana, (Paris, 1970) see chapter 2, particularly pages 35–57 for Augustine's position concerning the author and canonicity.

9. *Commentaries on the Psalms* 7.19. One can also glean the mention of

Ecclesiasticus (*Libri Ecclesiastici*) in *Commentaries on the Psalms* 37.8 but the date of this Commentary is imprecise.

10. M.A. Fahey, *Cyprian and the Bible: A Study in Third Century Exegesis*, pp. 40–41; Cyprian's Canon; pp. 177–184: A study of Cyprian's citations of Ecclesiasticus indicates that there are twenty–six quotes in thirty–five references.

11. See notes 1, 3 and 5.

12. Origen (Rufinus), *In Numeros*, Homilia 18.3; Athanasius *Lettre festale* 39, fragment 2 in 367; Epiphanius, *Panarion* 8.6.1–4; Epiphanius, *Des poids et des mesures*, 4 in 392; *Canons Apostoliques*, Canon 85 at the end of the fourth century in Syria; *Manuscrits Vaticanus, Sianaiticus, Alexandrinus*; Jerome, *Prologue au livre de Samuel et aux livres des Rois* in 389–392; Hilary of Poitiers, *Tractatus in Psalmum* 140.5; Filastre of Brescia, *De Haeresibus* 56.

13. Recommendation of this 'deuterocanonical' collection to catechumens is found in Origen, Athanasius, Rufinus and Jerome. Canon 85 of the apostolic canons states it in the following manner: "Take care that your young learn by heart the books of Wisdom which are attributed to the wise Sirach." This is the only case where Wisdom seems to be also atrributed to Sirach.

14. See A.M. la Bonnardière, "Le Livre de la Sagesse" chap. 3; and "Le Livre de la Sagesse dans la liturgie africaine", pp. 59–83.

15. *Sermon* 8.17: Here there is an allusion to the reading of Tobit 2:1.

16. It will suffice to cite *Sermons* 38, 39 and 41 which were respectively consecrated to a commentary on Sir. 2:1–2, Sir. 5:8–9 and Sir. 22:28. These were critically edited by Lambot in *CCL* 41. The word Ecclesiasticus is found in the title of *Sermon* 41.

17. *Speculum Quis Ignorat*. This notice preceded the section reserved for the book of Wisdom: "The Jews do not recognize the canonicity of Wisdom and Ecclesiasticus which the church receives. The author of the book of Wisdom is ignored. The author of Ecclesiasticus is Jesus Sirach, which is attested to by all who read the book to its end."

18. See *City of God* 18.26 (Judith); 18.36 (Maccabees); 18.36 (Esther); 13.22 (Tobit).

19. Augustine notes however, in *City of God* 17.20.1 that the prophecies of the books of Wisdom and Ecclesiasticus: "do not have the same force against our adversaries since they are not part of the Hebrew canon." Augustine knows henceforth that this is a current opinion.

20. This new opinion of Augustine concerning the literary genre of Ecclesiasticus is found in *Revisions* 1.10.3.

21. It should be kept in mind that 1 Kings and 2 Kings in Augustine's writings correspond to 1 Samuel and 2 Samuel in later lists. 3 Kings and 4 Kings correspond to the present day 1 Kings and 2 Kings.

22. It is interesting to study the perplexities of Augustine when confronted with books such as Job, Jonas or Judith. Modern research considers these

to be fiction which is not to detract from their canonical and inspired character.

23. A.M. la Bonnardière, "L'Epître aux Hébreux dans l'oeuvre de saint Augustin", RE *Aug* 3, 1957, pp. 137–162.

4

Did Augustine Use Jerome's Vulgate?

ANNE-MARIE LA BONNARDIÈRE

The "Vulgate", the very name is misleading: Jerome did not call his Latin translation of the Hebrew Old Testament and the Greek New Testament, the Vulgate. That would take centuries. It was because of its great diffusion during the Middle Ages that Jerome's translation received the 'Vulgate' title (probably as late as the sixteenth century). Prior to this the name had been reserved for the Latin version of the Septuagint.[1] Therefore it is not accurate to speak of Augustine's use of the "Vulgate" if one means by this term the modern Vulgate which is the official Latin version of the Roman Catholic Church.

Augustine and Jerome were contemporaries. It was during Augustine's life that Jerome worked upon and translated the scriptures in Palestine. In what measure and form was Jerome's work known to Augustine? From what date did he know it? Was Augustine favorably predisposed towards it? As far as we can tell, what was Augustine's attitude vis-à-vis Jerome's translations?

In order to fully understand Augustine's position vis-à-vis that of Jerome, it is necessary to map out the battleground, or in other words, the books of the Old Testament upon which Augustine had occasion to express his opinion. A certain number of the books of the Old Testament must be put aside since they fall into the following two categories:

a) The following books of the Old Testament are excluded since we find few traces of them in Augustine's surviving works: Ruth;[2] Lamentations and Baruch;[3] Esdras and Nehemiah;[4] Judith;[5] 1 Maccabees;[6] the minor prophets, Joel, Nahum and Obediah.[7]

b) Also excluded are the books which Jerome did not translate into Latin from either Greek or Hebrew. These were Baruch, Maccabees 1 and 2, Sirach, Wisdom and the Greek sections of Esther and Daniel. These books were not accepted into Hebrew canon and were later called 'deuterocanonical'.

Having eliminated these two categories of books, what remains to be examined? Which of Jerome's translations could Augustine have known and used? They were the Pentateuch, the historical books, the Prophets and the Psalter.

Our research for the *Biblia Augustiniana* allowed us to log progressively the works of Augustine that revealed a somewhat obvious knowledge of Jerome's biblical translations. They generally occur in later works where Augustine the exegete is armed with the tools of the trade (Greek and Latin manuscripts, works of authors that he consults or criticizes, the rules of Latin rhetoric) by which he elucidates as much as he can various obscure passages of Scripture. These works include, in my opinion, *Questions on the Heptateuch, City of God, On Christian Doctrine* and section 426 of the *Revisions*.

Since we are looking for the relationship between Augustine and Jerome, we cannot ignore their correspondence during the years between 394 and 405. This was marked by their debates on Jewish–Christians (the incident at Antioch: Gal. 2:14, the circumcision of Timothy found in Acts 16:3)[8] and the biblical versions of the book of Jonah.[9] We will not dwell upon these well–known quarrels.

1. Questions on the Heptateuch

As he usually does, Augustine provided in the *Revisions*, a description of this work:

> ...I also wrote books of questions on the same seven sacred books (Pentateuch, Joshua and Judges) and I wanted to give this title (*Questions on the Heptateuch*) because the points discussed in this work are presented more as questions to solve rather than solutions. For the most part these questions seem to me to have been examined in enough depth so that one can correctly regard them as being resolved and clarified.[10]

The work was written during the years 419–420. It contains seven books in which during the course of numerous discussions, Augustine compares a biblical citation from the Septuagint (the version upon which the work was based) with its corresponding Hebrew version *interpretatio quae est ex hebraico* a mere eighteen times.[11] Nowhere is Jerome named, although he was the only author of the period who had made a Latin translation from the Hebrew. Augustine tacitly reveals that he is in possession of the Latin manuscripts which Jerome had translated *ex hebraico* — from the Hebrew. How did Augustine procure these manuscripts? Should we assume that they were given to him by the letter carriers who traveled between Africa and Palestine? These critical references of Augustine wherein he compares the Greek and Hebrew versions include three passages from Genesis,[12] two passages from Deuteronomy,[13] six passages from Joshua,[14] and seven passages from Judges.[15]

Does this inclusion of several passages translated from the Hebrew *ex hebraeo* indicate some sort of conversion by Augustine to the Jerome texts? It is nothing of the sort. Actually his attempts at confrontation did not shake Augustine's regard to the Septuagint. It remained the text to which he referred. Its point of view is several times described as manifesting the prophetic intuitions of these authors.[16] In any case, the Greek text is always consulted even if, as Augustine clearly admits, the Hebrew text on many occasions is as authoritative or clearer.[17] Often Augustine lists the two translations without judging the value of either.

The essential interest of these eighteen Augustinian texts resides in the fact that they quickly introduce us to who uses the instruments of the trade that he has on hand in order to elucidate obscure scriptural fragments. One recognizes that Augustine manipulates one after the other Latin manuscripts translated from the Greek Septuagint and the Hebrew. Several times he alludes to those who knew the Syriac and Hebrew languages. One cannot give a better tacit description of Jerome.[18]

Definitively, with regard to our present research, the contribution of *Questions on the Heptateuch* resides in its value as a work occasioned by Augustine's desire to understand certain biblical obscurities.

We must keep in mind that for the first of the seven books, the *Questions on Genesis*, Augustine deals with Jerome's *Hebrew Questions on Genesis*. In his notable article, F. Cavallera[19] compared, question by question, the works of Jerome and Augustine. He illustrated that Augustine had certainly read the work of the older scholar. However, Augustine was not impressed by Jerome's criticism of the Septuagint. Cavallera writes:

> It is not surprising that Augustine, while using here and there the solutions of Jerome which he had closely read, never took recourse directly to the Hebrew text. He was satisfied with the resources offered him by the Septuagint, which he interpreted according to the rules set forth in the *On Christian Doctrine.*

J. Divjak's discovery of new Augustinian letters allowed us to discover how Augustine came into possession of Jerome's *Questions on Genesis*. *Letter 27* from Jerome is addressed to Aurelius of Carthage and congratulates him upon his accession to the episcopate probably in 392. During this letter, Jerome announces that he has sent several works to his correspondent and, in particular, the *Hebrew Questions on Genesis*.[20] This work, in Carthage by approximately 393, was therefore available to Augustine. We know that Jerome produced this work at the beginning of his stay in Bethlehem, between 389 and 392.

2. *The* City of God

The *City of God* reveals to an assiduous and curious reader the quantity of literature to which Augustine devoted himself and which constituted the sources for this great work. Certainly the writings of Jerome are one of the most important sources. Jerome's work had made Augustine aware, during the writing of *City of God*, of the Latin translations of the Hebrew version of the Old Testament. To begin with we turn again to Jerome's *Hebrew Questions on Genesis*. We know that in fact, from Book 9 to Book 16 in the *City of God*, Augustine engages in a generally constant commentary on Genesis from Gen. 4 onward. The lines of the commentary are often hidden by digressions that were somewhat necessitated by polemical issues of the period but never broken off entirely. We find it each time it emerges, sometimes concerning a somewhat obscure biblical fact or a discrepancy between the data of the Septuagint and that of some Hebrew text concerning which the reading appears quite natural when one refers to Jerome's work. We cite an example here. Regarding Gen. 12:4: "Abraham was seventy–five years old when he departed from Haran", Augustine adds the following personal commentary: "Abraham's seventy–five years when he left Haran, were calculated from the day that he was delivered from the 'fire of the Chaldeans and not the day of his birth'. (*City of God* 16.15.1). What was this fire of the Chaldeans? Jerome, in explaining Gen. 11: 28 which deals with Ur of the Chaldeans, translates the text as "in the fire of the Chaldeans". He uses the occasion to tell a Jewish fable. Abraham was forced to escape secretly a torture by fire that was being prepared for him by the Chaldeans in order to punish his refusal to sacrifice to idols. Abraham's age was calculated from that date by the Bible. This story is found in Jerome's *Hebrew Questions on Genesis* (11.28). Obviously Augustine had the text in front of him. An allusion to it had already been made in *Questions on the*

Heptateuch 1.12. In this case Jerome was not named but surreptitiously referred to: "*...aliter ista quaestio a 'quibusdam' solvatur; ex illo computari annos aetatis Abrai, ex quo liberatus est de 'igne Chaldaeorum', in quem missus ut arderet, quia eundem ignem superstitione Chaldaeorum colere noluit, liberatus inde 'etsi in Scripturis non legitur, iudaica' temen 'narratione' traditur.*"[21] The emergence of the dispute between the Septuagint and the Hebrew text is certainly important throughout books 15 and 16 of the *City of God*. Even if it indicates that Augustine is aware of Jerome's work, it does not prove his conversion to the Hebrew version of Genesis. Each time a comparison occurs, Augustine defends the Septuagint as having been produced under the influence of the Holy Spirit. He writes:

> When it is not an error made by a copyist, one must believe, if the meaning conforms to the truth and proclaims the truth, that under the influence of the Holy Spirit, the authors of the Septuagint, leaving their roles as translators and speaking in free prophecy wanted to explain in a different way. From there is the true title of apostolic authority invoked and not the Hebrew alone, when it calls upon the witness of scripture (*City of God* 15.14.2).

In the last section of the *City of God*, starting at Book 18, Augustine expands his position and we are surprised to read regarding the prophecy of Jonah: "But does someone object to the manner in which I knew what the prophet Jonah said to the citizens of Ninivah? Is it 'In three days Ninivah will be destroyed' or 'in forty days'? Who does not see that the prophet could not say the two at the same time when he was sent to threaten the city with imminent ruin? If the destruction should happen within three days, it is not forty days, and if it was forty days then it was certainly not three. If therefore someone asks me about what I think Jonah said, I am of the opinion that the which is read in the Hebrew; 'In forty days Ninivah will be destroyed'. The Septuagint, coming much later, could say something else, while still repeating the subject and concurring with it, but from another perspective to the same and only meaning. The reader was in this manner invited, without denigrating either of the two authorities to raise himself from the story in order to look for the reality *ad ea requirenda propter quae*, which the story itself means (*significanda historia ipsa conscripta est.*)" Augustine shows that it is Christ himself who is represented by both the forty and the three days. All this occurs, he continues:

> As if the Septuagint, prophets and as much translators *septuaginta interpretes idemque prophetae* had wanted to alert the reader, entirely preoccupied with the sequence of events, from his stupor and in inviting him to scrutinize

46

the depth of the prophecy *altitudinem prophetiae*, had offered him in some way with this language; 'Look in the forty days even for those that you will find in three; You will find the first in his Ascension, the second in his resurrection'. It was thus with great suitability that Christ could be prefigured in the two numbers, one from Jonah the prophet and the other from the prophecy of the seventy interpreters which the unique and same Holy Spirit made known (*City of God* 18.44).

Jerome, in his *Commentary on Jonah* rallied to the Hebrew text and showed the appropriateness of the number forty which was so particular to a prediction of penitence. He did not accept the Septuagint text. Was it Jerome's opinion which convinced Augustine of the value of the number forty which seemed like true *historia*, based upon actual events at that time? It is highly probable. In any case Augustine remained convinced of the prophetic mission of the writers of the Septuagint which he affirms soon after:

> I must be careful to emphasize, not wanting to support my demonstration of the numerous examples where the Septuagint seems to be removed from the Hebrew (*ab hebraica veritate*), when they are in agreement with each other. Since, following the footsteps of the prophets, in my own modest way, who were the first to invoke the prophetic witness found in the Septuagint as well as in Hebrew, I believe I can in my own way appeal to this double authority. Both are divine and are really one. (*City of God* 18.44)

To cite an authoritative modern testimony on Augustine's position:

> Augustine was moved by the audacity of Jerome. The preacher felt that his people were troubled by the critique... For his part he held fast to the canonical authority of the Greek Bible. These were the same proper theological considerations which we have already encountered in other Fathers: it (the Septuagint) was prepared by divine Providence for the conversion of the pagans (*On Christian Doctrine* 2.15); it had been received by the apostles (*Ep. 71; City of God* 18.44) and by them transmitted to the Church (*Questions on the Heptateuch* 1.169; *City of God* 18.43)...Augustine is interested in presenting the tradition of the church which resists Jerome's radicalism. He does it as a theologian who does not ignore the criticism. It is precisely the union of these two aspects found in Augustine, which produce a penetrating perspective, one which had never been presented before him with the same force. Both the Hebrew and the Greek texts are inspired and true. They are accepted as two stages intended by God in his ongoing revelation. Origen wanted as canonical only the Greek text, leaving the Hebrew for the Jews. Jerome wanted only the Hebrew, reducing the Greek to a less accurate tradition. Augustine retained the two as different, complementary, and desired versions of the same Spirit. It is a vision of singular depth and truth.[22]

47

The *City of God* illustrates clearly on several occasions that Augustine had arrived at this 'vision of singular depth and truth' by a comparison of certain Greek texts with the corresponding Hebrew as encountered in Jerome's works. Most specifically he read Jerome's *Commentary on the Prophets*. It appears that these works had been obtained by Augustine around 420. He explicitly names Jerome and his series of works in the *City of God* 18.43.1[23]. Augustine refers to Jerome's *Commentary on Malachi* in the *City of God* 20.25.1 and his translation of 4 Kings 5:26 from the Hebrew in Book 22.29.2 of the same work. In several other cases Augustine tacitly refers to Jerome, while not specifically naming him, when he cites Hebrew versions of scripture *sicut legitur in Hebraico*. This is the case for the following citations: Haggai 2:7b in the *City of God* 18.48; Zechariah 12:10 in the *City of God* 20.30.3; Malachi 4:6 in the *City of God* 20.29; and Isaiah 42:1–4 in the *City of God* 20.30.4. Does this mean that Augustine had thoroughly read all the commentaries by Jerome suggested by the citations listed above? One must resist jumping to conclusions too quickly. Let us merely say that Augustine had on hand the many works of Jerome mentioned in the *City of God* which he had at least partially read. Systematic analysis in each case will eventually determine all of the hieronymian material which was used by Augustine.

For the purposes of this paper we must enumerate the places in the *City of God* where one finds passages analogous to the Greek and Hebrew comparisons of Jonah 3:4. To my knowledge, and I hope that other researchers will pursue this, there are five similar cases where Augustine studies the two versions. These are Zechariah 12:10, Haggai 2:7b, 4 Kings (2 Chron.) 5:26, Is.42 n:1–4 and Malachi 4:6.

Let us take only one of these passages because of its importance for an illustration. In chapter 30.3 from Book 20 of the *City of God* Augustine comments upon the Septuagint version of Zechariah. He begins with the citation Zech. 12:10–11: "They will look to me because they have wounded; and they will mourn him as someone very dear, and they will cry bitterly for him as one cries for an only son." In the Latin version of the Septuagint, Zech.12:10a reads: *Et spicient ad me pro eo quod insultaverunt.* Augustine continues by citing and commenting upon the Latin version translated from Hebrew: "*Et aspicient ad me, quem confixerunt.* The word *confixerunt* (whom they have pierced) appears better in light of the crucifixion of Christ. However, the action of wounding, which was preferred by the Septuagint, is found throughout the Passion. When they arrested him, placed him in chains, dragged him to court, dressed him in a humiliating and ignominious cloak, crowned him in thorns, hit his head with a reed, knelt in mock worship of him, when he carried his cross and when he was hung upon it, most assuredly they wounded him. If furthermore, instead of one translation *interpretatio* we accept the two, reading both *insultaverunt* and *confixerunt*, we more fully understand the Passion of the Lord." (*City of God* 20.30.3)

We know that Zech. 12:10a is cited in John 19:37. Augustine is commenting on John's gospel, specifically John 19:37, in *Sermons* 120.3 during this period. He writes the following scriptural citation: "*Et iterum alia Scriptura dicit; Videbunt in quem confixerunt.*" The version of John's gospel, which in this case conforms to the Vulgate, provides a text for Zech. 12:10a which is given neither in the Septuagint nor the Hebrew version. There is more to be said. Before writing the *City of God* Augustine quotes this passage seventeen times, never indicating whether he is citing John or Zechariah. Fifteen times Augustine uses the version *Videbunt in quem pupugerunt*, which he applies in his pastoral writings. Ten of these fifteen occur in sermons. In many instances, Augustine attributed the phrase to the 'prophet'. He knows that it is a prophetic text and therefore he always applies it to Christ. Augustine relies here upon an old African tradition belonging to the old Latin version. This text is part of a theme related to the return of Christ at the end of time. He will be perceived as a man by both the good and the evil.

This example allows us to quickly grasp the difficulties surrounding Latin versions of the Bible. There are multiple variations. Here Augustine has witnessed to four Latin forms of Zech. 12:10a and two for Jn. 19:37b.[24]

Therefore, on at least six occasions, we find in the *City of God* a scriptural text cited using Jerome's Latin version and immediately compared to the corresponding text in the Septuagint. Augustine accepts the two versions without sacrificing the Septuagint text. He even defends the Septuagint formulation of the texts. But he allows that the Septuagint version is complemented by the Hebrew variation. One sees in perspective that the attribution of the *ex hebraico* translations due to Jerome amounted to several timely comments which have their source in the works of the priest of Bethlehem.[25]

NOTES

1. See *Dictionnaire Encyclopédique de la Bible*, article "Vulgate", 1959.

2. There are four allusions to Ruth found in the following: *On Christian Doctrine* 2.8.13; *On the Excellence of Widowhood* 4.5 and 7.10; *Questions on the Heptateuch*, quaestio 35 et quaestio 46.1.

3. See A.M. la Bonnardière, " Le Live de Jérémie", *Biblia Augustiniana*, Paris, 1972, pp. 11 and 102–103. Lamentations, except for Lamentations 3:30 (cited four times) and 4:20 (cited twice) are absent from the work of Augustine. Baruch, cited under the name of Jeremiah, is found in eight later citations.

4. There is one citation of Esdras 1 10:11 in *On Adulterous Marriage* 1.18.20; and an allusion to Esdras in *City of God* 17.241. There is nothing on Esdras 2 (Nehemiah). The apocryphal Esdras 3 is cited twice: 8:28 in *Against Two Letters of the Pelagians* 4.6 14 and is alluded to in *City of God* 18.36.

5. The book of Judith is named in *On Christian Doctrine* 2.8.13. The pericope Judith 5:5–9 is cited in *City of God* 16.13 and the book of Judith is alluded to in *City of God* 18.26.

6. The book of First Maccabees appears sporadically in several polemical works: 1 Macc. 4:42 in *Against the Letter of Parmenianus* II, 7 (14); 1 Macc. 2:61 in *Against Cresconius*.3.46.50; 1 Macc. 2:58 in *On the Merits and Remission of Sin* 1.3.3; 1 Macc. 2:65 in *On Original Sin* 2.30.35.

7. See A. M. la Bonnardière, "Les Douze Petits Prophètes", *Biblia Augustiniana*, Paris, 1963, p.33 (Nahum), p.25 (Obediah), pp. 21–22 (Joel). Joel 2:32 is only cited frequently through the Pauline text Rom. 10:13.

8. See *Letters* by Jerome: 39, 68, 72, and 81. See also *Letters* by Augustine: 28, 40, 71, 73, 74, 82 (following the numeration found in Augustine's work)

9. See *Letters*. 71, 75, 82 for discussion of the book of Jonah by Augustine. Also see A.M. la Bonnardière, "Les Douze Petits Prophètes", *Biblia Augustiniana*, Paris, 1963, pp. 27–29 and in particular Yves–Marie Duval, "Saint Augustin et le 'Commentaire sur Jonas' de saint Jérome" in *REAug* 12, 1966, pp.9–40.

10. *Revisions* 2. 55: Quaestionum libri septem.

11. According to *CSEL* 28^2, pp. 664–665: Hieronymus, t. XXIII, pp. 205 and s.

12. *Questions on the Heptateuch* 1, qu. 97 (Gen. 31:47–48); qu. 192 (Gen.41:50) qu. 162 (Gen. 47:31).

13. *Questions on the Heptateuch* 5, qu. 20 (Deut. 14:27–28); qu. 54 (Deut. 30:11–14).

14. *Questions on the Heptateuch* 6, qu. 7 (Jos. 5:13–15); qu. 15 (Jos. 10:5–6); qu. 19 (Jos. 16:10 and Jos. 6:26); qu. 24 (Jos. 23:14); qu. 25 (Jos. 24:3).

15. *Questions on the Heptateuch* 7, qu. 16 (Judg. 2:13); qu. 21 (Judg. 3:17); qu. 25 (Judg. 3:31); qu. 37 (Judg. 7:6); qu. 41 (Judg. 8: 26–27); qu. 47 (Judg. 10:1); qu. 55 (Judg. 15:8).

16. See 1.152; 6.19; 6.25; 5.54.

17. See 1.97; 1.162; 5.20; 6.7; 6.15; 7.37; 7.47.

18. See 1.97; 7.41.

19. F. Cavallera, *Les 'Quaestiones Hebraicae in Genesim' de saint Jérôme*, Rome, 1931 and "Les *Quaestiones in Genesim* de saint Augustin", in MA II, pp.359–372.

20. Jerome, *Letter* 27, CSEL 88, pp. 130–133; *"...tibi parva misi opuscula, id est in psalmum decimum et 'quaestionum Hebraicorum in Genesim commentariolos' quae legere te volo atque quasi amicum, non quasi iudicem."*

21. *Questions on the Heptaeuch* 1.25. see Cavallera, pp. 366–367 and *BA*, 36 footnote 21.

22. P. Benoit, "L'inspiration des Septante d'après les Pères", in H. de Lubac, *L'homme devant Dieu*, Paris, Aubier, 1963, pp. 184–185.

23. Concerning the book of Daniel in Augustine, see the article entitled "Daniel" which will appear in *Augustinus Lexikon*.

24. The text of *Against a Pamphlet of the Arians* 11.9 is the same as that of *Sermons* 102.3, which proves its late date.

25. To find the places where 'ex hebraico' is mentioned in the *City of God*, consult *Catalogus verborum Augustini*, volume *City of God*, by Eindhoven.

5

The Great Conference:
Augustine and His Fellow Readers

MARK VESSEY

The Science of Scripture: Jerome

We may begin by recalling some of the questions raised by Augustine in the first work he wrote as a priest, *On the Usefulness of Belief* (A.D. 392). Addressed to a friend and alter ego named Honoratus, the treatise combines an essay in hermeneutics with a sustained defence (against the Manichaeans) of the authority of the Catholic Church as interpreter of Scripture.[1] Augustine sets himself a limited goal and makes a show of saying more than would be needed to achieve it. Yet for all his bluster it is plain that he is grappling with problems more intractable than any ascribed to his correspondent. Granting the unity of the Old and New Testaments and trusting the Catholic Church to interpret them might be the first step for Honoratus, but for Augustine, who had taken this step and been ordained a teacher in that Church (2.4), other matters were already pressing. Many of them concerned the Bible. What kind of book was this that he now had to expound? How was it related to other books he knew? Why and how had it been promulgated? How did it fit into the (Christian Platonic) scheme of God's mediation of wisdom through Christ? Why was it often so difficult to understand? What were the constraints on its interpretation? How were reluctant readers to be reconciled to it? Some of these questions are raised explicitly, then deferred. Others merely suggest themselves. Few are convincingly answered. Behind them all, we sense, lies a single great unspoken question: what are the qualities that distinguish those ideal teachers, the *magistri, praeceptores* or *doctores* who embody the interpretative authority of the Catholic Church?

Only once in *On the Usefulness of Belief* is the anonymity of the ideal Christian teacher seriously compromised.[2] To read the Bible with understanding, Honoratus is told, one must find a qualified interpreter: "Is he difficult to find? Then search harder. Not to be found in your own country? Then travel. Not on the same continent? Take a boat. Not just across the water? Then go further, if necessary to the very land in which the events recorded in those books are said to have occurred"(7.17). Augustine's rhetoric then takes another turn. Nowhere else in this work does he suggest that in order to understand the Bible one must visit the holy places; such a radically "historicist" thesis would in fact be quite foreign to his thought. Unless the passage quoted is simply a flourish, we should suspect another reason for its eastward trajectory. The reason itself is not far to seek. The Holy Land could be recommended as a place to study Scripture, because Jerome was there.[3]

Augustine had missed meeting Jerome in Rome in the early 380s but would have had many opportunities since then to hear about him and his work. We know that as early as 392 Bishop Aurelius of Carthage took steps to secure copies of Jerome's biblical writings for the African church. A recently discovered letter of Jerome to Aurelius suggests that the author of *On the Usefulness of Belief* would already have had access to some of those texts.[4] When Augustine's friend Alypius returned from a visit to the Bethlehem monastery shortly afterwards, he probably brought more manuscripts with him. By then the Africans were in contact with one of Jerome's agents in Rome, from whom copies of his future works could be obtained. Thus, although it would be a few years before Augustine could claim close acquaintance with Jerome through his writings,[5] by the early 390s he would have had a strong impression of his literary persona and a fairly clear idea of his literary program.

Both persona and program were founded on emulation of Origen, the great third–century Alexandrian biblicist. "It is in your power," Augustine wrote to Jerome in 394/5, "to give us that man [sc. Origen] whom you so love to celebrate in your writings."[6] Jerome would not oblige the "studious society of the African churches" (as Augustine described himself and his learned colleagues) by producing a complete Latin translation of Origen's works, but he did aspire to the reputation for biblical science that Origen had acquired among the Greeks. The ideal of *scientia scripturarum* or "science of Scripture" that the Alexandrian represented for him, of a specialized or "professional" competence in biblical interpretation that was at once philologically and ascetically rigorous, is proclaimed repeatedly in the letters, prefaces and other promotional pieces that he published or republished in the late 380s and 390s after his removal from Rome to the East. Meanwhile, he sought to realize that ideal in his own major literary works, the biblical translations and commentaries.[7] No other Latin Christian writer had ever made so determined and exclusive a claim for interpretative expertise, or supported it with such impressive credentials. From all round the Mediterranean, Christian *studiosi* were now sending messengers, or going themselves to sit at the feet of the scholar of Bethlehem. The newly ordained priest of Hippo, who had lately begged his bishop for a little leisure for Bible study,[8] was bound to reckon with his example.

Jerome's work may have been one of the forces that impelled Augustine to focus his own intellectual and literary activity more closely on the Bible from the early 390s onwards. From the moment he began to write (and publish) on biblical topics he was inevitably engaged in a public dialogue with the man who had set himself up as a Latin exegete in "the very land" of the Bible. Part of that dialogue is clearly transcribed in letters between them, in which — despite mutual suspicion and misunderstanding — they came to exchange opinions on such important subjects as the contents of the biblical canon, the veracity of biblical narrative, the status of biblical commentary, and the desirability of a new translation of the Old Testament based on the Hebrew text (Jerome's great enterprise).[9] These letters are among our most interesting documents of early Christian approaches to the Bible. But they should not be read in isolation. Augustine's dialogue with Jerome on the aims and methods of biblical exegesis overruns the bounds of their formal correspondence. On his side it flows notably into two major works of the later 390s which, read in their historical context, can be construed as a justification or *apologia* for an activity of Christian teaching and writing on the Bible that was significantly different from the "Alexandrian" practice promoted by Jerome, albeit strongly influenced by it.

Before turning to those works, however, we should consider the role played by a third party.

Literary Conversation: Paulinus of Nola

At the same time as they worked to establish links with Jerome, the new men in the African church were opening channels of communication to the Christian elite of Italy. In the summer of 395, Aurelius' special envoy to Bethlehem, Alypius, took the initiative in writing to Meropius Pontius

Paulinus, a Gallo–Roman aristocrat with poetic ambitions whose ascetic conversion had caused a great stir a few years earlier, and who had now moved to Nola in Campania. In return for a service he asked of Paulinus, Alypius sent him a collection of Augustine's anti–Manichaean writings. The result, no doubt intended, was the beginning of a correspondence between Augustine and Paulinus which would continue with only brief interruptions for the next thirty years. Paulinus was the apostle of epistolary love (*caritas*). Believing more passionately than other men that letters were the portraits of their writers' souls, that letter–writing was true conversation, and that educated Christians had a duty to build up each other's spiritual strength by correspondence, this converted disciple of the poet–consul Ausonius (another zealot for epistolary reciprocity) had turned the hackneyed topics of late classical friendship (*amicitia*) into a sacrament of communion. Augustine positively reels under the shock of his first letter. He also recognizes at once the potential value of the Paulinian literary conversation or *conloquium litterarum* as a medium for religious instruction of the kind he was now called upon to dispense.

In his first letter Paulinus dilates upon his joy at receiving Augustine's writings, "not just for our own instruction, but for the use of the church in many of our cities." After acclaiming the author's services to Catholicism in the most extravagant terms, he continues with a characteristic figure of literary and spiritual refreshment:

> You see how intimately I have come to know you, how fondly I admire you, with how great a love I embrace you, who daily enjoy the converse of your writings (*qui cotidie conloquio litterarum tuarum fruor*) and feed upon the spirit of your words! For I may justly say that your mouth is a conduit of living water and a course of the eternal well–spring, because Christ has become in you "a well of water springing up into everlasting life" (John 4:14), in desire of which my soul's ground has thirsted for you and craved inebriation with the fullness of your flood.[10]

On the basis of the relationship thus evoked, Paulinus asks to receive more of Augustine's works and to be fostered and strengthened by him in his literary and spiritual endeavours. Though more restrained in its use of biblical language and imagery, Augustine's reply is scarcely less ecstatic: "O good man and good brother, you were hidden until now from my soul," it begins. Here indeed was a man he might have met sooner, one fit to have been an interlocutor in the dialogues of Cassiciacum, fitter perhaps than some who had been. A priest in a minor North African town could not expect to receive many such overtures, and Augustine makes the most of this chance to adapt the amities and aspirations of his Italian past to the realities of the present. Paulinus is enlisted to help with the difficult case of Licentius, the son of Augustine's patron Romanianus, who was excessively attached to secular learning. He is also fashioned into the ideal Christian reader. His own vision of himself as an ardent consumer of Augustine's works might be dangerously enthusiastic, but it could be modified. Reverting to the neo–Platonic pedagogy outlined several years earlier (ca. 389) in the *On the Teacher* and combining it with a traditional model of literary *emendatio* or friendly copy–editing, Augustine represents Paulinus as the reader who will discriminate critically but charitably between the words spoken by the divine Truth through Augustine's books and the words written in error by Augustine:

> When you read . . . I would not have you so transported by what the Truth speaks through our infirmity as to observe less carefully what I speak in my own right, lest in avidly drinking in the good and right things that I administer, having myself first received them, you neglect to pray for the sins and errors that I myself commit. For in those things which will rightly displease you if you take good notice, I am myself revealed; but in those which (by the gift of the spirit you have received) rightly please you in my books, he is to be loved and proclaimed, in whom is the well–spring of life. . . . For what have we that we have not received?[11]

In another context, such remarks could be dismissed as conventional modesty. Occurring in this case as the response to an impassioned appeal from an exceptionally qualified Christian reader, immediately after directions for obtaining copies of Augustine's works, immediately before the announcement of a project destined to form part of the *Confessions*,[12] and in the context of an exchange saturated on both sides with expressions of confidence in the virtue of "letters," they carry considerable weight. Here was a theory of Christian literary relations, already consistent with the most rigorous theology of grace (note the echo of 1 Cor. 4.7). All that was lacking in it was a clearly defined place for the biblical text.

In the event, Augustine's conversation with Paulinus had barely begun when Jerome broke in on it with an imperious reminder of the demands of biblical study as he conceived it. His Letter 53 to Paulinus, also written in 395, is a programmatic statement of his view of the science of Scripture as a distinct discipline, beyond the reach of any mere literary amateur.[13] In a long and rhetorically elaborate exordium Jerome piles up classical and biblical exempla designed to convince Paulinus and all other readers that they could never hope to enter the maze of Scripture without the help of a trained guide. Some scholars have detected a likeness of Augustine in the rogues' gallery of unqualified biblicists pilloried by Jerome in Letter 53. Even if no such reference were intended, Jerome's self–serving polemic would have run too close to the documented anxieties of the priest, soon to be bishop, of Hippo for the latter not to have felt himself implicated, had it come to his attention at this time. And apparently it did come to his attention.[14] Augustine responded by outlining a biblical pedagogy of his own, one which (in its final form) respected the demands of the Hieronymian science of Scripture without sacrificing the charms of the Paulinian literary conversation. His statement comes to us in two parts, the second of which significantly modifies the first: it begins with *On Christian Doctrine* of 396/7 and continues in the *Confessions.*

On Christian Doctrine

By 396 Augustine was ready to offer solutions to many of the problems raised five years earlier in *On the Usefulness of Belief.* Then he could only evoke the ideal of a Christian teacher, now he would lay down guidelines for his activity: *Sunt praecepta quaedam . . .* (Prol. 1: "There are certain precepts," etc.)[15] The new treatise would have to have a name. He had already written *On the Teacher;* to use that title again, or a variant of it, would be to invite confusion between the ultimate and proximate sources of true knowledge, an error that he was as keen to discourage now as ever. What was needed was a phrase that would encompass the whole economy of saving instruction, without prejudging relations between the divine and human agencies involved. Augustine's phrase is *doctrina christiana*, literally "Christian learning–and–teaching." As the prologue already makes plain, the ground of all such activity is the Bible.

To those who rejoice in a God–given ability to interpret Scripture without the use of such precepts as he is about to impart, Augustine opposes a carefully balanced theory of the instrumentality of human beings in the ministration of God's Word (prol. 4–9). The argument is built up of a number of elements: a characteristically Augustinian view of the mediation of transcendent truth, a demonstration of the social basis of language acquisition which anticipates the sign–theory outlined in Book 2, a series of biblical examples showing men of faith deferring to other men, and two *a priori* assumptions — that the human condition would be debased, and charity defeated of its aim "if human beings learned nothing through their fellow human beings" (prol. 6). Against whom is the argument directed? Several identifications of a hostile charismatic party have been proposed, but since none commands general assent we are free to entertain the suggestion (first made by R. Lorenz)[16] that Augustine is rejecting an extreme version of his own illuminism and that one purpose of the prologue is therefore apologetic. We should then suppose that the author of *On Christian Doctrine* chose deliberately to stress the outward or social aspect of Christian instruction in order to correct what might otherwise be perceived by readers of his works as a pastorally and ecclesially dangerous emphasis on its inward or psycho–logical aspects. Plausible as this argument is, it obliges us to consider why Augustine should particularly fear such an objection in 396. For while it is easy to see how a text like *On the Teacher* could be construed as hostile to the claims of professed (*a fortiori*, ordained) teachers of the gospel, those claims had been amply endorsed in *On the Usefulness of Belief* and other more recent works. Nor is there any reason to believe that Augustine's epistemology had itself changed significantly since the time of *On the Teacher*.[17] Thus when he goes out of his way to assert the validity of a human science of Scripture at the outset of *On Christian Doctrine*, he cannot be doing so merely for the purpose of *retractatio* or internal revision of his published opinions. Rather, he appears to be measuring his own approach to the biblical text against one that set more store than he ever would by the competence of the human interpreter.

As we have seen, Augustine's properly cautious attempt to establish his authority as a Christian teacher (writer and now bishop) had recently been crossed by Jerome's propaganda for a "professional" discipline of biblical interpretation. It can hardly be a coincidence that two of his four biblical examples of human instruction in the prologue (Paul and the Ethiopian eunuch) appear in exactly the same connection in Jerome's Letter 53 to Paulinus.[18] Like so much of Augustine's writing, *On Christian Doctrine* is visibly over–determined. As *correction*, the prologue and all that follows in 396/7 is directed at would–be charismatic or inspired interpreters of the Bible. As *defence,* it must contend with their arch–opponent, Jerome.[19]

Augustine's response to the Hieronymian theory of scriptural science is not only defensive, however. Even as he domesticates Jerome's polemic against amateur biblicists, he undercuts the social ambitions of the expert interpreter by assimilating his function to that of the humblest of the literary "professionals," the primary school reading–and–writing teacher or *magister litterarum* (prol. 9). The same process of reaction, adaptation, and critique can be observed throughout the two and a half books of *On Christian Doctrine* that were completed in the 390s. Augustine theorizes the *scientia scripturarum* more comprehensively than Jerome does, but is careful to place it no higher than the third step on a seven–rung ladder to *sapientia* (2.7.9–11). He accepts the importance of an acquaintance with Greek and Hebrew for the correct understanding of the Latin Bible, but subjects it to a general restraint on all knowledge of human conventions: *quantum satis est*, "as much as is necessary" (2.26.40; cf. 2.11.16–14.21). Perhaps most striking of all, at least to modern readers, is his subjection of secular literary and philosophical culture to the principle of *usus iustus*, "right use" (2.40.60), a criterion at once more generous and more rigorous than any hitherto proposed by Jerome. All these initiatives are fitted within the framework of a theory of the biblical text as consisting of "signs given by God but pointed out to us by men" (2.2.3). From first to last, Augustine's is a Christian *doctrina* simultaneously human and divine, historical and transcendent.

There are two other areas in which *On Christian Doctrine* (ca. 396–7) promises to correct or enlarge the notions that a Latin reader like Paulinus could have learnt from Jerome. First, it offers to shift the ethical conditions of acceptable or "successful" exegesis from the realm of asceticism to that of love or charity. Secondly, it announces precepts for the intepretation of Scripture (*tractatio scripturarum*) that would govern the enunciation of biblical meanings by human interpreters (*modus proferendi*) as well as their discovery (*modus inveniendi*). Neither promise is kept. Although Book 1 contains prolonged and often difficult discussion of the "rule of charity," it does not make good the providential connection between *caritas* and *doctrina* asserted in the prologue. And the first draft of the treatise breaks off before the author reaches the part devoted explicitly to the *modus proferendi*.[20]

On Christian Doctrine presents an anomaly with respect to Augustine's previous writings. For the first time he seems to have begun a major work without a named opponent or interlocutor, without a dedicatee, without even so much as an alter ego. In Jerome's continuing absence, the man who (in Peter Brown's words) "would never be alone" suddenly found he had no one to talk to. The strain on him is apparent from the start. Having announced the two parts of his subject at the beginning of Book 1, Augustine proceeds to a division: "We shall first discuss the discovery [of scriptural meanings], then the manner of their enunciation. A great and difficult task, *magnum opus et arduum . . . .*" A reminiscence of Cicero's dialogue of the *Orator* underlines the difference between the leisurely Ciceronian dialogues Augustine had himself composed at

Cassiciacum and immediately thereafter, and the heavy business of the present monologue. *Magnum opus omnino et arduum, Brute, conamur,* Cicero had written, *sed nihil difficile amanti* ("A great and difficult task it is that we attempt, Brutus, but nothing is difficult for one who loves his friend as I love you"). Ostensibly the expression of a friendship, the *Orator* is presented as a natural continuation of private conversations between Cicero and Brutus, conversations duly commemorated in the next sentence of that work. This fiction was one that Augustine had earlier used to great effect, but was now trying to do without. Perhaps not surprisingly, when the task of laying down "precepts" for the interpretation of Scripture finally proved too much for him, he transferred the matter in hand to a literary conversation already in progress between himself, his God, and his spiritual friends in Christ. In this respect as in others, the *Confessions* is the first and aptest sequel to the unfinished *On Christian Doctrine* of 397.

Conference and Confession

Paulinus' correspondence had reminded Augustine of the delights of epistolary conversation and suggested to him a way of turning them to religious account. It had also, as a result of Jerome's interference, made him acutely aware of the awkwardness of maintaining simultaneously a belief in the dependence of human insight on divine illumination and a public practice of scriptural exegesis. This difficulty, which his developing notions of divine grace could only exacerbate, was to exercise Augustine for the rest of his life. The immediate challenge, deferred at some cost in *On Christian Doctrine,* was to locate the activity of biblical interpretation within the literary–colloquial mode. Biblical theology, in the strict or etymological sense of "talking about God on the basis of his word in Scripture," had to be made part of a human dialogue conducted in writing. Thus formulated, the task confronting Augustine posed both a danger and a problem. The danger was that the dialogue would become merely human, mere chatter among men; this hazard he averts in the *Confessions* by the bold expedient of bringing God himself into the conversation.[21] The problem was that the message of a voiceless and at times barely intelligible text, the Bible in Latin, had somehow to be inserted into the current discourse of late antique men and women. It is (to adapt the terms of *On Christian Doctrine*) the problem of the *modus inveniendi et proferendi,* of discovering and enunciating the truth contained in Scripture — in reality a single complex procedure rather than two separable ones. The standard forms of biblical commentary, as Augustine who had lately begun to practice them knew only too well, represented at best a partial solution. A new theory and practice of the biblical text was required, for which recent experiments in Latin biblical poetry (e.g., those of Juvencus, Proba and Paulinus) and epistolography (e.g., those of Jerome and Paulinus) offered hints but no clear directions. The *Confessions* shows what such a new theory and practice might be like.

For the first seven of the ten books that he wrote "about himself,"[22] Augustine represents reading and conversation either as distinct and potentially opposed activities or as related forms of time–wasting. Learning to read and write might be useful; reading and reciting pagan poetry was a dangerous self–indulgence (1.12.19ff). When Monica asks the local bishop to speak with her son, he assures her that the latter will find his own way by reading (3.12.21). The society of the friends with whom Augustine is wont to talk, laugh and read is a snare (4.8.13). He reads Cicero, Aristotle and other difficult pagan texts on his own and has no trouble understanding them (4.16.28–31), but does less well with the Bible. The long awaited conversation with Faustus the Manichee is a disappointment; the two men end up studying classical authors together (5.6–7). Even Ambrose, reading silently apart, is unavailable for the talk that Augustine now so urgently desires to have (6.3.3).[23]

By this stage of the narrative, the reader of the *Confessions* already has a strong sense of the kind of talk that would be. It is represented in Augustine's text by a word which appears with remarkable frequency in Books 4–7, the verb *conferre* (past tenses: *contulisse, conlatum*; whence the noun *conlatio*). In his use of it, which largely exploits the range of meanings in the classical lexicon, this compound typically signifies one or more of the following: (1) to converse or confer, (2) to share or place something in common, (3) to compare ideas, opinions or impressions. In most instances in the *Confessions* it is applied in such a way as to emphasize the social and communicative implications of the *con–* prefix. Augustine was too good a grammarian to play idly with morphemes; as Kenneth Burke has shown, prefixes and their corresponding prepositions often mass with coercive force in the *Confessions*.[24] In this case the reiterated *conferre* inclines the reader surely if insensibly to accommodate the activity of *conloqui* ("to converse"), for which it is a common synonym, to that of *legere* ("to read"), with which it is regularly associated in the text. Three examples will serve to illustrate this process.[25]

1. As a student in Carthage, Augustine had read Aristotle's *Categories.* Ruefully he reflects on the experience:

> What did it profit me that, being scarce twenty years old, the book of Aristotle, called the Ten Categories, fell into my hands, and I read and understood it without a teacher? For when afterwards I conferred about them with others (*Quas cum contulissem cum eis*) they professed that they had much to do to understand them, though they had been instructed therein by most learned masters, and that not by lectures only but by means of many delineations drawn in the sand; yet could they not, for all that, tell me anything about the matter, which I myself had not learned, by reading them alone. (4.16.28)

In *On Christian Doctrine* Augustine had presented human intercourse as the normal prerequisite for any science, specified the relationship between teacher and pupil, and argued for the role of the human teacher in Christian instruction.[26] Now he presents himself as a brilliant autodidact, unable to engage in any productive discussion with his fellow students, in order to argue for a Christian "conversion" of secular science according to the principle of "right use" outlined in *On Christian Doctrine* 2.40.60. The object of his scorn in this chapter of the *Confessions* is neither Aristotle nor students less talented than himself, but his own motives as a reader and interpreter (discussant or expositor). His attempts at communication on secular literary and philosophical texts had failed because he was not aiming at their right use. Whereas Book 2 of *On Christian Doctrine* concentrates on the theory of the Christian use of pagan texts in relation to their contents, the *Confessions* strives for a vision of its practice in relation to the human parties involved.

2. For nine long years Augustine had looked forward to meeting Faustus the Manichee, in conversation with whom (5.6.10: *conlatoque conloquio*) he hoped to find solutions to the difficulties he was experiencing with the sect's doctrines. On finally hearing him speak, he was charmed by his eloquence. As described in the *Confessions*, Faustus' performance is comparable to that of the show–orators of the so–called Second Sophistic, men like his countryman Apuleius who had held earlier audiences of educated Africans spellbound with their verbal artifice. The mature Augustine takes him as a pretext for separating the claims of truth from those of eloquence, verbal form from doctrinal content, the human minister from the divine source. He also uses him to dramatize the problem of the "conference" evoked in connection with his own earlier readings of the poets and philosophers. The young Augustine, we are told, was not prepared just to listen to Faustus and applaud him with the rest, but was determined to put certain questions to him "in familiar conversation and the give–and–take of discussion" (5.6.11: *conferendo familiariter et accipiendo ac*

reddendo sermonem). The questions related to things he had read. There were particular Manichaean texts he wished to discuss, passages which he had marked because they contained statements in conflict with other authorities he had read (5.7.12: *conlatis . . . rationibus, quas alibi ego legeram*). The desired conversation or conference (*conlatio*, sense 1) would thus involve a comparison of ideas (*conlatio*, sense 3) based on a sharing or *mise–en–commun* (*conlatio*, sense 2) of relevant texts, extracted or summarized. Unfortunately, Faustus turns out not to be the conference–partner Augustine is looking for and he is once again confined to an unequal dialogue concerning texts he has already mastered (5.7.13).

   3. Incompetence or unwillingness to ventilate "secondary" texts is not the only failing for which Manichaean teachers are reproached in the *Confessions*. Their practice of the biblical text is also sharply criticized. Compelled by their philosophy to discount large portions of the Scriptures held canonical by the Catholic Church, they justified themselves by claiming that the excluded matter had been interpolated by judaizing heretics. In contending with this view, and finally rejecting it as untenable, Augustine was led into considerations of biblical philology:

> I thought that those things which the Manichees reprehended in the Scriptures could not be defended; yet I sometimes desired to examine them one by one with some man most learned in those books (*cupiebam cum aliquo illorum librorum doctissimo conferre singula*), and thereupon to see what he held. And I thought the answer of the Manichees was weak, for they would say that the Scriptures of the New Testament were falsified by I know not whom, but themselves did yet produce no copies thereof which were uncorrupted. (5.11.21)

This is as close as Augustine comes in the *Confessions* to using the verb *conferre* in the technical sense (4) of "collating" manuscripts. Even without such codicological precision, the passage is important testimony to the role played by the Manichees in shaping his view of the biblical text *qua* text, that is, as a set of verbal signs transmitted by writing, subject to the usual hazards of literary tradition in a manuscript culture. Interestingly enough, Augustine's dissatisfaction with the Manichaean view of the text and desire to confer with "some man most learned in those books" are recorded in the *Confessions* at a point just before his departure from Rome in 384. Their dramatic date thus coincides exactly with the launching in the same city of Jerome's career as a biblical philologist, an event closely associated with his collation (in the technical sense above) of Latin, Greek and Hebrew manuscripts of the Bible. Augustine's experience as a

Manichee undoubtedly helped make him receptive to Jerome's insistence on the philological aspect of the *scientia scripturarum,* while also ensuring that he would not follow him all the way in his editorial revisionism.

These examples from Books 4–5 by no means exhaust the implications of the verb *conferre* as used in the *Confessions.* They may suffice, however, to establish the importance of *conlatio* as a multivalent literary–theoretical concept in this context and to warrant our considering other scenes and episodes (including some from which the verb itself is absent) in the light of the "conference" paradigm. Indeed, they may even justify our taking a partial view of the *Confessions* as the record of a series of *conlationes* conducing to a literary–interpretative transaction or "text act" of potentially definitive type. By persistently associating human conversation with various kinds of comparison or collation involving texts, and gradually narrowing the range of texts considered to the Bible, Augustine contrives, first, to identify Christian discourse with attention to the biblical text and, secondly, to present the literary–colloquial mode as a natural vehicle for biblical exegesis.

The Discourse of Discovery

The autobiographical climax of Augustine's *Confessions* (or *Conferences*) is reached in the threefold conversion–narrative of Book 8.[27] Reading and conversation play decisive roles in the stories of Marius Victorinus and of the two imperial officials at Trier, but the privilege of conversion by biblical "conference" is reserved for Augustine and his life–long partner in God–talk, Alypius. The verb *conferre* does not appear in the surface text of the famous garden scene. Instead, as in the preceding description of Ponticianus' visit, the narrator uses the verb *sedere* ("to sit") in the first person plural to create the context for a shared activity of reading. In his distress, we are told, Augustine laid down the copy of St. Paul's Epistles that was to have been their study that day, got up from the place where he and Alypius were sitting together (*ubi sedebamus*), and prostrated himself under a fig tree some distance away (8.12.28). It is while he is lying there crying that he hears the childlike voice summoning him back to his reading: *tolle lege, tolle lege* ("take it up and read, take it up and read"). The singular imperative (*lege* not *legite*) can only apply to one reader, but since it is delivered more than once (*crebro*) by an invisible speaker, it could in principle be addressed to more than one person. We are not told whether Alypius heard the voice; the sequel suggests that, even if he did, he was less quick than Augustine to interpret it, else he would have been the first to pick up the book. Augustine, returning to stand or sit again beside his friend, opens the codex at random and reads in silence from Romans (*legi in silentio*). This is not a conversation, at least not between human beings, nor yet a conference.[28] Even now, in the close company of Alypius his fellow reader, Augustine (like Ambrose in the earlier scene) reads alone. The silence continues after he has finished reading and as Alypius reads in turn. The two men communicate over the text by facial expression and gesture:

> Then shutting the book, and putting my finger or some other mark between the leaves, I showed it to Alypius, my countenance now calm. And he also, in like manner, showed me what was in his heart, of which I knew nothing. He desired to see what I had read: I showed him, and he read on further than I had done. For I was ignorant of what followed, which was this: "Him that is weak in the faith receive ye" (Rom. 14:1). And this he applied to himself, as he then revealed to me. (8.12.30)

> [*Tum interiecto aut digito aut nescio quo alio signo codicem clausi et tranquillo iam vultu "indicavi" Alypio. At ille quid in se ageretur – quod ego nesciebam – sic "indicavit." Petit videre quid legissem: "ostendi", et adtendit etiam ultra quam ego legeram. Et ignorabam quid sequeretur. Sequebatur vero: "infirmum autem in fide recipite." Quod ille ad se rettulit mihique "aperuit".*]

Of course if one translates the verbs *indicare, petere, ostendere* and *aperire* as "to declare," "to ask," "to tell" and "to explain," as many good translators have, the silence is immediately broken. Augustine, however, seems to have gone out of his way to use deictic terms which in this instance do not require any speech to take place. The scene is more dramatically powerful, as well as more theologically significant, if no articulate sound is heard in the garden after the (divine) utterance from the neighboring house.[29] The subsequent "conversation" with Monica can also be seen as occurring in conditions of wordless rapture: "Thence we went in to my mother. We indicated to her [what had happened], she rejoiced." Only then, and with heavy emphasis, does Augustine introduce a verb that necessarily implies speech: *Narramus, quemadmodum gestum sit* ("We related how it had happened"). If this reading is accepted, the conversion of Augustine and Alypius appears as an example of what might be called the literary conference *degré zéro*, a text act involving two people who confer without speaking. Paradoxically but predictably, this minimal form of the literary conference is for Augustine also its highest form, unattainable without supernatural help. As shared human experience it is surpassed, in this life, only by such moments of textless communion as the vision at Ostia described in Book 9.

The deixis of the conversion–scene may be regarded as an epitome of the autobiographical part of the *Confessions*, Books 1–10 on the author's reckoning. Augustine's narration is self–indication. *Indicabo me* ("I will show myself", literally "I will point myself out," but with the possible further sense of "I will accuse myself"), he says repeatedly at the beginning of Book 10, in a passage of great importance for our understanding of his purpose in the work as a whole (10.1.1–4.6). We recall that in the *De doctrina christiana* Augustine had defined the contents of the Bible as "signs given by God but pointed out to us by our fellow human beings" (*signa divinitus data [sed] per homines nobis indicata*). Now he is intent on reading his own life as a divinely inspired narrative. By revealing himself, not merely as he once was but also as he now is, he hopes to induce in his readers a response comparable to Monica's at the end of Book 8: joy and praise of God, mingled with holy terror. As in the garden, so in the *Confessions* as a literary work, the act of self–indication is achieved through the medium of the Bible. The "Augustine" of 385 is reported to have revealed himself to Alypius and Monica by reading himself into (and out of) a passage in Romans in a manner suggested to him by the *Life of Antony;* the "Augustine" of ca. 397–400 reveals himself to his fellow human beings by writing himself into and out of a biblical narrative of loss and redemption artfully reconstituted from the Gospels and the Psalms. In neither case are the moment and means of discovering–himself easily distinguishable from the moment and means of discovering–himself–to–others, or from the moment and means of discovering–God–for–himself–and–so–to–others. The complex dynamics of this multiple process of discovery and indication is the main subject of Book 10, in which Augustine considers his own memory as the ground of his knowledge both of himself and (in an infinitely mysterious way) of his God, and as the source of all his utterances. Although the biblical text itself is conspicuously absent from the discussion, the return at a critical juncture of two key terms from *On Christian Doctrine* namely *invenire* ("to find, discover") and *proferre* ("to utter"),[30] reminds us that these reflections on discovery and declaration are the sequel to conferences textual (Book 8) as well as non–textual (Book 9), and prepares us for the transition from the ten books Augustine wrote about himself to the three he wrote about the Bible.

Book 11 of the *Confessions* resumes the unfinished business of the "apology against Jerome," inserting the act of biblical exegesis into the conference paradigm established in Books 1–9(10). The narrative of Augustine's life, we are given to believe, has delayed a more important enterprise:

> When shall I be able with this tongue of my pen to declare all thine exhortations and comforts and particular providences, whereby thou hast drawn me to preach thy word and to dispense thy sacrament to thy people? And although I should be able to declare these things in order, yet the very moments or drops of time are precious unto me; and for a long time have I been fired with a desire to "meditate in thy law" (Ps. 2:1), and therein to confess to thee both my knowledge and my ignorance (*tibi confiteri scientiam et imperitiam meam*). (11.2.2)

Whatever sense we attach to "confessing" in Augustine's previous uses of the verb, there is no mistaking the novelty of his idea of a *confessio scientiae* (sc. *scripturarum*), of a voluntary exposure of his limited expertise as an interpreter of the Bible. Five years after his initial correspondence with Paulinus of Nola, he is at last ready to challenge Jerome's theory and practice of the sacred text. As he turns from the narrative of himself to the mysteries of Scripture, his references to God's people and the preaching of God's word recall the theme of *praedicatio* announced in the opening sentences of the work, and can be — indeed have been[31]— taken as a sign that the confessional mode is now finally expanding to encompass the professional functions of the priestly interpreter. This is a legitimate inference, provided we respect the relations between *confessio* and *professio* implied in the work as a whole and do not try to read Augustine's exegesis of the Creation story in Books 11–13 as a specimen of the kind of sermon he might have preached to his congregation in Hippo. We do indeed see the "professional" biblicist at work in these books, but in a context dictated by the preceding parts of the *Confessions* rather than by the as yet unwritten fourth book of *On Christian Doctrine*.

When Augustine says he will "confess" before God whatever he "discovers" in the sacred text (11.2.3: *confitear tibi quidquid invenero in libris tuis*), he invites us to consider confession as a possible mode of discourse (*modus proferendi*) for the biblical interpreter. At the same time, he makes that possibility contingent on our own activity *as readers*. As a statement at the beginning of Book 11 reminds us once again, the aim of his personal narrative in the earlier books has been to turn each and every reader into a fraternal accomplice in the act of confession: "to stir up the affections both of myself and of others who shall read these things; that so together we may say: 'The Lord is great and greatly to be praised'"

(11.1.1).[32] That affective design does not lapse as confession turns to, or more fully becomes, biblical interpretation. When, a few lines later, the would–be exegete proclaims his desire not only to benefit himself but also to be "of use to fraternal charity" (11.2.3), we are meant to recognize the same symmetry between self–interest and altruism, feel the accumulated weight of innumerable *con–* prefixes, and understand that we (the fraternal reader) are to carry on participating in a speech act that is now manifestly a text act of the type prefigured in earlier books.

The last three books of the *Confessions,* Augustine's invitation to a charitable conference on the biblical story of Creation, rank among the hardest in Latin literature. "Anfractuous" one scholar has called them. They embrace *inter alia* an exegesis of Genesis 1, a demonstration of the multiplicity of possible exegeses of the same, and a discussion of the principles on which different exegeses (of this or any biblical text) should be rejected or accepted. Reduced to a set of precepts, a large part of what is said repeats statements already made in the unfinished *On Christian Doctrine.*[33] But Augustine is no longer giving precepts; he is working through examples with his imaginary fellows in conference, including some who he knows will want to contradict him. Problems of interpretation and adjudication raised theoretically in works such as *On the Usefulness of Belief* and practically by his earlier attempts to expound Genesis, problems which had become embarrassingly personal in the triangular correspondence with Paulinus and Jerome, and with which he had wrestled at length in *On Christian Doctrine* are now the subject of a debate that relentlessly solicits the reader's involvement. Although few late antique readers can have felt themselves wholly adequate to the task, none could doubt what was being required of him or her: to "seek, ask, knock" in company with Augustine, in the faithful and charitable hope of "receiving, finding, and entering" with him.[34] Oversimplifying slightly, we might say that the author of the *Confessions* had reverted to the manner of his earlier "literary debates with those present and with himself alone in the presence of God" (9.4.7), the dialogues of Cassiciacum or *On the Teacher* only this time with the biblical text as the center of conference.

Christian Literature as Biblical Conference

The *confessio scientiae* of *Confessions* 11–13 registers an important advance on the incomplete *On Christian Doctrine* of 396–7 and marks a turning–point in Augustine's relations with the Latin reading public. While the earlier treatise had laid an initial emphasis on the social aspect of biblical interpretation, only then to lose itself in semiotics, the *Confessions* finally envisages the act of discovering–and–announcing biblical truth as the joint work of two or more human beings gathered in the presence of God, as an *actus conferendi* or "conference" performed in the spirit of charity. It thereby deflects possible criticism of the author as one who would undervalue human instruction in the science of Scripture, without committing him to a narrowly "professional" conception of the interpreter's role. The *Confessions* defines an ideal context in which a recently elevated bishop could communicate on biblical topics with men like Paulinus, yet not fall victim to the philological–ascetic rigor of a Jerome. And it does all this without compromising Augustine's view of God as the only source of true knowledge, the inner teacher in conference with whom we discover what is true and what is false. The delicate balance between the respective claims of the external divine text and the internal divine voice is struck at the moment of approach to Genesis 1:1 in Book 11:

> Let me hear and understand how thou, "in the beginning created the heaven and the earth." Of this Moses wrote and passed away, he went hence from thee, to thee, and he is not now before me. For if he were, then would I hold him fast and beg of him for thy sake that he would discover these things to me; and I would lay these ears of mine to the sound that should break out of his mouth. Yet if he should speak Hebrew, in vain would it fall upon my ears, nor would aught of it reach unto my mind; but if he spake Latin, I should know what he said. Yet how should I know, whether he said true or no? And if I knew this also, should I know it of him? Indeed I should not. For within me, in that very house of my thought, neither Hebrew, nor Greek, nor Latin, nor any barbarous tongue, but Truth itself, without instrument of mouth or tongue, and without the noise of any syllables, would say unto me, "It is the truth"; and I, being assured thereof, would confidently avow to that man of thine, "Thou speakest truly" (11.3.5).

The ground on which Augustine rejects an imaginary conversation with Moses is the ground on which he joins in an imaginary conference with his readers. Responding to Jerome in *On Christian Doctrine*, he had stipulated a limited knowledge of the original biblical languages, *quantum satis est*. Now even that requirement is tacitly lifted. Jerome, who in his recourse to the "Hebrew verity" (as he called it) could be thought to have identified biblical "truth" with the language of its first expression, might converse with Moses in Hebrew if he wished. The author of the *Confessions* is not interested in that kind of conversation. Less than a decade earlier, in *On the Usefulness of Belief*, he had briefly hinted that the aspiring

69

Christian biblicist should seek a master in the Holy Land, by implication someone like Jerome. The experience of the intervening years, in particular his epistolary converse with Paulinus, had convinced him of the pointlessness of such expedients. Augustine was in Hippo, and there would remain, the animator of a biblical conference of ever–growing dimensions that would go on for centuries after his death. The third chapter of Book 11 of the *Confessions* marks the end of Augustine's apology against Jerome and the beginning of one of the greatest conversations in history.

NOTES

1. Ed. J. Zycha, *CSEL* 25(1): 3–48; trans. C. L. Cornish, *NPNF*, 1st ser., 3: 347–66.

2. Teaching of Ambrose is briefly evoked at 8.20 but his role is restricted to that of one who helped Augustine reach a conviction of the value of *auctoritas* in the Christian religion; he is not yet cited as an exemplary teacher, as he was to be in the *Confessions*.

3. Compare Jerome's preface to his translation of Chronicles according to the Septuagint (*PL* 29: 423): "Just as the histories of the Greeks are better understood by those who have visited Athens, or the third book of Virgil's *Aeneid* by those who have sailed from Troy to Sicily by way of Leucadia and Acroceraunia and thence to the mouth of the Tiber, so the sense of Holy Scripture will be clearer to one who has seen Judaea with his or her own eyes." This work is traditionally dated between 389 and 392.

4. *Letter* 27*, ed. J. Divjak, CSEL 88.

5. In his *Letter* 40 of ca. 397 he speaks of knowing the "whole Jerome" (*te totum*) through his books and urges him to engage more closely in a "literary conversation" (*litterariam conlocutionem*). Augustine's letters of the period ca. 391–401 are quoted from the edition of A. Goldbacher, *CSEL* 34. There is an English translation of his correspondence with Jerome by Carolinne White (Lewiston: The Edwin Mellen Press, 1990).

6. *Letter* 28.2.

7. H. F. D. Sparks, "Jerome as Biblical Scholar," in *The Cambridge History of the Bible*, vol. 1: *From the Beginnings to Jerome*, ed. P. R. Ackroyd and C. F. Evans (Cambridge: Cambridge University Press, 1970), 510–41, is an excellent introductory survey.

8. *Letter* 21.3.

9. See now Ralph Hennings, *Der Briefwechsel zwischen Augustinus und Hieronymus und ihr Streit um den Kanon des Alten Testaments und die Auslegung von Gal. 2, 11–14*, (Leiden: E. J. Brill, 1994). References to earlier studies are given by White (note 5 above).

10. *Letter* 25.2 in Augustine's correspondence, 4.2 in that of Paulinus (ed. W. Hartel, *CSEL* 30). Paulinus' letters have been translated by P. G. Walsh in *ACW* 35–36.

11. *Letter* 27.4.

12. *Letter* 27.5 concerns the project of a "life" of Alypius; see now James J. O'Donnell, *Augustine: Confessions*, 3 vols. (Oxford: Clarendon Press, 1992), 2: 360–2, who suggests that Paulinus' habit of weaving biblical imagery and allusions into the texts of his letters "was surely one element in the forging of the distinctive style of [the *Confessions*.]"

13. Also containing a summary of the biblical canon, the letter subsequently appeared as a general prologue to the Vulgate. Text ed. I. Hilberg, *CSEL* 54; trans. W. H. Freemantle, *NPNF*, 2nd ser., 6: 96–102.

14. For evidence, see Jean Doignon, "'Nos bons hommes de foi': Cyprien, Lactance, Victorin, Optat, Hilaire (Augustin, *De Doctrina Christiana*, II, 40, 61)," *Latomus* 22 (1963): 795–805.

15. Citations of the *On Christian Doctrine* follow the edition of J. Martin, *CCSL* 32. There is now a convenient edition of the Latin text with English translation and commentary by R. P. H. Green (Oxford: Clarendon Press, 1995).

16. "Die Wissenschaftslehre Augustins," *Zeitschrift für Kirchengeschichte* 67 (1955–56): 29–60, 213–51, here 237. See now Charles Kannengiesser, "Local Setting and Motivation of *De doctrina christiana*", in J. T. Lienhard, S.J., E. C. Muller & R.J. Teske, S.J., *Augustine Presbyter Factus Sum* (Collectanea Augustiniana 2), New York: P. Lang, 1993, pp. 331–339; and "The Interrupted *De doctrina christiana*," in *De Doctrina Christiana: A Classic of Western Culture*, ed. Duane W. H. Arnold and Pamela Bright (Notre Dame: University of Notre Dame Press, 1995), 3–13.

17. A. D. R. Polman, *The Word of God according to St. Augustine* (Grand Rapids, MI: Eerdmans, 1961), 30, correctly observes that "The . . . interpretation of the Logos as the inner teacher who shows us how to contemplate truth was never rejected by St. Augustine, and made its influence felt throughout his writings on the Word of God as Holy Writ and as proclamation."

18. Prol. 6–7; Jerome, *Letter* 53.2, 5.

19. The crossing at this point of Jerome's and Augustine's purposes as biblical interpreters is shrewdly observed by Christoph Schäublin, "*De doctrina christiana*: A Classic of Western Culture?" in Arnold and Bright (note 16 above), 47–67, at 54–5.

20. The break between the unfinished treatise of 396–7 and its later continuation occurs at 3.25.35/36. For evidence that the work circulated in this unfinished state, see now Kenneth Steinhauser, "Codex Leningradensis Q.v.I.3.: Some Unsolved Problems," in Arnold and Bright (note 16 above), 33–43. Augustine returned to the work and finally completed it ca. 427, in the course of reviewing his lifetime's literary output in the *Retractationes* or *Revisions*.

21. The best discussion of this device is by Reinhart Herzog, "'Non in sua voce': Augustins Gespräch mit Gott in den 'Confessiones' – Voraussetzungen und Folgen," in *Das Gespräch*, ed. Karlheinz Stierle

and Rainer Warning, *Poetik und Hermeneutik* 11 (Munich: Fink Verlag, 1984), 213–250. On his analysis, Books 1–8 of the *Confessions* enact the gradual fulfilment of the conditions for the *beginning* of a dialogue between Augustine and God, one of which is the exclusion of other, human partners–in–conversation. That dialogue begins in the garden in Milan and continues thereafter in confrontation with the text of Scripture. Once *begun*, it immediately expands to include Augustine's fellow readers.

22. In *Revisions* 2.6.1 (ed. A. Mutzenbecher, *CCSL* 57), Augustine speaks of his *Confessions* as "written about me from the first to the tenth book, and in the other three books about Holy Scripture, from the point where it is written: 'In the beginning God created heaven and earth.'"

23. See now Brian Stock, *Augustine the Reader: Meditation, Self–Knowledge and the Ethics of Interpretation* (Cambridge, MA: Harvard University Press, 1996).

24. *The Rhetoric of Religion: Studies in Logology* (Berkeley: University of California Press, 1970), 43–171.

25. Translations are from the version by Tobie Matthew (1620), rev. Dom Roger Hudleston (London: Burns Oates and Washbourne Ltd., 1923), adapted where necessary. For the Latin text I follow the *editio minor* of M. Skutella, rev. H. Jürgens and W. Schaub (Stuttgart: B. G. Teubner, 1981).

26. The argument is already well developed in *On the Usefulness of Belief*, e.g., 7.17 where it is followed by the passage evoking the ideal teacher of Scripture.

27. See Stock, *Augustine the Reader*, 75–111, for a nuanced account of these events.

28. Cf. Joseph Anthony Mazzeo, "St. Augustine's Rhetoric of Silence," *Journal of the History of Ideas* 23 (1962) : 175–97, esp. 189–92.

29. Cf. Pierre Courcelle, *Recherches sur les "Confessions" de saint Augustin*, 2nd edn. (Paris: De Boccard, 1968), 306–10, for whom the voice saying *"Tolle, lege"* is an internal voice heard only by Augustine. Whether this point is granted or not, Courcelle is surely right to say that *"Il s'agit matériellement d'une scene muette, d'une histoire sans paroles [humaines]"* (307).

30. At 10.14.22 (on the recovery and production of concepts from memory): *"Sed ecce de memoria "profero", cum dico quattuor esse perturbationes animi . . . et quidquid de his disputare potuero . . . , ibi "invenio" quid dicam atque inde "profero" nec tamen ulla earum perturbatione perturbor, cum eas reminiscendo conmemoro; et antequam recolerentur a me et retractarentur, ibi erant . . . . Forte ergo sicut de ventre cibus ruminando, sic ista de memoria recordando "proferuntur". . . Quis enim talia volens loqueretur, si quotiens tristitiam metumve nominamus, totiens maerere vel timere cogeremur? Et tamen non ea loqueremur, nisi in memoria nostra non tantum sonos . . . sed etiam rerum ipsarum notiones "inveniremus". . ."* These reflections lead naturally to a discussion of the problem of finding (*invenire*) and uttering (*confiteri, praedicare*) God or the Truth.

31. E.g., by Burke, *Rhetoric of Religion*, 123, 135.

32. Similarly, Augustine writes in his *Revisions* (2.6.1): "The thirteen books of my *Confessions* praise the justice and goodness of God in both the good and evil of my life, to stir up human understanding and love for him. For myself, I can say already that they had that effect on me when they were being written and continue to move me in the same way when they are read [i.e. when they are read aloud to a group]. As for what others think, that is for them to decide; I know, however, that they have greatly pleased and continue to please many of the brothers."

33. While some of what is said anticipates the still–to–be–written second part of Book 3.

34. *Conf.* 13.38.53 (the closing sentences of the work): "And what human being is there that can make another human being understand this? Or what angel, an angel? Or what angel, a human being? Let it be asked of thee, let it be sought in thee, let it be knocked for at thee; so shall it be received, so shall it be found, so shall it be opened [*A te petatur, in te quaeratur, ad te pulsetur: sic, sic accipietur, sic invenietur, sic aperietur*]." The final phrase is potentially ambiguous. Although the biblical subtext implies that the "opening" will be made *to* the human postulant by God, the passive form of the Latin verbs hints at the possibility that one human "recipient" will (by the grace of God) "open" what has been "found" to another. We may compare the opening sentences of *On Christian Doctrine* prol. 1: "There are certain precepts for the interpretation of the Scriptures, which I consider may usefully be transmitted to those who are studious of those books, in order that they may profit, not only by reading the [works of] others who have opened things that lie hidden in the divine writings but also by opening [such things] to others themselves." Note that one's capacity to profit from Scripture is here (as in 1.1) conceived partly as a function of one's ability or willingness to assist others in understanding it (cf. the text quoted at note 11 above). At its close the *Confessions* comes back to the point–of–departure of *On Christian Doctrine* in order to "retractate" – i.e. revise and supplement – the statements made in the earlier work about the role of the human teacher in the transmission of saving doctrine.

6

The Christological Substructure
of Augustine's Figurative Exegesis

MICHAEL CAMERON

Introduction: Tracking Augustine the Exegete

Augustine's experience of conversion in the year 386 was momentous but not unique; he was a man of several large conversions and a number of small ones. Reading Cicero's *Hortensius* ignited him with the love of wisdom; the books of the *Platonici* uncovered for him the panoply of the spiritual world; the necessity of authority for understanding truth devolved on him all at once; and within his catholic experience he suddenly moved to a radical understanding of operative grace. But Augustine's development is a story, not of vacillation, but of change through the accumulation of insights.[1] This paper will track one thread of change in the ten years between *On Genesis Against the Manicheans* (388) and *Against Faustus* (398), which reveals development in his approach to the figurative exegesis of the Old Testament. Eventually his approach represented a creative synthesis of the two major strands of early Christian exegesis, traditionally called the allegorical and the typological.[2]

Because of the symbiotic relationship in his thought between human language and the Word of God,[3] correlations exist between Augustine's christology, theory of signs and practice of figurative exegesis, and suggest a field of coherence within his theology. How to describe such fields and their changes is a challenge, but recent interest in adapting Thomas Kuhn's language of "paradigms" to the concerns of historical theology suggests one option. Since Kuhn's definition of paradigm stresses not only a constellation of meaning but the exemplary form and the revisionary power of a "concrete puzzle solution" such as Augustine labored to find, "paradigm" will be the term used here for describing the bishop's shifting interpretive structures.[4] This paper will argue that in the period after his conversion Augustine's understanding of signs, figurative exegesis and christology are identifiable as elements of a "spiritualist" paradigm, and that in the early 390's they gradually and coordinately shift to an "incarnational" paradigm which, as the name implies, was generated by an advance in his christology.[5]

In the mid–380's Augustine broke free from what might be called a "materialist" paradigm and achieved a conception of immaterial and immutable spirit (*Conf.* 7.17.23). Though releasing him from the Manichaean strain of dualism, the new spiritualist paradigm carried its own pronounced disjunction between the world of spirit and the world of sense. In its wake, Augustine formed a disjunctive theory of signs which radically distinguished the signifying realm of sense from the signified world of true being. After he became a catholic Christian, this theory privileged a practice of figurative exegesis in which Old Testament events, characters, rites and texts served as signs pointing either to eternal realities or to the future advent of Christ. Meanwhile Augustine's christology, while orthodox from the time of conversion, emphasized the distinction between the Word in heaven and the assumed man Jesus on earth. He understood the divinity of the Word to have used the man Jesus didactically as an exemplar of humility who opened the way to the spiritual realm. But in time Augustine's restless desire to understand what he believed forced a revision of that disjunctive perspective, because it only partly explained the function of the Word's assumed mutability and weakness. The incarnational paradigm interrelated the eternal and temporal by embracing Christ not only as exemplar but also as mediator whose ensouled flesh was the nexus of a saving exchange between immutable divinity and mutable humanity. The conceptual conjunction of the temporal and eternal correlatively produced a conjunctive theory of signs which acknowledged the ductility of God's power for the world of history and language. In turn, the Old Testament appeared not only to anticipate but also to dispense the grace of the New, though made to wear a "veil" because of its different place in salvation history. Becoming less distinguishable from the New, the Old began to function pastorally and polemically in Augustine's figurative exegesis as the first book of the New Testament.

I. Exegesis, Signs and Christology in the Spiritualist Paradigm

A. Exegesis: History and Prophecy

Augustine wrote the two books of *On Genesis Against the Manicheans* about 388, shortly after his return to Africa following his baptism by Ambrose at Easter Vigil the previous year.[6] This work defended the Old Testament against Manichaean objections to its anthropomorphisms and immoralities by showing the possibility of interpretation along the allegorical lines he learned from the bishop of Milan. In the main it followed a "rule of contradiction" which authorized figurative interpretation where the literal sense clashed with the spiritual understanding of God.[7] Augustine intended to give both a literal and spiritual interpretation for the first three chapters of Genesis, but the end product heavily weighted the spiritual. The treatise proposed a two–fold schema for interpretation according to the contrasting perspectives of history and prophecy. "According to history past events are narrated, according to prophecy future events are foretold."[8] *Historia* envisioned the visible, time-bound, corporeal world of matter, sense, and serial events, as contrasted or linked with the invisible, timeless, incorporeal world of spirit, understanding and truth (*On Genesis Against the Manicheans* 1.1.1–1.22.33; 1.25.43; 2.1.1–2.23.35). *Prophetia* related the events, characters, rites and texts of salvation history to the schema of promise and fulfillment of God's self–revelation on the temporal plane (1.23.35–24.42; 2.2.3; 2. 24.37ff.). History and prophecy each contained a literal and figurative sense.

A text may be read as a straightforward chronicle, "according to history," a text's referent being understood to reside within ordinary parameters of verbal meaning. But for Augustine *historia* was patient of both a literal and a figurative sense, much the way lexically the same word may carry a proper and a transferred sense. In contrast to modern definitions, this history deals not only with events and people in the flow of space and time, but by virtue of its verbal medium includes figurative meanings which extend from the literal descriptions. Figurative expressions can point either to an indescribable literal event or to spiritual truth, e.g., as the authority over animals granted to Adam may represent an actual command or the stages of the soul's ascent (1.20.31). In the former case the reality referred to by the verbal signs of the text resides in the visible world, in the latter the invisible. Augustine's usual word for the figurative sense was allegory (*allegoria*), which despite some inconsistent language functioned at this time within Augustine's sense of *historia*.

76

But the same text may also be read "according to prophecy." After many pages of literal and spiritual interpretation of the days of creation, Augustine declared the need for God's rest on the seventh day to be considered "more carefully" (*diligentius;* 1.23.35). The seven days are reconsidered first as a literal prophecy foretelling the six ages of salvation history followed by a seventh age of eternal rest (1.23.35–41); then as figurative prophecy focusing on "the sixth age" of Christ and the Church which extends from the incarnation to the current moment of the Church's temporal journey (1.23.40; 2.24.37–26.40). Augustine's figurative approach attempted to "explain all those figures of things according to the catholic faith, either those which belong to *historia* or those which belong to *prophetia*" (2.2.4). As the figures belonging to history were characteristically discovered by reason and observation, figures belonging to prophecy were laid down through "the apostolic authority by which so many enigmas in the books of the Old Testament are resolved" (2.24.37).

Augustine's immediate reference was to the Pauline declaration of Eph. 5.32 that Genesis 2.24 ("the two shall become one flesh") refers to Christ and the Church; but he took this as a "clear sign" (*signum manifestum*) to interpret the remainder of Genesis 1–3 within a christo–ecclesiological frame. This frame sharply differentiated the figures of history and prophecy. Augustine said that Genesis narrative considered as *historia* signified Adam, but as *prophetia* portrayed Christ and the Church (2.24.37ff.). As *historia* the creation of woman from the side of sleeping Adam figuratively described either an actual event or the spiritual reality of the human carnal appetite; but as *prophetia* it foresaw the emergence of the Church from the sleep of Christ's death. As *historia* the serpent signified evil, but as *prophetia* it anticipated heresy's attempt to draw the Church from pure devotion to Christ. As *historia* the coats of skin signified the mortality merited by sin; but as *prophetia* they foretold the enslavement to carnal images of spiritual things.

B. Signs: Anagogic and Dramatic

In *On the Teacher* (389) Augustine imagined language "running parallel to the stream of experience and alongside it, so to speak, rather than within it."[9] The mind's images arise from within human captivity to the senses, alerting and fitting the mind for a movment of understanding which occurs entirely in the intelligible realm. A sign (*signum*) indicates a certain intelligible or spiritual reality (*res*), and prompts the mind to seek the immediate contact which creates understanding. Spiritual interpretation is possible because a likeness (*similitudo*) exists between the sensory images conveyed by verbal signs in Scripture, and the truth of either the intelligible world or salvation history. But likeness only juxtaposes sign and reality; understanding remains incommensurate with expression, coming not from the sign *per se* but from enlightenment by God, who readies the soul by co–opting its capacity to be moved by likenesses. This disjunctive theory of signs is operative in the figurative exegesis of both history and prophecy in *On Genesis Against the Manicheans.* On the one hand the visible *signum* of history invites either an inward look to an immanent *res* of the spatio–temporal world (literal history), or an upward look to a transcendent *res* of the eternal spiritual world (figurative history); on the other hand the visible *signum* of prophecy invites a forward look to a *res* of the future, either to the events of salvation history (literal prophecy) or its culmination in Christ and the Church (figurative prophecy). The figurative signs of history and prophecy possess no revelatory value of their own, but are as it were windows, "diaphanous" to the realities of which they speak.[10]

The spiritualist paradigm's correlation of signs, exegesis and christology comes to expression in parts of Augustine's energetic, rambling synthesis of neoplatonism and catholic Christianity, *De uera religione* (390). In this construction of the faith, the main concern is with "the history and prophecy of the temporal dispensation" which providence made for salvation (7.13). Pride had turned the human soul outward to the things of sense, perverted its love and numbed its capacity for spiritual understanding. This diseased condition blocked the soul's immediacy to truth and necessitated both serial existence and communication by signs. But God accommodated to the fragmented human condition by sending his Wisdom into the world, who assumed and lived a perfect human life in order to remind humanity demonstrably of its original perfection (16.30), not by force but by persuasion and admonition (16.31). His life, death and resurrection were lessons in right conduct and hope (16.32). He taught both clearly and obscurely in order to incite the search for truth, a strategy which encapsulated the divine method in all the Scriptures; this showed that the obscurities of the Old Testament remained valid for faith through figurative interpretation (17.33). The unity of Old and New Testaments is rooted in their common subject, the one God who revealed through them the stages of movement from the imperfect to the perfect (17.34). The play of human language in their parables and similitudes used events, characters, rites and texts to create a stairway to heaven.

These "visible words" configure spiritual reality as words in a sentence configure semantic meaning (50.98). The incommensurability of the eternal and temporal realms, as well as the differing capacities of human understanding, is reflected in the contrasting modes of human response to these likenesses, spiritual faith and historical faith (50.99). The modes are hierarchically ordered; the historical is the lowest step in the climb to the spiritual, and *allegoria* provides the thrust of ascent in Scripture's "ennobling and uplifting game" (51.100).

Rather than a finished product of neoplatonic Christianity, *De uera religione* is the report of that work in progress. In particular the mood of the eloquent culminating passage of 50.98 – 51.100 can only be described as interrogative. He wonders about the ends of allegorical exposition, whether the realities underlying the words of Scripture reside in visible events or in the intelligible world of the soul—referring to either movements of the affections, decisions of the will, or images of the mind—or whether the texts may refer to all of these. He asks about the kinds of allegorical exposition which differ depending on whether the text is a history–like narrative, the report of a real event, speeches or dialogues of characters, or the description of a rite.[11] He seeks to understand the function of the relativities and cultural idiosyncrasies of figurative representation in finding the truth which transcends the particularities of space and time.

Augustine's fluid categories suggest the need to import some terminology for the sake of clear analysis. He attempted during this time to assimilate the Church's traditional language about the four senses of Scripture, but it never was a comfortable fit.[12] His early language about figurative interpretation continued to contrast history and prophecy in a way roughly approximating the modern distinction often made between allegory and typology. But Augustine eventually grew restless with distinguishing these categories too sharply and gradually amalgamated them under the comprehensive term "figure" (*figura*).[13] The opposition between these traditional terms seems to undermine their usefulness for describing the synthesis of Augustine, who yoked them in a comprehensive figurative approach which operated often in the same passage and sometimes in the same sentence. Therefore I propose to consider his approach as a unified practice with two aspects which I will call the *anagogic* and *dramatic* perspectives of figurative exegesis. The anagogic perspective focuses on a synchronic, upward movement of understanding which is driven by a likeness, usually discerned by rational observation, between a visible figure in the temporal, corporeal world of sense and an invisible referent in the supratemporal, incorporeal world of understanding. The figurative sign incites the soul to engage the world of spirit and truth, but is essentially *ad hoc*, incidental to its reality and obsolescent because of its incommensurability with the intelligible world. By contrast the dramatic perspective focuses on a diachronic, back–and–forth movement of understanding which is driven by a likeness, usually posited by authority, between a figure and a referent which both belong to the visible world of history and language.[14] The anagogic and dramatic perspectives share the pattern of the sign pointing beyond itself to a complete manifestation of its reality; their major difference is that the dramatic perspective indicates a *res* which belongs to space and time. But there is also the difference that within the dramatic perspective the relation between a prophetic sign and its reality occurs in either of two ways. The first is analogous to anagogic signs of history and characteristic of the spiritualist paradigm: both literal and figurative prophetic signs are interpreted disjunctively, pointing forward to a fulfillment in future space and time. The sign is obsolescent; after its fulfillment the sign serves only as a support for faith by proving the prophecy's credibility. But the second relation breaks new ground that is characteristic of the incarnational paradigm: figurative prophetic signs are also interpreted conjunctively, not only indicating but also somehow mediating the power of the signified reality, the *res* itself as it were present within the *signum* and anticipating its own full disclosure. For this sign the medium is the message, and intrinsic to the reality it signifies. It is therefore also permanent, because after fulfillment in Christ and the Church it serves not only as a proof for faith but also as an interpreter for understanding. Because of the close relation of signs, exegesis and christology for Augustine, I argue that his expansion of the theory of signs to include the conjunctive, and with it the practical interrelation of the anagogic and dramatic perspectives of figurative exegesis, derives from a paradigmatic reconfiguration of his exemplar christology to include the idea of mediator.

C. Christ as Exemplar

In the christology of the treatises Augustine wrote within the spiritualist paradigm, God approaches lost humanity especially through the mind, sending the Word into flesh and history in order to reveal the way to the spiritual realm. God circumvented diseased human patterns of perception by using Christ, a human being on the plane of history, to prompt and fit the dormant higher part of the soul to choose to seek the spiritual realm. Christ's humility formed a prototype or *exemplum* of humility from which humble faith retrieves enough health for the eye of the soul that spiritual beauty breaks in, stirs love, and initiates the rise into the spiritual world. The historical images of the Savior provide a framework, but the locus of salvation is the free response of the one who believes. The words which describe Christ's function at this time are predominantly didactic; he "teaches" *(On the Teacher* 11.38), "admonishes" *(On Free Choice* 3.10.30), "persuades" *(De uera religione* 16.31), "demonstrates" *(On Faith and the Creed* 4.6).[15]

On Faith and the Creed, originally an address to the Council of Carthage in October 393, contains the longest sustained reflection on christology to date among the early writings. In 2.3 Augustine explains that in his divine nature Christ is called the Word because he makes the Father known as a person uses words to make thoughts known. In 4.6 he says that the Word assumed the garb of humanity in order to demonstrate a certain way of humility by offering the soul a dynamic "example of living" *(uiuendi exemplum).* But in 4.7 he juxtaposes images of black and white, hot and cold, fast and slow, to rhetorically generate wonder at the incarnation's mysterious intersection of time and eternity, change and changelessness, being and non–being. For the time being in 4.8 he explains the unity of opposites in Christ as the result of a *temporalis dispensatio.*

> But through what I have called a temporal dispensation—because by a work of God's goodness our mutable nature was assumed by that immutable wisdom of God for our salvation and restoration—we adjoin *(adiungimus)* faith in temporal things done with a view to our salvation when we believe in him, "the Son of God who was born through the Holy Spirit from the virgin Mary."

Augustine's underlying restlessness to understand better what he believed concerning the functional association of the divine and human in Christ made for an uneasy alliance of conceptual paradigms. The disjunctive christology of the spiritualist paradigm was under stress, perhaps from the countervailing conjunctive language of Scripture, the inner logic of creedal claims, and his own sacramental ministry. His difficulty interrelating the two realms continued to contrast spiritual and historical faith as in *De uera religione;* their "adjoining" points to the juxtaposition rather than interrelation of the temporal and eternal. This spiritualist understanding of christology and faith corresponded to his separation of the sign and the reality, with divinity running alongside the stream of humanity rather than within it. While the reality remained above, the sign remained below, displaying humility by its appearance in the world, and pointing the way to heaven. The organizing principle was synchronic and anagogic, subordinating the diachronic and dramatic as the first step on the way of spiritual ascent.

Through the early 390's Augustine's project of synthesis affirmed antinomies which inspired faith but vexed reason, and put his thought on parallel tracks related by juxtaposition rather than coordination. Faith held the two perspectives in tension, but his longing for synthetic under-standing made this tension increasingly difficult to sustain. Constitu-tionally dissatisfied with contradiction and paradox, Augustine contin-ued to search for the way conceptually to bring the two planes together. Like his trial use of spiritualist language about Christ as "the Lord's man" (*homo dominicus*; see *Revisions* 1.19.8), Augustine's experiment with the phrase "temporal dispensation" to explain the incarnation fell into vir-tual disuse after 396.

II. Christology, Signs and Exegesis in the Incarnational Paradigm

A. Christ the Mediator

Imaginative projections of a newer understanding begin to appear in 392 among Augustine's first homilies and notes on the Psalms, in which he continued an already ancient Church tradition of reading the Psalter as the transcript of Christ's inner life. It opened the design of the incarnation by graphically displaying the movements of his human soul, which "so inhered and somehow coalesced with the surpassing excellence of the Word when it took up a human being that it was not laid aside even by a humili-ation as great as the passion."[16] The texts injected images of seething hu-man passions into the neat christology of the spiritualist paradigm, and pressed Augustine beyond mere affirmation to a more exact understand-ing of the function of Christ's full humanity. The sixteenth psalm pictured for him the soul of Christ as the instrument of God's power:

> "My soul is your weapon" which your "hand"—that is, your eternal power—assumed in order that through it your power might conquer the kingdoms of iniquity and divide the just from the ungodly. (*Commentaries on the Psalms* 16.3)

These notes on the Psalms mark the first appearance, without elaboration, of the image of Christ as mediator (e.g., *Commentaries on the Psalms* 25.1). In the meantime study of Christ the teacher proceeded in 393 with an exposition of the Sermon on the Mount (*De sermone Domini in monte*).

But the year 394 marked a turning point in Augustine's integration of christological faith and understanding. In studying Paul's letter to the Galatians he explored the complex of ideas associated with Christ as mediator in order to answer the essentially dramatic question of how the old covenant saints were justified through faith before his advent.[17] Paul declared in Gal. 3.19 that, because God's promises were based on faith, the law had been given pedagogically for the sake of transgressions until the promised seed of Abraham should come, who is Christ; to this he appended the rabbinic idea that, unlike the promise given directly to Abraham, the law had been "ordered" through angels by the hand of a mediator, i.e. Moses. In Augustine's *Expositio epistulae ad Galatas* (394), the interpretation of this text combined certain elements of the bishop's preunderstanding and a mistake in translation to crystallize decisive ideas relating to christology and the exegesis of the Old Testament.

First, Augustine out–christologized even Paul with his understanding of Scripture as a unified verbal mosaic, according to which the word "mediator" referred not to Moses but to Christ, in light of 1 Tim. 2.5, the first quotation of this critical text in Augustine's works. Well understanding Paul's dramatic transposition of the story of Israel into Christian salvation history, Augustine saw Christ mediating the interrelation of the old and new covenants. This image of interrelation, fertilized by his neoplatonic fascination with the number one, gave him conceptual ground for joining rather than merely juxtaposing the eternal and temporal realms.[18] Because the Word is eternally one with God he is excluded from functioning as a mediator, who by definition belongs to two parties and so "is not of one, whereas God is one" (Gal. 3.19). But the mediator was nevertheless also "one," according to the text in which the apostle speaks "more clearly" (*planius*), 1 Tim. 2.5: "God is one, one also is the mediator between God and humans, the human Christ Jesus." For Augustine this text legitimated the unity of God with a trinity of persons as a pattern for conceiving the unity of the mediator with a duality of natures. However, it was applied to speculation, not about the unity of the two natures in Christ's person, but about their reciprocity in his work. Conflating the image of the mediator with the self–emptying christology of Phil. 2.6ff., Augustine articulated a saving "exchange" between human weakness and divine strength.[19] Instead of the Word assuming flesh only in order to exemplify and incite the human will to humility, the mediator was a double agent who also cured human weakness and injected divine strength. Christ's power not only enlightened the mind but remade the will; therefore his humanity was not only the theater but also the protagonist of the drama of redemption.

> So the only Son of God was made a mediator of God and the human, when the Word of God, God with God, both laid aside his majesty in descent to the human, and bore aloft human humility in ascent to the divine, so that he might be the mediator between God and humans, through God a human beyond the human. (*Expos. ep. ad Galatas* 24)

After 394 the power of the exchange based on the unity of God and humanity in the mediator was soon reflected in the appearance of a word group built around the image of "transfiguration."[20] Lexically the verb *transfiguro* denoted the act of changing the appearance or form of a thing, a sense Augustine often used in quoting New Testament references to Satan's self–transformation into an angel of light (2 Cor. 11.4), Jesus' transfiguration before the disciples (Matt. 17.2ff. and parallels), and bodily change at the resurrection after the pattern of the glorified Christ (Phil. 3.21). His first use of the concept occurred about this time in reference to the Word's immutability in the incarnation, which occurred not by transforming his deity (*non transfiguratione*) but by wearing humanity as a garment (*83 Diverse Questions*, qu. 73.2). However, the word also carried a metaphorical sense which rhetorically subsumed a constellation of people or things "under the figure of" some other person or thing. Thus Paul's references in Rom. 7.14ff. to being "under the law" were not literally autobiographical, but typical of every person enslaved to the letter of the law (*On Diverse Questions to Simplicianus* 2.3.2). The transition from the reality to the figure was emphasized by appending the phrase "into oneself" (*in me, in se*); understanding was conveyed by "carrying over" the subject into the type. So Paul wrote (1 Cor. 4.6), "I have carried over the figure of these things into myself and Apollos for your sake" (*haec transfiguraui in me et Apollo propter nos*), in order to project the Corinthians' attitudes onto a larger screen (*Against the Letters of Petilianus* 3.2.3). The critical use of the word in Augustine appears in reference to Christ's passion in which he "transfigured us in himself," or more sharply, "transfigured our weakness in himself."[21] Christ assumed in his suffering not only the condition of humanity's finitude, but also its sinful self–absorption. The classic text in this regard is Matt. 26.39 where Christ confesses, "my soul is sorrowful even unto death," and prays "may this cup pass from me." According to Augustine, Jesus spoke not from himself but from the weakness and fear which he "carried over" into his humanity from every person's mortal desperation.

This representational use of "transfiguration" recurs throughout his writings and especially fits the exemplary emphasis which dominated the spiritualist paradigm. However the powerful double agency of the one mediator is also reflected in Augustine's contention that Christ not only *demonstrated* change for the human will, as in the second sense of *transfiguro*, but also *effected* change within it, as in the first sense. Both senses are carefully delineated in a comment on the agony in the garden from a homily of 403:

> Wherefore Christ, carrying the human and laying down a rule for us, teaching us to live and granting us to live (*docens nos uiuere et praestans nobis uiuere*), displays as it were a private human will ... But because he willed the human to be upright in heart, so that whatever in the human that was somewhat crooked he should bend (*dirigeret*) toward the One who is always upright, he says, "nevertheless not what I will, but what you will, Father" ... In the person of the human he assumed, transfiguring his own in himself, he displayed as it were humanity's own will. He showed you, and he rectified you (*ostendit te et correxit te*). Look, he says, see yourself in me. (*Commentaries on the Psalms* 2.32, sermon 1.2)

Augustine understands the incarnation to have collected chaotic human striving into a single entity and remarkably united it to the will of Jesus, who displayed its characteristic self–concern in the agonized words, "let this cup pass from me." But his passion not only revealed the human will, but "bent" it flush with God's straightedge; Christ taught *and* gave, showed *and* rectified. Humanity so embraced the divinity of the mediator that the sign of his deed cured the infirmity of all, and divinity so inhabited the humanity of the mediator that the same sign bestowed God's strength upon all. It was in order to convey the full impact of this exchange that Augustine conflated the literal and transferred senses of *transfiguro*.

The second insight of 394 generated by Augustine's study of Galatians concerned the exegesis of the Old Testament. Latin translators had garbled Augustine's text by rendering the Greek masculine participle *diatageis* ("ordered") by the neuter *dispositum*, thus referring the action not to the law but to the corporate seed who is Christ.[22] This moved him toward a nuance of the Latin which construed the angels as having "prepared" Christ and the Church in the time of the Old Testament. This trajectory of interpretation pushed him toward taking the preposition "in" with a locative rather than with Paul's instrumental sense, so that the hand or power of the mediator became the superintendent rather than the instrument of the angels' work. In other words, the angels did not use Moses as their agent but were themselves used as agents by Christ, whose divinity acted proleptically through them to prepare its own advent.

The angels' service as temporary surrogates for the incarnation implied a dramatic unity between the Old and New Testaments that was deeper than the anagogic. Expanding Paul's salvation–historical focus, Augustine explained that "through the angels was administered the entire dispensation of the Old Testament" in the stead and for the sake of the mediator to come.[23] Through the various elements of this dispensation the Spirit revealed Christ's future humility to the spiritual people of that age— the patriarchs, the prophets and their followers. They were justified by a "prophetic faith" which was no less effectual before the incarnation as Christian faith was after it. For the carnal people of Abraham's seed, the law generated an awareness of sin which positioned them to seek the grace to come. For this the angels became visible agents, quasi–incarnate mediators who were sometimes called by divine names because "the Spirit of God was acting in them, along with the Word of Truth himself, who though not yet incarnate, never withdrew from any part of the process of dispensing the truth."[24] The angels' activity was exactly analogous to that of the prophets who acted sometimes in their own person, at other times in the person of God, in order to indicate that God was acting in them.

Through the same assimilation of persons Augustine understood the traditional "prosopological exegesis" of the Psalms in which the psalmist prophetically but actually spoke the words of the mediator.[25] Augustine began to unfold his earlier intuitions more fully about 395, especially through the use of Psalm 21, whose first line ("My God, my God, why have you abandoned me?") the mediator had spoken "in the psalm and on the cross."[26] In the Psalm the Word anticipated his future exchange of human weakness for divine strength in a mysterious conjunction of sign and reality which united his voice with that of the prophet. On the cross Jesus' words signified not only his burden of sins but the burden of the old human nature itself, "as though he were saying, 'these words were transfigured in me from the person of the sinner'" (*Commentaries on the Psalms* 37.27). Based on Augustine's vision of the whole Christ of head and body (*totus Christus*), the exchange was predicated on the inference that "if there is 'two in one flesh' why not also two in one voice?"[27] For Augustine this act of bedrock exegesis from the lips of the dying Savior disclosed of the voice of Christ in all of Scripture; the rest of the Psalter and the whole Old Testament accordingly indicated not only that the mediator would appear on the earth, but also that he himself was secretly acting in all the persons, events, rites and texts of the prophetic people. He gave New Testament grace in human history and language both before and after his advent; the signs of the old covenant were fragmentary but effective means of grace for people of their time by which the Holy Spirit conveyed incomplete but genuine knowl- edge of the mediator's future humility. Augustine took a number of years to polish his language for this, but eventually spoke of the Old as "the secret of the New," the New in the Old "like fruit in the root," the grace of the New "hidden" in the Old, and, in the famous couplet, "the New is in the Old concealed, and the Old is in the New revealed."[28]

The new perspectives on christology and exegesis which came to expression in the commentary on Galatians imply a correlative shift in Augustine's understanding of signs. Prophecy's fulfillment meant that the New Testament neither contradicts nor cancels but unveils and completes the Old; this conclusion was pressed immediately into service against the Manichaean claim of antithesis between Old and New. Augustine's treatise *Against Adimantus* (394), rooted the counterclaim of their harmony primarily in the literal sense, but also explored fresh ground regarding figurative interpretation, in particular Paul's "rule" for figurative exegesis found in 1 Cor. 10. 4.[29] The assertion that the Israelites "drank from the spiritual rock which followed them, and the rock was Christ," drew him to reflect on a nuance of the relation between sign and reality that was different from the disjunctiveness characteristic of the spiritualist paradigm.[30] He noted that Paul used a copulative verb rather than a transitive: "he did not say, 'the rock signifies Christ,' but 'the rock was Christ.'" Of course Paul meant the statement to be taken in a spiritual sense; but Augustine seems to have thought further that it suggested two modes within the spiritual sense which are confused if the word "signify" is taken to imply a disjunction which makes the sign obsolete.[31] Signifying power is generated from the qualities of an already existing thing in such a way that sign and reality intimately meet in a relation which the bishop increasingly reserved for the idea of "sacrament." It is sacramental because in the same way "our Lord did not hesitate to say 'this is my body' when he gave the sign of his body," the same conjunction operative in the Old Testament rite whose reality he understood to have been "placed within" the sign.[32] This conjunctive understanding binds a reality of the spiritual world to its sign in such a way that, despite their incommensurability, the effectiveness of the reality depended on the presence of this particular sign. Therefore, even if "the flesh's blood is its soul"—the text

of Deut. 12.23 which generated the discussion of *Against Adimantus* 12—
is literally true only with respect to animals, its interrelation of sign and
reality is paradigmatic for the sacraments of the Old Testament which
anticipate redemption and those of the New which recall it.[33]

Ultimately the difference between disjunctive and conjunctive
signs lies in discriminating between a reality which is merely signified
and the signified reality which in turn signifies some other reality; e g. the
geological reality which is signified by the word "rock," but which in
turn also signifies Christ. In this case the geological reality and its image
in Scripture is a hybrid which he eventually called a "signifying reality"
(*res significans*) and treated as a special class of sign (*On Christian Doctrine*
3.5.9). Like "the seven corn ears which are seven years" (Gen. 41.26), or
the building called "church" because it houses the Church, the bond of
sign and reality is so close that the signifying thing takes the name of the
signified thing, and that which contains is named by that which is contained (*Questions on the Heptateuch* 3.57). His reflections are ultimately
rooted in rhetorical analysis of figures of speech, especially metonymy.[34]

B. *On Christian Doctrine*: Movement between Paradigms

In light of his path of development the *On Christian Doctrine* of
396 is paradoxically both profound and puzzling, because it seems to catch
Augustine midway between the spiritualist and incarnational paradigms.
It works with the anagogic view of christology, signs and exegesis, but
also reflects a dramatic christology and conjunctive understanding of
signs.[35] But the anomaly of the incomplete *On Christian Doctrine* is that it
does not go on to articulate a method of prophetic and christological exegesis of the Old Testament. Whatever its merits on theological and philosophical grounds, this omission made the treatise an inadequate theoretical representation of Augustine's practice of figurative exegesis even as it
was being written.[36]

Augustine proceeded anagogically in both passages relating to
christology, 1.11.11–15.14 and 1.34.38. In 1.11.11, while discussing the freedom from moral obstruction needed for loving enjoyment of the Trinity,
Augustine declared that human purity was impossible except that the Word
deigned to conform to human weakness and to offer "an example of living" (*exemplum uiuendi*). The second passage, following the anagogic distinction between "use" and "enjoyment," invoked the incarnation to speak
of the important but impermanent role of visible and temporal things in
the spiritual ascent. Because human beings are unable to seek the invisible

God, their believing perception of the visible humility of the incarnate Word brings them humility and strength; Christ launches the return to the invisible. The process was exemplified in the apostle Paul, who declared that having once known Christ "according to the flesh" he knew him thus no longer (2 Cor. 5.16), referring to humbly believing the Gospel narrative's picture of Christ's abasement in the world.[37] Linking this text in typical cumulative fashion with Phil. 3.13, Augustine saw Paul "forgetting what is behind," transcending Christ's humanity as the starting point of faith, and "straining for what is before," attaining to immediate knowledge of his divinity. The Word assumed a practical obsolescence by submitting to use as a vessel, making possible the soul's enjoyment of God and prompting the "forgetting" which leaves the earthly form behind. The humanity of Christ is one of those *transitoria* to be used rather than enjoyed, a vehicle whose beauty transports a person to enjoyment of the Trinity:

> … we ought to use such things not with an abiding but a passing love and delight, like that for the road, like that for vehicles or some other means of transportation. Or if it can be said more accurately, let us love those things by which we are carried for the sake of that to which we are carried.

The transitional love and delight honors Christ's actual though ultimately temporary capacity to reveal God. Incarnation did not compromise the Word's nature because its eternal will was to assume serial existence; when the Word accepted temporality and "wore it for our salvation," it included accepting the transitional human love which is appropriate to momentary things. This anagogic approach conforms to the *exemplum* christology of the spiritualist paradigm.

Correlatively, *On Christian Doctrine* continues the spiritualist discussion about signs of *On the Teacher*. Augustine's statement of 1.2.2, "things are learned by means of signs" (*res per signa discuntur*), summarizes the anagogic, utilitarian interpretation; in biblical language of Rom. 1.20, "the invisible things of God are understood from the things that are made" (1.4.4). Incommensurability in the spiritualist paradigm between "things" (book 1) and "signs" (book 2) is reflected in his intention to separate their discussions. Further, charity is the pervasive end of interpreting the signs of Scripture, the achievement of which relativizes any technical errors made by the interpreter and relativizes even Scripture itself among those whose perfection has obviated the need for external instruction (1.39.43). This anagogic pattern is displayed in Christ who taught us to relativize temporal things, for "although he deigned to become our way, he did not want us to clutch (*tenere*) but to move along (*transire*) this way lest we cling weakly to temporal things, although he assumed and bore them for our salvation" (1.34.38).

On Christian Doctrine's focus on the anagogic perspective is a product of the spiritualist paradigm. However, Augustine's concessive language, "although he became our way" and "although he assumed and bore temporal things," is a tip that the other, dramatic perspective on the humanity of Christ is also present. Cardinal elements of the dramatic perspective appear in both christological passages. In 1.11.11 a new instrumental use of John 14.6 is unveiled in which Christ is declared not only to reveal but to be himself the way to God: "Therefore, while he himself is the home country, for us he also made himself the way to the home country."[38] In 1.14.13 the new note is struck again by modifying a familiar medical image; the humanity of the Word brought not merely knowledge of possible healing but also the actual healing itself. Like a physician who applies different remedies for different maladies, Wisdom brought a medicine which is nothing other than his own being.

> The medicine of Wisdom accommodated to our wounds by assuming a human being ... So the Wisdom of God in curing humanity furnished (*exhibuit*) himself for the healing; the doctor was himself the medicine (*ipsa medicus, ipsa medicina*).

Compared with earlier formulations the originating point of saving health has shifted from the will of the enlightened soul to Christ; the way to healing has been paved by the power of his virtue.[39] The early idea of the *exemplum* has quietly widened from being a mere source of knowledge to include a healing power which inheres in the knowledge; in terms of Augustine's brief exposition of 1 Cor. 1.24, Christ gives not only the wisdom but power to act. The Word took flesh "so that what he shows us should be done we might do."[40] He says further in a summary passage that divine providence engineered the temporal dispensation—here referring to all of salvation history—in order to provide both knowledge and ability to obey the twofold command to love God and neighbor: "that we might know and be able [to so love], the whole temporal dispensation was made through divine providence for our salvation."[41]

Because of the relationship of christology and language for Augustine, we expect that a modification in christology will be registered in a modified theory of signs. In 1.2.2 Augustine had defined a thing from the anagogic perspective as a brute reality "which is not used to signify something else, like wood, stone and cattle." The disjunctive sign–thing relation which is characteristic of the spiritualist paradigm can be diagrammed as follows:

$$S\ (\text{``ox"}) \text{———} R\ (\text{ox–animal})$$

But brute realities can signify other realities. For the sake of separating his treatments of signs and things, Augustine bracketed this category of signs by insisting that for the sake of clarity his discussion could not concern things such as the wood Moses threw into the water, or the stone Jacob placed under his head, or the animal Abraham sacrificed in place of his son, "for these are things in such a way that they are also signs of other things." However, in 2.10.15 the concept of metaphoric or figurative signs (*signa translata*) compromised that intention and dissolved the brackets by reintroducing the complex sign–thing relation in which signification is predicated on the reality of a thing previously signified.

> Figurative signs occur when the things themselves, which we signify by literal words, are also taken over (*usurpantur*) for signifying some other thing, as we say "ox" and through this syllable we understand a herd animal because it is usually called by this name, but again through that animal we understand an evangelist, which Scripture signified when the apostle interpreted it, saying "You will not muzzle the ox who is threshing." [1 Cor. 9.9; cf. Deut. 25.4]

Augustine's term for this hybrid is "signifying thing" (*res significans*; 3.9.13). Analogous to the interrelation of divine and human in the incarnation, the disjunctive relation of sign and reality has given birth to a conjunction in which a *signum* points to a *res* which acts as *signum* for yet another *res*. The original relation conjoins with another so that the *res* of the first equation becomes the *signum* of the second, diagrammed as follows:

$$S\ (\text{``ox"}) \text{———} R\ (\text{ox–animal})/S\ (\text{``ox"} [\text{Scripture}]) \text{———} R\ (\text{evangelist}).$$

The distinguishing characteristic of the figurative prophetic sign is that it is both thing and sign, *both* literal *and* figurative (cf. 3.12.20, 3.22.32). Similarly, the Sabbath was not merely a diaphanous image of a heavenly reality; literally obeying the command for physical rest generated its signifying force as prophecy of the Christ who gives heavenly rest, as the patriarchs, prophets and writers of Scripture recognized. In "the prophetic sacrament"[42] the Sabbath and the whole Old Testament in a sense mediated the mediator to come, as the angels prepared Christ in the hand of the mediator; for each the reality and its sign is one ("R/S"). Their paradigm was the incarnate Word whose humanity mediated his divinity, and was therefore both the prophesied "reality" of the Old Testament signs from the dramatic perspective, and effective human "sign" of the divine reality from the anagogic perspective. Christ's Sabbath cures worked in both ways, revealing him "to have come from God," anagogically signifying spiritual rest, but also that "he was himself God," dramatically signifying that one resorts to him for rest (3.6.10). The conjunctive crucible of the incarnation was at work in Augustine's understanding of signs in *On Christian Doctrine* when the anagogic disjunction of thing and sign was qualified by the conjunction of a second sign–thing relation whose middle term was both figurative and literal, witness of grace and medium of grace.

But *On Christian Doctrine* leaves this conversation dangling. Though conjunctive signs combine the literal and the figurative, Augustine was very concerned to prevent the fatal mistake of understanding spiritual things carnally; his formulations therefore concentrate on their distinction. His rule for preventing confusion between the literal and figurative ("Whatever cannot be referred to virtuous behavior or the truth of faith you should understand to be figurative," 3.10.14) does liberalize the rule of contradiction to include superfluities among legitimate material for figurative interpretation.[43] But it still limits such interpretation to a separate non literal sphere, and does not explain the presence of both literal and figurative in a *res significans* such as the Sabbath. Contradiction and superfluity simply indicate the limits of the literal sense and warrant the necessity of finding a figurative sense. But figurative exegesis based on such dissimilitude discloses an underlying likeness between a sign and its reality whose discovery is possible before it is necessary. If Augustine had written from the dramatic perspective, a rule for figurative exegesis recognizing things which are also signs would have concerned not only the narrow hermeneutical conditions which make figurative interpretation *necessary*, but the broad conditions which make it *possible*; not only how an anagogic sign must be *either* literal *or* figurative, but also how a dramatic sign may be *both* literal *and* figurative. In the end it would not only negatively concern the contradiction or superfluity which *discloses* figurative relationships, but would also positively concern the similitude which *forms* them. Further, since the incarnation paradigmatically shows that temporal things conduct grace, then the capacity for grace in prophetic signs should have been apparent, and prophecy and christology should have been analyzed as mutually interpreting. Book 3 should have gone on to use this two–way hermeneutical key to explore Moses' wood as a sign of the cross, Jacob's stone as a sign of the incarnation, and Abraham's ram as a sign of redemption. But an explanation of the relation prophecy and christology to exegesis is conspicuous by its absence in the treatise of 396.

Why did Augustine not further develop his conjunctive understanding of figurative signs in *On Christian Doctrine*? And why did he give no analysis of the dramatic perspective which is evident everywhere in his actual practice of interpretation, particularly the homilies? Augustine may have been concerned primarily to present first the less familiar method of anagogic figurative interpretation, to which he intended later to append the dramatic. It is intriguing to consider the possibility that the dramatic perspective was to be the subject of the latter part of book 3 when he suspended the work. An oblique piece of evidence for this is the summary of Tyconius' rules of interpretation which eventually completed the book when he resumed writing in 426. The "keys and lamps" of the Donatist exegete's *Book of Rules,* as the bishop understood them,[44] offer what had not been discussed thus far in *On Christian Doctrine,* namely a prophetic, christological and indeed christo–ecclesiological hermeneutic. But Augustine may have needed more time to achieve theoretical clarity about the dramatic figurative perspective; the challenge of Tyconius' ideas may well have been a major factor in stalling the progress of writing his handbook of scripture interpretation.[45]

C. *Against Faustus*: Flowering of the Dramatic Perspective

Signals of the emerging dramatic perspective multiply in the *Confessions,* in which conjunctive language telescoped the new bishop's understanding of the 390's with his faith of the 380's. In 5.14.24 he reported having listened before conversion to the preaching of Ambrose in order to critique his eloquence; but "together with the words, which I was enjoying, came into my mind the realities (*res*), which I was ignoring—because I could not separate them" (*dirimere*). After narrating his neoplatonic enlightenment in book 7, Augustine recounted his inability to enjoy God until "embracing the mediator" of 1 Tim. 2.5, who had been secretly calling to him in the words of John 14.6, "I am the way" (7.18.24). He had taken charge of redemption by building himself a humble "cottage of clay" in the incarnation, and "mixing" (*miscentem*) divine food with our flesh. His humility wrenched humans from their pride and "carried them across" (*traiceret*) to the sphere of his wisdom and power, where he healed their hearts and nourished their charity. To the extent Augustine once saw in Jesus only "an example of despising temporal things for the sake of gaining immortality" he did not realize "of what reality (*res*) his weakness was the teacher (*magister*)," or what mysterious depths lay hidden in John 1.14, "the Word was made flesh" (7.19.25). But having embraced the mediator Augustine remembered seeing past the Manichaean charge of contradiction between the Testaments, and descrying in them the simple unity of "one face" (*una facies*; 7.21.27) which not only admonished him to see God, but healed him to hold God. In the figurative exegesis of book 13, Genesis 1 is explored first anagogically for its vision of the Trinity attained through charity (1.1–11.12), then dramatically with reference to Christ and the Church (12.13ff.).

With *Against Faustus* (c. 398) the dramatic perspective came into its own and indeed dominated Augustine's interpretation of the Old Testament. In it Augustine explored the ancient books of Israel exactly as one whom Tyconius had described, "walking through an immense forest of prophecy."[46] But he did so with an anti–Manichaean agenda in hand, exploiting the hints of the commentary on Galatians and the treatise against Adimantus on grace in the Old Testament springing from Christ its deep center: "everywhere Christ meets me and refreshes me" (12.27); "not only some things but everything Moses wrote pertains to Christ" (16.26); "everything there was written either about him or because of him" (12.7). Augustine had argued for the necessity of the Old Testament to launch the anagogic process of understanding heavenly realities; however by itself this argument was vulnerable to the Manichaean claim to have rendered such launch points superfluous. *Against Faustus* argued assiduously from the dramatic perspective that the Old Testament was necessary because it not only launched but sustained the understanding of Christ, supplying not one but both poles of what modern thought would call the hermeneutical circle. When a Gentile inquirer reads the Old Testament, "from the present accomplishments of Christian realities the true prophecy of the books is proven to him, while from those very books the Christ to be revered is understood."[47] Augustine said in effect, "If you say 'our understanding of Christ is the only key we need,' then you should know that the Old Testament is key for understanding Christ." The reason is that while the promise needed fulfillment in order to be confirmed, the fulfillment needs the promise in order to be understood, as was evident from the citations of the Old Testament on every page of the New. Augustine worked consecutively through each passage to which Faustus had objected, showing its dramatic inner unity with the New Testament, first treating the possibility of figurative prophetic interpretation based on authorized likenesses between Old and New (especially book 12), and then the necessity of prophetic interpretation based on likenesses disclosed by contradiction and superfluity, i.e. the prophetic significance of even the immoral acts and unintelligible rites of Old Testament figures (especially book 22). In both its practice of interpretation and its theoretical reflections *Against Faustus* fully exploits the figurative exegetical implications of the incarnational paradigm.

It is instructive to compare *On Christian Doctrine* and *Against Faustus* for their differences of emphasis. Anagogic unity between the Old and New Testaments emphasized by the spiritualist paradigm and presupposed in *On Christian Doctrine* came from their participation in the same invisible spiritual reality; dramatic unity of the incarnational paradigm and *Against Faustus* was based on the hidden presence of the New within the Old through figurative prophetic signs. While *On Christian Doctrine* left the field virtually untouched, *Against Faustus* explored the dynamics of prophecy and fulfillment as a primary design of revelation. *On Christian Doctrine* concentrated on *caritas* as the end of Scripture interpretation; *Against Faustus* focused on the centrality of Christ and the Church. *On Christian Doctrine* posited contradiction and superfluity as warrants for the necessity of figurative exegesis in certain texts; *Against Faustus* also explored the possibility of figurative interpretation inherent in any text. *On Christian Doctrine* concentrated on likenesses between signs and things discerned by extratextual reasoning and experience; in *Against Faustus* authority licensed the lines of intratextual correspondence between dissimilar constellations of meaning. Finally, *On Christian Doctrine* was concerned primarily with explaining the anagogic perspective of figurative exegesis; *Against Faustus* so interrelated the anagogic and the dramatic perspectives that, while *caritas* remained the ultimate goal of interpretation of Scripture, christo–ecclesiological exegesis emerged as the key to *caritas*.

Characteristically, *Against Faustus* displays these advances not only in theoretical reflections but also in the actual exegesis of specific texts. Book 12 contains a brief but complex interpretation of the story of Jacob dreaming as he slept on the stone at Bethel (Gen. 28.10–22). Augustine saw the unity of the two Testaments in Paul's expression of longing for his kinfolk, the Israelites, to whom belonged "the covenants," of which the apostle would not have spoken in the plural unless "they had been given both the old covenant as well as the new figured in the old" (12.3). Because the New is in the Old, a Christian cannot fail to see the figures foretelling the Christ of head and body in the pages of Old Testament, because "these pages teem (*uiligant*) with such foretelling" (12.25). The stone which Jacob anointed signified nothing but Christ, the head of "the Man," the whole Christ of head and body. In John 1.49 the apostle Nathanael was a new Jacob who "anointed the Stone" by confessing Jesus as the Christ (12.26). Jesus' response to him authorized the similitude between himself and the Jacob story in the plainest possible terms (*apertissime*) when he portrayed himself as the ladder of the angels. Christ in his humanity was therefore to be seen as the (dramatic) fulfillment of the promised ladder which initiates the (anagogic) rise to his divinity. In both the descent to the visible and the ascent to the invisible Christ is the destination to be reached (*ad ipsum*) as well as the given means of reaching (*per illum*). "In him is the ladder reaching from earth to heaven, reaching from the flesh to the spirit, because by progressing or ascending in him the fleshly–minded become the spiritually–minded."[48]

Conclusion: The Old Testament as the First Book of the New

Augustine first attacked the Manichaean disregard for the Old Testament from the anagogic perspective, perhaps believing that to demonstrate even the possibility of such interpretation was to conquer their objection. Through a deeper understanding of the incarnation Augustine saw more clearly not only the initiating but the continuing role of faith in Christ for generating the love which made spiritual understanding possible. A corresponding increase of attention to the dramatic perspective developed the second christo–ecclesiological line of interpretation. As Christ in his flesh effactually offered God to the world, so sacramental signs effectually offered spiritual reality to the soul. This critical turn of mind so interrelated the two realms that reality could be said to inhabit the sign. If Christ as the *res significans* of God had acted within history, and was not merely witnessed by history, then in principle every historical sign was open to bearing something of its *res*, either before or after his advent. This revision made the Old Testament into a bearer of New Testament grace, and opened prophecy to sacramental interpretation. Where Augustine had once thought the prophetic sign acted as the diaphanous and obsolescent pointer to the future reality, Christ was now understood to have been present within the sign both to denote and to communicate his power. The ancient saints did not merely anticipate but actually partook of him; salvation came to the patriarchs and prophets who witnessed through the Spirit the mediator's future humility, and the Church itself was constituted among the people of the Old Testament (cf. *On Catechizing of the Uninstructed* 3.6).

This interrelational view explains the superficially contradictory assertions that the end of Scripture interpretation is *caritas*, and the meaning of Scripture is Christ (e.g., *On Christian Doctrine* 1.36.40, *Commentaries on the Psalms* 45.1). Augustine disclosed the relationship between the dramatic and anagogic perspectives by joining them so that each became essential to the other. If charity is the prerequisite for rising to God, then Christ is the prerequisite of arousing charity, and all Scripture "proclaims Christ and enjoins love" *(On Catechizing the Uninstructed* 4.8). *Caritas* is the end of Scripture from the anagogic perspective, and Christ is the end from the dramatic. In contrast to the sharp distinction between prophecy and history in *On Genesis Against the Manicheans*, their interrelation gradually blurred these categories and Augustine eventually came to speak of "prophetic history."[49]

Augustine's development of the figurative exegesis of prophecy in the 390's infused life into what had become a tired argument with Manichaeism over the canonicity of the Old Testament. Certainly the thirty–three books of *Against Faustus*, some of which are themselves as long as entire treatises, as Augustine himself noted *(Revisions* 2.33.1), stand as evidence that the schema of prophetic promise and fulfillment filled his mind and heart in the late 390's. The length and energy of this work freshly reveals a dimension of Scripture interpretation which had been only hinted in earlier works. The advance in understanding the incarnation and its correlative advance to a conjunctive theory of signs led to a new appreciation of the possibilities of prophecy as a tool of argument along the lines of a dramatic and figurative—specifically christo–ecclesiological—interpretation of Old Testament. What facilitated Augustine's advance at this time? His immersion in the life of the Church had certainly modified his outlook from that of retiring religious philosopher to active Catholic bishop. Primary impetus surely came from the work of ministry, perhaps especially his responsibility for instructing catechumens.[50] The reading of Scripture by all accounts became a constant preoccupation *(Letters* 21.3). The narrative structure of Genesis, the impassioned voices of the Psalms and the salvation history of Paul's letters each in their own way challenged the neat anagogic distinctions of the spiritualist paradigm. At the same time his search for aids to reflection on Scripture introduced him to theorists like Tyconius *(Letters* 41.7). This reading was not unique, but seems to have fed a larger hunger to assimilate the tradition of the Church, at least the part that was accessible to him in Latin. Through Ambrose and translations, he was exposed to Philo and Origen, and by the time of his elevation as bishop, Augustine had been reading Tertullian, Cyprian, and Hilary.

The enemies of the faith were a constant spur to his strong apologetic streak. A major resource for polemical work, as well as a strong impetus toward a conjunctive understanding of the incarnation and of figurative exegesis, may have come from reading Irenaeus' *Aduersus Haereses*.[51] With full development of the christological substructure of Augustine's figurative exegesis, the Old Testament functioned as a prologue of the New, and therefore became legitimate territory for apologetic controversy concerning Christ and the Church. In a sense the Manichaean controversy prepared the ground for argument with the Donatists which intensified in the mid 390's. The dispute with Manichaeism was over *whether* the Old Testament was to be received; with Donatism the controversy turned on *how* the Old Testament was to be received. In other words, the dispute with the Manicheans concerned canonicity; the dispute with Donatists concerned hermeneutics. And by a kind of organic growth the conclusions harvested in the former controversy germinated seeds of arguments for the latter.

In the end Augustine's strongest goad, as in other matters, may have been the experience of his own life. Early dreams of spiritual perfection receded over the years under the press of daily living and the growing understanding of the power of grace. Book 10 of the *Confessions* amply shows his painful sensitivity to continuing imperfection. But that book's culminating reflection on the power of the mediator (42.67 – 43.69) also reveals the presupposition of his new understanding of operative grace. And an almost offhand pair of quotes from the Psalms (54.23, 118.1–8), just before turning to consider Scripture in the next three books, reveals the role of christological spirituality in his work of exegesis. "Look, Lord," he says, "I have cast my care on you that I may live, and I will consider the marvels coming from your law" (43.70).

NOTES

1. Eugene TeSelle elegantly characterizes Augustine's theology as a "continuity in process of becoming … a coherence always changing." *Augustine the Theologian* (New York: Herder and Herder, 1970), p. 20. Augustine himself said, "I count myself one of the number of those who write as they progress and make progress as they write" (*Letters*. 143.2). *Revisions* prologue 3 invited readers to retrace his progress.

2. Erich Auerbach, "Figura," trans. Ralph Mannheim, in *Scenes from the Drama of European Literature*, Theory of History and Literature Series, vol. 9 (Manchester: Manchester University Press, 1984 [orig. 1944]), p. 36f.

3. See, e. g., *On Faith and the Creed* 4.6, *On Christian Doctrine* 1.13.12

4. Thomas S. Kuhn, *The Structure of Scientific Revolutions*, 2d ed. (Chicago: University of Chicago Press, 1970), p. 175; cf. *Paradigm Change in Theology*, ed. Hans Küng and David Tracy, trans. Margaret Köhl (New York: Crossroad, 1989), pp. 3–33.

5. This thesis goes against standard scholarly opinion of Augustine's christology. Joanne McWilliam says, "Christology did not lead the way but changed in response to other changes in his thinking." See "The Study of Augustine's Christology in the Twentieth Century," in *Augustine: From Rhetoric to Theologian*, ed. Joanne McWilliam (Waterloo, Ontario: Wilfrid Laurier University Press, 1992), p. 197.

6. Roland J. Teske, S. J., *St. Augustine on Genesis*, The Fathers of the Church, vol. 84 (Washington: Catholic University of America Press, 1991), p. 4ff.

7. In 2.2.3 he intends to interpret literally "unless no way out (*exitus*) is given for what is written to be understood reverently and worthily of God" (*pie et digne Deo*).

8. 2.2.3: *Secundum historiam facta narrantur, secundum prophetiam futura praenuntiantur*. Cf. Robert A. Markus, "History, Prophecy and Inspiration," appendix A in *Saeculum: History and Society in the Theology of St. Augustine*, revised edition (Cambridge: University Press, 1988), pp. 187–96.

9. Robert A. Markus, "St. Augustine on Signs," in *Augustine: A Collection of Critical Essays*, ed. R. A. Markus (New York: Doubleday, 1972 [orig. 1957]), p. 72. The treatise enlarges on views first advanced in *De dialectica* (386).

10. Ibid., p. 76.

11. 50.99: *et quid intersit inter allegoriam historiae, et allegoriam facti, et allegoriam semonis, et allegoriam sacramenti?*

12. *On the Usefulness of Belief* 3.5.391 and *On the Literal Interpretation of Genesis: An Unfinished Book* 2.5.393; note the revision in *On Genesis Literally Interpreted* 1.1.1.

13. Robert W. Bernard, "*In Figura*: Terminology pertaining to Figurative Exegesis in the Works of Augustine of Hippo" (Ph.D. diss., Princeton University, 1984), p. 105ff.

14. The movement is forward from the angle of the prophetic sign, and backward from the angle of its fulfillment; i.e., the prophetic sign of the rock from which Israel drank points faith to Christ (Num. 20.8, 1 Cor. 10.4), but the Church looks back to the rock both to confirm faith and to deepen its understanding of Christ.

15. Cf. Wilhelm Geerlings, *Christus Exemplum: Studien zur Christologie und Christusverkündigung Augustins* (Mainz: Matthias–Grünewald–Verlag, 1978), p. 173ff.

16. *Commentaries on the Psalms* 3.3: ... *ita inhaesit et quodammodo colauit excellenti supereminentiae Uerbi hominem suscipientis, ut tanta passionis humilitate non deponeretur.* Cf. J. M. Dewart, "The Influence of Theodore of Mopsuestia on Augustine's *Letter 187," Augustinian Studies* 10 (1979), pp. 113–15.

17. *Expositio epistulae ad Galatas* 24. On the importance of this text see Gérard Remy, *Le Christ mediateur dans l'oeuvre de saint Augustin,* vol. 1 (Lille: Université de Lille, 1979), pp. 46–52. Augustine's text of Gal. 3.19–20 reads as follows: *Quid ergo? Lex transgressionis gratia proposita est, donec ueniret semen cui promissum est, dispositum per angelos in manu mediatoris. Mediator autem unius non est, Deus uero unus est.*

18. Cf. Augustine's remarkable development of the theme of Christ's mediation between the one and the many in the plan of redemption in *On the Trinity* 4.2.4–7.12.

19. William S. Babcock ("The Christ of the Exchange," [Ph.D. diss. Yale University, 1971], p. 331ff.) articulates Augustine's "identity–action structure" in which "human weakness and suffering have as their grammatical subject the Word himself, and not the man or the human nature assumed by the Word." The contention here is that this was the achievement of the incarnational paradigm.

20. M.–J. Rondeau, *Les commentaires patristiques du Psautier,* vol. 2, Orientalia Christiana Analecta 220 (Rome: Pont. Institutum Studiorum Orientalium, 1985), pp. 380–88; cf. T. J. van Bavel, *Recherches sur la christologie de saint Augustin,* pp. 116–18.

21. A series of such references may be found in *Letters* 140.6, 10, 11, 12 and 13.

22. Many years later he recognized the mistake in reading the Greek text, *Revisions* 2.24.2. But this translation was still operative for the latter books of the *On Genesis Literally Interpreted* (5.19.38; 9.16.30, 18.35).

23. *Expos. epist. ad Gal.* 24: *per angelos autem ministrata est omnis dispensatio ueteris testamenti ... per angelos disposita est illa dispensatio legis* Cf. F. Edward Cranz, "The Development of Augustine's Ideas on Society before the Donatist Controversy," in *Augustine: a Collection of Critical Essays,* ed. Robert A. Markus (New York: Doubleday, 1972 [orig. 1954]), p. 355f.

24. *Expos. epist. ad Gal.* 24: *... agente in eis spirito sancto, et ipso uerbo ueritatis, nondum incarnato, sed numquam ab aliqua ueridica administratione recedente.*

25. Rondeau, *Les commentaires patristiques du psautier,* vol. 2, *Exégèse prosopologique et théologie,* 7–14; on Augustine, p. 365ff.

26. See especially *Commentaries on the Psalms* 37, delivered in Lent of 395. The quote is from *On the Trinity* 4.3.6.

27. *Commentaries on the Psalms* 30, sermon 1.4; cf. *Commentaries on the Psalms* 49.4: "the two Testaments have one voice."

28. Respectively, *On Catechizing the Uninstructed* 4.8 (c. 400); *Commentaries on the Psalms* 72.1 (c. 411); *Letters* 140.3.6 (c.412); and *Questions on the Heptateuch* 2.73 (c. 419).

29. *Against Adimantus* 12.5; cf. *Against Faustus* 12.29, where Paul's statement authorizes christological interpretation of other phenomena of the Exodus.

30. At this point the following interpretation steps away from C. P. Mayer's magisterial work, *Die Zeichen in der geistigen Entwicklung und in der Theologie des jungen Augustinus*, 2 vols. (Würzburg: Augustinus–Verlag, 1969, 1974). Mayer traces the neoplatonic ontology of sign and reality which was characteristic of what I have called the spiritualist paradigm (I, 141–49), but contends that Augustine's encounter with biblical understanding did not affect it (I, 287), and that the salvation–historical understanding was "integrated into" his neoplatonic structure (I, 248ff.). The different view offered here is that after he studied Paul this perspective seemed to Augustine, as Prof. Mayer's thesis applied to *On Christian Doctrine* seemed to H. J. Sieben, to be one–sided ("Die 'res' der Bibel: eine Analyse von Augustinus, *De doctr, christ.* I–III," *Revue des études augustiniennes* 21 (1975), p. 73). This was remedied by an advance in the dramatic perspective which gave it integrity as the condition of the anagogic. Even if the continuing power of the anagogic makes it an exaggeration to speak of "a radical conversion of [Augustine's] platonism" provoked by the discovery of the mediator (Remy, *Le Christ mediateur*, p. 175), the critical and distinctive role of the dramatic perspective makes it misleading to call its christo–ecclesiological focus the "flipside" *(Kehrseite)* of his philosophy (Mayer II, 438). In the incarnational paradigm, both of these irreducible perspectives on signs were operative, as in his reflections on the Paschal and Christmas feasts in *Letters.* 55.1ff., and in the different nuances of *sacramentum* and *exemplum* in *On the Trinity* 4.3.6 (cf. B. Studer, "'Sacramentum et exemplum' chez saint Augustin," *Revue des études augustiniennes* 10 [1975] pp. 89–93, 106–109). In themselves contrary, they came to function as complements in a single process. This development allowed Augustine's different strategy for defending the unity of the Old and New Testaments against the Manicheans. A purely neoplatonic ontology of signs could only argue for the possibility of retaining the Old Testament. Like the signs of *On the Teacher* the Old Testament possessed "no semantic function," serving only as reminder of knowledge to be gained elsewhere. The "weakness" of such a view of signs (I, 330: "This disjunction (*Auseinanderfallen*) of sign and reality is the ontological weakness of signs.") was also the weakness of this view of Scripture's unity. Only an interlocking understanding in which the reality *necessitated* the given sign, in which to deny the Old is to deny the New, could defend the bond of the Testaments. That necessity was emerged in the wake of the fuller christology of the mature dramatic perspective. See the reflections on *Against Faustus* below.

31. See Jolivet and Jourjon's *notes complémentaires* 27, 29 to *Against Adimantus*, *BA* 17, 775. But cf. Augustine's distinction in *On the Trinity* 2.6.11 between signs of Christ and signs of the Spirit. The former signify through

a symbolic (= sacramental) action performed upon an existing reality, like Jacob anointing the stone; the latter such as a dove or fire come into being *ad hoc* and pass away.

32. 12.3: *possum etiam interpretari praeceptum illud in signo esse positum.*

33. The reciprocity of the anagogic and dramatic in the incarnational paradigm comes into view when Augustine views a dramatic sign anagogically. In *Questions on the Heptateuch* 2.139 [c. 419] Augustine says that eternal rest remained in God while the Sabbath was given as a sign of the eternal reality "just the way (*quodammodo*) 'the rock was Christ' because the rock signified Christ." Note that *Questions on the Heptateuch* 3.57 repeats the statement of *Against Adimantus* that Paul avoids the word "signified."

34. Quintilian, *Institutio oratoria* 8.6.23f.

35. H. J. Sieben similarly sees in the hermeneutic of *On Christian Doctrine* the twofold goal of charity and the whole Christ of head and body; "Die 'res' der Bibel," 90.

36. In the categories of *On Genesis Against the Manicheans* 2.2.3ff., *On Christian Doctrine* does not adequately interpret "the figures of things which belong to prophecy."

37. 1.34.38; Augustine takes this phrase adverbially in reference to Paul's "fleshly" manner of knowing, and not adjectivally as if to speak of the Christ of flesh, i.e. the Jesus seen by humans.

38. Cf. Cranz, "Augustine's Ideas on Society," p. 375f. L. C. Ferrari noted the use of this text "as early as 396" ("'Christus Via' in Augustine's Confessions," *Augustinian Studies* 7 [1976], 49). But because the early writings often used other parts of the verse, "I am the truth" (*De beata vita* 34), "I am the life" (*On Two Souls* 1.1) and "no one comes to the Father but through me" (*On the Morals of the Catholic Church*. 16.28), the question would seem rather to be why "I am the way" does not appear any earlier. (Cf. Ferrari, "Young Augustine: Both Catholic and Manichee," *Augustinian Studies* 26:1 [1995], p. 117.) I suggest he avoided the quote until his understanding concerning the saving role of Christ's humanity fully matured, particularly because of the Manichaean invocation of Christ as "the way."

39. 1.11.11: *exemplo uirtutum eius uitia nostra curantur*; cf. Geerlings, *Christus Exemplum*, 213–15.

40. 1.15.14: *ut id quod ostendit esse faciendum ... faciamus.*

41. 1.35.39: *ut nossemus atque possemus, facta est tota pro salute nostra per diuinam prouidentiam dispensatio temporalis.*

42. In *Against Faustus* 16.23 Moses is called the "absolutely faithful dispenser of the prophetic sacrament"(*fidelissimus dispensator prophetici sacramenti*).

43. H.–I. Marrou, *Saint Augustin et la fin de la culture antique*, 4th ed. (Paris: Éditions E. de Boccard, 1958), p. 479; cf. J. Pepin "L'absurdité, signe de l'allégorie," in *Tradition de l'allégorie* (Paris: Études augustiniennes, 1987 [orig. 1957]), p. 173ff.). I use the term "liberalizes" rather than R. Teske's

"maximizes" ("Criteria for Figurative Interpretation in St Augustine," in *De Doctrina Christiana: A Classic of Western Culture*, ed. Duane W. H. Arnold and Pamela Bright [Notre Dame: University of Notre Dame Press, 1995], 110, 116ff.) because dramatic figures are not included. But the rule certainly maximizes the field of anagogic figures.

44. *Liber regularum*, preface: *regulae mysticae … claves et luminaria;* cf. Pamela Bright, *The Book of Rules of Tyconius* (Notre Dame: Notre Dame University Press, 1988), p. 119ff.

45. Charles Kannengiesser, "The Interrupted *De doctrina christiana*," in *De Doctrina Christiana: A Classic of Western Culture*, 3-13.

46. *Liber regularum*, preface: *prophetiae immensam siluam perambulans.*

47. 16.20: *illi ex rerum christianarum iam praesentatis effectibus librorum prophetia uera probaretur; ex librorum uero prophetia Christus colendus agnosceretur.*

48. 12.26: *In illo enim scalae a terra usque ad caelum, a carne usque ad spiritum, quia in illo carnales proficiendo uelut ascendendo spiritales fiunt.*

49. *City of God* 16.2.3; cf. Markus, *Saeculum*, pp. 188–92.

50. His first known homily, *Sermon 214*, explained the creed to catechumens.

51. Cf. Berthold Altaner, "Augustinus und Irenäus," in *Kleine patristische Schriften* (Berlin: Akademie Verlag, 1967 [orig. 1949]), p. 203, who dates Augustine's first exposure to Irenaeus in the mid 390's.

7

Augustine, Sermon 21

On the Verse of Psalm 64:
"The Just One Will Take Delight in the Lord and Hope in
Him, and All The Upright of Heart Shall be Praised"

Edmund Hill O.P. *The Works of Saint Augustine–A Translation for the 21st Century:
Sermons II (20–50)* (New York Press, N.Y.: 1990, pages 30; 36–37).

—Date: 400-420

1. The just man will take delight in the Lord and hope in him, and all the upright of heart shall be praised (Ps 64: 10). We have certainly sung this with voice and heart. Christian consciences and tongues have spoken these words to God: The just one will take delight, not in the world, but in the Lord. Light has dawned for the just, it says somewhere else, and for the upright of heart delight (Ps 97:11). You may ask where delight is to be found. Here you have it: The just one will take delight in the Lord. And somewhere else: Delight in the Lord and he will give you the aims of your heart (Ps 37:4). What are we being shown? What's being granted us? What are we being told? To take delight in the Lord. But can you take delight in what you don't see? Or perhaps we do see the Lord? We have that safely promised us; but now we walk by faith, as long as we are in the body we are away from the Lord (2 Cor. 5: 6–7). By faith, not by sight. When will it be by sight? When another thing John says is fulfilled: Beloved, we are children of God, and it has not yet appeared what we shall be. But we know that when he appears we shall be like him, because we shall see him as he is (1 Jn 3:2). Then there will be great and perfect delight, then joy will be full, when it is no longer hope suckling us with milk, but the real thing providing us with solid food....

2. However, we have the first fruits of the Spirit and in another way, perhaps, we are near to the one we love, and now already, even if only slightly, we have a first lick and foretaste of what we are avidly going to eat and drink. How can we show this? Well, God whom we are commanded to love, in whom we are commanded to take delight, isn't gold, or silver, or earth or sky, or this light of the sun or anything that shines in the sky, or anything that glitters when bathed in light on earth. He is no kind of body at all. God is spirit. Therefore, he goes on, those who worship him must worship in spirit and in truth (Jn 4:22–24). Not in some place for a body because he isn't a body: you shouldn't imagine, for example, that you can get nearer to God on a high mountain or by the height of a mountain. The Lord is indeed high, but he looks on the lowly, while high things he knows from afar (Ps 138:6), low things not from afar. Certainly he is high, and of course if he knows high things from afar, he ought to notice low things from even further. "If he is far from high things in his highness," someone says, "so that he knows them from afar, how much more is his highness withdrawn a long way away from low things." But it isn't like that. For the Lord is high but he looks on the lowly. How does he look on them? The Lord is near to those who have broken their hearts (Ps 34:18). So don't look for a high mountain, where you may kid yourself that you are nearer to God. If you lift yourself high up, he withdraws far away from you; if you humble yourself low, he bends down to you. The tax collector stood a long way off, and that made it all the easier for God to draw near to him; he didn't even dare to raise his eyes to heaven, and he already had with him the one who made heaven. So how are we to take delight in the Lord if the Lord is so far away from us? But don't let him be far away! It's you who make him be far away. Love and he will draw near; love and he will live with you. The Lord is very near, do not be anxious at all (Phil 4:5–6).

You want to see how he is with you if you love? God is love (1 Jn 4:8–16). Why let your thoughts and fancies fly far and wide, as you say to yourself "Can you imagine what God is? Can you imagine what God is like?" Whatever you suppose, he isn't that: whatever you grasp with your thoughts, he isn't that. If it were what he is, it could not be grasped by thought. But so that you may have a taste of him, God is love. You are going to say to me, "Can you imagine what love is?" Love is what we love with. What do we love? A good beyond words, a good that does good, a good that is the creator of all goods. Let him delight you from whom you have whatever else delights you. I don't mean sin, because sin alone you do not have from him. Apart from sin, it is from him that you have whatever else you have....

9. Therefore, delight in the Lord, take pleasure in the Lord, not in the world. That man used to take pleasure in the Lord who, after losing all the pleasure of the world, still had the Lord with him to take pleasure in. He kept a wonderful, simple, perfect, unutterable pleasure in his heart. He possessed what he used to have, wasn't possessed by it, but he was possessed by the Lord. He trod down all that, he depended on him. When everything he trod down was taken from him, he clung to the one on whom he depended. Here is what it means to take pleasure in the Lord. The Lord has given—notice him taking pleasure—The Lord has taken away (Jb 1:21). Did he take himself away? What he gave he took away, he who gave offered himself. So he takes pleasure in the Lord. The Lord has given, the Lord has taken away: as it pleased the Lord so it has come to pass; blessed be the name of the Lord. Why should the slave be displeased with what has pleased the Lord? "I've lost my gold," he says, "I've lost my family, I've lost my herds, I've lost everything I owned. The one I am owned by I have not lost. I have lost my belongings, I have not lost the one I belong to. He is my delight, he is my riches." Why? because he isn't perverse, he isn't upside down, he hasn't thought lightly of the one who is above him and highly of the things that are below him. That, you see, is the perversity of using created things badly.

10. Why blame the one who gave you gold, when you are rightly to be blamed for wrongly loving gold. Have your gold, God says to you, I have given it to you, use it well. You want to adorn yourself with gold, think rather of adorning the gold; you want to be honored, you want to be graced by gold, think rather of gracing the gold, and not being yourself a disgrace to gold. He's got gold: he goes whoring, fornicating, leching, he puts on flashy shows, he gives outrageous presents to actors, he gives nothing to the starving poor, he is no credit to gold. Won't anyone say, who assesses the matter rightly, "I'm sorry for the gold that comes his way?" And what about you, if you have got gold? Now you are saying, "I'm sorry for the gold that comes his way. Oh, if only I had it!" What would you do with it? "I would take in strangers, I would feed the needy, clothe the naked, redeem captives." Fine talk before you have it; how will you talk when you do have it? If you are really like that, gold will be an adornment to you. If you really use gold like that, because you love him more who created gold, then you will be upright, loving higher things more, rightly using lower things. And you will delight in the Lord, as a just person you will take delight in the Lord. You will not be accusing your creator, you will be thanking your redeemer. Amen.

PART II

A Conflict of African Hermeneutics:
Augustine and Tyconius

8

"The Preponderating Influence of Augustine":
A Study of the Epitomes of the
Book of Rules *of the Donatist Tyconius*

PAMELA BRIGHT

1. Augustine's patronage of the Book of Rules

In his contribution to the Colloquy held at the Center for Hermeneutical Studies in Hellenistic and Modern Culture (Berkeley, 1989) on the differences between the hermeneutics of the Donatist Tyconius and Augustine, Henry Chadwick observed:

> Tyconius's influence on Augustine was something that he handsomely acknowledged from the 390's to the end of his life. Soon after Augustine had become a bishop, Alypius and he were badgering Aurelius of Carthage in repeated requests for an authoritative view of the merits of Tyconius. They found their diffident metropolitan singularly reluctant to offer them guidance. (Aug. *Letter* 41.2) Years later Augustine is found recommending the study of Tyconius to a deacon named Restitutus, exercised about the problem of the apparent incompatibility between purity and unity in the Church. (*Letter* 249) His commendations of Tyconius in the third book *On Christian Doctrine* ensured for the Rules not only mere survival but a serious influence on many later writers of great eminence.[1]

There is no doubt about the importance of Augustine's patronage on the subsequent reception of Tyconius's ideas. However, the following study of three very early summaries of the *Book of Rules*, prepared for the Berkeley Colloquy, demonstrate that Augustine's transmission of Tyconius's hermeneutical theory was a mixed blessing for the Donatist exegete.[2]

In the Preface to the critical edition of the *Book of Rules* of Tyconius published in 1894, F. C. Burkitt notes that it was mainly "the corrupt state of the text which has prevented the recognition of the important place which Tyconius holds in the history of Biblical interpretation of western Europe."[3] However, one of the sections of Burkitt's Introduction to the critical edition is devoted to a survey of the literary history of the *Book of Rules*. This survey clearly demonstrates the "preponderating influence"[4] of Augustine on the subsequent interpretation of the hermeneutical system which was proposed by Tyconius in the *Book of Rules* and applied with consistent logic in Tyconius's own commentary on the Apocalypse.

Burkitt's review of the numerous references to the seven rules of Tyconius in authors from the fifth to the fifteenth century suggests that Tyconius was read through the eyes of Augustine. Through the overwhelming popularity of Augustine's summary of the seven rules in *On Christian Doctrine*,[5] the *Book of Rules* itself was relegated to the status of an unread classic.[6]

> ...the sole reference to Tyconius' book independent of the review in *De Doctrina Christiana* is that by the author of the *De Promissionibus*. He was an African, and perhaps for that reason familiar with the book which his fellow countryman had written less than a century before. But Cassian and John the Deacon quote the *Book of Rules* only to illustrate a passage where Tyconius's explanation had already been noted by S. Augustine; Cassiodorus names Tyconius only in the sentence in which he recommends the study of the *De Doctrina Christiana*; S. Isidore follows S. Augustine's remarks more than the original seven rules. Therefore it is not unlikely that the frame of the book in the Middle Ages and its preservation to the present time is entirely due to S. Augustine. It was his recommendation, rather than the intrinsic merit of the work of a Donatist, that secured the respect of Latin Christendom.[7]

The purpose of the present work is not to duplicate Burkitt's fine analysis, already a century old, but to examine the consequences of Tyconius's being read through a series of interpretative summaries, beginning with that of Augustine.

This first and most renowned of the epitomes of the *Book of Rules* was written by Augustine in 427 as the concluding section of Book 3 of the *On Christian Doctrine* which had been begun thirty years before. This unprecedented approbation of the exegetical system of a schismatic theologian by a Church Father was undoubtedly, in Burkitt's terms, "the most important event in the history of the *Book of Rules*."[8]

Burkitt refers to a second epitome, published by Dom Pitra in the third volume of the *Spicilegium Solesmense*.[9] In 1975, Pierre Cazier published a critical edition, with commentary, of this epitome of the *Book of Rules* in which he draws principally upon eight manuscripts dating from the twelfth to the fourteenth century.[10] Cazier dates this epitome after that of Augustine and argues that it originated in circles that experienced the double influence of Augustine and Cassian. Cazier does not rule out the possibility of authorship by Cassian himself.[11]

A third summary of the *Book of Rules*, known as the Monza Epitome, was included as an appendix to Burkitt's critical edition of the *Book of Rules*.[12] This summary of the seven rules of Tyconius was found in the Codex Modoetianus, a ninth-century manuscript in the Cathedral Library at Monza near Milan. It was bound together with the commentaries of "Ambrosiaster" on the Pauline epistles.[13]

An important question in examining the adequacy of these epitomes of the *Book of Rules* to convey the sense of the original is to ask if the authors of these summaries understood the purpose of the *Book of Rules*, let alone the hermeneutical theory that stood behind it.

In the carefully crafted preamble to the *Book of Rules*, Tyconius tells us that he intended to write a "libellus" to introduce the reader to the logic of seven "mystical" rules which obscured the "treasures of truth" from some people. If the logic of these rules were understood, then the reader would be led along "paths of light" through the "immense forest of prophecy."[14] *Lucis tramitibus deductus ab errore defendatur*.

In my earlier work, the *Book of Rules of Tyconius: Its Purpose and Inner Logic*,[15] there is a study of the biblical citations chosen by Tyconius to illustrate the "logic" of the seven "mystical" rules. Since Tyconius draws equally from the Old and the New Testament — particularly from the Pauline texts — it is clear that the "forest of prophecy" is not to be identified with the prophetic books of the Old Testament as such. An analysis of his selection of texts reveals a thematic bias towards texts that speak words of comfort and encouragement or that speak words of threat and admonition.

Tyconius's own commentary on the interpretation of these texts in the light of the "logic" of the seven "mystical" rules lays constant stress on the presence of the "mystery of evil" in the Church (2 Thess. 2:7), a mystery that is sealed, "held back," in the "recesses" of Scripture by the seven rules of the Spirit.[16] The Spirit, as Author of Scripture, reveals that, because of this "mystery of evil," there is an "invisible" separation already at work in the church, separating some of the members of the church from Christ. The time of the "visible" separation of those on the right and on the left is not till the Judgement. In the meantime, in the time of the church, the Scriptures address words of promise and, at the same time, words of warning to the church which Tyconius describes as "bipartite" in its very nature.

The following survey of three epitomes of the *Book of Rules* will attempt to assess the fidelity of the various summaries of the seven rules to both the ecclesiological and exegetical concerns expressed by Tyconius in his explanation of the logic of the seven "mystical" rules. First (a) there will be a brief discussion of the individual rules according to the *Book of Rules*, (b) Augustine's treatment of the same material in *On Christian Doctrine*, (c) the epitome published by Cazier, and (d) the Monza epitome.

It will be argued in the following analysis of the three epitomes of the *Book of Rules* that Augustine's interpretation of the *Book of Rules* obscured for future generations of exegetes the very purpose and logic of Tyconius's *Book of Rules*.

2. The Seven Rules

Rule 1: Of the Lord and His Body

(A) TYCONIUS, THE *BOOK OF RULES*: RULE 1

In the first section of Rule 1, Tyconius illustrates the logic of the scriptural text in relation to the mystery of the union of Christ and the church. He discusses problems concerning certain sections of scriptural texts traditionally interpreted christologically *quae in Dominum convenire omnis Ecclesiae ore celebratur*. Tyconius cites the suffering servant of Isaiah 53 (*Liber Regularum* henceforward *LR* 2:4–14) and the stone from the mountain of Daniel 2 (*LR* 2:15–3:11).

According to Tyconius, when the text contains elements that are unfitting or unsuitable to refer to Christ, then the proper reference has "crossed over" to the church, the Body of Christ. It is the church that is in need of the gift of prudence, not Christ, "the Light and the Wisdom of God" (Is. 53:11). It is the church that "fills the whole world," not Christ who may fill the world with His power but not "palpably" (Dan. 2:35, *LR* 3:2)

Tyconius's objections may seem overscrupulous unless one takes into account his overriding concern for the universality of the church. Against the whole force of Donatist ecclesiology, Tyconius teaches that

112

the church, with sinners and saints in its midst, is to be found beyond the confines of Africa. Like the stone that is growing until it "fills the world" the church grows daily through Baptism, but the "mystery of evil" is also secretly increasing.

In the second part of Rule 1, Tyconius draws attention to more difficult texts where the logic of the rule is less clear *sunt alia in quibus huiusmodi ratio minus claret,* (*LR* 4:13). Problems of interpretations of the christological titles, Son of Man and Son of God, form a literary inclusion (*LR* 4:13–7:24). Where the reference "crosses over" from Christ to the church, that is, from a christological to an ecclesiological interpretation, Tyconius explores his constant theme of the revelation of the "mystery of iniquity" (2 Thess. 2:7, *LR* 8:3) and the need for awareness of its insidious growth "in the midst" of the Church.

(B) Augustine, On Christian Doctrine: Rule 1

Of the seventy biblical citations in Rule 1 of the *Book of Rules,* Augustine chooses a single verse of Isaiah, "as a groom he places a crown upon me, as a bride he adorns me with ornaments" (Is. 61:10). To this sole Tyconian quotation Augustine adds a second text from Galatians, "Therefore you are the seed of Abraham" (Gal. 3:29). Using these two texts to illustrate the first Tyconian rule, Augustine explains that through the union of Head and Body, the biblical text may refer either to Christ as Head of a Body, or to the Church.

Augustine's summary fails to convey Tyconius's focus on the question of the presence of evil "in the midst" of the church which is to be found "throughout the world." Neither does Augustine's treatment give an adequate idea of Tyconius's careful selection of texts whose ecclesiological rather than christological interpretation prepared for the logic of Rule 2, the "bipartite" church.

(C) Spicilegium Solesmense, Cazier's Critical Edition: Rule 1

The second epitome of the *Book of Rules* follows Augustine's choice of the single text of Isaiah (Is. 61:10) to illustrate Rule 1, but omits Augustine's reference to Galatians. This summary also follows Augustine's tendency to ignore Tyconius's ecclesiological concern with the question of the "mystery of evil" in the midst of the church.

The most notable difference between this epitome and that of Augustine in *On Christian Doctrine* is that the anonymous author suggests a three–fold distinction in discerning the reference of the biblical

113

text. Because of the unity of Head and Body, according to the context, the text can refer (i) to Christ only, (ii) to both Christ and the Church, (iii) to Christ or to the Church.

In arguing for this three–fold method of interpretation, the author of the epitome demonstrates a certain independence from Augustine, but is not thereby any closer either to the letter or the spirit of the Tyconian exposition.

(D) THE MONZA EPITOME: RULE 1

The Monza Epitome presents a striking contrast with the two previous summaries. Every scripture citation in the *Book of Rules* is given, even if only the first verse of a fairly lengthy quotation, for example, verse 11 of Ps 90 (LXX) instead of verses 11–16 quoted in the *Book of Rules* (LR 3:14–23). Sections to Tyconius's commentary are omitted, for example the introductory comments to Rule 1, but without detriment to the sense of the argument as a whole. When one considers the economy of Tyconius's style, this is no small achievement. The Monza Epitome may best be characterized as an abbreviation of the *Book of Rules*, faithfully and intelligently executed.

Rule 2: Of the Bipartite Body

(A) TYCONIUS: THE *BOOK OF RULES*: RULE 2

In Rule 2, Tyconius addresses the problem of interpreting scriptural texts that, within the space of a few verses, seem to "blow hot and cold," that is, to heap praise and blame on the same person, or city, or nation (Is. 33:20; 33:23; 42:16, 17). For Tyconius this is the biblical confirmation of the "bipartite" nature of the church. In addressing both comfort and warning to the church through scripture, the Spirit reveals the double nature of the church as a community in which one part is already invisibly separate from their fellow christians.

(B) AUGUSTINE, *ON CHRISTIAN DOCTRINE*: RULE 2

Augustine strongly disagreed with the Tyconian concept of the "bipartite" church:

> The second rule is about the twofold division of the body of the Lord; but this is not a suitable name, for there is really no part of the body of Christ which will not be with him in eternity. We ought therefore to say that the rule is about the true and the mixed body of the Lord, or the true and the counterfeit, or some such name; because, not to speak of eter-

114

nity, hypocrites cannot even now be said to be in him, although they seem to be in His Church.[17]

Apart from a concluding reference to the doom awaiting these "hypocrites" for which he turns to the Tyconian interpretation of Matthew 24:50–51, Augustine follows the general line of the argument of Rule 2 of the *Book of Rules*. However, an additional comment relating to the "seeming" union of the "hypocrites" in the Body of Christ underlines the difference between the ecclesiology of Augustine and that of Tyconius.

> Now this rule requires the reader to be on guard when scripture, although it has now come to address or speak of a different set of persons, seems to be addressing or speaking of the same persons as before, just as if both sets constituted one body in consequence of their being for a time united in a common participation of the sacraments.[18]

For Tyconius, it is not a question of the "true church" and the "counterfeit church." It is a question of the "bipartite" church in which the "right" and the "left" will be visibly and irrevocably separated at the judgement when the time for repentance is over, but until the Judgement there is no visible separation (Mt. 13:29) of the membership of the church. It was this repudiation of the necessity of a withdrawal from a "tainted" church that made Tyconius's ecclesiology such an anomaly in Donatist circles.

(c) Specilegium Solesmense, Cazier's Critical Edition: Rule 2

The second epitome follows Augustine rather than Tyconius in almost every respect. It refers to the church as *"vero et permixto"*; it cites three of the biblical quotations chosen by Augustine (Cant. 1:4; Mt. 13:47–48; 24:51), and refers to the "common participation in the sacraments" of the good and the bad.

(d) The Monza Epitome: Rule 2

The Monza reading of the Tyconian Rule 2 is again distinguished for its close attention to the scriptural quotations of Rule 2 of the *Book of Rules* as well as Tyconius's concept of the bipartite church.

Rule 3: Of the Promise and the Law

(a) Tyconius, the Book of Rules: Rule 3

With its dense quotation from Romans and Galatians, Rule 3 underlines the importance of Tyconius among the Pauline commentators of the fourth century as he tackles the question of justification and the Law.

However, Tyconius's attention does not waver from his notion of the church as "bipartite." This is demonstrated in his exegesis of the "sons of Promise" and the "sons of the Law" in Romans and Galatians. The separateness of the destiny of these two "orders" in the church is emphasized by citations from 1 John 4:3 (*LR* 30:26) and 1 John 4:18 (*LR* 25:14) and from 2 Thessalonians 2:3, 7, 8, 9 (*LR* 30:27; 31:4, 11).

(B) AUGUSTINE, *ON CHRISTIAN DOCTRINE*: RULE 3

Augustine's whole attention in Rule 3 is galvanized by Pelagianism. He suggests alternative titles for the Tyconian rule — "the spirit and the letter" or "grace and the law" *de gratia et mandato*. Since Tyconius wrote before the outbreak of the Pelagian dispute, Augustine excuses him for a certain lack of watchfulness and precision in considering the question of faith and works. Augustine draws on Ephesians 6:23, Philippians 1:29, 1 Corinthians 9:19, but selects only one citation from Romans (Rom. 12:3). There is not one biblical citation drawn from Rule 3 of the *Book of Rules*, nor is there any allusion to the two "orders" in the church, the "sons of promise" and the "sons of law", a concept that is linked with Tyconius's constant theme of the secret presence of evil in the church.

(C) *SPICILEGIUM SOLESMENSE*, CAZIER'S CRITICAL EDITION: RULE 3

The second epitome does not cite a single biblical text either from the *Book of Rules* or *On Christian Doctrine*. The author proposes a series of dichotomies: letter and spirit *de littera et spiritu*, law and grace *de lege et gratia*, historically *historice* and spiritually *spiritualiter*, and finally, law and faith *ut lex fidei et fides iungatur legi*. An obvious omission from the dualities of the second epitome is the Tyconian "promise and law" which is at the very center of the discussion in Rule 3 of the *Book of Rules*. The comparison and the contrasts with Augustine's commentary obviously would be more fruitful than a comparison of this epitome with the Tyconian original.[19]

(D) THE MONZA EPITOME: RULE 3

As was observed in Rule 1 and Rule 2, the Monza Epitome once again demonstrates a remarkable fidelity both to the argument and the biblical citations of Rule 3 in the *Book of Rules*.

Rule 4: Of Species and Genus

(A) TYCONIUS, THE *BOOK OF RULES*: RULE 4

In Rule 4, Tyconius examines the ecclesiological implications of oracles addressed to individuals whether a king (Solomon, 2 Kings 7:12–16) or cities (Babylon, Isaiah chapters 13 and 14), or nations (Egypt, Isaiah chapter 19). A "species" prophecy is addressed both to the historic reality, Solomon or Jerusalem, and to the church of which they are "figura" or types. Where the prophetic text exceeds historical reality (the throne of Israel to last forever) Tyconius speaks of "genus" prophecy, that is the immediate referent is the church throughout the world.

Whether through "species" or through "genus" type prophecy, the Spirit addresses the double word of comfort and admonition to the "bipartite" church. Egypt is "bipartite," Tyre is "bipartite," Jerusalem is "bipartite." In this way the church is warned against the "spiritual wickedness in heavenly places" (Eph. 6:12 *LR* 54:23). Once again the *Book of Rules* is concerned with the scriptural call to repentence of the sinful members of the church.

(b) Augustine, *On Christian Doctrine*: Rule 4

Augustine's commentary on Rule 4 follows the Tyconian original more closely than his treatment of Rule 3. Augustine explains the need for careful attention to the transitions of referent from species to genus in the reading of scripture. He illustrates these transitions in an exegesis of chapter 36 of Ezekiel where the prophet first speaks of Israel's infidelity and its dispersal among the nations (Ezek. 36:17–19). Then, with the prophecy to collect Israel once again from "all the nations," Augustine notes[20] that the "species has been overstepped and the genus taken in." Augustine is obviously approving of the strong emphasis on the catholicity of the church in the Donatist's exegesis and concludes the first part of his summary of Rule 4 with the comment:

> And thus the spiritual Israel is made up, not of one nation, but of all the nations which were promised to the fathers in their seed, that is, in Christ.[21]

It is precisely at this point, where Augustine introduces the opposition between the "spiritual" Israel and the "carnal" Israel,[22] that Augustine's summary departs from Tyconius's concept of the "bipartite" church. Augustine concludes his commentary on Rule 4 by insisting that the "unrighteous" have no abode in the "spiritual" Israel. On the other hand Tyconius had concluded his treatment of Rule 4 with citations from Jeremiah 32:15–29, which warns of the evil found in Jerusalem and the cities of Judah, and from Ephesians 6:12, which speaks of spiritual wickedness in heavenly places. For Tyconius, the "heavenly place" is the "spiritual world which is the Church" (*LR* 61:31).

(c) *Spicilegium Solesmense*, Cazier's Critical Edition: Rule 4

This section of the epitome shows independence from Augustine in selecting Isaiah 13:5, 17 to illustrate the transitions of the biblical referent from genus to species, from species to genus, and from genus back to species. This text is quoted by Tyconius, not by Augustine.

Ironically, Tyconius uses this oracle against Babylon to introduce his concept of an evil species, that is, one that is a "figure" or "type" of the "left" side of the "bipartite" church, to which the warning oracle is addressed. The second epitome ignores Tyconius's focus on the warnings addressed to the sinners in the church.

(d) The Monza Epitome: Rule 4

While the treatment of Rule 4 is more abbreviated than the previous rules, the author pays careful attention to Tyconius's preamble to Rule 4 which is passed over by the other two epitomes. This preamble is of particular significance for understanding the pneumatology underlying Tyconius's system of exegesis.[23]

The Monza Epitome also notes the important Tyconian commentary on Ezekiel 37:11–14, the valley of dry bones. Tyconius's interpretation of the "first resurrection" as Baptism was accepted by Augustine in Book 20, chapter 6 of the *City of God*.

The Monza Epitome also refers to the Isaiah oracle against Babylon (Is. 13), but unlike the second epitome, this document remains faithful to Tyconius's focus on the presence of evil "in the midst" of the church.

Rule 5: Of Times

(a) Tyconius, the *Book of Rules*: Rule 5

Tyconius describes two different methods of interpreting biblical "times." The first is "synecdoche," the part for the whole, or the whole for the part. With this method, Tyconius deals with the problem of computing the "three days" between the crucifixion and the Resurrection. According to the logic of Rule 5, a part of day counts as a whole day. Tyconius deals in a similar way with conflicting accounts of the duration of Israel's sojourn in Egypt (Exod.1:6–10 *LR* 55:13; Exod. 12:40 *LR* 55:9).

The second method of interpreting biblical "time" concerns "legitimate" numbers. Here the duration of time is symbolic rather than quantitative. There are certain favored numbers for time in scripture. Forty "days" or "years," seven "days" or "years," multiples of ten, especially a thousand "years," are times that are to be interpreted not quantitatively but as referring to the "whole time" of God's work of salvation.

In the context of his understanding of the double nature of the church, Tyconius explains that frequently these "legitimate" numbers are double *haec bona et mala duplicis temporis, LR* 64:16), that is, they are mentioned sequentially in scripture, for example, the waters of the Deluge rising then receding for forty days, and the seven years of plenty followed by seven years of famine. However, in the "bipartite" church the "times" of life and death occur simultaneously (*LR* 65:8–21).

Tyconius further explores the concept of the "bipartite" church in the exegesis of the injunctions for observing the Sabbath in Jeremiah 17:19–27 *Hierusalem bipertita est, et portae eius bipertitae,* (*LR* 63:2). As in the previous Rules, this study is remarkable for its ecclesiological focus. Time is precious because "now is the acceptable time" (2 Cor. 6:2, *LR* 60:15,19), the time for repentance for the sinners in the church.

(B) AUGUSTINE, *ON CHRISTIAN DOCTRINE*: RULE 5

In his summary and commentary of the fifth rule, Augustine describes the two kinds of biblical times: "synecdoche," the whole for the part, and the part for the whole, and "legitimate" numbers. "Synecdoche" solves the problems of discrepancies in the scriptural narrations of the transfiguration (eight days, Luke 9:28; six days, Matthew 17:1, Mark 9:2) as well as the three days in the tomb (Mt. 12:40).

The "legitimate" numbers are those numbers which are highly favored in scripture, seven, ten, twelve and their multiples. Augustine explains that these numbers are to be interpreted spiritually as referring to the "whole time" — the time of the church. This "whole time" is the time when the church remains a "sojourner among the aliens" (Jer. 25:11). The difference between Augustine's interpretation and that of Tyconius is that for Tyconius the church is not among the aliens, but the "aliens" are the left side of the "bipartite" church.

Augustine concludes his discussion of Rule 5 with a reference to the 144 thousand saints of the Apocalypse (Rev. 7:4). He remarks that Tyconius's concept of the "legitimate" numbers of scripture could well apply to the interpretation of numbers of "persons" in the scripture as well as "times." This comment ignores Tyconius's concentration on the ecclesiological theme of the invisible separation of the left and the right side of the church during the "time" of the church.

(c) *Spicilegium Solesmense*, Cazier's Critical Edition, Rule 5

While both Tyconius and Augustine explain "synecdoche" as the part for the whole, or the whole for the part, the author of the second epitome speaks of "greater" and "lesser" time. *Quinta est de temporibus, per quam aut pars maxima temporibus per partem minorem intelligitur, aut pars minima per maiorem.*

After referring to the interpretation of the three days in the tomb, the author introduces a brief discussion about the "legitimate" or favored numbers of scripture *quos eminentius divina scriptura commendat*, a direct quotation from Augustine. Seven, ten, twelve and their multiples, according to the author, may be equally interpreted as a reference to a totality of "persons" or of "times." Apart from the novel use of "major" and "minor" times, the debt of the author of this epitome to Augustine is obvious.

(d) The Monza Epitome: Rule 5

Once more the Monza Epitome is a model of fidelity in following the ecclesiological interpretation and the scriptural citations of the *Book of Rules.*

Rule 6: Of Recapitulation

(a) Tyconius, the *Book of Rules*: Rule 6

Tyconius declares that of all the rules that "guard the way to light" the rule of recapitulation is the most subtle.[24] There are two kinds of recapitulations, that is, similarities that link the present situation in the church to something described by scripture either in the past or in the future. As an example of the first kind of recapitulation, Tyconius shows that the present situation resembles that of the destruction of Sodom. Just as Lot was separated from the sinners of Sodom, so the faithful Christian is separated from the spiritual death of the sinners in the church.

The second kind of recapitulation links present and future events. Tyconius cites the prophecy in Matthew 24:15–16 of the signs of the end–times and remarks that the sign of the "abomination of desolation" is already discernible in the Africa of his own day, in the presence of evil "in the midst" of the church, and yet "the end is not yet" (*LR* 67:11).

For Tyconius the "signs" of the coming separation of the Judgement are already present in the church. There are those members of the church who are already "separate from Jesus" (1 John 3:14, 15 *LR* 68:26; 1 John 4:1–3 *LR* 67:31). Once again through the understanding of the "logic" of a mystical rule of scripture, the Spirit reveals the presence of the "man of sin" in the midst of the church.

(B) AUGUSTINE, *ON CHRISTIAN DOCTRINE*: RULE 6

Augustine understands the term "recapitulation" as a summary inserted into the biblical narrative. In the first part of his discussion of Rule 6, Augustine concentrates on problems of the order of the biblical narrative, especially in the creation narratives in Genesis (Gen 2:8–9, 15) and then in narratives of the Deluge and tower of Babel (Gen 10:2–32, 11:1). The inconsistencies in the biblical account are explained by the presence of a "recapitulation" of events outside the narrative.

In the second part of the Rule, Augustine turns to a "more obscure" kind of recapitulation, for example when the Gospels urge, "Remember Lot's wife!" (Luke 17:29–32). Augustine claims that the biblical warning not to look back and to long for that which has been renounced in the past is to be needed now, not on the last day:

> "In that day" the time for giving heed to these sayings, unless the reader be watchful and intelligent so as to understand the recapitulation, in which he will be assisted by that other passage of scripture which even in the time of the apostles proclaimed: "little children, it is the last time."[25]

Although Augustine's treatment of this rule is sensitive to Tyconius's consistent ecclesiological interpretation of the scriptural texts, yet Augustine's understanding of recapitulation as a summary, rather than as a prophetic sign addressed to the church, obscured the "logic" of the Tyconian rule.

(C) *SPICILEGIUM SOLESMENSE*, CAZIER'S CRITICAL EDITION: RULE 6

The influence of Augustine upon the subsequent interpretation of the Tyconian rules is all too evident in this section of the epitome. The rule is viewed as a method of interpreting problems in the order of the biblical narratives. Following Augustine, the author of this epitome illustrates the rule with texts from the second chapter of Genesis.

Unlike Augustine, the author does not include any reference to the scriptural warnings of discerning the signs of being "separate from Jesus" even before the day of Judgement. The shortcomings of this section of the epitome as a vehicle for understanding the Tyconian concept of recapitulation are all too obvious.

(D) THE MONZA EPITOME: RULE 6

The summary of Rule 6 of the *Book of Rules* in the Monza Epitome is the most problematic section of the work. The careful and intelligent summary of the previous five rules is interrupted by insertions of Augustinian material, not only from *On Christian Doctrine* but also from the *Enchiridion*, Augustine's "handbook" on faith, hope, and charity prepared for Laurentius around the year 421.[26]

The section on Rule 6 begins with Tyconius's remarks about the need for care in discerning the recapitulations of scripture because of the subtlety of this rule, but then it turns from the Tyconian text and summarizes Augustine's commentary on the sixth rule with the same fidelity to the argument, the vocabulary, and the biblical citations of *On Christian Doctrine* that was formerly lavished upon the text of the *Book of Rules*.

After including the summary of Augustine's own summary of Rule 6, the Monza Epitome then turns back to the text of Tyconius, but not without a significant change in the text where Tyconius had spoken of *two* kinds of recapitulations. The first occurred when the past was united to the present by certain similarities; the second was when the present was linked to the future by a likeness of event. *Aliquotiens autem non sunt recapitulationes huius modi sed futurae similitudines.* (LR 67:7, 8)

The Monza Epitome renders the same text thus: *Aliquoties autem non sunt recapitulationes sed futurae similitudines.*[27] The Monza Epitome speaks of "recapitulations" and of "future likenesses," not of two different forms of recapitulations that Tyconius insisted upon.

After introducing this change in the interpretation of the Tyconian rule, the Epitome concludes the section of Rule 6 with an abbreviated but a faithful interpretation of the rest of the Tyconian text.

At this point the Epitome breaks off its summary of the *Book of Rules*. It concludes the whole work with a summary of a passage from Augustine's *Enchiridion* 103 concerning the will of God for the salvation of all and the evil will of those who reject this salvation.

Rule 7: Of the Devil and His Body

(A) TYCONIUS, THE *BOOK OF RULES*: RULE 7

Tyconius introduced Rule 7 by recalling the kind of "logic" that was required in the discernment of Rule 1, Of the Lord and His Body, that is, to discern through the logic of the rule whether the biblical text refers to the Head, in this case the Devil, or to the members of the "opposing" body, the left side of the church.

In Rule 1 it was noteworthy that though Tyconius first selected texts in Rule 1 that referred to either Christ or the Church and then concentrated upon only the ecclesiological interpretations, in this seventh rule he does not even allow one illustration to apply to the Devil. Every text is referred to the Antichrist, "the man of sin," the "mystery of iniquity" "in the midst" of the church.

Tyconius selects two long passages from the prophetic books for detailed exegesis. The first, Isaiah 14:12–21, describes the blasphemous pretentions of the King of Babylon who thought to place his throne in the heavens. The second is from Ezekiel 28:1–17, in which the Prince of Tyre claims to be as God in the heart of the sea. Both of these texts are perfectly fitted to the Tyconian theme of the "mystery of evil" at work in the church, stealing "precious stones" from Christ, and establishing a "princely" throne in the heart of the church.

The final words of the *Book of Rules* are a prophetic denunciation of the evil–doers who separate themselves from Christ. Yet even these grim warnings are intended as an admonition to the sinner to return to Christ before the finality of the visible separation of the Judgement.

(B) Augustine, *On Christian Doctrine*: Rule 7

Augustine selects only one verse from those cited by Tyconius, Isaiah 14:12, the fall of Lucifer from heaven. According to Augustine this text refers to the Devil, whereas in the second part of the verse the reference is to the Devil's body, "ground down on the earth." This interpretation ignores Tyconius's focus on the establishment of evil "in the midst" of the church and his insistence upon the salvific purpose of the double word of Scripture: the word of comfort to the faithful and the word of warning to the sinner.

(C) *Spicilegium Solesmense*, Cazier's Critical Edition: Rule 7

The second epitome contains a very brief discussion of Rule 7. It refers to the relationship between Rule 1 and Rule 7. It follows Augustine in interpreting the fall of Lucifer from the heavens as a reference to the Devil, but independently from Augustine interprets Babylon (rather than the King of Babylon) as the body of the Devil. There is no attempt to convey the close attention that Tyconius devotes to the question of the "revelation" of the "man of sin" "in the midst" of the church.

(D) The Monza Epitome: Rule 7

Although the manuscript of the Monza Epitome commences with

the words *"vii.Ticonii,"*[28] there is neither a summary nor even a reference to the seventh rule of the *Book of Rules*.

3. Augustine's Legacy

The pioneering studies of the *Book of Rules* initiated by Burkitt, T. Hahn,[29] and P. Monceaux[30] earlier in the century have paved the way for the needed reassessment of the place of Tyconius in the history of Christian exegesis. At the same period that Burkitt was beginning his study of the manuscript tradition of the *Book of Rules*, J. Haussleiter published the findings of his study of the African commentary of the Apocalypse.[31] While the present century has seen a growing attention to the history of the reception[32] of Tyconius's commentary of the Apocalypse from the closing years of the fourth century on through the medieval period, there is a need for a better appreciation of the relationship between the *Book of Rules* and the *Apocalypse Commentary*. The complementarity of the two works may well have been appreciated by Bede when he prefixed his own *Explanatio Apocalypsis* with a short account of the *Book of Rules*. However, Bede's description of the rules is entirely dependent upon Augustine's summary of the *Book of Rules* in *On Christian Doctrine*.

The present study of three epitomes of the *Book of Rules* is a further witness to what Burkitt terms "the preponderating influence" of Augustine upon the reception of Tyconius's hermeneutical system. This influence is clearly demonstrated in the epitome from the *Spicilegium Solesmense* edited by Cazier. While the author shows independent judgement at times in his terminology and his understanding of certain facets of the Tyconian rules, for the most part, in his choice of biblical citations and particularly in his acceptance of Augustine's concept of the "true" and the "counterfeit" church, the epitomist obscures the meaning of the *Book of Rules*.

The Augustinian legacy is apparent in the *memoria technica* of the seven rules of Tyconius. This summary of the seven rules in hexameters reflects Augustine's interpretation of the Tyconian rules, and even more so, it reflects the terminology of the epitome which Cazier attributes to the circle around Cassian in Southern Gaul in the fifth century.

> *Regula prima caput nostrum cum corpore iunguit;*
> *corpore de vero loquitur mixtoque secunda;*
> *tertia describit quid lex quid gratia possit;*
> *quarta genus speciem, totum partemque rependit;*

tempora disiungit maiora minoraque quinta;
sexta refert iterum quae primo facta fuerunt;
septima serpentis sibi membra caputque resoluit.[33]

The changed readings of the Rules since the time of Tyconius can be noted in a number of the rules:

(Rule 2)
Tyconius: *bipartite corporis*
Augustine: *De Doctrina Christiana*: *corpore vero et permixto*
Cazier's edition: *corpore vero et permixto*
memoria technica: *corpore de vero...mixtoque*

(Rule 3)
Tyconius: *de promissis et lege*
Augustine: *gratia et mandato*
Cazier's edition: *lege et gratia*
memoria technica: *lex...gratia*

(Rule 5)
Tyconius: *a parte totum, aut a toto pars*
Augustine: *a parte totum, aut a toto partem*
Cazier's edition: *pars maxima...minorem; pars minima...maiorem*
memoria technica: *pars minima per maiorem*

The *memoria technica* shares the disregard of both the epitomes for Tyconius's concept of the bipartite church upon which the whole understanding of his hermeneutical system is based.

The Monza Epitome is the exception that proves the rule. As a summary of the seven "mystical" rules, it is astonishingly faithful to the Tyconian original. However, Burkitt knew of only a single manuscript copy of this epitome. Not only is there the problem of the availability of such a tool for medieval exegetes but there is the question of the inclusion of Augustinian material in the concluding sections.

One may ask why was the seventh rule omitted in the Monza Epitome. An obvious explanation is that it was missing from the manuscript available to the author of the epitome, but, since the Augustinian material was inserted into the middle of the confused summary of Rule 6, it may be that the epitomist did not understand the Tyconian concept of recapitulation, and turned to the Augustinian material for clarification. Again one may wonder if Augustine's own misunderstanding of reca-

125

pitulation blinded the author of the Monza Epitome to the logic of the Tyconian rule. Aside from such speculations, the Monza Epitome is further evidence for the influence of Augustine on the reception and the transmission of Tyconius's hermeneutical theory.

Conclusion

How was the purpose and the meaning of the *Book of Rules* obscured by its well–meaning and diligent interpreters?

The brief analysis of the difference between the Tyconian text and its earliest summaries, whose authors were Tyconius's younger contemporaries, demonstrates the radical changes introduced into the reading of the rules within fifty years of its composition. The details of these changes have been outlined in the study of the individual rules, but in general terms, these earliest interpreters of the rules, beginning with Augustine, shifted attention from the precise ecclesiological focus of Tyconius.

Tyconius wrote his *libellus* to guide the reader to an understanding of the "logic" of the "mystical" rules of scripture. These seven rules seal the mystery of the presence of evil growing secretly "in the midst" of the church. The Spirit, the Author of Scripture, through prophetic denunciation of the evil members who are "separate from Jesus" calls the whole church to repentance and fidelity before the Judgement, the time of the visible manifestation of the "opposing" party that would seek to usurp the place of Christ in the heart of the church.

It may be argued that when the first commentators of the *Book of Rules* failed to understand the criteria behind the selection of biblical texts for illustrating the logic of the mystical rules, they failed to understand the very purpose of the *Book of Rules* as well as the hermeneutical theory that lay behind it.

From Augustine onwards, the interpreters of the *Book of Rules* did not recognize the "keys" or the "windows" which Tyconius provided as an access to the understanding of the mysteries of the church sealed within the "recesses" of scripture by the Spirit. It may well be that Tyconius's pneumatological and ecclesiological understanding of the task of biblical exegesis still awaits the unbiased consideration he appealed for in the preamble to the *Book of Rules*:

> Should the logic of these rules be recognized as readily as we communicate it, then anything closed would be opened, and what is dark would be illuminated, so that the one walking through the immense forest of

126

prophecy, guided as it were on paths of light, would be protected against error (*LR* 1:5–9).

A careful analysis of the differences of approach by the two African exegetes to the same ecclesiological themes is a rare opportunity for watching Augustine at work over a long period of time precisely within the framework of hermeneutics. He struggles not so much with the Donatists but with a subtle version of *African* exegesis.[34] For all Augustine's magisterial command over the scriptural texts, for all his ability to communicate the Word in vivid and compelling immediacy, here in rhetorical combat with the elder (possibly defunct!) Donatist he is not so sure–footed. Tyconius was a worthy opponent/conversationalist who challenged Augustine for many decades to understand an approach to hermeneutics that had developed in Africa especially in response to the Novatian schism where Cyprian and his bishops faced the question of the inclusion of the "lapsed" into the communion of the church. Because of the disputes and continuing schisms, Augustine lived with the pastoral and doctrinal question of the "holiness" of the church throughout his episcopate. In consequence, it is not surprising to observe the Tyconian undercurrent that periodically surfaces in Augustine's hermeneutical concerns.

NOTES

1. H. Chadwick, "Tyconius and Augustine," C. Kannengiesser and P. Bright, eds., *A Conflict of Christian Hermeneutics in Roman Africa: Tyconius and Augustine: Protocol of Fifty–Eighth Colloquy*, (Berkeley, 1989) 49–55.

2. P. Bright, "Tyconius and His Interpreters: A Study of the Epitomes of the *Book of Rules*," *A Conflict of Christian Hermeneutics* (Berkeley, 1989) 23–39.

3. F. C. Burkitt, *The Book of Rules of Tyconius* (Cambridge: University Press, 1984).

4. Burkitt, *Book of Rules*. xxiii.

5. Augustine, *On Christian Doctrine* 3.30–37, PL 34: 16–121.

6. See the chapter entitled: "The Book of Rules, A Neglected Classic" in *The Book of Rules of Tyconius: Its Purpose and Inner Logic* (Notre Dame, IN: University of Notre Dame Press, 1988).

7. Burkitt, *The Book of Rules*, xxiii, vi.

8. Burkitt, *Book of Rules*, xviii.

9. Burkitt, *Book of Rules*, xxii.

10. Pierre Cazier, "Cassien auteur présumé de l'épitomé des Règles de Tyconius," *Revue des Etudes Augustiniennes* 21:1–2 (1975,6), 267.

11. Cazier, "Cassien auteur présumé de l'épitomé des Règles de Tyconius," 263.

12. Burkitt, *Book of Rules*, appendix 89–98.

13. Burkitt, *Book of Rules*, xxvii.

14. Burkitt, *Book of Rules*, LR 1:1–9.

15. Pamela Bright, *The Book of Rules of Tyconius: Its Purpose and Inner Logic*, chapter two: "The Immense Forest of Prophecy."

16. *LR* 1:4.

17. Augustine, *On Christian Doctrine*, Book 3.45. The Nicene and Post–Nicene Fathers, first series 3, ed. by P. Schaff, trans. J.F. Shaw, (Grand Rapids MI: Eerdmans, 1956), 569.

18. Augustine, *On Christian Doctrine*, Book 3.45, *NPNF*, 2, 569.

19. Cazier, *L'Épitomé des Règles de Tyconius*, 276–279.

20. Augustine, *On Christian Doctrine*, Book 3.48.

21. Augustine, *On Christian Doctrine*, Book 3.48.

22. Augustine, *On Christian Doctrine*, Book 3.49.

23. See chapter five, P. Bright, *The Book of Rules of Tyconius*.

24. Burkitt, *Book of Rules*, 66:11–13.

25. Augustine, *On Christian Doctrine*, Book 3.54; *NPNF*, 573.

26. Augustine, "The *Enchiridion* to Laurentius," trans. C.K. Cornish, *Seven Short Treatises of S.Augustine* (Oxford: J.H. Parker; London: F.and J. Rivington, 1847), Introduction.

27. Burkitt, "The Monza Epitome," 98.

28. Burkitt, *Books of Rules*, 98.

29. T. Hahn, *Tyconius–Studien*. Studien zur Geschichte der Theologie und der Kirche, vol.6, no.2 (Leipzig: Dietrich, 1900).

30. P. Monceaux, *Histoire Litteraire de l'Afrique Chrétienne: Depuis les origines jusqu'à l'invasion arabe*, 7 volumes (Paris, 1901–1923).

31. J. Haussleiter, "Die lateinische Apokalypse der alten afrikanischen Kirche," *Forschungen zur Geschichte des neutestamentlichen Kanons und der altkirchlichen Literatur*, ed. Theodor Zahn, vol. 6 (Erlangen: Deichert, 1891).

32. K. Steinhauser, *The Apocalypse Commentary of Tyconius: A History of Its Reception and Influence* (Frankfurt: Peter Lang, 1987).

33. Cazier bases a critical text on five manuscripts: London: British Library 3 C III; Laon: 89; Munich: Bayerische Staatsbibl., 22239; Vatican: Vatican latin, 4296; Vatican: Palatine, 841.

34. See P. Bright, "Biblical Ambiguity in African Exegesis," *De Doctrina Christiana: A Classic of Western Culture* ed. Duane W.H. Arnold and Pamela Bright (Notre Dame, IN: University of Notre Dame Press, 1995).

9

Tyconius's Mystic Rules *and the* Rules *of Augustine*

ROBERT A. KUGLER

In recent years there has been renewed interest in the work of the fourth century North African lay theologian, Tyconius. Tyconius's "work", in fact, amounts to a book on hermeneutics entitled the *Book of Rules (Liber regularum)* and fragments of a commentary on Revelation, scattered throughout the Apocalypse commentaries of later authors, and in fragmentary manuscripts of questionable value.[1] Of particular interest in the study of Tyconius and the *Book of Rules* has been Augustine's appropriation of Tyconius's book.[2] Much has been said in the recent past regarding the effect of Augustine's reception of Tyconius on later comprehension of Tyconius's work.[3] However, one particular aspect of Augustine's appropriation which has escaped close examination is his use of Scripture in adducing Tyconius's hermeneutical rules, in comparison with Tyconius's own use of Scripture in the *Book of Rules*.[4] In what follows I intend to make that comparison and thereby show that both authors' understanding of the Church and Scripture can be deduced from the way they use Scripture in the presentation of the rules. Stated most briefly, Augustine sees Scripture as that which contains God's Word to humanity, but also obscures God's Word by its sign-nature and thus gives rise to the need of interpretation by means of human reason to be understood. Tyconius understands Scripture to be a seamless, living oracle of God, made incomprehensible only by the human failure to grasp its logic. In turn Augustine comprehends a Church which in the end time will be one in its predestined election by God, and untainted by evil within itself. However the Church as it exists presently, though ontologically separate from evil and hypocrisy, is mixed with such matter which is a "counterfeit church", to be eliminated in the age to come. Tyconius on the other hand adheres to the notion of the Church's unity, yet asserts it is of a bipartite nature whereby evil and good, faithfulness and faithlessness coincide in the present age together in the one Church. Therefore, those who dwell on the evil side of the Church of the present age have the opportunity to make the transition to the right side before the dawn of the New Age by comprehending the Scriptures through acceptance of the logic of those Scriptures which Tyconius provides for them in his *Book of Rules*.

1.

Before turning to the examination of the respective authors' presentations of the rules a few brief observations regarding each author's background are in order. The purpose of these observations will be to show in what ways their respective backgrounds laid the foundations for their unique views of Scripture and the Church.

Augustine's youthful education in North Africa, though perhaps inadequate by the standards current in the rest of the Empire of his day, nevertheless established in him a clear appreciation and love of the Classical tradition as filtered through the Latin authors. In this educational system Augustine was trained from the very first to be a rhetor, a wordsmith seeking from his sources adequate material for the creation of pleasing and effective speech.[5] There is little doubt that Augustine clung to these educational roots established so firmly in his early years. In fact, in *On Christian Doctrine* one finds Augustine praising the eloquence of the Scriptures, in response to those who might suggest they lack erudition; but he concludes and supports his own comments with a citation of Cicero![6]

In addition to his early education, Augustine seems also to have learnt quite a great deal during his sojourn in Milan in the mid and latter portion of the ninth decade of the fourth century. It was there (and no doubt to some extent also later in Thagaste where he engaged in conversation with his friends) that Augustine gained acquaintance with the depth of the Greek tradition and the premium it placed on intellectual exchange. As a result Augustine came to know the notion of the critical relationship between subject and object. In the Greek tradition that relationship is defined by the subject acting upon the object to analyze, manipulate and utilize the latter.[7] This comprehension of the subject-object relationship made a lasting impression on Augustine, and as we shall see, was critical in shaping his understanding of Scripture.

130

What of Augustine's background could have shaped his vision of the Church? The most likely answer to the last question is the most simple one: Augustine's experience in the Church shaped his comprehension of the nature of that Church. It is important to remember that Augustine went from being a mere priest to the role of bishop in a very short period of time.[8] As a result, his experience of the Church was, almost from the very beginning, as one of its appointed guardians.[9] It is little wonder that Augustine can be found to have been impassioned in his defense of the notion of the Church's purity and oneness, and of its ontological distinctness from that which was evil and faithless in the world.

But perhaps even more important in shaping Augustine's vision of the Church was once again his Classical education. There he learned the values of the "school" setting, where the intellectual sought the ultimate experience of love — intellectual communion with one's fellow learners. Augustine seems to have transferred this notion to the Church; it became his new school wherein Jesus was the headmaster and the objective was perfect love of God.[10] However, under the influence of Platonism Augustine recognized the Church in the present to be a mere shadow of the ultimate "form" to be realized in the end of time.[11] Add to this Augustine's thoroughgoing predestinarian views and it is quite natural that Augustine would understand the true Church to be invisible in the present, but aimed for visibility in the end time when the hypocrites would be eliminated by judgment.

What of Tyconius? We have little to go on in reconstructing Tyconius's life. In fact, all we know of him is what he left to us in his own meagre writings and the few things Augustine and others tell us of him.[12] Nevertheless, we do know that he was a North African, apparently deprived of the exposure to the outside world to which Augustine was privileged. We also know that he was a member of the Donatist movement. Given these facts we may ask what in the North African and Donatist contexts might have contributed to his view of Church and Scripture.

The influence of Donatism cannot be gainsaid. Quite generally Tyconius seems to have been influenced in his conception of the Church by the embattled ecclesiology of the Donatists. However, Tyconius made a unique and damning, as far as his contemporaries in the movement were concerned, twist on this siege mentality. Rather than seeing the Catholic attackers of the Donatist church to be outside the Church, he perceived them also to be part of the one Church. In this sense, as is well known, Tyconius was quite distinctive. Nevertheless, he was at one with the

Donatist movement following in the theological and ecclesiastical heritage of Cyprian[13] and conforming to a large degree with the man who cast him from the movement, Parmenian.[14] Tyconius insisted on the oneness of the Church; though bipartite it was one and undivided. In this sense Tyconius inherited his ecclesiology from his intellectual forefathers in North Africa.

It is likely there was some Jewish influence on North African Christianity. The evidence for this suggestion is wide-ranging and varied. The material evidence suggests that the North African context was home to many Jews at least into the late third century, and almost certainly well beyond;[15] Rabbi Akiba (ca. 135 CE) is said to have come from North Africa, and there was a tradition of rabbis coming from there into the amoraic period. The importance of the Jewish influence is its possible contribution to Tyconius's view of Scripture. Shortly before Tyconius's time one can find evidence of Jewish communities which understood Scripture to be a living oracle of God speaking to them across the centuries as though it was given long ago expressly to address their circumstances.[16] More importantly the rabbinic movement which was coming to full flower in Tyconius's time saw Scripture in much the same way that Tyconius did.[17] It amounted to God's living voice speaking directly to them and their context. In some senses one can understand the whole of rabbinic literature as an extended commentary on what this living voice has to say to the present reality.[18] Finally, it is within Judaism of this age that one finds the persistent view of all of Scripture beyond the Law as prophecy; as I will make clear this was Tyconius's view of Scripture as well.[19]

Before turning to Tyconius's and Augustine's presentations of the rules, I examine the rest of each author's work in which the rules are discussed to see what that material can contribute to our understanding of their views, particularly of Scripture.

Besides the rules themselves, and a short listing of them in the Preface to the *Book of Rules* Tyconius leaves us but sixty-six words.[20] Nevertheless, they are very well chosen words, conveying already a good deal about the author's view of Scripture and the Church.[21] I reproduce Charles Kannengiesser's translation of the Preface here.[22]

> All things considered I found it most necessary to write an essay about the rules, and to fabricate, so to speak, keys and windows appropriate to the secrets of the Law. There are namely certain mystical rules, which withhold the hidden parts of the universal Law and render invisible for some people the treasures of the truth; should the logic of those rules be

recognized as readily as we communicate it, then anything closed would be opened, and what is dark would be illuminated, so that on the way through the immense forest of prophecy one would, as guided on paths of light, be protected against error.

What springs to one's attention is the notion that the rules about which Tyconius intends to write actually hold back the hidden parts of the "universal Law" and render invisible to some the treasures of truth. The "rules" are therefore not the keys to the meaning of the text, as Augustine was to understand them; rather they are the logic of the Scriptures themselves. Therefore, says Tyconius, if one accepts the *ratio* of the rules one will be able to comprehend Scripture, the "vast forest of prophecy," and in so doing make the transition from the left to the right hand side of the Church.[23] That Tyconius discerns a division within the Church is also already made evident in his Preface by the statement that the rules restrain "for some" the treasures of truth: there are those who understand Scripture and so know the nature of the Church, and there are those who do not.

Augustine, for his part, leaves us far more material with which to work in our reconstruction of his view of Scripture and the Church, apart from his presentation of Tyconius's rules. In fact, the material is so vast as to force a rather arbitrary limitation for the sake of brevity. In what follows I will refer only to the remainder of *On Christian Doctrine*.

In the Preface to the work, Augustine makes clear that he is about the task of teaching others to read Scripture, and to use that reading for the service of the Church. As such, the treatise is often thought of as a textbook of hermeneutics for leaders in the Church.[24] This he does particularly in opposition to one of the groups against whom he protests in his Preface, namely those who would read purely by the aid of the Spirit.[25] In Book 1 Augustine goes on to make clear that human persons are called to enjoy but one "thing," that being God who presents himself to us in Scripture. But God, as a thing to be enjoyed, conveys himself to us in the word-signs of Scripture, word-signs which can be obscure in a number of ways.[26] Thus to understand that which we are to enjoy requires that one decipher the obscure signs of Scripture.

In his introduction to Tyconius's rules Augustine betrays in yet another way his understanding of Scripture. While Tyconius's Preface, as I have already indicated, reveals that his "rules" are not keys to opening Scripture, but rather the logic of the Scriptures, Augustine misunderstands Tyconius in exactly this direction. Before quoting Tyconius's Preface he calls the rules "keys to open the secrets of the Scriptures."[27] Furthermore, he concludes his presentation of the rules by saying that, though Tyconius's "rules" do not contend with all the figurative forms of speech in Scripture they address many, and so are useful for the interpreter. In other words, Augustine understands the rules clearly to be useful tools for excavation — a sure sign of his understanding of Scripture, the object of such excavation.

2.

It is time now to turn to the examination of Tyconius's and Augustine's presentations of the rules themselves. While there has been no previous study of Augustine's Bible use in his review of Tyconius's rules, Pamela Bright has provided a convenient summary of Tyconius's Scripture citations in her presentation of his rules.[28] Accordingly I will rely to a good degree on Bright for my discussion of Tyconius's use of Scripture, while providing a first close reading of Augustine's use of the Bible in his discussion of Tyconius.

Rule 1: The Lord and His Body[29]

In the first "rule" Tyconius asserts the unity of the Head — Christ — and the Body — the Church; this is plainly indicated by Scripture, says Tyconius (1 Cor. 12:27 and Eph. 1:9–10). Assuming such unity allows one to understand the prophecies of Scripture (which as we will see throughout the review of Tyconius's *Book of Rules* include the whole of Scripture) as applying to both Christ and the Church. In order to demonstrate this Tyconius cites, in particular, verses from Is. 53 and 56, Dan. 2, Ps. 91 (MT), Rev. 22 and Mt. 24 and 26, as well as material from Eph. 1 and 2 Thess. and 1 John.[30] While Bright highlights the way in which Tyconius uses these texts to undergird his christological, ecclesiological and eschatological concerns,[31] what is important for my purpose is to affirm one of these observations and note one other aspect of Tyconius's use of Scripture in this regard. In the first instance, it is immediately apparent that Tyconius understands all of Scripture to be "prophetic" insofar as it can speak to the state of the Church in his day; thus the "immense forest of prophecy" he describes in the Preface to his book is not *just* the collection of Hebrew Bible prophecies with which modern readers are familiar.[32] Secondly, I agree with Bright that Tyconius's choice of texts reflects his view of the Church in his day; it is one, but divided within itself, containing both wicked and good persons. Indeed, at the conclusion of his discussion of the rule Tyconius cites, pastiche fashion, Eph. 2:21, Mt. 24:2

and 2 Thess. 2:7, to prove that the body/temple/Church is bipartite and that the evil portion will suffer destruction in time, but meanwhile the faithful must be on guard against its evil.[33] However, I believe what this shows is that Tyconius's selection of texts did indeed reflect his theological interests — that is his christology, ecclesiology and his eschatology — only insofar as he arranges them in a fashion which betrays his theology. The passages he adduced in the section just noted, taken alone and separately, say little or nothing reflective of his "theology."[34] Thus it seems that what is most obviously revealed from the outset is that Tyconius selects Bible passages not so much because of their theological content, as he does on the basis of an underlying preconception of what Scripture is: a set of oracles of God, which when read with the proper logic in mind, address contemporary reality as if they were composed precisely to address it, and it alone. The fact that the texts remain fundamentally unrelated to his theology when read in their own right, apart from the "logic" of the rule, provides compelling testimony to the notion that Tyconius is able to abstract the text of the Bible, word for word, phrase for phrase, regardless of its "contextual meaning."

Meanwhile Augustine, in his presentation of Tyconius's first rule, adduces but two passages of Scripture (compared to Tyconius's forty-five), Is. 61:10 and Gal. 3:29.[35] He does so to affirm in its bare essence what Tyconius asserted in his work; that Scripture can be understood to address, with reference to the same person, both the Head (Christ) and the Body (the Church). In this Augustine confirms Tyconius's view of the unity of the Church with Christ. However, he completely disregards Tyconius's concern to show that the body is bipartite (further elaborated by Tyconius in the second rule; see below), and that that reality further complicates one's comprehension of Scripture. In this it is already evident, in small part, that Augustine holds a different view of the Church from that of Tyconius.

In this first rule an initial clue is also given regarding Augustine's very different view of Scripture. Augustine can be seen here to marshall texts to show that the rule is a useful key to understanding Scripture: often in Scripture the subject of a sentence appears to shift in mid-verse and this rule aids one in comprehending this literary phenomenon in the Bible. So while for Tyconius Scripture is something which speaks plainly, according to a perceptible logic, for Augustine it is an often obscure document, filled with ambiguous and unknown signs, all of which require "keys" for their proper interpretation.

135

Rule 2: The Lord's Bipartite Body[36]

Noting the fact that texts seem to make contradictory statements regarding the same person or entity (e.g., Is. 45:3–5[37]), leading justifiably to confusion, Tyconius reminds his readers of the bipartite nature of the body of Christ. With that in mind, confusion becomes a thing of the past; the references to good coming to or from a person or entity refer to the faithful half of the Church, while references of an opposing nature pertain to the evil portion of the Church.[38] Promise is for the right hand side of the Church; threat for the left hand side.[39]

Augustine agrees with Tyconius that Scripture addresses both the wicked and the faithful; however the two, according to Augustine's view, are not united within the same Church.[40] In order to make this clear Augustine cites some of the same Scriptures as those cited by Tyconius, while adding two of his own.[41] Augustine's additions separate him from Tyconius on the matter of the nature of the Church. He invalidates the use of Songs 1:5 (a text used by Tyconius) as evidence of the bipartite nature of the Church by going on to say that "the tents of Kedar [to which 'black and beautiful' are likened in the second half of the verse] pertain to Ishmael, who 'shall not be heir with the son of the free woman' (Gal. 4:30)."[42] That is, the wicked never were actually part of the "body." Nevertheless, Augustine admits, at the present time "the good fish and the bad are...mixed up in the one net (Mt. 13:47, 48)."[43] But the fact remains that the true Church exists in the midst of this reality, but is not imbued by the evil of the "bad fish." The hypocrites of the false church, though appearing to be a part of the true Church at the present, will be revealed in the last judgment as having always been separate. What Augustine has done in this instance is to use a few of the texts Tyconius proffered, but adds two of his own choosing which allow him to reinterpret Tyconius's view of the Church. Additionally, while Tyconius consistently cites texts in order to show their conformity with the logic he is constructing in the rules, we find Augustine bringing texts forward to reinterpret Tyconius's view, and confirm his own; therefore for Tyconius the text is a living subject, acting on the Church, while Augustine sees it as an object, obscured by its sign-nature, needful of reawakening at the hands of the interpreter to make its voice useful for the Church. Two different views of Church and Scripture were clearly at work here.

Rule 3: The Promises and the Law[44]

In this long section Tyconius reveals the logic of Scripture whereby law and promise embedded in the text address the Church, calling it to

136

faith, and calling especially to the faithless to see the futility of attempting to gain God's mercy by their actions, and to see the proper logic of Church and Scripture. Again Tyconius suggests that the logic of Scripture centers around the bipartite nature of the Church and the need for the faithless to hear and perceive a call to repentance. In support of this view Tyconius mentions around one hundred different passages of Scripture, with the great majority coming from the New Testament. He neatly draws into relationship with one another key passages of promise in Genesis with passages of "fulfillment" in Romans and Galatians.[45] What Tyconius wants to show is that the whole of Scripture is a model of what God intends for his contemporary reality. In that the promises in Genesis are said to have been fulfilled in Romans and Galatians, one can perceive in this biblical pattern, this "biblical logic" if you will, the logic and pattern by which contemporary reality in Tyconius's Church is governed. The right hand side of the Church lives out the pattern of promise and fulfillment while the left hand side continues to exist under the power of law and without the benefit of the fulfillment of God's promises. The Church is proved by Scripture and its logic once again to be bipartite and those on the left hand side are shown to be in need of the rules as an aid to comprehension of that fact that they may share in life on the right hand side.

Augustine was clearly excited by this rule, and for obvious reasons, given his preoccupation some time before the completion of *On Christian Doctrine* with Pelagianism. But his excitement gets the better of him, it seems. While in the case of the other six rules it seems arguable that Augustine did not so much misunderstand Tyconius as did he correct him,[46] in this instance he genuinely seems to have been so preoccupied with his earlier encounters with Pelagius that he simply speaks past Tyconius and his consistent ecclesiological concern.[47] Instead he lauds Tyconius for his viewpoint and offers his own four texts to second the general notion of the relationship between promise and law.[48] In an oblique way even this attests to Augustine's view of the Church; the defeated Pelagians represent the faithless and the evil, and they are *outside* the Church. Furthermore, in a more direct way his use of Scripture confirms the notion that he understands it as being useful as proof of views already held, and in this instance, of views held by the orthodox Church.[49]

Rule 4: Genus and Species[50]

In this rule Tyconius suggests that the prophecies of Scripture are of two types; those which refer both to their immediate referent and to the Church (species) and those which refer first and last to the Church in the present (genus).[51] Once again, in order to demonstrate that this is the logic of the Scriptures, Tyconius cites Scripture itself. The texts come predominantly from Isaiah, Jeremiah and Ezekiel, with additional citations from the New Testament. What is important to note here is that yet again Tyconius's own discussion reveals that he sees all of Scripture to be *prophetic* of the nature of the Church in his day, and therefore perfectly clear in its own speech so long as one understands the logic by which it speaks. Furthermore, the prophecies of the Scriptures attest to the bipartite nature of the Church with prophecies of salvation and judgment pertaining to the two halves of the Church. By selection of particular texts relating both promise and threat Tyconius is able to show that Scripture does, indeed, concern itself with the nature of his contemporary Church situation.

It is in relationship to this rule that Augustine's different understanding of Scripture and of the Church come most to the fore.[52] While Tyconius cites about sixty passages, Augustine is very selective in his citations, limiting himself to only nine strategically chosen texts. He begins by agreeing with Tyconius on the notion that there are two types of "prophecy" in the Bible, namely species and genus texts.[53] However, when he moves beyond this to address the referent of the prophecies more specifically Augustine does a very interesting thing. He adduces Ezek. 36:17–19 as a proof text, as does Tyconius, but instead of finding its fulfillment in the life of the Church in his day he finds its corresponding fulfillment in a New Testament passage not adduced by Tyconius, namely 1 Cor. 10:18. So he can say with reference to Ezek. 36:23–29,

> Now that this is a prophecy of the New Testament, to which pertain not only the remnant of that one nation of which it is said elsewhere 'For though the number of the children of Israel be as the sand of the sea, yet a remnant of them will be saved' (Is. 10:22, cited in Rom. 9:27) — but also the other nations which were promised to their fathers and our fathers — no one who looks into this matter can doubt.[54]

Augustine cites the text from the Hebrew Bible, calling it "a prophecy of the New Testament"! He does the same with Ezek. 38:26 and 2 Cor. 3:2, 3. This shows clearly that for Augustine the prophecies under consideration are from the Old Testament and their fulfillment is in the New Testament story, which for him is the story of the Church. In this way Augustine is typical of early Christian comprehension of the promise-fulfillment schema in the Old and New Testaments. The promises made in the Old Testament are fulfilled by the New Testament story which is constitutive for the Church. Promise and fulfillment are on a historical trajectory which has its penultimate completion in the Church of the present age, and its ultimate completion in the Church of the coming age when all counterfeit elements will be eliminated.[55]

Additionally, Augustine parts ways with Tyconius in a very distinct manner with regard to the nature of the Church in his discussion of this rule.[56] He asserts that the "carnal Israel" and the "spiritual Israel," though perhaps appearing to be mixed, have always been separate entities, never of one body. Proof of the eternity of this state of affairs lies in 2 Tim. 1:9 and 10, a passage not used by Tyconius in his discussion of the rule, and one which suggests that those destined for grace have been known since before creation. It appears from this that Augustine is intentionally aligning himself against Tyconius's view of the Church, and that this self-alignment dictates his choice of texts.

Rule 5: Times[57]

Tyconius notes the frequent use of temporal designations in Scripture and offers in this rule the logic of these designations. In the first instance those temporal indicators which are problematic in that they contradict other temporal indications (e.g., Gen. 15:13 indicates a four hundred year stay in Egypt for the Israelites, while Exod. 12:40 enumerates four hundred thirty years) can be resolved by means of synecdoche, taking the part for the whole and the whole for the part. Tyconius also identifies "mystical numbers" used repeatedly in Scripture, such as seven and forty. These are not to be taken as literal expressions; rather they are expressive of a complete segment of time in the life of the Church leading to a particular goal — ultimately to the eschaton. As in the case of the other rules Tyconius adduces a large number of biblical texts to show that this is the logic of the Scriptures. In this case his nearly ninety citations are almost evenly divided between the Hebrew Bible and the New Testament. Furthermore, where there are double temporal designations (for instance, the seven years of prosperity and seven years of famine in the Joseph story in Genesis) one refers to the time of goodness for those who are faithful and the other to the time of distress for the faithless. However, according to Tyconius, these time periods are not successive, but simultaneous and occur in the present life of the Church.[58] In this regard Tyconius's eschatology comes to the fore. However, it remains unclear as to whether it is an eschatology which anticipated an imminent coming of Christ, or was more concerned to suggest that, though the precise time of

Jesus' coming again might not be determinable, the Church was nevertheless living in eschatological times in the present day.[59]

Augustine, meanwhile, adopts Tyconius's means of resolving temporal contradiction in Scripture, accepting the view that synecdoche and the notion of "ideal numbers" contend with the temporal ambiguities in Scripture.[60] In doing so he uses three of the passages cited by Tyconius and adds four of his own. While three of the additions do not contribute to a divergence of Augustine from Tyconius, one does. Augustine cites Rev. 7:4 (where the 144,000 refers to all the *saints*) in the course of a discussion of temporality in the Scriptures, and points to it as an indication that the saints — and therefore the Church by extension — was and is in the "midst" of iniquity. In this subtle way Augustine was able to counteract once again Tyconius's bipartite ecclesiological perspective: according to this Scripture, the evil is not in the true Church; rather the true Church exists in its midst, and is even mixed up with it in the present age.

It is also particularly clear in this rule, as in those already examined, that Augustine and Tyconius have two very different views of Scripture. While Tyconius suggests that the matter of temporal designations in Scripture is speaking directly to the Church in the present age, and one merely needs to understand the logic of such designations to comprehend their intended pertinence for the present day, Augustine believes that only after one has deciphered the signs, arriving at a comprehension of the "thing," can they be *interpreted* for the Church.[61] For Tyconius the text is its own voice, speaking as subject over against the Church; for Augustine the Scriptures are an object in need of the subject Church's careful study and analysis prior to its appropriation of them for its own consumption and self-definition.

Rule 6: Recapitulation[62]

This rule in Tyconius's formulation concerns those recurrent phrases in Scripture such as "in that hour," "on that day," or "at that time."[63] It is Tyconius's contention that these resumptive clauses are marks in the text calling one's attention to what lies in the Church's future, or is the present reality of the Church.[64] Thus, while some of the phrases denote an address to the Church concerning its present reality (so, for example Luke 17:29–32, calling the Church to remember Lot's wife), others refer to the Church's future (so, for example Daniel, seen through a citation from Matt 24:15–16, refers to the Church's future). Throughout the discussion of this rule Tyconius uses almost all New Testament passages to support his view. He also brings in his concern for the bipartite nature of the Church in this rule; the texts he cites allow him to do this.

Augustine turns this "mystical rule" of Tyconius into a mere rule of reading Scripture: when these resumptive phrases turn up in biblical literature they indicate that the author is merely retelling what was already briefly alluded to. Thus Augustine points to the creation account and the Noah story in Genesis, wherein one finds an abundance of these resumptive phrases.[65] They stand as proof of the helpfulness of the "rule" as far as Augustine is concerned.

However, Augustine also goes on to show that the Luke 17:29–32 passage adduced by Tyconius is meant for the life of the Church in its present reality. The admonitions of Scripture regarding watchfulness refer not to some future time but to the present life of the Church as it awaits the eschaton. He proves this by citing 1 John 2:18 ("...it is the last time"). By this Augustine manages to betray a little of his eschatology, but even more of his ecclesiology; he seems to view the true Church as a single body, undivided and united in itself, on the journey to the New Age, and needful at every step of the way to be careful in its way of life. He acts the role of the elderly bishop, concerned for the readiness of his Church for judgment day when the true Church will be made evident apart from the counterfeit church.

The same observations that I have repeatedly made with regard to the respective authors' views of Scripture and the Church are pertinent here and need not be repeated. What does bear scrutiny is the similarity that the authors exhibit at this point. Both clearly see Scripture as the pastoral voice calling to the Church to be ready for its future and both are concerned that the voice be heard by the members of the Church. The difference remains in how they think Scripture's voice comes to be heard by its audience, and in what the nature of that audience is.

Rule 7: The Devil and His Body[66]

Tyconius focuses on the prophecies in Ezek. 28 and Is. 14 concerning the kings of Tyre and Babylon respectively in order to show that just as there is Christ and his body (the Church) there is the Devil and his body (the Church too!). While the body of Christ is the faithful part of the Church, the faithless and evil part is the body of the Devil in the world. To support this contention, founded on reading the prophecies by the logic of this mystical rule, Tyconius cites nearly ninety other Scripture passages. This remarkable chapter of his book shows most clearly the style in which he treats Scripture as oracle of God. The ninety citations or allusions are merely plucked from the Bible with little concern for their original context, so that they might serve to support his view of the central passages. This may seem capricious to the modern reader. But to Tyconius the Scriptures are God's voice speaking directly to the Church and thus may certainly be found to say what he hears them saying.

Meanwhile, Augustine radically transforms this rule. While Tyconius sees it clarifying for us the nature of the Church, Augustine simply makes it a rule like the first; we must be aware that while Scriptures may speak of the Devil in one half verse the next half may be referring to the body of the Devil. Thus Augustine points to Isaiah 14:12a and 12b as an example of just this sort of reality in Scripture.[67]

Conclusion

To conclude I offer a brief synopsis of what has been discovered regarding the respective authors' views of Church and Scripture.

It has become clear that Tyconius understands the Church to be one, but bipartite, including within itself the faithful and faithless, the good and the evil. At the judgment the division will be made, but until then the Church is one, *ontologically* undivided. Meanwhile Augustine understands the Church to be of two kinds in the present age: the true Church and the counterfeit church, the two being *ontologically* distinct from one another. However, the distinction between these two "churches" is not apparent in the present age, and will only become so in the end time when judgment will be rendered and the true Church will become evident in its glory.

As for their views of Scripture, it has become apparent that Tyconius understands it to be (1) an extended prophecy of the contemporary reality of the Church and (2) therefore a living oracle of God. (3) As such it is an active subject, able to address the reader on its own power. (4) In light of this Scripture is obscure only in so far as the reader does not comprehend its logic; those who do not comprehend its logic of "Church description" are on the left hand side of the bipartite Church and so need illumination regarding its *ratio* that they may share in the joy of life on the right hand side of the Church now and in the future age. (5) Finally it may be said of Tyconius's view of Scripture that it is normative of the Church; Scripture describes and prescribes for the life of the Church. For Tyconius the Church is merely a mirror image of what God announces it to be in the Scriptures. Augustine, on the other hand, views Scripture as

(1) prophetic promise and the story of its penultimate fulfillment in the present reality of the Church. (2) As such it is an objectified voice of God which tells the story of the Church, a story which is, however, entrapped in word-signs, a story which is needful of liberation. (3) In this manner Scripture is an object on which the subject-actor is called to exert his or her skill to release God's voice from its prison of written words. (4) Therefore Scripture is obscure by its very nature; it requires illumination achieved by the exercise of human reason in deciphering the word-signs of the text. (5) Scripture is in a dialectical relationship with the Church in so far as the Church is the result of the Scripture's story, and as such, though being to some extent a product of Scripture, also is normative of the meaning derived from Scripture.

One very interesting issue remains: did Augustine misunderstand Tyconius, and therefore appropriate his work in the manner he did? Or did he intentionally reshape Tyconius's insights to meet his own understanding of Church and Scripture? With respect to his understanding of Scripture I am inclined to agree with Charles Kannengiesser and say that Augustine simply misunderstood his forerunner.[68] He came to Tyconius with all the tools of a Classical thinker and a rhetor of his age. Thus he was predisposed to see texts as objects, not living subjects with active voices of their own. As for his view of the Church, I think that he quite purposefully set out to correct, or at least reinterpret, what he saw to be a tragic flaw in Tyconius that damned him to both the Donatists and the Catholics. Specifically by his choice of Scriptures in illustrating Tyconius's rules Augustine corrected or reinterpreted the ecclesiology of the latter to make it more like his own. Interestingly enough, the modern reader must admit that had Augustine not had the generosity to correct or reinterpret instead of reject altogether we might not be so presently enriched by Tyconius's work.

Notes

1. For the most recent discussion of the manuscript evidence for the Apocalypse commentary see Kenneth B. Steinhauser, *The Apocalypse Commentary of Tyconius: A History of its Reception and Influence* (Frankfurt am Main: Peter Lang, 1987).
2. *On Christian Doctrine* 3.42–56.
3. See especially Charles Kannengiesser and Pamela Bright, *A Conflict of Christian Hermeneutics in Roman Africa: Tyconius and Augustine* (Berkeley, Cal.: The Center for Hermeneutical Studies in Hellenistic and Modern Culture, 1989).

4. Observe the striking disparity in use of Scripture texts; Tyconius quotes 728 verses of Scripture to Augustine's 29. Augustine uses nearly ten texts of his own choosing in spite of the wealth from which to pick in Tyconius's work.

5. For a brief discussion of Augustine's education as a youth see Peter Brown, *Augustine of Hippo* (Berkeley: University of California Press, 1967) 35–39.

6. 4.10.

7. For a convenient and lively contemporary discussion of the Classical mindset see E. G. Weltin, *Athens and Jerusalem* (Atlanta: Scholars Press, 1987) 59–112.

8. See Brown, 74–76. Baptized in 387, Augustine was ordained in 391 and consecrated to succeed Valerius as bishop in 395.

9. Consult Brown for the details of Augustine's elevation to Bishop and his concern while Bishop for the unity of the Church in the face of opposition from Donatists and later Pelagians. See especially 212–225, and 330–339, for the Donatist controversy.

10. For this conceptualization of Augustine's view of the Church I am indebted to Charles Kannengiesser who articulated it in a seminar meeting on December 6, 1990.

11. For the influence of Platonism, see Brown, 222, note 3.

12. Augustine, *Letter 93*, informs us that Parmenian excommunicated Tyconius. We also learn only a few details in his introduction to the rules in *On Christian Doctrine* 3.42–43.

13. For details regarding Cyprian's view of the Church see J. Quasten, *Patrology* (Westminster Md.: Newman, 1950–60) 2.343–383. See also Boniface Ramsey, *Beginning to Read the Fathers* (New York: Paulist Press, 1985) 99ff.

14. For a discussion of Parmenian, with special reference to his views on Tyconius, see A. Mandouze, *Prosopographie chrétienne du Bas–Empire: Prosopographie de l' Afrique chrétienne* (303–533) (Paris: CRNI, 1982) 1122–1127.

15. See especially W. H. C. Frend, "Jews and Christians in Third Century Carthage," in *Paganisme, Judaisme, Christianisme. Influences et affrontements dans le monde antique* (Paris: Editions E. de Boccard, 1978) 185–194.

16. See John Barton, *Oracles of God* (Oxford: Oxford University Press, 1986), 179–213.

17. For example see *Genesis Rabbah: The Judaic Commentary to the Book of Genesis* (Jacob Neusner, trans.; Atlanta: Scholars Press, 1985) 63:10, where Esau in Gen. 25 is equated with the Rome of the rabbis' time (about 400 CE). It must be admitted that while the rabbis can carry on in this vein for some length they can also read Scripture as a referent to its own time, something Tyconius cannot do, as we will see.

18. See especially Jacob Neusner, *Midrash in Context: Exegesis in Formative Judaism* (Philadelphia: Fortress Press, 1983). Neusner's argument throughout the book is that the rabbis' interpretations of Scripture were

largely meant to show Scripture's paradigmatic and explanatory power for the Jewish experience under the rise of Christianity. They shared the siege mentality Tyconius and his Donatist contemporaries possessed.

19. Ibid., 35–95.

20. As counted in William Babcock, *Tyconius: The Book of Rules* (Atlanta: Scholars Press, 1989), 2.

21. For a full discussion see Charles Kannengiesser, "Quintilian, Tyconius, and Augustine," *Illinois Classical Studies* 19 (1994) 1–14 (Fs. Marcovich), as well as the work of Pamela Bright, *The Book of Rules of Tyconius: Its Purpose and Inner Logic* (Notre Dame, Ind.: University of Notre Dame Press, 1988), 35–38.

22. Kannengiesser, 5.

23. That comprehension of the rules leads to proper understanding of the Church makes Tyconius's work a very pastoral piece of literature; he writes with the specific intention of offering a road–map from the evil half of the bipartite Church to its righteous half.

24. See Preface, 9. This is rather transparently so in the section which Augustine wrote after the resumption of activity on the *On Christian Doctrine* in 426. However, for the section up to that point in the work (3.36) one can question such a judgment. A legitimate alternative would be to conceive of that section having been authored as Augustine's personal exercise of devising an approach to Scripture for himself as he embarked on the bulk of his ecclesiastical career. For a taste of the range of opinion regarding the nature and purpose of *On Christian Doctrine* see E. Hill, "*De doctrina christiana:* A Suggestion," *Studia Patristica* 6 (1962) 443–46; E. Kevane, "Paidea and Anti–Paidea: The Proemium of Augustine's *De doctrina christiana,*" *Augustinian Studies* 1 (1970) 153–180; and G. Press, "Subject and Structure of Augustine's *De doctrina christiana,*" *Augustinian Studies* 11 (1980) 99–124.

25. Preface, 4.

26. There are essentially four types of obscurity in Scripture according to Augustine. They may be represented graphically as follows:

Unknown literal signs	Unknown figurative signs
Ambiguous literal signs	Ambiguous figurative signs

The degree of obscurity increases as one moves to the right and the bottom of the diagram. While unknown literal and figurative signs can be cleared up by a simple gain of knowledge, ambiguous signs require something more to be adequately deciphered; they require a method or a set of rules for their interpretation. Because of this Tyconius's rules no doubt appeared attractive to Augustine at this point.

27. 3.42.

28. Bright, 43–49.

29. Babcock, 3–15.

30. It is useful to note that once he has established a base text from which he hangs his theological point Tyconius feels free to cite any text from the body of the Bible to continue illustrating his idea.

31. Ibid., 43–44.

32. I will return to this notion of prophecy being the whole of Scripture. Suffice it to say at this point that Tyconius's view of Scripture beyond the Pentateuch as "prophecy" was not unique in his day, and seems to have been a controlling factor in his use of Scripture.

33. Babcock, 13–15.

34. For example the Mt. 24:2 citation is from Jesus' prediction of the destruction of the temple; its usefulness lies in the key word and key notion of destruction. Otherwise the passage itself has little to say to Tyconius's theological statement in this instance.

35. 3. 44.

36. Babcock, 15–21.

37. Babcock, 15.

38. It is interesting to note that the predominant text selection with reference to this rule is from Second Isaiah, a bit of Scripture notoriously full of condemnation followed by promise in the same sentence. The prophet was addressing the exiled community explaining the reason for their exile (condemnation) and extending a message of hope (promise). These were natural texts for Tyconius to be drawn to as a means of illustrating his second "rule" regarding Scripture. Therefore their predominance ought not raise the suspicion that he meant "prophecy" in the canonical sense after all. They merely happened to be the best illustrations of his point. Not to be forgotten is the fact that he also adduces passages from the New Testament and, notably, from Song of Songs (1:5 especially) as well.

39. Bright, 44.

40. 3.45.

41. The texts from Tyconius include Is. 42:16, Songs 1:5 and Mt. 24:50–51. The last refers to the fate of the faithless. The Songs text is the famous "I am black and comely" passage (see below how Augustine transforms Tyconius's interpretation by one of his additional texts), and the first text he cites as one of those reflecting the dual interest in promise and threat identified by Tyconius. Augustine adds Gal. 4:30 and Mt. 13:47, 48.

42. 3.45.

43. Ibid. Note also that Augustine transforms Tyconius's use of Mt.. 24:50–51 to suggest that the wicked servant will be cut off from the rest of the faithful, and therefore never was destined to be a part of the one Church. Therefore if it ever appears that there are evil bodies present in the Church, it is mere deception; they never were nor never will be a part of the one body of Christ.

44. Babcock, 21–55.

146

45. Bright, 45.

46. To this question of Augustine's "misunderstanding" of Tyconius I shall return below.

47. For speculation that Augustine derived his radical view of the gift–character of God's mercy from his reading of Tyconius on this point, see William Babcock, "Augustine's Interpretation of Romans (A.D. 394–396)," *Augustinian Studies* 10 (1979) 55–74, and "Augustine and Tyconius: A Study in the Latin Appropriation of Paul," *Studia Patristica* 17 (1982) 1209–1215. Though Babcock seems somewhat more inclined to think so in 1982, in general he appears to set aside the notion that Augustine derived his theological perspective from Tyconius.

48. Rom. 12:3; 1 Cor. 11:19; Eph. 6:23; and Phil. 1:29.

49. As I will only intimate in the conclusion of this paper, this might be characteristic of Augustine's understanding of the relationship between Church and Scripture; the former was of such authority and authority that it could be the norm for understanding of the latter! This is in sharp contrast to Tyconius's view that Scripture provides the blueprint for the Church.

50. Babcock, 55–89.

51. Bright, 53, suggests that genus prophecies also refer to the Church in the Last Days, in parallel with the cataclysm announced in the prophecy. This is certainly true of Tyconius, but seems to be a secondary dimension of this type of prophecy for Tyconius.

52. 3.47–49.

53. So he cites, in agreement with Tyconius, 2 Sam. 7:14–16 as an example of the species type.

54. 3.48.

55. This is the view to which I alluded above in the discussion of Tyconius's understanding of promise and fulfillment. It is clear how the two views differ; Tyconius understands promise and fulfillment in the Bible to be paradigmatic and prophetic of contemporary reality, while Augustine understands the schema as the historical trajectory which leads to and beyond the present reality.

56. 3.49.

57. Babcock, 89–109.

58. Most startling here is Tyconius's failure to use Is. 65:13–15 in this instance. The passage is the single instance in the Hebrew Bible where the destinies of a faithful and faithless people are juxtaposed not only in the literary context, but are also understood by the text to be juxtaposed in the temporal dimension as well. Tyconius's logic of Scripture in this respect is compelling; yet he fails to adduce the text.

59. For the view that Tyconius was not anticipating an immediate parousia, see Paula Landes Fredriksen, "Tyconius and the End of the World," *Revue des études augustiniennes* 28 (1982) 59–75. Fredriksen reviews the evi-

dence for an imminentist view on Tyconius's part and concludes that it is not unambiguous enough to allow such a conclusion. I find her arguments largely convincing, and for that reason have refrained from suggesting in this paper that Tyconius's selection of Scripture texts is reflective of an eschatological perspective. However, it may be said that Tyconius is most concerned with the notion of judgment at the end time; thus he writes his work as a missionary tract for those he considers to be in danger of receiving a negative review on judgment day. In this sense Tyconius might be thought to operate with a sense of "permanent immanence." (The phrase in quotations is the suggestion of Charles Kannengiesser, made in oral communication regarding the issue of eschatology in Tyconius.)

60. 3.49–51.

61. This distinction needs to be elucidated. While Tyconius does not see a need for "Scripture interpretation" because Scripture can speak for itself, Augustine is up to just that task in *On Christian Doctrine*. Augustine understands Scripture to be in need of elucidation. Tyconius sees the *believer* to be in need of the light to see.

62. Babcock, 109–115.

63. These phrases denote something different for Tyconius than the temporal designations addressed in the previous rule. It is interesting to note that Tyconius picked up on something in the text that modern critical scholars have focused on. Their concern with these sort of phrases has suggested that they denote secondary additions to the text. Obviously Tyconius can be expected to find a completely different sort of significance in the phrases at hand.

64. It seems, upon a careful reading of the text, that there are only these two senses in which Tyconius takes the phrases. This is challenged, I believe wrongly, by Kenneth Steinhauser, "*Recapitulatio* in Tyconius and Augustine," *Augustinian Studies* 15 (1984) 1–5. Steinhauser seems to think there are three senses in which Tyconius takes these phrases, the third being, that they mean what they say; they have no referent to the present or future reality of the Church. Beside the fact that this relies on Steinhauser's misconstrual of one of Tyconius's phrases in his discussion of the matter, it is entirely inconsistent with Tyconius's view of Scripture. As far as he is concerned Scripture simply cannot be understood, ever, to mean *only* what it might appear to have meant in its strictly historical context. As living oracle of God it speaks always to the contemporary situation.

65. So, for instance Gen. 2:8, 9, 15; 10:20, 32.

66. Babcock, 115–145.

67. 3.55.

68. Kannengiesser, "Tyconius and Quintilian," 3.

10

Augustine and Tyconius: A Conflict of Christian Hermeneutics in Roman Africa[1]

CHARLES KANNENGIESSER

Augustine's Opponents in 397

After returning as a Christian convert from Italy to his African homeland in the Fall of 388, Augustine, thirty–five years old, was disinclined to face the complex realities of his native province.[2] In particular, he showed at first no interest at all in the dramatic tensions and inner divisions proper to the Christian church in Africa since the first decade of the fourth century. For two and a half years Augustine preferred living in a community of dear friends, who shared his newly developed mystical devotions and were ready to cultivate with him a common remembrance on the kind of metaphysics and ethics assimilated by them in Rome and Milan. It was a form of private elitism, or, in more prosaic terms, a comfortable way for educated laymen to forget that they were lost in the obscure town of Numidia. This "holy leisure" could have lasted longer, had the converted rhetor not been spurred on by the desire for a more monastic setting. He made the mistake, in the Spring of 391, to travel, for about forty–five miles away from his retreat in Thagaste, to the small port of Hippo Regius, in search of a possible monastery. The paradigmatic figure of Anthony the Hermit, who had played such a decisive role in his still recent conversion, should have channeled him to search toward more deserted horizons as a candidate for possible monastic adventures. In Hippo, Augustine found himself chosen, quite unexpectedly, by the parishioners of a Catholic community for serving them as a priest. Even then he tried to keep his heart and mind cleared of all the bewildering concerns of the troubled local Christianity. He now claimed overtly that he was called to become a monk, which was just another way to stay by himself with a few chosen companions, despite the church–life to which he had to pay more and more attention.[3] In 395 or 396, the old bishop Valerius of Hippo, a Greek who had never felt at ease in Latin, managed to have this very learned priest and would–be monk consecrated as his coadjutor. Augustine assumed the unwanted and burdening appointment in the most consistent way, namely in dedicating, during his first three episcopal years, the best of his energies to a composition of personal *Confessions*, ideal as a choice of activity for keeping his inner self, introspective and self–sufficient as it was, free from the pressing realities of African church life. From 397 on, he was the sole head of the diocese and his involvement with Aurelius, the elderly primate of Carthage, was soon to announce the dawn of a new era for African Christianity as a whole.[4]

In that same year 397, in the midst of writing what could have been the ninth book of his *Confessions*, and when he was on the verge of assuming full pastoral responsibilities, Augustine conceived the project of a programmatic survey, *On Christian Doctrine*.[5] Given the frame of mind by which he had withdrawn, as much as circumstances allowed it, from political and social engagements in church affairs during the past decade after he had returned to Africa, it is not surprising to find the author of *On Christian Doctrine* biased by his own cultural background to the point of sounding defensive in his polemical prologue. He introduced his "doctrine" as a specific set of "precepts for interpreting scripture, *praecepta tractandarum scripturarum*,"[6] which he intended to analyze at length, and to prescribe, in the two parts of the book as projected. With a bold assertiveness, strengthened by his fresh pastoral zeal, Augustine was able to invest past professional skills and a whole teaching experience in handling the notion of such *praecepta*. He was seemingly less confident on the side of the *tractatio scripturarum* itself, being still a neophyte in the field. Therefore he felt obligated to protect himself against three categories of readers whose responses would certainly be those who were too ignorant to grasp the very meaning of his precepts; in other words, people without formal education. Secondly, there would be those who would accept the new precepts, inculcated by the rhetor transformed into an exegete, but who would fail in their application. Finally, in Augustine's own words, "detractors of a third type"[7] were to be expected, who would bluntly oppose their own hermeneutic to his precepts, for they were people "who either treat the sacred scriptures well, or think they do" (Prol. 2). The allusion is extremely cautious and discreet.

The recently appointed bishop of Hippo was still, in 397, in the process of discovering the real hermeneutical situation of his ecclesiastical environment all over the province of Carthage. For about ten years, driven by personal reasons, he had avoided plunging into the puzzling pecularities of the African church, unfamiliar to a sophisticated rhetor like himself coming from the high Romanitas and converted in Milan. In short, he was still a cultural stranger among the home trained African Catholic clergy, not to speak about the schismatic clergymen of the Donatist Church. What he faced was a disconcerting local hermeneutic inspiring "those who exalt in divine assistance and who glory in being able to understand and to treat the sacred books without precepts of the kind which I have undertaken to supply herewith" (Prol. 4). Thirty years later, writing his *Revisions* in 427, at the end of a prestigious and powerful career as an intellectual leader, the aging bishop became much more explicit. The aggressive proscriptions perceptible in the prologue of *On Christian Doctrine* had vanished together with the presumed "detractors." In the meantime, Augustine had matured, learning from his pastoral experience. In the process of engaging into a bitter fight against the Donatist establishment in African Christianity, he had recovered somehow his own African identity as a Christian. Now he was able to witness a thoughtful interest in the biblical hermeneutic which he had rejected in the prologue as arbitrarily charismatic: "A certain Tyconius wrote a book which he called *Book of Rules*, since in it he explained seven rules with which, as if with keys, the obscurities of the divine scriptures might be opened" (*On Christian Doctrine* 30.42).[8] Augustine adds that Tyconius himself, whom he quotes, said that these rules are "*mystic* rules which *reveal* what is hidden in the whole Law,"[9] a perfect Tyconian expression indeed of the "divine assistance" claimed by the anonymous interpreters of Scripture considered as "detractors" in the prologue of *On Christian Doctrine* written thirty years earlier. And, in the same way as he had denounced in that prologue the pretension of "those who glory in being able to understand and to treat *the sacred books*," the books being taken all together, Augustine observes now, in the final section of *On Christian Doctrine*, in Book Three, chapter 30, par. 43, that "when Tyconius commended these principles as rules, he attributed such virtue to them that they would help us understand almost all those things which are said obscurely in the Law, *or in the divine books*" (30.43).[10]

One of the most neglected aspects of the study of *On Christian Doctrine* is the thirty–year interruption of the composition. The change in the circumstances of authorship is crucial to such a study. Thirty years earlier, Augustine had been on the defensive in launching *On Christian Doctrine* because at that time he had to oppose a traditional, typically African and rather old–fashioned way of interpreting scripture, which had been appropriated by the Donatist church, and was best expressed in Tyconius's recent *Book of Rules*. The author was galvanized by a hermeneutical purpose, which would not so much call on a liberal and educated exegesis of scripture for the Christian humanists of all times, as Henri Marrou and many others after him repeatedly insisted,[11] but which would more directly address the peculiar biblical mentality of Augustine's African contemporaries whom he saw trapped in unwisely charismatic categories of exegesis, as well as in the institution of Donatism.[12] Such a polemical context, denounced anonymously in the prologue of *On Christian Doctrine* and critically evaluated by Augustine thirty years later in the final stage of composing *On Christian Doctrine*, makes it easier also to admit the obvious reasons of Augustine misunderstanding Tyconius.

A Neglected Question: Augustine's Quotation of Tyconius

In *On Christian Doctrine* 30.42, Augustine enumerates the titles of the seven Tyconian rules, starting with a brief description of them. They are, he says, "seven rules with which, as with keys, the obscurities of the divine scriptures might be opened."[13] But Augustine's main concern was obviously to relativize Tyconius's authority from the start, claiming that the author of the *Book of Rules* was as "absurd" in his life as he was in his doctrinal endeavour. For, observes Augustine, Tyconius remained a Donatist despite writing against Donatism, and, if he attributed to his rules a clarifying power capable of eliminating any obscurity from Scripture, he, Tyconius himself, interpreted many obscure places by using other methods. More than that, in his commentary on the Apocalypse, he did not apply them at all. Par. 42 ends with a rather pessimistic denial of the very relevance of Tyconius's rules: "To collect all the examples of places in the Scriptures, which are obscure in such a way that no one of these seven rules applies, would be too laborious and tedious."[14] So far, Augustine's preamble to the quotation of Tyconius could hardly be more prejudiced. Why did the seventy–three–year–old bishop feel obliged to dedicate to the Tyconian rules as many as fourteen paragraphs, from chap. 30 through chap. 37, in writing the last part of Book Three of *On Christian Doctrine* at the time of his *Revisions*, when he had dismissed those same rules as inappropriate? The answer is given in paragraph 43 of *On Christian Doctrine* where Augustine declares in all candor: "I thought that this should be said so that this book [by Tyconius], which is of great assistance in understanding the scriptures, might be read by students."

There is something puzzling in the reluctant, and even hostile way, by which the Tyconian quotation is introduced, and even much more puzzling is the very fact that Tyconius *is* quoted by Augustine. For we have to deal here with a phenomenon that is unique, not only in the writings of Augustine himself, but probably in all Patristic literature. A vigilant supervisor of a strict form of ecclesiastical orthodoxy undertakes to introduce a hermeneutical system of a man excluded from the Catholic communion and well–known as a life–long schismatic, in order to give "to such an elaborate and useful work"[15] a paradigmatic value in the Catholic exegesis of scripture! If the Roman Church authorities, two centuries earlier, had publicly recommended Marcion's understanding of the Christian canon, they would have fairly anticipated the initiative of Augustine quoting Tyconius.

The prologue of Tyconius's essay is first quoted verbatim in par. 43, and the seven Tyconian rules are summarized in the next chapters. But in the very text of Tyconius's prologue, as quoted by Augustine, we read as a matter of fact an astonishing translation of Tyconian thought into Augustinian categories. For having omitted a discussion of this fact, the learned commentators of *On Christian Doctrine*, from the fifth century down to the present day, neglected to analyze Augustine's quotation of Tyconius. Let us read the passage under scrutiny, not in the *Book of Rules* itself, but as quoted by Augustine: "He [Tyconius] introduced his book with these words: 'I thought it necessary before all the other matters which occurred to me to write a book of Rules, and to fabricate, as it were, keys and windows for the secrets of the Law. For there are certain mystic rules which reveal what is hidden in the whole Law and make visible the treasures of truth which are invisible to some'[16] etc." The translation shows clearly that, in conformity with Augustine's understanding, the Tyconian rules, assimilated to "keys" and "windows," operate as explanatory principles fixed by the exegete who faces grammatical or lexical obscurities in the books of scripture. In other words, they are equivalent to the *praecepta* recommended by the author of *On Christian Doctrine* himself. Their main function is to clarify, in a rhetorically consistent way, the text to be interpreted. The whole Augustinian treatise, in which the Tyconian rules are highlighted through the present quotation, serves precisely to teach similar precepts. After all, it may well be the case that in 427 the author of *On Christian Doctrine* was paying a literary tribute to that famous *Book of Rules* which had provided him, as *he* had read it, with a systematic pattern akin to his own hermeneutical enterprise. And it may be more than plausible that Augustine, in his seventies, was only willing to refer to Tyconius by spontaneously projecting himself into the very text of Tyconius which he was quoting.

A quick glance at the Latin text of Burkitt's edition of the *Book of Rules* imposes a text critical observation which may help to illustrate the Augustinian attitude. In the Latin original, — which means in the manuscript tradition of the *Book of Rules* independent from the tradition of *On Christian Doctrine*, — one reads the second sentence of the prologue, which Robertson Jr. translated by the words: "For there are certain mystic rules which reveal what is hidden, etc.," as follows: *Sunt enim quaedam regulae mysticae quae universae legis recessus obtinent et veritatis thesauros aliquibus invisibiles faciunt*. In stark contrast to Robertson Jr., I propose the following translation: "For there are certain mystic rules, which withhold the hidden parts of the universal Law and render invisible for some people the treasures of the truth."

The text of the prologue in Burkitt's edition is perfectly secured. It allows us now to make a curious observation on this same text in Augustine's quotation, if we go back to Joseph Martin's edition of *On Christian Doctrine* in the *Corpus Christianorum*. Martin's apparatus, for line 35, shows that, in the seventeenth century, *visibiles* was added to *invisibiles* in the Editio Benedictina of the Parisian Maurists. This addition was made against the unanimous consensus of the many manuscripts of *On Christian Doctrine*, a consensus indicated by Martin's capital O in italics. In a similar attempt to change the meaning of the text, an earlier hand, between the tenth and the seventeenth century, maybe also the hand of a Benedictine, had replaced *invisibiles* by *visibiles*, just scratching out the prefix *in* on a Vatican manuscript from the late 9th century. In both cases, the intention was simply to make the quoted text more compatible with Augustine's comments, framing the quotation in par. 42 and 43 of *On Christian Doctrine*. For the Tyconian rules could only be understood, in the light of these comments, as a device for *clarifying* scripture's message in line with the Augustinian "precepts" themselves.

Unfortunately, if such corrections were imposed on the prologue of the *Book of Rules* by Augustine's commentary in *On Christian Doctrine*, and if *visibiles* was finally printed after *invisibiles* in standard editions like the French *Bibliothèque Augustinienne*,[17] or even the *Corpus Christianorum*, there is no way that *visibiles* could stay, even by sheer hypothesis, in

Tyconius's very carefully and artistically knotted prologue. We must now briefly consider the prologue, and with it the whole *Book of Rules*, putting to one side, for the moment, their traditional Augustinian reading.

Mystic Rules: The Key Notion of Tyconian Hermeneutics

In the prologue of the *Book of Rules* the author started by declaring his intention to write what he called a *"libellus regularis"*[18] an "essay on rules." In the same first sentence, he uses the additional metaphors of "keys" and "windows" in order to illustrate his purpose. Then his second sentence includes, as expected, a definition of the rules which he has in view. Both propositions are strictly symmetrical, inside themselves, and in comparison with each other. In the first proposition, *scribere* is in line with *fabricare*, the direct complements of each verb, *libellum* and *claves et luminaria* as well are in line with each other. And so are the qualifications of both of these complements, *regularem* or *regularum*, and *secretorum legis*. Thus writing an essay about rules equals, in Tyconius's metaphorical terms, fabricating "keys and windows" about the *"secreta,"* the inner and hidden parts of the Law. The author intends to produce a work which would obviously deal with rules assimilated to the inner structuring of the Law. That is precisely what he makes explicit by his second sentence. For as he says, the rules in question are "mystic" rules. They govern all the *recessus* of the Law, *recessus* in the plural being paralleled by the plural *secreta* of the same Law mentioned before. As a consequence, the rules render invisible for some the "treasures of the truth." Again, *veritatis thesauros* is in line with *legis recessus*, and *obtinent* with *invisibiles faciunt*, the meaning of these symmetrical terms being always the same: "truth" equals "law," *"thesauros"* equals *"recessus,"* and *"obtinent"* equals *"invisibiles faciunt."* The metaphors of the first sentence come back in an additional third sentence, which explicates the author's expectations. If his book should be well received: "what is closed," — in the plural *clausa* parallels *claves* in the first sentence, — would be "opened," and "what is obscure," — in the plural *obscura* parallels *luminaria*, — would be "cleared up."

The central notion, around which the whole prologue makes sense, is the notion of "mystic rules." The unique purpose of the prologue itself appears to be to introduce the notion of these normative principles of a mystic nature, regulating the whole scripture by securing the needed secrecy of its message in preserving the "treasures of truth" dispensed by this message from all profane curiosity.

Because Augustine had, quite innocently from the start of par. 42, identified "book" and "rules," "rules" and "keys," it never crossed his mind that the Donatist theologian was explaining a coherent pattern which would structure scripture itself, in other words, a system of revelatory procedures woven into the very texture of the "universal Law." In short, mystic rules were a core institution of God's supernatural message in scripture which had nothing to do with the properly human precepts of an exegete trained by secular grammarians and rhetoricians. Therefore a sarcastic Augustine could only demur at Tyconius's final expectation at the end of the prologue in hoping that, "should the logic of those rules be recognized as readily as we communicate it, then anything closed would be opened, and what is dark would be illuminated." The author of *On Christian Doctrine*,[19] assimilating Tyconius's rules with what he himself had announced in his own prologue as "precepts of the kind which I have set out to make,"[20] took no notice of Tyconius's exact phrasing in his final wish: "should the *logic* of those rules (*quarum ratio regularum*) be recognized, etc." Tyconius meant by it that the *Book of Rules* would not "fabricate" the rules themselves. He would have resented such a thought as blasphemous or as sheer nonsense. His book would only offer "keys" and conceptual insights assisting the recognition of "the logic of those rules." Being a *liber regularis*, it would provide its readers with a *ratio regularum*. Again, far from producing the rules themselves, the author of that *liber regularis* would only assist in detecting them in "the immense forest of prophecy." Thanks to a correct identification of the mystic rules, his book would offer a rational and systematic guidance. It would keep the faithful on "paths of light," like a radar beam, through the dark forest of scripture.

Before having a closer look at the seven rules outlined by Tyconius, an additional criticism of Augustine's pervasive influence in their current reception seems to be in place here. In the series Sources of Early Christian Thought, Karlfried Froelich published, in 1985, a most welcomed volume entitled *Biblical Interpretation in the Early Church*.[21] If I am correct, the volume includes the first translation ever printed in a modern language[22] and for a broader public of Tyconius's *Book of Rules*, at least of a part of it. We should now recognize without difficulty how the Augustinian attitude imposes its bias unwillingly on Prof. Froelich's translation of the Tyconian prologue. I give first the translation: "I thought it necessary before anything else which occurred to me to write a brief book of rules providing something like keys and windows to the secrets of the Law" (p.104). Here, "providing" complements "book of rules," and therefore "keys and windows" are now describing the "rules" themselves, exactly as was the case in Augustine's comment, preliminary to his quotation of the prologue in *On Christian Doctrine* 30.42. As we have already seen, in Tyconius's own symmetrical definition of rules, "providing," which translates *fabricare*, was parallel to *scribere*, and its subject was obviously the *author* of the *Book of Rules*, not the *book* as here. In other words, it was *Tyconius* himself who claimed to offer "keys and windows" in presenting his book "on Rules."

Tyconius identified only the divine Spirit as the appropriate and effective author of divine scripture. For him, the Law was a divine book, as a means of salvific revelation, but it was also, in a very pre–Augustinian, or better, *non*–Augustinian way, divine as a cultural product. For the Spirit, according to Tyconius, regulated the whole communication of God's message. By using a human language and creating a style proper to scripture, the Spirit directly caused the actual truth of scripture in its written form. This scriptural Spirit operated as an author according to rules, and it is the proper task of a Christian exegete to identify and explain the mystic rules instituted by the Spirit and followed by the Spirit, when the message of scripture in its final draft addressed the community of the faithful.

Seven Rules: The Spirit Addresses the Church

The key notion of *mystic* rules is applied by Tyconius in a system of *seven* rules. On this issue I can limit myself to a few formal remarks, the whole system of the seven rules having been submitted to a thorough analysis by Pamela Bright in her book on Tyconius.[23] This monograph, completely dedicated to the Tyconian hermeneutic in the *Book of Rules*, has broken the silence imposed on the topic by Augustine's powerful and fatal influence. My present interest would only focus on the question: What more do we learn about the very *nature* of the mystic rules in letting them operate through the sacred scriptures as a consistent system of *seven* rules? Engaged as we are in studying a pattern of hermeneutic which was theologically so properly African that the young bishop Augustine himself could not perceive it correctly around 397, we must content ourselves by catching only the most elementary data in the matter. But let me anticipate the conclusion of this analytical investigation here: "It belongs to the *nature* of the mystic rules to be *seven*."

Rule 1

First, the Rules produce what Tyconius's prologue called in the first place a withholding of "the hidden parts of the universal Law," *universae legis recessus obtinent*. Rule 1, "On the Lord and His Body," withholds the clear distinction to be made in biblical terms between the Lord and his body, the Church. Only if correctly perceived does rule 1 allow the appropriate rational discernment of the scriptural statements where such a distinction must intervene. In Tyconius's words, the rule is by itself "scripture speaking" in its own mysterious way, but the rule categorizes at once scriptural speech so that a rational perception of its phrasing becomes possible. Thus the rule is proper to the scriptural Spirit's divine self–communication, and it is a rule because the Spirit calls for a rational interpretation of what is said in the *recessus* of the biblical terms. Tyconius states as basic evidence that "only reason discerns if Scripture speaks about the Lord or about his body, which is the church," *dominum eiusne corpus, id est ecclesiam, scriptura loquatur sola ratio discernit* (1:19–20). What "reason" does in this case is to distinguish between "head" and "body" by crossing over (*transitum fecit*) with the Spirit from one mystic reality to another, in a way properly determined by the rule. I quote: "Only by reason can one see what a shift happens from the head to the body," *sola ratione videri posse quando a capite ad corpus transitum facit* (2:13–14). Then the *recessus* of scripture is disclosed, because the *transitus* has been secured by the rule in a correct way, and what happens is this: "God opens an access to the invisible measures of Christ's body," *Deus aperit corporis Christi thesauros invisibiles* (4:7–8). Invisible treasures are thus made available by God operating in rule 1. Tyconius had alluded in the prologue to this same procedure, but the preventive negative statement, *regulae mysticae, quae universae legis recessus obtinent et veritatis thesauros aliquibus invisibiles faciunt*, now becomes a jubilant recognition of what the rule produces positively when *ratio* provides the needed and correct hermeneutical "key."

Rule 2

In rule 2, which applies again "throughout all scripture," *per omnes scripturas* (8:6), the *recessus* of divine revelation takes another form, namely "from one part of the body of Christ to another," *a parte corporis ad partem* (8:8–9), and, this *recessus* calls for "shifts on and back," *transitus reditusque*, as operated by the Spirit and elucidated by the Christian interpreter, namely shifts "from the right side to the left, or from the left to the right," *a dextera ad sinistram vel a sinistra ad dexteram* (8:6), when scripture mentions the body of Christ, alias the Church, in symbolic terms, Tyconius insists on the fact that, with rule 2, we are again introduced into a divine mystery of God's self–revelation throughout the scriptures.

Rule 3

Rule 3, "On Promises and Law," is immediately declared another revelatory category. It is "a divine authority," *Auctoritas est divina* (12:2). The *recessus* proper to rule 3 is characterized by a *transitus* in which the universal church participates, namely the "shift" between *repromissio* and *lex* (14:13–19): "For the Law itself was referring to the Abrahamic faith," *Lex inquam fidei erat demonstratrix* (18:9), in such a way that the Church has ever since engaged in a transit from one status of grace into another: *ab eadem namque imagine gratiae et Spiritus in eandem transisse ecclesiam* (19:8–9). Tyconius stresses, with a strong systematic rigor, the fact that only such a "mystic rule" overcomes the apparent contradiction between the distinct levels of salvation, the one of "promise" and the other of "law."

Rule 4

The title given to rule 4, "On Species and Genus," refers to rhetorical categories. But the initial statement of the chapter, paraphrasing 1 Cor.1, locates this new *regula* expressly among the "mysteries of heavenly wisdom," *mysteria caelestis sapientiae*. More than that, Tyconius explicitly defines rule 4 as a norm stated by the magisterial authority of the Holy Spirit, *magisterio spiritus sancti* (31:11–12). And Tyconius feels the need to add, still in line with 1 Cor.1, that rule 4, in being one of his seven rules, does not belong, by any means, to what he calls the "help and ornament of *human* speech," *auxilio atque ornamento sermonis* (31:7–15). As a matter of fact, the *recessus* seems to deepen here in its complex mystery (31:15–17). All sorts of *transitus* between generic and specific statements start now to be practiced by the scriptural Spirit (31:17–32:12). Therefore a huge diversity of biblical realities and situations show up *spiritualia*. They all result from the specifically multiform *transitus* proper to rule 4. A special "faith seeking for God's grace," in Tyconius's own terms, is required here, more than it was presupposed by the other rules: *Haec varietas translationis et ordinis exigit fidem quae gratiam dei quaerat*, (32:11–12). For the divine Spirit, operating with rule 4, imposes on the interpreter's mind such a constant *translatio* of meanings, and such a subtle *ordo* in the way the semantic shifts happen, that only an authentic *fides quaerens gratiam Dei* may be able to do the job. One cannot help distinguishing such a *fides quaerens gratiam Dei* from the Anselmian *fides quaerens intellectum*, anticipated by the whole hermeneutic system of Augustine's *On Christian Doctrine*. As all the biblical realities become *spiritualia* when processed by the Spirit according to rule 4, God speaks scriptural prophecy in old times and in the present day. Jeremiah, for instance, delivered his message in the past as well as in the Church of now, *tunc quoque et nunc in ecclesiam locutus est* (54:18). Thus, rule 4, like the former ones, is identified ultimately with a divine statement addressed by the Spirit to the Church of now.

Rule 5

In introducing rule 5, "On Times," Tyconius declares that "the space of time in scripture is often a mystical reality," *temporis quantitas in scripturis frequenter mystica est* (55:2). Here the *recessus* of scripture asks for a rational inquiry catching the manifold *transitus* possible between "whole" and "partial" times included by the Spirit in numerical symbols. Only the Spirit knows how to make sense out of such a bewildering diversity of times. Tyconius limits himself to using a definition from an elementary manual of rhetorics: the figure of speech called *synechdoche* consists in signifying "the whole from a part, or one part from the whole," *synechdoche vero est aut a parte totum, aut a toto pars* (55:4–5). One of the "paths of light," mentioned at the end of the prologue, is thus opened, giving a free way to experienced people who would find more out of rule 5: "We leave open the way for further inquiry by wise people," *quod prudentibus plenius investigandum data via relinquimus* (66:6–7).

Rule 6

The metaphor of the "path of light" comes back at the beginning of the next chapter, dedicated to rule 6, "On Recapitulation." Rule 6 is also recalled in the preamble of rule 6 by a mention of the "Spirit" whose acting is marked by a peculiar "subtlety," when the *narratio* shifts over discreetly into a *recapitulatio*: *ea subtilitate, ut continuatio magis narrationis quam recapitulatio videatur* (66:11–12). Finally the introductory sentence of rule 6 alludes to a more secret feature of the sacred rules, a feature carefully kept out of sight by Tyconius until now, namely the mystic *recessus* of the *recapitulatio* proper to rule 6, calling for its appropriate interpretation, as a sealing. The opening sentence of the chapter on rule 6 exemplifies the style and the logic proper to Tyconius. "Among the rules by which the Spirit sealed the Law so that one would keep steadfast on a way of light, He or She took special care of the seal of recapitulation, with such a subtlety that one would see a continuation of the narrative rather than a recapitulation," *Inter regulas quibus spiritus legem signavit quo luminis via custodiretur, non nihil custodit recapitulationis sigillum ea subtilitate, ut continuatio magis narrationis quam recapitulatio videatur* (66:11–14). Thus the rules, as understood in Tyconius's *Book of Rules*, are not only explicitly called divine operations, proper to the Spirit, but, for the first time, their operative power is also called a "sealing of the Law" (*legem signavit*). The Law is sealed by the Spirit's rules in order to have its many *recessus* well withdrawn and even kept unseen by the unfaithful. The sealing of scripture results in a consistent network of seven rules structuring the whole Law as a divinely codified message. Further on in this chapter, Tyconius speaks of rule 6 as the "seal of recapitulation," *recapitulationis sigillum* (66:12), so that each rule appears now to be a "seal" of a proper type, and the whole scripture a book with seven seals. Each "seal" is of a different type, wherefore seven different sorts of *recessus*; but the seven seals function in a coordinate and complementary way, like security locks on our attaché–cases. The fourth seal, placed in the middle of their concentric system, plays a leading role.

The objective and supernatural reality of the scriptural rules according to Tyconius now becomes obvious. They are the seven seals of the heavenly scroll mentioned in Revelation 5:1. In the second half of the fourth century Tyconius transfered the celestial symbolism of the sealed scroll (Revelation 5–10) into the rhetorical culture of Roman Africa. The *ratio* of the rules, understood throughout the *Book of Rules* in the light of rhetorical categories, refers constantly to the supernatural nature of these rules, open to a theological investigation. Thereby the heavenly "seals" became, at least in Tyconius's mind, out of the archaic form of apocalypticism proper to the Johannine Revelation, *regulae* submitted to a rational inquiry. Hence the Spirit was then seen as addressing the Church in the cultural framework of the educated Roman middle–class society in Africa, and Tyconius's new categories of thought gave scripture a new voice.

Rule 7

About rule 7, "On the Devil and His Body," Tyconius observes that the *recessus* of rule 1 and of rule 7 are symmetrical, their *ratio* being the same: "For the shift from head to body is identified by the same logic," *transitus namque a capite ad corpus eadem ratione dinoscitur* (70:13–14). Allegorism had been discussed already in rule 7 (67:29–30). Here it becomes clear that allegorism belongs to the common rhetorical culture shared by the author with his audience (72:20–73:15). It does *not* belong to the scriptural "shifts," those many *transitus* made possible by the Spirit's procedures, at the opening of each "seal" when the *ratio* of each rule is correctly perceived. By itself, allegorism would not allow any access to

161

the mysterious *recessus* proper to each rule. There is indeed nothing Origenian in Tyconius's system of *regulae*. The Tyconian hermeneutic, with *regula mystica* as its key–notion, seems rather to derive entirely from a personal meditation on the Johannine Apocalypse, a meditation which turned into an intellectual exercise of rare systematic acumen. From the Book of Revelation Tyconius received the very notion of a divine "book" sealed by "rules," as well as his other basic notions, that of a coherent diversity of *recessus*, and of the divine Spirit addressing the decisive needs of the present Church through the opening of the sealed *recessus*.

Tyconius's Apocalypse Commentary

It is precisely at this point where the conflict of Christian fourth–century hermeneutics in Roman Africa became the most dramatic. One should remember Augustine's final objection when he introduced his quotation of Tyconius in *On Christian Doctrine* 30.42: the Donatist exegete was absurd in his contradictory behaviour observed the elderly Augustine emphatically, because on one side he pretended to solve all the obscure problems of interpretation in the whole Law, but on the other side he did not even think about using his own *Book of Rules* when he wrote his commentary on the *Apocalypse*. Needless to say, this categorical judgement has been canonized by the whole tradition. The twentieth century developed a new interest in the study of Tyconius as a witness of the *Vetus Latina*,[24] but the renewed interest ignored the logical linkage and the close partnership between the *Book of Rules* and the *Apocalypse Commentary* of Tyconius.

The Tyconian commentary on the *Apocalypse* is practically lost. Kenneth Steinhauser's careful conclusions in his study on its textual transmission through the Middle Ages underline the problems of any attempted reconstruction. But I cannot help observing in the Turin Fragments of Tyconius's *Apocalypse Commentary*[25] a massive and constant use of the technical terminology elaborated in the *Book of Rules*. I claim that Tyconius's interpretation of the famous seven letters addressed to the Churches in the Johannine Apocalypse conforms closely to the logic and the sequence of the Tyconian seven rules.

The commentary on the seven letters builds up the logical and lexical basis of Tyconius's whole work on Revelation. It runs in a continuous series of short–phrased notations from par. 1 to around par. 200 in a text including about 500 paragraphs.

In par. 1 the "angel" of Apoc. 2 is said to be "bipartite," because this angel refers on one side to the leaders of the church people, and on the other side to the people themselves: *Angelus ergo bipartitus est, cuis utraque pars et praepositos habet et populos.* The notion of "bipartite" was introduced in the chapter on rule 1. In par. 2 of the *Apocalypse Commentary* Tyconius claims that the angel's message addresses at once "in a single person either one of his/her members, or the whole shape of the person," *Sermo itaque designat in uno homine et membrum et indolem.* Thus Tyconius applies here explicitly the category proper to rule 2, which he had entitled "On the Body and Its Parts."

He continues to use the technical terms proper to rule 2 until par. 7; *generaliter*, in par. 3, as opposed to *speciali*, in par. 4; in the same par. 4 he adds that "only by reason does one distinguish the *transitus*, the shift, from the *species* (namely the ancient Jerusalem) to the universal church"; and in par. 7 he refers to the "left part of the followers" (*sinistram sequentium*). All these terms have been noted above as proper to rule 2. In par. 8, the precision with which Tyconius goes over to illustrating rule 3, which was entitled "On Promises and Law," is just as striking. I quote: "Like the angel, so the members [of the community addressed] are also bipartite, for future times are mixed up with times past. In what remains specific, the generic is introduced, so that it is only in catching the *ratio* of what is said that one could verify what is proper to each and at what time," *Ut enim angelus, et membra bipartita sunt; ita ut temporibus praeteritis futura permixta sunt. In specie genus insertum est, ut nonnisi dicti ratione perspici possit, dum consideratur quid cui et quando conveniat.*

As rule 3 had been introduced in the *Book of Rules* by the initial statement, *Auctoritas est divina*, so here, and only in this sequence, does Tyconius conclude, in ending par. 11, that what the angel's message announces is supposed to serve "as *exemplar et auctoritas* for the future." Then, in par. 13 and 15, he introduced his notion, also introduced in rule 3, of human realities becoming "spiritual" when a symbolic meaning is given to them by the Holy Spirit: *idolatriam significat spiritalem* (par. 13), *contegens corporale et spiritale adulterium ...Sicut spiritus sanctus per apostolum definivit* (par. 15).

In rule 4, "On Species and Genus," Tyconius discussed for itself the interplay of what he called "specific" and "generic" statements in scripture. He starts to apply this rule in his *Apocalypse Commentary* from par. 18 on, and he concentrates on it until par. 23: *Est autem quod nonnisi in specie <m> conveniat, aut in genus* (par. 18), *sequens vero in genus convenit* (par. 19), *sicut specialiter,... ita ... apud omnes ecclesias* (par. 22), *et David hanc separationem fecit speciei et generis ... omnis terra ... specialiter. Adiecit etiam*

speciem ... Erant vero et spiritales qui credebant . . . (par. 23). The density of
the allusions and the explicit references made to rule 4 in this section of
the *Commentary* are obviously intended by the author. Then, in par. 26,
comes the unique mention in the *Apocalypse Commentary* of the figure of
speech called *"synecdoche,"* which served for defining the *transitus* characteristic of rule 5: *Non est dicere quod totum pro parte increpet.* Later on, in
par. 58 and following, the sixth angel of the Apocalypse who addresses
the church in Philadelphia is focused on. In par. 65, Tyconius feels obliged
to observe that the address of the angel was not just valid "for Philadelphia alone," exactly as he had noticed, about rule 6, "On Recapitulation,"
that "what Daniel said, is now experienced in Africa": *Notandum quia non
Philadelphiae tantum ... sicut in Actibus Apostolorum invenimus scriptum* (par.
65), *quod autem Danihel dixit in Africa geritur* (Rule 6). Also as in rule 6, but
at the same time as a preamble to the next section in his *Apocalypse Commentary* which matches rule 7, Tyconius describes the sixth angel as the
messenger of future things which will happen before the end comes:
"Therefore things are predicted by the sixth [angel] which will happen
before the end," *Sexto itaque quod est ante novissimum futura praedicit* (par.
69). One is reminded of the *futurae similitudines* mentioned in the chapter
on rule 6 (Burkitt, 67:8). Finally, rule 7 is clearly applied in regard to the
seventh angel of the Apocalypse. This angel will signify the "end of time,"
and introduce the "ultimate king" as a "member of the Anti–Christ":
novissimo tempore ... rex novissimus unum sit membrorum antichristi (par. 74),
in conformity with the notion of "the devil's body" (*corpus diaboli*, 72:23),
or "the devil and his man" (*diabolus et homo eius*, 84:12) in the last chapter
of the *Book of Rules*.

  After par. 74 of his *Apocalypse Commentary*, Tyconius introduces
the notion of the "seal," exactly as he had waited until rule 6 had been
discussed before speaking of "seals" in the *Book of Rules*: "For the narrative of the seventh seal, which he had omitted to tell earlier, is closed up,"
Concluditur namque septimi sigilli narratio quam ante praetermiserat enarrando
(par. 127). He also becomes more explicit about the Holy Spirit as author
of Scripture and active subject of its rules, a notion which was really one
of the most fundamental in his systematic theory of the *Liber Regularum
(Book of Rules)*: "This genre of narrative deserves careful attention because
the Holy Spirit often gives a brief account and concludes in a way different from what was announced, and He/She returns to the issue at stake
in presenting what had been interposed in order to obscure," *Ad hoc quoque
narrationis genus sollicite advertendum est quia spiritus sanctus frequenter aliter*

164

quam proponit breviter narrat et finit, et illud quod <ad> obscurandum interposuerat disserendo, ad propositum redit (par. 132).

My analysis of Tyconius's *Apocalypse Commentary*, sketchy and incomplete as it may be, should suffice at least to question Augustine's pointed criticism at the end of *On Christian Doctrine* 30.42, where he stated explicitly that Tyconius "himself explains many obscure places without recourse to them [his rules] because they do not apply." And in order to stress this point Augustine had added what he considered as the best example of Tyconius's failure: "For example, none of the seven rules was used or brought in question when he sought to discover how we should understand in the Apocalypse of St. John the seven angels of the church to whom John is commanded to write" (Tr. Robertson, Jr., p.104).

As Kent Emery, my colleague at Notre Dame, observed after I had given an oral presentation of these data in our Christianity and Judaism in Antiquity Seminar: It looks almost as if the author of *On Christian Doctrine* had confused Tyconius's *Apocalypse Commentary* with another work of the same author, which we would no more be able to identify, when he affirmed that Tyconius had not used his *Book of Rules* in that commentary. More probably, Augustine had never read the Tyconian commentary, when he referred to it at the end of his career in order to show that the Donatist author was "absurd."

A Classical Background: Cicero, Quintilian, The Jurists

That Augustine was a genius as a rhetor, after his conversion even more than before, needs no comment. By his *Confessions*, at the start of his public ministry in the church, and by his *Retractationes*, at the end of his episcopal career, the bishop of Hippo posed, for many generations to come, as an outstanding artist of the written word, and as a professional writer gifted with a prodigious literary vitality.[26] In the case of Tyconius, talent and audience were much more modest. Nevertheless he was a rhetor as well. His *Book of Rules* conforms to a classical pattern.

The Rhetorical Composition of the Liber Regularum

Rules 1 and 2 are two chapters of *inventio*, closely linked together with a continuous crescendo deliberately stated between them. In Aristotle's *Rhetoric*, a first part was filled with statements about society at large, as the place and context out of which arguments or statements originated for forensic communications. Tyconius starts by exploring the complex reality of the church at large. His basic categories (*scriptura*, *regula, transitus, recessus*) are introduced in the light of the social body of the church.

Rule 3 continues the same *inventio*, in an argumentative way. Tyconius discusses the moral institutions of *repromisso* and *lex* out of which the body of the church came into existence. At the same time, he gives a psychological turn to his analysis. Rule 3 opens an access to the inner experience of people in the church, with their passions, their memories, their expectations. A similar turn may be noted in Aristotle's *Rhetoric*, where the psychological behaviour of people is constantly referred to in order to explain and to legitimate juridical procedures. After rules 1 and 2, rule 3 intends to prove the legitimacy of the social body of the church.

Rule 4, the central "seal" in the combination of the seven Tyconian "seals," announces by its title *De specie et genere*, a rhetorical distinction. It could as well be stated as a chapter "On Style," according to a genre of rhetorical essays popular in late Antiquity. The style examined by Tyconius is proper to the divine Spirit whom he considers as the real author of scripture (I mentioned earlier that, contrary to Augustine, Tyconius never considers a *human* author or redactor of the sacred books). The Spirit told his stories in mysterious ways, in hiding the genus in the species, *mysteriis narravit in speciem genus abscondens* (31:13). That is precisely the way in which *mysteria caelestis sapientiae* are delivered *magisterio Spiritus Sancti* (31:11–12). For instance, talking of *veterem Hierusalem*, the Spirit tells us something of the new one which is now spread all over the world, *totam quae nunc est per orbem* (31:13–14). The idea itself is Pauline, the words sound extremely common, but the category out of which the rule proceeds in this case is formally rhetorical: *in speciem genus*. Quintilian, as we will see, was indeed very interested by the shifts in a narrative between specific and generic notions. Tyconius notes that the most striking characteristic of the Spirit as an author is his subtlety. The Spirit is particularly subtle in the genus–species shifts spread all over his Old Testament narratives. Therefore the biblical narratives become necessarily obscure for readers without any knowledge of the Spirit's "rules."

Rule 5 adds a classical chapter on the ornamentation of the style. The biblical ornaments are figures and arithmological symbols. The chapter is introduced by a rhetorical definition, already noted and partly translated above, *Temporis quantitas in scripturis frequenter mystica est tropo synecdoche, aut legitimis numeris, qui multis modis positi sunt et pro loco intelligendi; synecdoche vero est aut a parte totum, aut a toto pars* (55:2–5).

166

Rule 6 can only be correctly understood in the light of rule 4, the same subtlety of the Spirit operating here "with that peculiar kind of recapitulation," *ea subtilitate, ut continuatio magis narrationis quam recapitulatio videatur* (66:13–14). The narrative apparently continues speaking about Lot escaping from Sodom (Luke 17:29–32), but its warning (*illa hora*) addresses us now; or we listen to the story of the prophet Daniel, in Matt. 24:15–16, but *tunc* recapitulates in it all the centuries since Daniel's day, and actualizes the story: *quod autem Danihel dixit in Africa geritur* (67:10–11). Tyconius completes rule 5 on ornamentation by additional remarks on analogy and allegory (67:29–31).

Rule 7 serves for the purpose of a deliberate inclusion, being paralleled with rule 1 by the initial statement of the chapter: "The *ratio* about the devil and his body can be stated at once, if only one notices here also what has been said about the Lord and his body," *Diaboli et corporis eius ratio breviter videri potest, si id quod de domino et eius corpore dictum est in hoc quoque observetur* (70:11–13). The adverb *breviter* needs to be taken here in a figurative sense, as meaning "easily" or "at once," for this final chapter has more than twice the length of the preceding one, and it is longer than the chapters of rules 1, 2 and 5. It is filled with remarks on allegorical and symbolic forms of speech in *scriptura*, in addition to what was noted about it in rules 5 and 6. Thus the three last rules, after the central rule 4, seem to present a continuity of their own.

Quintilian's Use of *Regula*

The notion of *regula* plays a role in Book 1 and in the four Books 9–11 of Quintilian's *Institutio Oratoria*,[27] which means at the start and in the final part of the Roman rhetor's *opus magnum*. In order to evaluate adequately Quintilian's originality, and Tyconius's debt to him in this matter, one must remember that Cicero ignored the technical term *regula* in his rhetorical theory, whereas the Ciceronian *praeceptum* is devotedly taken over by the *Institutio Oratoria*. My thesis, stated very briefly, would be that not only the term but the whole logical value of Quintilian's *regula* was transferred by Tyconius into the theological framework of his Christian hermeneutic.

In Book 1, chapter 5.1, of the *Inst.Or.* the three main qualities of a speech, considered as a whole, are, *ut emendata, ut dilucida, ut ornata sit*, in other words "correctness, lucidity and elegance." Quintilian adds the following advice: "The teacher of literature therefore must study the rule of correctness of speech (*loquendi regulam*), this constituting the first part of his art" (ed. Loeb, vol. 1, p.78–79). The phrase *loquendi regulam*, in the singular, equals *recte loguendi scientia* in the first sentence of the former chapter, each phrase being part of initial statements or definitions. In the same Book 1, Quintilian presents in Chapter 6.33 the merits of studying etymologies. It is a basic requirement for interpreting a text, for it helps to define the meaning of words, and it delivers the *ratio* of familiar names, like *Latium, Italia, Capitolium*. Even in small matters it makes sense, for instance when one single letter differs from one word to another, as in *tegula* and *regula*. Thus Quintilian is mainly interested in the logic behind the play with words: how does etymology help to catch the *ratio* which imposes such and such a name, or a given spelling. The notion of regula crosses his mind in this context.

Next, in chapter 6.44, "usage" needs to be stated as normative, and the wise Quintilian concluded: "In speech we must not accept as a rule of language (*pro regula sermonis*) words and phrases that have become a vicious habit with a number of persons" (p. 132–133). Here *regula* replaces *praeceptum*, used at the start of 6.44. It refers to the consistency of an educated speech, which needs tradition for its ruling, and rests on the *consensus eruditorum* (6.45).

7.1 follows immediately, with a repeated use of *regula*: *Nunc, quoniam diximus, quae sit loquendi regula, dicendum, quae scribentibus custodienda*, and Quintilian goes on translating *orthographian* by *recte scribendi scientiam* (p.134). It shows once more the semantic equivalence of *regula* and *scientia*, which could as well be completed by adding *ratio loquendi* in the initial statement of 9.1. *Regula* as used by Quintilian does not mean a "grammatical rule," in the modern sense. It has a different extension, and it rests on a form of abstraction which expresses the *ethos*, or the cultural institution of human speech in a well educated society.

In the last part of his immense work, Quintilian has still more to state about the rhetorical *regula*, as he understands it. In 9.4.4, where he celebrates the merits of an "artistic structure" (*compositio*, in language), he opposes those who would prefer to speak about any education at all: "For the first men did not speak with the care demanded by that art (the *ars orandi*) nor in accordance with the rule that it lays down," *Neque enim locuti sunt ad hanc regulam et diligentiam primi homines* (p.506–507). They had no rhetorical culture at their disposal. Pretending to imitate them would mean the end of civilization. In short, *regula* maintains firmly its general and normalizing meaning, as applied in Book 1.

In Book 10.2.13, *On Imitation*, the use of chosen words is said to be determined by their traditional value. Nevertheless no servile copy will ever work, "the one sure standard being contemporary usage," *ut quorum certissima sit regula in consuetudine* (Vol. 4, pp.80–81). In Book 13.12, Quintilian justifies his distinction between "what is expedient" and "what is becoming": "I have followed rather the usage of common speech than the strict law of truth," *Et nos secundum communem potius loguendi consuetudinem quam ipsam veritatis regulam divisione hac utimur* (Vol. 4, p.160–161). At the time of Tyconius, the Latin translator of Irenaeus' *Adversus Haereses*, would use the same phrase *regula veritatis*, as synonymous of *regula fidei*. And Tyconius himself would use it with the same semantic value.

Finally, in Book 12.10.50, one reads: "on the other hand, the written speech which is published as a model of style must be polished and filed and brought into conformity with the accepted rule and standard of artistic construction (*ad legem et regulam compositum esse oportere*) since it will come into the hands of learned men .... These subtle teachers (*subtiles magistri*)..." (Vol. 4, p.478–479).

Regula equals *lex* in the present occurrence. It serves as a ruling and structuring principle of written communication. The latter's content results from the rule's application as *compositum*, put together in a unified disposition. It should be clear now that *regula* was used by Quintilian consistently in order to state a global ruling and structuring of such written communications. Even the magisterial *subtilitas* of its experts is mentioned at the end. There are indeed "subtle teachers" (*illi subtiles magistri*: 12.10.51) who are praised for their subtlety, because they know how to identify correctly what is distinctive of the *regula* in oral and/or written speech. The word *regula* is used by Quintilian only in the singular. Tyconius would introduce the plural *regulae* while keeping the logical pattern and the value of the *regula* exclusively singular in the *Institutio*. Maybe Quintilian ignored the plural because the classical ideal of the *regula* called insistently for unity and clarity in any oral or written speech. Tyconius needed the plural for theological reasons.

Quintilian on Genus and Species

Quintilian's first concern about *genus* and *species*, in Book 4 of the *Institutio Oratoria*, is to recommend their consistent distinction. One should not mingle realities of a generic nature with others, specifying them, as if all of them were of the same value: "Redundance as a rule occurs through our dividing into species when it would be sufficient to divide into *genera*,

169

or through the addition of *species* after stating the *genus*. The following will serve as an example: 'I will speak of virtue, justice and abstinence.' But justice and abstinence are *species* of the *genus* virtue" (5.27). Just before giving that example, Quintilian had disapproved those who multiply distinctions "by which they seem to divide the case in a more subtle and abundant way," *quo subtilius et copiosius divise videantur* (5.25). As a final result, those people would end in an "obscurity" equal to the one they had tried to overcome when they started distinguishing. It is worth noting that Quintilian, like Tyconius, apparently links "subtlety" with the grammatical and rhetorical use of the distinction between *genus* and *species*.

In Book 5 still dedicated to the *inventio* of cases, the dominance of *genus* over *species* leads to some general remarks which could well illumine Tyconius's fourth rule: *genus ad probandam speciem minimum valet plurimum ad refellendam* (10.56) ... *contra species firmam probationem habet generis, infirmam refutationem* (10.57) ... *Numquam itaque tolletur a specie genus, nisi ut omnes species, quae sunt generi subiectae, removeantur* (57). If a grammarian, who would also act as a theologian in a community of educated believers, assimilated *genus* with church, and *species* with the ancient Jerusalem, the logic of generic and specific definition would remain untouched in becoming a theological vision of the relationship between church and Israel.

The problem of keeping clear-cut distinctions between *genus* and *species* was already discussed by Cicero in his *Topics* (3:13, 5:17). One may improve the Ciceronian theory, as Quintilian suggests it very discreetly, in giving an explicit account of the "differences" proper to each *species*: "the term difference is applied in cases when the *genus* is divided into *species* and one species is subdivided. Animal, for instance, is a *genus*, mortal a *species*, while terrestrial or biped is a difference" (10.61).

And the analysis goes on, with this chapter becoming one of the longest (125 paragraphs!) and most elaborate of the *Institutio*. The reasoning of the Roman rhetor seems to bring us into the vicinity of the fourth century African grammarian–theologian: *Ac mihi quidem sufficeret hoc genus, sed in species secatur. Nam et ex pluribus ad unum et ex uno ad plura—et ex parte ad totum et ex genere ad speciem et ex eo quod continet ad id quod continetur, aut ex difficilioribus ad faciliora et ex longe positis ad propriora et ad omnia, quae contra haec sunt, eadem ratione argumentia ducuntur* (90).

In Book 7 Quintilian goes into examining the many questions about the *dispositio* of a speech or of a written essay. He allows some autobiographical glances: *Solebam et hoc facere, ut ab ultima specie . . . retrorsum quaererem usque ad primam generalem quaestionem, vel a genere ad extremam speciem descenderem, etiam in suasoriis* (1.23). Tyconius's fascination would develop on the same analytical line, when he shows in the *Book of Rules* how much attention one must dedicate to watching the Spirit circulating between *species* and *genus*. In Book 7 also Quintilian discusses at length the case, directly taken over from textbooks, of an exiled son who fails to appear in court to assist his father, and who finds himself disinherited for that reason. At the end of the argument he notes: "Still the time is not yet come to relax our efforts ..." and he gives a new swing to the whole discussion: "A little ingenuity will lead us to look further afield, for as *species* comes after *genus*, so *genus* precedes *species*," *qui subtiliter quaeret, aliquid spectabit ultra; nam, et genus species sequitur, ita speciem genus praecedit* (1.59). Again, "subtlety" is recommended particularly for perceiving the *ordo* between *genus* and *species*.

In Book 7.6, on tropes, the *synecdoche* is mentioned, as apt to introduce more diversity into a narrative: *haec [synecdoche] variare sermonem potest, ut ex uno plures intellegamus, parte totum, specie genus, praecedentibus sequentia* (6.13). Tyconius's vital interest, in rule 5, was also to show how the *genus*–church could be understood in prophetic statements about the *species*–old Jerusalem, and he rested his argument in introducing at first a similar definition of what a *synecdoche* means. Later on in the same context, Quintilian examines how allegorical elements can serve to give a more metaphorical shape to the distinction *genus–species* (6:48), and he persists in elaborating a theoretical stance about the many possible links between the two categories: *Cui accedit hoc quoque, quod genus, cum dividatur in species, nihil habet proprium, . . . et ipsius per se nulla proprietas, allegoria vero habet aliquid proprium* (6:58).

Tyconius's own theory matches the style and the focus of Quintilian in this kind of ruminating clarification. In the *Institutio* (9.2:61), the notion of *ratio* would deserve a closer look, in order to establish more connections with the *Liber Regularum,* just as we tried it for the notion of *regula.* Even *transitus* may be worth comparing: "Such methods will also provide us with elegant transitions (*transitus*), although transition is not itself to be ranked among figures" (9.2:61).

Cicero and the Jurists[28]

Cicero, except by a few short remarks in his *Topica,* has nothing to say about the grammatical distinction of *genus* and *species,* nor does he describe its rhetorical use in *Orator, De Oratore,* or in *De partitione oratoria.* In fact, the same silence could be observed already in Aristotle's *Art of*

Rhetoric. The distinction *genus–species* was thoroughly worked out in Aristotle's *Metaphysics*, mainly in Book 3, but it never entered the scope of his *Rhetoric.* One must wait for Quintilian's building up on the Aristotelian distinction for finding a rhetorical equivalent of Tyconius's theological use of *genus* and *species.*

In Cicero's *De Oratore* 42 the distinction *genus–species* developed into a fundamental principle of the future theory of Roman Law. M. Villey's penetrating remarks and the brillant survey by Peter Klein, *Regulae Iuris,* would open more views on the Tyconian categories in the light of Rome's juridical tradition.

6. Conclusion: Augustine and Tyconius in 426–427

(This post–script follows the publication of *Augustine. De Doctrina Christiana,* Edited with an Introduction, Translation, and Notes by R. P. H. Green (Oxford Early Christian Texts), Oxford: Clarendon Press, 1995).

When deciding in 426 to complete the interrupted *On Christian Doctrine* after thirty years filled with other engagements the elderly bishop started as best as he could by making use of notes for such continuation kept in his folders since 396–397.[29] First he rounded up his exposition of figurative expressions by adding to the 'leaven' (25.35) other examples of images with diverse meanings, like 'lion,' 'serpent,' and even 'bread' and 'wine' (25.36), not without some complementary guidance for the use of such biblical utterances, which betrayed the wisdom he had accumulated in the matter during the past decades (26.37–29.40). He also added a special note for the *litterati,* those among his readership with formal education, by which he expressed a professional concern that had not been on his mind thirty years earlier. As he mentions the frequent use of figures of speech in Christian literature, he feels the need to specify: "I do not wish to look as if I am giving a course of grammar" (Green, 171), and he ends this transitional section with some observations on tropes in scripture.

In his decisive attempt to complete the *On Christian Doctrine* in 426, Augustine quotes Tyconius with a confidence unthinkable thirty years earlier. "A certain Tyconius" (30.42; Green, 92): from the first two words, *Tyconius quidam,* until the end of book 3 (37.55; Green, 135), the citation and discussion of the *Book of Rules* is conducted in a decidedly depreciative and antagonistic spirit. Augustine's final observations about "all these rules" states that what the Tyconian rules have in common "is the characteristic of metaphorical diction, which is too broad a category, it seems to me, to be embraced in its entirety by a single person" (Green, 133). In other words, considered one after the other the rules seem unable to provide the proper meaning of scripture. Such negative judgment matches Augustine's initial reaction, following the very first enumeration of Tyconius's rules: "Of course not everything that is written in a way that makes it difficult to understand can be clarified by these rules, there are numerous other methods not included in his seven" (Green, 93) "so–called rules" (*has velut regulas*, Green, 95). The restrictive criticism immediately added to the citation of Tyconius's prologue sounds negative in the same way: "Had he said here, 'There are *certain* mystic rules..., he would have been telling the truth without raising false hopes in his readers and disciples" (Green, 95). The bishop justifies his severe judgment about the *Book of Rules*: "I thought that this needed saying so that students would actively read the book itself,... but not expect from it more than it had to offer. It must certainly be read with caution, not only because of certain things which, being human, he gets wrong, but especially because of things which he says as a Donatist heretic" (Green, 97).

After so many years still on the defensive in taking over Tyconius's work, the bishop distances himself from the "Donatist heretic" with the rigour of his own personal involvement in the destruction of Donatism, successfully achieved under his leadership since the end of the fourth century. He has no reason to become properly polemic, he does not attack Tyconius nor does he expressly refute him; he contents himself with treating "readers and disciples" of Tyconius as a phenomenon of the past, neutralized by time and prejudice. His immediate pastoral concern is to recuperate a still well–known and quintessentially African essay on biblical hermeneutics — actually the only one on the market — for his own convenience.

If Augustine's whole approach to the *Book of Rules* is marked by a depreciative evaluation, it also reflects the life–long love–hate relationship between those two interpreters of scripture who never actually met, the rhetor who became a bishop and the other educated African who became a "Donatist heretic." Tyconius was too old, if not already dead, for meeting the newly appointed bishop of Hippo, but the latter never freed himself from the challenge imposed on him by the *Book of Rules*. Now himself in old age, the bishop would have the last word on this vexed issue. He would offer a version of the Tyconian rules acceptable to him, because adjusted to what he calls in the preface of *On Christian Doctrine* the "rules of the kind that I have now undertaken to give" (Green, 4). His reception of the seven Tyconian rules would be entirely infused by his own vision of the church and his own notion of Christ. The whole doctrinal substance of his thought would weigh on his short description of each of the seven rules, to the point that he would not even be aware of missing their real focus. As a consequence, his initial misreading of the "mystical rules" as being the interpreter's "keys" prevented him from perceiving the truth enunciated by Tyconius in the notion of the "bipartite church." In the same way, he sincerely protested against Tyconius's claim that through acceptance of the rules, "all closed doors will swing open" (Prologue: Green, 95) because he confused the "mystical" nature of the Tyconian rules with the arrogance of a carrier of "false hopes" (Green, 96). In the same way Augustine now rewrites the rules of Tyconius in conformity with his own theological disposition. His procedure, while far from being innocent, is by no means ill–meaning; rather, it is therapeutic in view of an orthodox rendering of the rules. Therefore it is not enough to observe that "as a rule Augustine takes one or two of Tyconius's shorter examples" (Green, 176, n.87); the fact is that biblical examples offered by Tyconius from one rule to another are not only eliminated, they are also replaced by other quotations deliberately chosen by Augustine in line with his own concerns.

As a result the Tyconian rules are emptied of most of their proper signification in Augustine's *On Christian Doctrine*. In her contribution to *A Conflict of Christian Hermeneutics in Roman Africa*, reprinted in this volume, Pamela Bright gives a detailed account of the use of scripture in the Tyconian rules, and she convincingly demonstrates how Augustine manipulated those scriptural data. She shows that a different christology and ecclesiology explains the changes operated by Augustine in the summary of each rule, not to speak of Rule 3: Of the Promises and the Law, which calls for a special bias in *On Christian Doctrine*, as "Augustine's whole attention in Rule 3 is galvanized by Pelagianism." From one misunderstanding to another the Augustinian reception "obscures the 'logic' of the Tyconian rules."

The fourth book of *On Christian Doctrine* on the "process of presenting" (*modus proferendi* 1.1; Green), very different from the three earlier books dedicated to the "process of discovering" (*modus inveniendi*), may be considered as Augustine's final response to the Tyconian challenge. For it is in the *delivery* of his personal understanding of scripture that the bishop of Hippo had, over several years of laborious apprenticeship, forged his own hermeneutic. By *preaching* the Word of God to common believers, not in a confined circle of scholars, he had invested the sum of his cultural and theological gifts in a hermeneutical framework of his own, able to let him find in scripture Truth itself. Now, with Book 4, the longest of *On Christian Doctrine*, the clear–minded rhetor and the Christian lover of spiritual values in him found a final opportunity to profess with one voice their life–long fascination with scripture. The fusion of secular culture and ecclesiastical awareness resounds in these pages in a perfect harmony. Augustine's insights and recommendations become paradigmatic by the quality of their personal diction more than by their content. It no longer makes sense to compare him with Tyconius or with anyone else, as he celebrates rhetorical skills for their usefulness in communicating the meaning of divine scripture, and scripture itself for transfiguring the style and eloquence of secular culture.

NOTES

1. A provisional form of the present essay can be found in *A Conflict of Christian Hermeneutics in Roman Africa: Tyconius and Augustine*. Protocol of the Fifty–Eighth Colloquy: 16 October 1988. Center for Hermeneutical Studies in Hellenistic and Modern Culture, Berkeley, California, 1989, ed. W.Wuellner. The text has been revised and completed with a conclusion.

2. "For some years he remained perched between two worlds," Peter Brown, *Augustine of Hippo: A Biography* (London: Faber, 1967), 152.

3. "He wanted to be a monk, not a busy town parson continually beset by unreasonable people." Henry Chadwick, *Augustine* (Oxford, 1986), 56.

4. "Aurelius I," Andre Mandouze, *Prosopographie de l'Afrique Chrétienne* (303–533), Prosopographie Chrétienne du Bas–Empire I (Paris: C.N.R.S, 1982), 105–127.

5. *Sancti Aurelii Augustini. De Doctrina Christiana* (= DDC) ed. Joseph Martin, in *Corpus Christianorum Series Latina* vol. XXXII (Turnhout: Brepols, 1962).

6. DDC, *Prooemium* I (1:1). A.A.Press, "The Subject and Structure of Augustine's *De Doctrina Christiana*," *Augustinian Studies* II (1980), 99–124.

7. *St. Augustine. On Christian Doctrine*, Trans. by D. W. Robertson, Jr. (Indianapolis: Bobbs–Merrill Educational Publishing, 1958), 3.

8. Ibid., 104.

9. Ibid., 105.

10. Ibid.

11. Henri–Irénée Marrou, *S. Augustin et la fin de la culture antique* (Paris, 1958), 331–540; "le traité sur la culture chrétienne," 343. *A History of education in Antiquity* (New York, 1956). E.Kevane, "Paideia and Anti–Paideia: The *Prooemium* of St.Augustine's *De Doctrina Christiana*," *Augustinian Studies* I (1970), 153–190. E.L.Fortin, "Augustine and the Problem of Christian Rhetoric," *Augustinian Studies* 5 (1974), 85–100.

12. Other interpretations of the anonymous opponents mentioned in the prologue of *On Christian Doctrine*: Christian Monks (U.Duchrow, "Zum Prolog von Augustins De Doctrina Christiana," *Vigiliae Christianae* 17 (1963), 165–172); Pelagians (I. Opelt, "Doctrina und doctrina christiana," *Altsprachlicher Unterricht* 9:4 (1966), 5022; "Zur Nachwirkung von Augustins Schrift De doctrina christiana," *Jahrbuch fur Antike und Christentum* (1974), 64–73; "konsequente Charismatiker," (P. Brunner, "Charismatische und methodische Schriftauslegung nach Augustins Prolog zu De doctrina christiana," *Kerygma und Dogma* 1 (1955), 59–69, 85–103).

13. Trans. D.W.Robertson, Jr., 104.

14. Ibid., 105.

15. Ibid.

16. Ibid.

17. "Aliquibus invisibiles visibiles faciunt," *Bibliothèque Augustinienne. Oeuvres de saint Augustin*, vol.XI. Le Magistère chrétien, ed.G.Combès et M. l'abbé Farges (Paris, 1949), 396.

18. In fact, we repeat Augustine's quotation and comment in using the traditional title *Liber Regularum*. The ancient meaning of *regularis* was material, "in form of a bar." C.Plinius Secundus (the Elder, d.79 CE), in *Naturalis Historia* 34:94, mentions a *regulare aes*, "a bar of copper."

19. Trans. D.W.Robertson, Jr., 105. M. A. Tilley, "Understanding Augustine Misunderstanding Tyconius" : E. A. Livingstone, ed., *Studia Patristica*, vol. XXVII Leven: Peeters, 1993, 405–408, explains the "misunderstanding" between Tyconian "typology" and Augustinian "allegorism" on the basis of a complete identification of "rules" and "keys" in the prologue of the *Book of Rules*.

20. Ibid., 3.

21. Philadelphia: Fortress Press: 1985, 105.

22. A further observation needs to be made on the first complete translation of Tyconius's work in a modern language, William S. Babcock's *Tyconius: The Book of Rules*. Translated with an Introduction and Notes (SBL Texts and Translations 31 Early Christian Literature, Series 7) Atlanta, GA: Scholars Press, 1989. The Introduction starts by repeating the Augustinian equation of "keys" and "rules" in Tyconius's prologue: "Like keys, they (the rules) will open..." (ix), and the translation of the prologue, based on Augustine's *liber regularum* (Green, 92; instead of Tyconius's *libellum regularem)* says: "...I considered it necessary to write a book of rules, and so to fashion..." (3) by which "and so" conforms to the pre–established equation, but lacks any support in the original text. (A few lines further, rule 4, *De specie et genere*, is rendered by "The particular and the General", which misses Tyconius's rhetorical categories.)

23. P. Bright, *The Book of Rules of Tyconius: Its Purpose and Inner Logic*. (Christianity and Judaism in Antiquity Series) University of Notre Dame Press, 1988.

24. A study linked with the names of W.Bousset, J. Haussleiter, H. L. Ramsay, A. Souter, I. M. Gomez. Traugott Hahn, *Tyconius–Studien* Ein Bitrag zur

Kirchen–und Dogmengeschichte des 4. Jahrhunderts (Studien zur Geschichte der Theologie und der Kirche). Leipzig, 1900 (Aalen, 1971), represents a rare essay extending the study of Tyconius to a broader doctrinal scope.

25. F. LoBue, ed. *The Turin Fragments of Tyconius' Commentary on Revelation.* (Cambridge, 1963).

26. I enjoyed particularly the praise of Augustine as a writer by W.R. Johnson, "Isocrates Flowering: The Rhetoric of Augustine," *Philosophy and Rhetoric* 9 (1976), 217–231.

27. *The Institutio Oratoria of Quintilian.* With an English translation by H.E.Butler (The Loeb Classical Library, 4 vols.) Cambridge, MA: Harvard University Press, 1920–27 (1980). Helpful for the present comparative purpose were G. Assfahl, *Vergleich und Metaphor bei Quintilian* Stuttgart, 1932; J. Cousin, *Etudes sur Quintilien*, Paris, 1936.

28. M. Villey, *Recherches sur la littérature didactique du droit romain*, 1945; Peter Stein, *Regulae Iuris. From Juristic Rules to Legal Maxims.* Edinburgh, 1966; see in particular chap.4: "The Classical Books of Rules," p. 74–89, and chap.5, "The Classical Jurists' Ideas of *Regulae Iursi*," p.90–108.

29. This post–script follows the publication of *Augustine. De Doctrina Christiana* Edited with an Introduction, Translation, and Notes by R.P. H. Green (Oxford Early Christian Texts), Oxford: Clarendon Press, 1995.

11

Augustine, Sermon 23

A Sermon Preached in the Faustus Basilica on the Vision of God

Edmund Hill O.P. *The Works of Saint Augustine–A Translation for the 21st Century: Sermons II* (20–50) (New York Press, N.Y.: 1990, pages 56-57; 64–65).

—Date: 413

1. Let us take it that what we have been singing to the Lord has been proposed to us as a subject to talk about. Let my sermon to you be on this point. And may the one to whom we have said You have held my right hand, and led me along according to your will, and taken me up with glory (Ps 73:23), may he take our minds up to a clear understanding, and assist us with his mercy and grace: me as I talk, you as you judge. For although to all appearances I am standing in a higher place than you this is merely for the convenience of carrying my voice better, and in fact it is you who are in the higher place to pass judgment, and I who am being judged. We bishops are called teachers, but in many matters we seek a teacher ourselves, and we certainly don't want to be regarded as masters. That is dangerous, and forbidden by the Lord himself, who says Do not wish to be called masters; you have one master, the Christ (Mt 23:10). So the office of master is dangerous, the state of disciple safe. That's why the psalm says, To my hearing you will give joy and exultation (Ps 51:8). Hearing the word is safer than uttering it. That's why that man feels quite safe as he stands and hears him, and rejoices with joy at the bridegroom's voice (Jn 3:29).

2. The apostle had taken on the part of teacher because his stewardship obliged him to, and just see what he says about it: With fear and much trembling was I among you (1 Cor 2:3). So it is much safer that both

we who speak and you who listen should realize that we are fellow disciples under one master. Yes, it's unquestionably safer, and it helps enormously if you listen to us not as your masters but as your fellow pupils. Just see how anxiety is drummed into us by this text: Brothers, let not most of you become masters, for all of us slip up in many ways. Who wouldn't shudder at the apostle saying "all of us"? And he goes on, Whoever does not slip up in speech, this is a perfect man (Jas 3:1–2). And who would ever dare to call himself perfect?

Well at any rate, the one who stands and hears does not slip up in speech. As for the one who is speaking, even if he does not slip up, which is difficult enough, imagine what he suffers from his dread of slipping up! So what you have to do is not only listen to us speaking, but also feel for us dreading; in this way for whatever we say that is true (since everything true is from Truth) you will praise not us but him, and wherever being human we slip up, you will pray to the same him for us.

3. The scriptures are holy, they are truthful, they are blameless. Every divinely inspired scripture is useful for teaching, for reproving, for exhortation, for doctrine (2 Tm 3:16). So we have no grounds at all for blaming scripture if we happen to deviate in any way because we haven't understood it. When we do understand it, we are right. But when we are wrong because we haven't understood it, we leave it in the right. When we have gone wrong, we don't make scripture wrong, but it continues to stand up straight and right, so that we may return to it for correction. And yet the self–same scripture, in order to give us some mental exercise, appears to speak in a crude, materialistic way in many places, though the law is always spiritual. For the law, as the apostle says, is spiritual, but I am carnal (Rom 7:14) or materialistic. So while scripture is spiritual in itself, nonetheless it often, so to say, goes along with carnal, materialistic people in a carnal, materialistic way. But it doesn't want them to remain carnal and materialistic....

17. So if we don't understand very much about these extremely difficult and impenetrable questions, let us be peaceable as we try to find answers. No one should be puffed up in favor of one against another (1 Cor 4:6). For if you have a bitter zeal and there are disputes among you, this is not the wisdom coming down from above, but is earthbound, unspiritual, diabolical (Jas 3:14–15). So we are God's children, and we should be recognizable as his children, and we won't be recognizable as such unless we are peacemakers. You see, we shall have nothing to see God with if by quarreling we put out the necessary eye in us.

179

18.   Notice what he says, which is why I speak with fear and trembling. Pursue peace with everyone and sanctification, without which no one can see God (Heb 12:14). How he does terrify his lovers! Here he doesn't terrify anyone except his lovers. Did he say "Pursue peace with everyone and sanctification, because whoever doesn't have it will be thrown in the fire, will be tormented with eternal fire, will be handed over to tireless torturers"? It's all true, but he didn't say it. He wanted you to be a lover of the good not a dreader of the bad, and so he terrified you by means precisely of what you were longing for.

You will see God. Is that a reason for showing contempt, a reason for wrangling, a reason for raising a hubbub? Pursue peace with everyone and sanctification, without which no one can see God. Two people want to see the sun rise; how stupid they would be if they started arguing about which side it would rise on and how it could be seen, and the argument turned into a quarrel, and in the quarrel they struck each other, and in striking each other they put out one another's eyes, so that they couldn't see it rise after all! So in order to be able to see God, let us cleanse our hearts with faith, let us heal them with love, let us strengthen them with peace, because this thing with which we love each other has already come from him whom we are longing to see.

PART III

The Sword of the Word:
Augustine and Polemics

12

The Bible and Polemics

ANNE-MARIE LA BONNARDIÈRE

"It is necessary that there be heresies so that proven men among us should be made manifest" *Oportet et haereses esse, ut probati manifesti fiant in vobis.* 1 Cor 11:19 turns to these words of the Psalm 67:31: "So that will be made manifest those who are proven by silver" *ut excludantur ii qui probati sunt argent.* That is to say those who have been put to the test *probati* by the Word of God; in truth: "The words of the Lord, pure words, proven silver by the fire of the earth" *Eloquia Domini eloquia casta, argentum igne probatum terrae* Ps. 11:7, because *excludantur* means that they will appear *appareant,* that their eminence *emineant* will be visible. In other words as the Apostle says they will be made manifest *manifesti fiant.* In the art of gold smithing one calls *exclusores* those who know how to form a vase from the formless mass. For many meanings of holy scripture remain hidden and are only known to a few people who understand them in a better way. They become explicit with greater accuracy and convenience for those who must face the task of answering heretics. Then even those who have neglected the study of doctrine give up their indolence, hasten to listen to them (the multiple meanings of scripture) in order to confound their adversaries. Thus many understandings of holy scripture have been made explicit about the divinity of Christ against Photinus, many about the humanity of Christ against Mani, many about Trinity about Sabellius, many about the unity of the Trinity against Arians, Eunomians and Macedonians, and many about the church *catholica,* spread over the whole world, as well as about the promiscuity with evil–doers until the end of time that they do not cause damage to good people in society in the sacraments of the church. This latter is against Donatists, Luciferians and any others who because of a similar error deviate from truth. Finally many (meanings of scripture) have been explicated against other heretics which would take too much time to enumerate and to recall to memory. The experienced defenders of these meanings (of scripture) either would have remained completely ignored or would not have been recognized distinctly as they were through the contradictions of the haughty mentioned by the Apostle where he asks that the candidate chosen for the episcopacy should be capable both of exhorting to sound doctrine and of refuting those who contradict it. (Titus 1:9) (*Commentaries on the Psalms* 67.39).

This passage from Augustine's *Commentary on Psalm 67* was dictated at the beginning of 415, as *Letter 169* addressed to Evodius that same year informs us. This learned commentary upon Psalm 67 which contains an explanation of verse 31 (Ps. 66:10) was already found in two other *Commentaries* (*Commentaries on the Psalms* 54.22 and 106.14; see also *On the Spirit and the Letter* 10.17). In these three cases the similarity between 1 Cor. 11:19, Ps 11:7b (Ps 12:6) and Ps. 67:31 (Ps. 66:10), allows Augustine to develop the same theme. Heresies are useful in that they manifest the "goldsmiths" of God's word, those who are made of proven silver are capable of expressing solutions to difficult scriptural questions. Nevertheless these "goldsmiths" would have been ignored for the lack of an adversary to reduce to silence. The poet in Augustine was not ill–pleased with his analogy drawn from the art of goldsmithing. It pleased him to describe the great interpreters of the Bible as the goldsmiths who had the courage to oppose the subversive opinions of heretics. One notes Augustine's precise information in his enumeration of the three categories of errors as christological heresies, trinitarian heresies and ecclesiological heresies. He knows their main lines of argument and the very clear error in each one of them. This little exposition is framed by two Pauline texts. The first is 1 Cor. 11:19 which is cited more than twenty times in the work. Each time Augustine reminds the reader of the usefulness of heresies which allow for the deepening of sound doctrine *doctrina sana* and the education of the uninformed.[1] The second text, Titus 1:9 underlines the role of mission of bishops who become the goldsmiths vis à vis the Word of God, their congregation and those who have been lost.

Augustine had adopted this mission to defend and manifest the Word of God on the day of his ordination as a presbyter. He had already, since the time of his conversion, prepared himself for it in the solitude of Thagaste. From then on, he took to heart the work that was imposed upon him by the numerous controversies caused by the heterodox doctrines he encountered during the course of his ministry. All of these controversies had a common characteristic. From Mani to Julian of Eclanum, passing through the Donatists, the Arians, the Eunomians, the Priscilianists, the "Compassionists" *misericordiae*, the Pelagians, etc. All those who existed on

184

the margins in some way or another of the Catholica threatened the Word of God. Indeed, and this fact is a constant focus, Augustine's polemical discussions are undertaken most often, (and on occasion uniquely) upon the bases of scriptural texts. The desire to reduce Augustine's polemics to quarrels based upon more or less theological concepts would falsify the position of the adversaries. In some way or another, even when the Bible is not the specific arena of confrontation, it always furnished the arguments for the dialogue or the battle. It is impossible, when studying Augustine's polemical works, to minimalize the study of scriptural citation.

Heterodox Writings Transmitted by Augustine

As the point of departure we will consider this first fact: Augustine's work has conserved for us a number of documents and archival pieces of all sorts which would have disappeared if he had not taken the care to have copies made either by himself or others. Among these documents are found the entire or partial works of heterodox writers who expressed their objections to scripture or found scriptural backing for their arguments. These were the two different ways that scripture might be attacked or compromised.

1. Manichean Writings transmitted solely by Augustine

a) The *Acta* were the result of public debate between the priest Augustine and the Manichean priest Fortunatus which occurred on the 28th and 29th of August 392 at Hippo. These *Acta*, immediately written down by the notaries, bear witness to the scriptural citations of Fortunatus as well as those of Augustine (*Against Fortunatus the Manichean*, see *Revisions* 1.16).

b) In 394 the "disputations" *disputationes*, to use the description which would be frequently employed, of the Manichean Adimantus fell into Augustine's hands. Adimantus had been a disciple of Mani and his work illustrated the opposition of Old Testament and New Testament texts. Augustine selected a certain number of these antitheses and strove to resolve them by revealing their true concordance (*Against Adimantus*, see *Revisions* 1.22).

c) From the end of 399 to 402–403, Augustine, having become bishop and already written his *Confessions*, engaged himself in refuting the thirty–three *Capitula* of the Manichean Bishop Faustus of Mileve. He writes: "In reply to Faustus the Manichean who, in blasphemous fashion, was attacking the Law and the Prophets, and their God, and the Incarnation of Christ, and who was also saying that the writings of the New Testament, by which one refutes them, are false I wrote a lengthy work in which I give my responses to the words I cite." (*Against Faustus*, see *Revisions* 2.7)[2]

From this work we possess a complete list of the objections and scriptural citations used by Faustus.[3]

d) From December 7 to 12, 404, a second public debate took place between the bishop Augustine and the Manichean Felix. As always in such circumstances *notararii* transcribed the *Acta*.[4]

e) Shortly after, Augustine received a letter from the Italian Manichean, Secundinus, wherein he is criticized for his conversion to Catholicism and in particular, for defending in his writing the books of the Old Testament. Augustine saved Secundinus' letter and answered him.[5]

Apart from all of this, Augustine remembered the criticisms of scripture which he had heard during his years as a Manichean. These are found in his *Confessions*.

2. Writings of the Donatists transmitted solely by Augustine

Augustine did not transmit in their entirety all the Donatist writings which came his way. It should be further noted that a fair number of his works addressed to the Donatists have also been lost.[6] In order to glimpse the biblical contribution of these works, one must return to the brief notices found in the *Revisions*.

a) The judgment of the Donatist council of Bagai (April 24, 394) was the work of the Donatist, Emeritus. Its grandiloquent style seems influenced by Augustine's verve particularly since it has woven together unexpected scriptural reminiscences.[7]

b) In the pastoral letter of Petilianus, the Donatist Bishop of Cirta, which was addressed *ad presbyteros et diaconos* of his own church, Augustine is out of the question. This vehement letter against the Catholics concerns the period prior to 400. Around this date a fragment of the letter is delivered to Augustine by friends from Cirta (Constantine). Aware of the danger it represented, Augustine writes *Against the Letters of Petilianus 1* and shortly after when he had access to the complete document, *Against the Letters of Petilianus 2*. During these two refutations, Augustine transcribes the entire pastoral letter of Petilianus. The work was finished near the end of 401.[8] Petilianus' letter is rich in scriptural references.

c) Shortly after 404, Augustine, in his three books *Against the Epistle of Parmenianus*, partially conserved the letter which Parmenianus, the old Donatist Bishop of Carthage, had sent to Tyconius reproaching him for playing into the hands of the Catholics in his writings. Books 2 and 3 discuss in depth the biblical arguments of Parmenianus.[9]

d) In 406 Augustine answered the second letter of Petilianus and added a book 3 to *Against the Letters of Petilianus* of which Book 1 and 2 date from the end of 401. The census in *Revisions* 2.25 of the three united books registers their union in 406.

e) After the anti–Donatist laws of 405, Augustine received a letter from the Donatist grammarian, Cresconius, wherein he is taken to task for having criticized the pastoral letter of Petilianus. Augustine, while writing *Against Cresconius*, highlights part of the Donatist letter. (*Against Cresconius*, see *Revisions* 2.26)

f) Augustine's *De unico baptismo*, written shortly before 411, is a response to a book *On the One Baptism* by Petilianus of Cirta. (*De unico baptismo*, c. Petilianus, see *Revisions* 2.34)

g) Later, during 419–420, Augustine preserves in his two books, *Against Gaudentius*, several elements of the letters of Gaudentius, the Donatist Bishop of Thamugadi. (*Against Gaudentius*, see *Revisions* 2.59)

Independent of Augustine, the official acts of the Conference of Carthage (411) preserved the two *mandata* (official declarations) of the Catholic and Donatist bishops. They are two real professions of faith based upon biblical documentation to which we will return later on.

3. Arian Writings transmitted solely by Augustine

The work of Augustine includes two Arian texts which he alone transmitted. The first is the *Sermo Arianorum* which he transcribes and responds to in the autumn of 419 while at Hippo.[10] The second are the speeches of the Arian Bishop Maximinus, debates which took place in 428 at Hippo pitting Augustine and Maximinus. A study of the scriptural citations attributed to Maximinus was made by Roger Gryson.[11]

4. Gnostic Writings transmitted solely by Augustine

We classify under the general term of gnostic, several heterodox writings which passed occasionally through Augustine's hands. In 415, Orosius sent him from Spain a consultation including Pricillianist opinions and Origenist tendencies.[12] Around 419 or 420, in Carthage, Christians sent Augustine a suspect book which attentive audiences had listened to at the maritime square *in platea maritima*. The manuscript did not contain its author's name. Augustine recopied and refuted it under the title *Against an Enemy of the Law and the Prophets* (See *Revisions* 2.58). Bishop Ceretius of Grenoble sent Augustine a Priscillianist hymn to critique.[13] Consentius, a Spaniard from the Balearic Isles, sent Augustine a Priscillianist work of Bishop Dictinus called the *Libra*.[14] These four heterodox works threaten scripture each in their own way. Those who discovered them immediately consulted Augustine.

5. Pelagian Writings transmitted solely by Augustine

Among the numerous Pelagian writings, several have been preserved solely by the work of Augustine.

a) In *On the Perfection of Human Justice*, Augustine seems to have completely taken over the *Definitiones* written by Pelagius' disciple Caelestius. The work was rich in biblical references to the Wisdom writings.[15] The *Definitiones* itself had been sent to Augustine by the priests Eutropus and Paul.

b) Augustine transcribed none of Pelagius' works in their entirety. He cites fragments of *On Nature*, and *Pro liberto arbitrio* and the responses he made to those who questioned him at the Council of Diospolis (Lydda) in 415. These later words are found in Augustine's *On the Proceedings of Pelagius*.[16]

c) Julian of Eclanum, with whom Augustine entertained a long debate between 419 and 430, was saved from oblivion by the transcribing of two long works at the end of a commentary. These were *Epistula ad Turbantium* in four books and *Epistula ad Florum* in eight books. Only six of the eight *ad Florum* books were copied and criticized by Augustine. This extensive critique constitutes the *Against Julianus* and *Opus imperfectum contra Julianum*. The latter book was interrupted by Augustine's death on the 28th of August 430. While it was in process the town of Hippo beleaguered by the Vandals had become a refuge for numbers of Christians from the surrounding area.[17]

Even the dry enumeration of the heterodox texts which have been uniquely preserved in the Augustinian works gives an idea of the breadth of polemical treatises found in his works. Even so, another category of treatises has not been mentioned: those initiated by Augustine himself. These works are essentially those which he undertook from the time of his conversion against Manicheism and which he pursued without respite until

405. One can also recognize, as in the case of the refutation of Donatism, that a number of works and perhaps transcriptions have been lost.

In the face of such industry on the part of Augustine, one cannot but feel overwhelmed, not only by the sheer volume of the writing, but also because of a sense of fragmentation of the discussions.

For the moment we will pursue the discussions from the perspective of the scriptural documentation. This is definitively the undisputed richness in these works and often perhaps their "Ariadna's thread."

The Biblical Versions from the Polemical Documentation

In preserving some of the heterodox texts, Augustine also preserved their "bible" or, in other words, the scriptural citations found in these texts. Consequently we have a sheaf of biblical documents to which Augustine is witness but not author. Coming from diverse horizons, these biblical sequences present a wide variety of versions. The critical study of these versions is far from complete. We already possess the work of François Decret concerning the Manicheans, Fortunatus, Faustus and Felix[18] and Roger Gryson's study of the scriptural citations of the Arian Maximinus.[19] The masterful research of these scholars points the route which must be followed if knowledge of the heterodox "bibles" recorded by Augustine is to be achieved.[20] Despite their variety, all these versions of the Bible display, at the very least, a common characteristic. They are all prior to the Hebrew translation of Jerome. In any case, they should not be judged and criticized on the basis of the Vulgate. One can say that as a whole, they come from the *Vetus latina* (Old Latin), or better yet the *Veteres latinae* (Old Latin versions) which is being edited by the prestigious Vetus Latina Institute at Beuron.[21] The term *Vetus latina* covers a mass of data furnished by the manuscript and the scriptural citations gathered one by one from the works of the Fathers of the Latin Church. Augustine, like all the other Latin Fathers, is a witness to versions of the Bible which he had on hand and subsequently the heterodox versions which he had gathered. The variety of versions depended not only on the authors of these writings, but also upon each of the books of the Bible themselves. Today we are more familiar with the studies of this "old Latin" thanks to the *Bulletin de la Bible latine* annually edited by P. Maurice Bogaert from the Abbey of Maredsous, in the *Revue Bénédictine*.[22]

Perhaps a quick example taken from the work of Augustine will allow the reader some concrete insight into the difficulty with which the "goldsmithing" of God's word was debated. We will use the case of the book of Ecclesiasticus.

In the French edition of the *Pleiade*, we read under the reference Sirach (Ecclesiasticus) 34:25 the following as translated by Jean Habot from the Septuagint: *"Qui se purifie de la souillure d'un mort et le touche encore, qu'a–t–il gagné en son bain de pureté?"* (If a man washes after touching a dead body, and touches it again, what has he gained by his washing?). This particular text alludes to a ritual interdiction found in Numbers 19:11. The French translation given here corresponds to a text cited by Augustine in 389 found in *On Genesis against the Manichees* 2.21.31. Augustine wrote: *Qui baptizatur a mortuo, et iterum tangit illum, quid proficit in lavacro suo?* Augustine uses these words to prove that according to scripture sin is often called death. One sees that he possesses a version of this fragment of Ecclesiasticus based upon the Septuagint version. In 394, in a work called *Contra epistulam Donati haeretici* which has been lost, Augustine reproached Donatus for having altered Ecclesiasticus 34:24 by amputating *"et iterum tangit illum."* In the listing of this work in *Revisions* (1.21.3) Augustine rescinds his accusation of Donatus. He points out that when he wrote the work, he was not aware that old African manuscripts from Donatus' time did not include the long version of Eccl. 34:25. Augustine in 394 only knows of the long version.

From 410, successively under the pens of Petilianus (*Answer to Letters of Petilianus* 1.9.10, 1.16.47, 2.7.9.15), Parmenianus (*Against the Epistle of Parmenianus* 2.10.20), Quietus of Buruc,[23] Cresconius, (*Against Cresconius* 2.24.29, 4.16.18), the Donatist letter writer (*Letter 108* 2.6), and Gaudentius (*Against Gaudentius* 1.39.54), Augustine found Eccl. 34:25 cited in its following short version: *Qui baptizatur a mortuo non ei prodest lavatio eius* "He who is baptized by death, his purification serves him nothing." The Donatists considered as dead those who had not received true baptism, or in other words, a baptism in the church. For them Catholic baptism was useless since they argued that Catholics were descended from the "traditors," those people who had surrendered the scriptures to the Diocletian persecutors. These traditors *traditores* were sinners and spiritually dead. In criticizing Petilianus, Augustine wrote:

> He uses in an unintelligent and lying way a text he remembers: "To him who is baptized by a death of what use is his washing?" He tries to show us that the traditor should be considered as dead and he adds: "He is dead, he who did not merit the birth of true baptism, dead also is he born of legitimate baptism who mixes with the traditors." (*Answer to Letters of Petilianus* 1.16.17)

It is remarkable that in all these passages of the Donatist treatises, the incriminating fragment is never attributed to Ecclesiasticus and it is never linked to the Numbers verse to which it alludes. Where did the Donatists find this version and interpretation of the shortened Eccl. 34:25? The source is Saint Cyprian's *Epistula 71* (*Letter 70 ANF*), which unhesitatingly taught that heretics needed to be rebaptized. He wrote:

> But again some of our colleagues would rather give honour to heretics than agree with us; and while by the assertion of one baptism they are unwilling to baptize those that come, they thus either themselves make two baptisms in saying there is a baptism among heretics; or certainly, which is a matter of more importance, they strive to set off before and prefer the sordid and profane washing of heretics to the true and only and legitimate baptism of the Catholic Church, not considering that it is written, "He who is baptized by one dead, what availeth his washing?" Now it is manifest that they who are not in the Church of Christ are reckoned among the dead; and another cannot be made alive by him who himself is not alive, since there is one Church which, having attained the grace of eternal life, both lives forever and quickens the people of God.[24]

Transposing Cyprian's words to their benefit, and considering themselves to be the only legitimate church, the Donatists applied Cyprian's reading of Ecclesiasticus 34:25 to their contemporary conflict about baptism with the Catholic Church.

It seems that around 406, when he started the *On Baptism*, Augustine was made aware of the Cyprianic origin of the short version of Ecclesiasticus 34:25 and the danger of its use by the Donatists. *On Baptism* starts in this way:

> Also this work undertakes, with the help of God, not only to refute the Donatist objections on this subject (baptism) but also to illustrate that which God will give me to say on the problem of the authority of the sainted martyr Cyprian. It is from him that they attempt to support their error for fear that it will collapse under the shock of the truth. This work will make clear to all souls in whom bias has not blinded their judgment that the authority of Cyprian is not on their side and that it not only disputes but perfectly ruins their theories (*On Baptism* 1.1.1.).

The whole of *On Baptism* is based upon Cyprianic documents such as his letters and the episcopal judgments of the council held September 1, 256. It is from one of these judgments, attributed to Bishop Quietus of Buruc, that the shortened version of Eccl. 34:25 is found.

Augustine was in a delicate position. Regarding the textual version of Eccl. 34:25, Augustine never brought to the attention of the Donatists that their text was inaccurate. He simply tactfully admits that Cyprian and his disciples did not alter the text which they had been given by their manuscripts.[25] However, concerning the fundamental question at stake, Augustine recognized that Cyprian had made a mistake in asking for the rebaptism of heretics. Furthermore, in his dispute with Pope Stephen, Cyprian was never schismatic or troublesome to church union. Finally, Augustine repeated tirelessly, that in all baptism it is Christ who baptizes even if the priest visibly performing the sacrament is a sinner.

Returning to Eccl. 34:25, according to the long version of the verse, we are surprised to find it cited once in question 161 of *Questions on the Heptateuch 1*. Augustine writes:

> Now there is no doubt that in the Law the dead body is the sign of sin, since whosoever touches one for whatever reason must purify himself as with a stain. From that it was written: *Qui baptizatur a mortuo et iterum tangit illum, quid proficit lavatio eius? Sic et qui ieiunat super peccata sua et iterum ambulans haec eadem facit.* (Eccl. 34:25–26)

The tomb of the dead signified therefore the remission of sins and belongs to the word. Augustine writes: "Blessed are those whose iniquities are remitted and whose sins are covered" (Ps. 31:1) (*Questions on the Heptateuch* 1, qu. 161). Here Augustine naturally combines Eccl. 34:25 and Numbers 19:11–12,[26] which is its source. He makes no allusion to the previous discussion with the Donatists. It is a characteristic example of the distinction between literary genre typical of Augustine.

The history behind Eccl 34:25 in Augustine's writings is only one example of the type of study required of the biblical material included in the polemical documentation. It is a complex study which is full of promise for researchers who are interested in the problematics of "old Latin."[27]

The Structure of the Biblical Polemical Treatises

Each of Augustine's polemical works, listed at the beginning of this chapter, corresponds to a particular problematic question. Nevertheless, almost all (and certainly those works that transmit heterodox texts) follow a structure which is important to highlight if one wishes to understand Augustine's method for writing them. The literary construction of these works can disconcert and even lead to misunderstanding for the uninitiated. The heterodox documents which Augustine received one after the other were complete works or continuous texts such as the *Capitula* by Faustus of Milevus, the letter by Petilianus to his priests and deacons and the letter by Parmenianus to Tyconius to mention only three. Augustine, the accomplished Latin rhetor, accustomed to explaining the works of Virgil or Cicero phrase by phrase, transmits these heterodox texts in the same way. They are presented piece by piece with critical glosses, scriptural citations and all sorts of comments. Since Augustine did not have the scientific goal of criticizing a whole work, but rather the pastoral goal of preserving Catholics from subversive biblical interpretations, he transcribes what he perceives as dangerous. Therefore his transcriptions are often partial. He warns us himself in the *Revisions* that he did not have time to finish his study of the *Antitheses* of Adimantus. He answers Petilianus's second letter citing only a small number of sentences.

Such a method of debate presents some inconveniences which Augustine did not foresee and which tend to weaken his arguments. Furthermore, this method can give the illusion of a real disputation which is echoed in the written work. Petilianus reproached Augustine for using his work in this way and giving the impression that an actual dialogue had occurred. Without a doubt there were real public debates such as the *Acta contra Forunatum*, the *Acta contra Felicem*, the debate with the Arian Pascentius, and the *Acta* of the Conference of Carthage in 411.These public controversies were duly documented by the chancellery notaries. But works such as *Answer to Letters of Petilianus, Against the Epistle of Parmenianus, Against Faustus*, and *Against Julianus* are of another sort. Their "dialogue" is fictional. This was an accepted literary style at the time, which Augustine adopted. However readings of these works could imply that the opponent whom Augustine argues against had personally attacked him. This is the case for the second letter of Petilianus, the letter of Cresconius, the letter of Secundinus and certainly in the writings of Julian of Eclanum. Aside from these specific examples, Augustine treats in his polemical writings, documents which had been transmitted to him by the faithful of Cirta, Hippo and Carthage. These include Petilianus' first letter, Pelagius' *De natura*, the *Sermo Arianorum*, and the book, *An Opponent to the Law and the Prophets*. As for works intended to refute the Manicheans, Augustine certainly took the initiative since the writings upon which he comments were written prior to his conversion and certainly not personally directed at him. One should not commit the reversal of thinking that Faustus in the *Capitula* attacks Augustine. Challenged ceaselessly in many ways, the Bishop of Hippo considered it a duty of his pastoral charge to satisfy those who wanted a quick answer. He provided it using the method which he had learned in his old profession as rhetor.

We should not neglect to mention a circumstance which upon occasion further aggravated the situation we have just described. For various reasons Augustine found himself obliged to write the same refutation twice because he had received the first version of the document in incomplete or truncated form. This was the case with the letter of Petilianus to his clergy hence *Answer to Letters of Petilianus 1* is followed by *Answer to Letters of Petilianus 2*. The same thing happened with Julian of Eclanum's *Ad Turbantium* which Augustine partially refuted in *On Marriage and Concupiscence 2*. When he received the complete document he wrote *Against Julianus*. In the same way Augustine produced *De adulterinis conjugiis* and later *Against Gaudentius*.

The whole of the situation surrounding the redaction of the polemical treatises is played out against layers of biblical controversies. These were translated into a repetition of the arguments. On the one hand all the Donatists, to use one example, frequently cited the same texts. Augustine on the other hand used the same collection of scripture texts in his refutations. This phenomenon of repetition is particularly trenchant in the Augustine/Julian of Eclanum works even though the duel had only one participant. Controversies like these necessitate chronological reconstruction of the arguments of the protagonists verse by verse. In this manner one can uncover the historical and thematic progression within a polemical treatise. Thematic reconstitution allows for the following:

1. On one side, there are those debates which are isolated, closed, without resonance with the rest of Augustine's work, and on the other, there are those which are constantly taken up, and open and gush forth even in such works as the *City of God* and the commentaries of the Psalms.

2. The recognition of the borrowings made by each party from their predecessors, so that one can speak of what might be described as a call to the Fathers, particularly on the part of the Donatists and the Pelagians.

3. The highlighting of the doctrinal issues which both parties discuss by focusing on their pondering on the scriptures. They pull from these reflections what would today be called "theology" and upon which they base their concepts of God, Christ, and Church.

Closed Debates

Many of Augustine's biblical controversies are the result of isolated and unique circumstances or a theme which is narrowly tied to a specific polemical work. These are called closed debates. They are numerous and difficult to categorize prior to making a definitive inventory of the scriptural citations found therein. Even so, several constants can be isolated.

Characteristically these closed debates are frequently based on books of the Bible which will later be called "deuterocanonical." Such is the case for 1 Maccabees, the unique citation or allusion to Esdras and the Greek version of Esther which is evoked and cited in the anti–Pelagian controversies.[28] No portion of these three books is taken up in *Speculum quis ignorat*.

The closed debates also frequently correspond to biblical books which are rare in Augustine's work. For example the book of Chronicles, which Augustine calls Paralipomenon, plays an important role in Augustine's dialogue with the monks of Hadrumetum and Marseilles who were awkwardly termed semi–Pelagian.[29] A cluster of citations, quite new in Augustine's writing, even though one or two other fragments from Chronicles make their way into *Against Julianus 5*. This cluster includes 1 Kings 12:15, 2 Chron. 21:16–17, 2 Chron. 25:7–8, 2 Kings 14:9–10, 2 Chron. 25:20, Esdras 14:9, four citations from Esther, Prov. 21:1, Ps. 104:25, Rom. 1:24–26–28 and 2 Thess. 1:10–11. The introductory sentence for this cluster of citations illustrates their significance : "Who would not tremble before the divine judgments by which God does His will, even in the heart of evil men rewarding each according to his works."[30] We know from Augustine himself as found in *Revisions* 2.66, to whom *On Grace and Free Choice* was addressed (Abbot Valentinus and the monks at Hadrumetum) and what was the intention of the work. Augustine writes:

> I wrote a book whose title is *On Grace and Free Choice* because of those persons who, by thinking that free choice is denied when the grace of God is defended, defend free will in such a manner as to deny the grace of God by affirming that it is bestowed according to our merits. I addressed it, however, to those monks of Hadrumetum in whose monastery the controversy on this subject started; as a result, some of them were compelled to consult me (*Revisions* 2.66).[31]

We have here the proof (and this is not the only case) of a well–structured, but new study by Augustine of biblical themes which, as a matter of fact, have no previous data to rely on before the polemical discussion on the Bible between himself and Julian of Eclanum and the monks of Hadrumetum and Marseilles.[32] These themes are questions which are disputed between learned theologians. They were never part of Augustine's pastoral or catechetical works.

Not only do books which Augustine rarely cites nourish the closed biblical debates. We have already had occasion, while working through the installments of the *Biblia Augustiana* to point out themes from Proverbs, Jeremiah and Deuteronomy, etc. which were from time to time the object of discussion with an opponent.[33] This work needs to be pursued particularly regarding the gospels and epistles of the New Testament.

Due to limited space I propose to use four short Epistles which appear in Augustine's polemical work for examples. They are the Epistle of Jude, the second and third Epistles of John, and the Epistle of Philemon.

1. The Epistle of Jude

Augustine cites Jude very rarely. The first citation occurs in 394–95 in an incomplete commentary on Romans. Augustine minutely analyzes Paul's introductory salutations. Paul writes: " Grace to you and peace from God our Father and the Lord Jesus Christ." Augustine explains the absence of the Holy Spirit in these salutations. It is not surprising since grace and peace in Paul's words were gifts of the Father and Jesus Christ, consequently these two terms, grace and peace mean the Holy Spirit. Therefore Paul's greeting includes the entire Trinity. He writes: "*Et ideo ipsa Trinitas pariterque incommutabilis unitas in ista salutatione cognoscitur.*" Reviewing the greetings of Paul and those of the other Apostles, Augustine shows that, despite some variations (the principal one being the introduction of the word "mercy"), all the greetings, by naming grace and peace as being a gift of the Father and the Son, are affirmations of the Trinity. Jude is no exception. It names God the Father and the Lord Jesus Christ and in order to indicate the Holy Spirit, lists the gifts of God with the three words charity, peace and mercy. Jude begins: "*Judas, Jesu Christi servus, frater autem Iacobi in Deo Patre dilectis, et Jesu Christo conservatis et vocatis, misericordia vobis, et pax et charitas adimpleatur*" (Jude 1:1) Augustine adds that grace and peace cannot be understood without mercy and charity. It is therefore under the auspices of the Holy Spirit that the work of Jude is found in Augustine's writing (*Ep. ad Romanos inchoata expositio* 10–12).

We know that Jude was admitted to canon with difficulty. In the fourth century, Eusebius of Cesarea indicated that some people contested Jude. However, it was accepted by the Muratorian Canon (slightly before 200) and by Tertulian (around 200). The Council of Carthage in 397 cites it. Augustine affirms its canonical authenticity on several occasions. These are found in the discussion of canon inserted into *On Christian Doctrine* 2.8.15 and later in the *City of God* books 15.23.4 and 18.38. In the latter two instances Augustine affirms that the Apostle Jude in his canonical epistle bore witness to certain text as far back as Enoch, the fifth descendant of Abraham. By this affirmation Augustine alludes to Jude 14 and 15.[34] A last time, in treatise 76 on John's Gospel, Augustine reiterates that Jude is part of the canon of scripture. In this case he is discussing Jude's question to the Lord during the Last Supper: "Lord, how is it that you will manifest yourself to us and not to the world?" Augustine reminds his readers that according to scripture this Judas is not Judas Iscariot and he adds that this Judas is *cuius epistula inter scripturas canonicas legitur* (*Treatises on the Gospel of John* 76.1).

In *De fide et operibus* Augustine fulminates against a certain group called the "Compassionists" who wanted to baptize catechumens before they left adulterous relationships. This regularization had always been necessary for admission into the last stage of the catechumenate. Augustine cites texts from Paul (Gal. 4:31 and 5:13) and the Second Letter of Peter (2 Pet. 2:17–22) which he quotes at length. In this situation he notices a coincidence between 2 Peter. 2:13a, 14a and Jude 12. He writes:

> For he said earlier about such men: "...those who take part in your meals whose eyes are filled with adultery and unremitting sin" 2 Peter 2:13,14. Hence he calls them "dried up wells" because they have received the grace to know the Lord Christ; but "dried up" because they are not consistent in their way of life. It is also to such men that the apostle Jude alludes: "They come all stained mixing with your fraternal meals with the purpose of getting their fill without shame...clouds without water..." When Peter says: "those who take part in your meals, with eyes full of adultery" Jude goes on to say: "all stained, they mix with your fraternal meals" because they mingle with the good people in sacramental meals and in the agapes for the congregation, and here Peter says: "dried up sources." Jude goes on: "clouds without water," and James: "dead faith." (James 2, 20)[35]

Up to now the citations from Jude which we have discussed are rare. The only verse which is accorded a place of importance is verse 19 which states: "It is these who set up divisions, worldly people, devoid of the Spirit" *Hi sunt qui se ipsos segregant, animales, Spiritum non habentes*. Without hesitation, Augustine identifies Jude's "Spirit" and the Holy Spirit. This verse is quoted eight times in the anti–Donatist controversy. The first citation is found in a short work by Augustine which has been lost but is listed in *Revisions* 2.27. Augustine had published a pamphlet entitled *Proofs and Testimonies Against the Donatists* which was posted on the walls of the Donatist basilica in Hippo. This fact is dated to 408 or 409. In his listing Augustine noted:

After I recalled the testimony of Jude the Apostle where he says: "These are they who set themselves apart, sensual men, not having the Spirit" I also add the words: "The Apostle Paul says about them: But the sensual man does not perceive the things that are of the Spirit of God. These should not be placed in the same footing as those whom schism separates completely from the church. For the same Apostle Paul says that the former (those described by Jude) are "little ones in Christ" whom, nevertheless, He nourishes with milk because they are not yet strong enough to take solid food; but among the dead and the lost, so that, if any one of them, after amendment, be reconciled with the Church, it can rightly be said of him : "He was dead, and has come to life; he was lost, and is found"(Luke 15:32). (*Revisions* 2.53)

With these two examples, we see the first and last Augustinian interpretation of Jude 19. We see that Augustine changed his mind between these commentaries and that he, at a certain point, no longer placed Jude's text on the same level as Paul's 1 Cor. 2:14.

The six commentaries written between these examples belong to five sermons, and *Letter 185* addressed to Count Boniface.

The five sermons are the following: *Sermon 285* preached at Pentecost 411 at Carthage, *Sermon 8* (Frangipane I) preached it seems in 411 at Carthage, *Sermon 265* preached for Ascension Thursday May 23, 412, in an unspecified location, *Sermon 285* preached sometime between 405 and 410 in Carthage for the May twenty–second celebration of the Martyrs Castus and Emilius, and *Sermon 71*.[36] This last sermon concerned sinning against the Holy Spirit (Mt. 12:31–32) and was preached sometime in 417–418, probably in Carthage. This simple listing of these five sermons serves to illustrate that each one was concerned in some way or another with questions about the Holy Spirit. The common thrust of the preaching was the insistence upon the indissoluble relationship between the unity of the Church and the presence of the Holy Spirit. Such a link was so strong that those who did not adhere to the unity of the body of Christ did not possess the Spirit. It was in this context that Augustine had recourse to Jude 19: "It is these who set up divisions, worldly people, devoid of the Spirit." This verse is used by Augustine to condemn the Donatist schism. Jude argues against dissension and schism by which one loses the presence of the Holy Spirit, since the Spirit belongs uniquely to the unity of the Church. In sermons 269, 3 and 17 written in 411, Augustine links Jude 19 and 1 Cor. 2:14 as though they provided an equal witness. 1 Cor. 2:14 is absent from sermons 265, 285 and *Letter 185*. In *Sermon 71.18.30* Augustine refuses to consider that Jude 19 and 1 Cor. 2:14 deal with the same men.

Sermon 71 presages the exposition described in *Revisions* 2.27. Furthermore, *Sermon 71*, almost certainly dates from 417, the same year as *Letter 185*. In *Letter 185* Augustine expresses to Count Boniface in the following manner what one should think about the situation of the Donatists vis à vis the Catholic Church.[37] One cannot participate in divine charity and at the same time be an enemy to unity. That is why those outside the Church do not have the Holy Spirit. It is of them that it was written: "It is these who set up divisions, worldly people, devoid of the Spirit." (*Letter 185*.50)

In *On Rebuke and Grace* (6,10) in the course of a long collection of spiritual texts proving that perseverance is a gift from God, Augustine cites Jude 24: "Now to him who is able to keep you from falling and to present you without blemish (*immaculatos*) before the presence of his glory with rejoicing." This is the only time the verse is cited.

In *Speculum quis ignorat*, Augustine selects Jude 4, 12, 16 to 23. This is the only time that Jude 19 is cited in its context.

2. The Second Epistle of John

As with the opening greetings of Jude's letter, the salutation from 2 John is cited in *An Unfinished Explanation on the Epistle to the Romans*. Augustine comments that this greeting corresponds to those found in the letters to Timothy. He writes: "*In secunda vero illis quae ad Timotheum sunt consonat, dicens: "Sit vobiscum gratia, misericordia, pax a Deo Patre et Jesu Christo Filio Patris*" (Grace, mercy and peace from God the Father and Christ Jesus our Lord.) (*An Unfinished Explanation on the Epistle to the Romans* 12) The trinitarian value of this greeting is evident since it includes "grace" and "peace" which are gifts of the Holy Spirit.

The canonical character of the second Epistle of John is affirmed in *On Christian Doctrine* 2.8.13 and by the Council of Carthage in 397.

2 John 10–11 had been used by one of the eighty–seven bishops (which included Cyprian) attending the council held in Carthage (September 1, 256) to support the re–baptism of heretics. Augustine included the eighty–seven judgments of the bishops attending the council in *On Baptism*. Judgment 81, by Bishop Aurelius of Cillavi stated:

> The apostle John has written in his letter: "Anyone who comes to you without the doctrine of Christ, do not welcome him, do not even salute him. If one salutes one participates in his evil doings." (2 John 10–11) How can one easily welcome into God's house those forbidden to be admitted in our private house, and how can we enter into communion with them before they have received the baptism of the church, as it

would merely suffice to salute them to become compromised by their evil doings?" (Judgment 81 *De Baptismo* 8.45.88–89)

Augustine refused to accept 2 John 10–11 as a reference to baptism. In effect, heretics who abandoned their errors, and converted to the doctrine of Christ, had already something of that doctrine. They had had the sacrament (*sacramentum*) or, in other words, visible baptism. When they converted they found that which they had not possessed. That was the peace and charity arising from a pure heart with good conscience and an open faith (1 Tim. 1:5). The Johannine text, on the other hand, was intended for those who possessed nothing of Christ's doctrine. Augustine writes: "John declares, in effect, that one should not greet those holding strange doctrines."[38]

In *On Grace and Free Choice*, addressed in 426 to Abbot Valentinus and his monks, Augustine quotes 2 John 5 in the midst of a series of biblical citations affirming charity as the fullness of the Law. The following verses (1 Peter 4:8, James 2:8, 1 John 2:10, 3:23, 4:21 and 5:2–3,) were followed by 2 John 5 which says: "And not as though I were writing you a new commandment, but the one we have had from the beginning, that we love one another."[39]

In the *Speculum*, section 48, Augustine has occasion to return to his previously cited 2 John 2:5 and 10–11.

3. The Third Epistle of John

Third John is extremely rare in Augustine's work. The exordium from third John is cited in *An Unfinished Explanation of the Epistle to the Romans*. Augustine writes: "*In tertiae principio, de Trinitate penitus tacetur, credo, quod sit omnino brevissima. Sic enim incipit: 'Senior Gaio dilectissimo, quem ego diligo in veritate'* (3 John 1:1). *Quam veritiatem pro ipsa Trinitate positam puto.*" (*An Unfinished Explanation of the Epistle to the Romans* 12) The epistle is canonical according to *On Christian Doctrine* 2.8.13 and the Council of Carthage in 397. Section 49 in *Speculum* contains 3 John 5–8 and 11.

4. The Epistle to Philemon

The Epistle to Philemon was included in sacred canon by Augustine in *On Christian Doctrine* 2.8.13 and by the Council of Carthage in 397. *On Christian Doctrine* 1.34.37 includes a citation of Philemon 20 by which Augustine attempts to express the nature of rejoicing among people in God. Paul wrote: "Therefore, brother I will take joy of you in the Lord" *Ita frater, ego te fruar in Domino*. Verses 13 and 14 of the epistle belong to the

Pelagian conflict. Celestius, in his *Definitions*, which Augustine gathers into *De perfectione justitiae nominis*, cites Philemon 13–14 in a series of texts favouring the free will of man. Paul wrote to Philemon concerning Onesimus: "...but I preferred to do nothing without your consent in order that your goodness might not be by compulsion but of your own free will."[40] Augustine takes up a portion of the text used by Celestius. Concerning Philemon 14, he notes that there can be no good voluntary actions unless, "God is at work in you, both to will and to work for his good pleasure. (Phillippians 2:13)"[41] However, in *On Grace and Free Choice* 2.4 Augustine cites Philemon 14 in a series of scriptural texts which prove human free will.[42] Augustine writes: *Et ad Philemonem: Ne bonum tuum velut ex necessitate esset, sed ex voluntate*. Philemon 7, 13 and 14 are gathered in *Speculum*.

The study of four short epistles of the New Testament proves that during a period when the Eastern Church was suspicious of their authenticity, there was not doubt in the African church about their canonicity. However they served no pastoral purpose.

Polemics and Theology

We are concerned here with the polemics which disputed fundamental questions of Christian doctrine of institution and sacramental aspects of the Church. They loom large in Augustine's theology. Some are the point of departure for his theological reflection such as the debate upon Pelagianism. In such a vast field we will limit ourselves to delineating a number of key points.

In the course of his debates with heretics, we see Augustine's formulation and elaboration of his christological convictions. Against one and all Augustine defends the realism of that which will later be called Christ's human nature. Christ was truly a man. He was incarnated and genuinely resurrected. Based upon a text from 1 John, Augustine taught that all heresies either explicitly or implicitly denied the physical aspect of Christ. *Sermon 183* analyzes in the face of heretical propositions 1 John 4:13 which states: "Beloved, do not believe every spirit, but test the spirits to see whether they are of God..." One recognizes the Spirit of God in the following manner. All who confess that Christ came in the flesh from God are of the Spirit. Those who divide Christ are following the spirit of the anti–Christ. From this analysis Augustine deduces that each heresy, in its own way, denies the Incarnation and consequently the Resurrection. This constitutes his principal argument against the Manicheans and all the Gnostics.

On the other hand, to combat the subordinationists, such as the Arians, the Sabellians, the Apollinarists, etc., Augustine cites Phillippians 2:6–11. With this hymn, Augustine teaches that Christ is God and of the same nature as God. It would be enlightening to research the use of these Pauline verses alone in *On the Trinity*.[43] In fact this treatise elaborates the richest collection of New Testament quotations in the whole of Augustine's works in support of the unique nature of the Trinity. By defining his own theological vision, without becoming a polemist, Augustine accumulates here an important scriptural arsenal directed against specific heterodox groups, in particular the Arians.

One notable point of divergence between Augustine and the heretics concerns the Old Testament. This is certainly the case with the Manicheans and is witnessed to in *Against Faustus*.[44] An impressive biblical collection, consecrated to this polemic, is found in this work. The issue is strongly highlighted in *On the Catechizing of the Uninstructed*.[45] It also forms the exegetical teaching in *On Christian Doctrine*[46] where it is vigorously highlighted against heretical denials of the prophetic nature of the Old Testament. It is definitive in announcing Christ's coming and the preparations for His arrival.[47]

Augustine's thinking on baptism, as we already know, was formulated in the face of Donatist and Pelagian doctrines, attacks, and refutations which he encountered. Donatist doctrines in particular were concerned with the administering of baptism. A monograph about the whole question would need to research on the one hand anti–Donatist works such as *On Baptism*[48] and *On the Uniqueness of Baptism*[49] and on the other hand the abundant anti–Pelagian writings. While such a synthesis is lacking, there is an abundant bibliography available. For information about this see the notes where I point out a certain number of significant elements.[50]

Again while confronting the Pelagians, Augustine is lead to be more specific concerning his interpretation of the Lord's Prayer. Several of the treatises devoted to this controversy discuss Mt. 6:9–13 which states: "And forgive us our debts, As we also have forgiven our debtors; And lead us not into temptation, But deliver us from evil."[51] It should be pointed out here that it appears that someone praying the Lord's Prayer recognizes himself as a sinner and asks God's help to avoid sinning.

Finally, we mention in passing the need for an in–depth study of the biblical citations of the Pelagian debate. Noteworthy on this point is the dialogue between the seemingly deaf Augustine and the equally deaf Julian of Eclanum.[52] Such a study would highlight a series of scriptural texts borrowed from Paul and a number of Old Testament works such as Ezekiel, Deuteronomy, and the Wisdom books. It would determine the degree of dependence upon Jerome by the two opponents. (It seems that Julian followed Jerome's Vulgate no more closely than Augustine did). It would compare their respective interpretations, and underline the seemingly intractable positions of the authors upon the problem of theological implications.

These brief notes merely skim the surface of the wealth of biblical citations found in the polemical debates. They do not do justice to Augustine's virtuosity nor, upon occasion, that of his adversaries found in these works (one thinks particularly of Julian of Eclanum). They provide only the briefest of synthesis of the preponderance of Pauline literature in Augustine's work. According to the insight of Pascal, Paul is Augustine's master since the "scene in the garden." (*Confessions* 8.19, 12.28) Without a doubt it is this profound agreement and unconditional admiration for the Apostle, which accounts for a certain excess in Augustine's anti–Pelagian position.

Incomplete as it is,[53] our survey raises the suspicion of the long echoing of polemics in the use of the scriptural texts. This topic has already entailed a vast literature over the centuries, the study of which far exceeds the limits of the present essay.

NOTES

1. In the *Confessions* 7.19.25, Augustine writes: "As for me, I must confess that it was not until later that I learned how true Catholic doctrine differs from the error of Photinus in interpreting the meaning of incarnation. It is indeed true that the refutation of heretics gives greater prominence to the tenets of your Church and the principles of sound doctrine." *Opotuit enim et haereses esse, ut probati manifesti fierent inter infirmos.* (1 Cor. 11:19)

2. *The Fathers of the Church: A New Translation* Vol. 60. Ed. Roy Joseph Deferrari. "Saint Augustine, The *Retractations*," translated by Sister Mary Inez Bogan, RSM, Ph.D. (The Catholic University Of America Press, Washington, D.C., 1968.)

3. See the analytical and extremely suggestive study in François Decret's book *Aspects du Manichéisme dans l'Afrique romaine. Les controverses de Fortunatus, Faustus et Félix avec saint Augustin*, Études Augustiniennes, Paris, 1970.

4. *Against Felix the Manichean*, see *Revisions* 2.8 and the Decret work already mentioned above.

5. *Against Secundius the Manichean*, see *Revisions* 2.10: "At the beginning of this writing was also a copy of the letter from Secundius."

6. All that remains is the references in the *Revisions*: 1.21 (Against the Epistle of Donatus); 2.5 (*C. partem Donati*); 2.19 (*Against the ideas of Centurius*); 2.27 (Proofs and Testimony against the Donatists); 2.28 (*Against the unnamed Donatist*); 2.29 (*Warnings to the Donatists*); 2.35 (*Maximinianists against the Donatists*).

7. See A.–M. la Bonnardière, "Psaume 13:3 et l'interprétation de Rom. 3:13–18 dans l'oeuvre de saint Augustin" in *Recherches Augustiniennes* 4, 1966, pp. 49–65 and particularly pp. 55–65.

8. *Answer to the Letters of Petilianus* 1, 2 and 3. To understand the structure of the whole of these three books see *Revisions* 2.25 and A. Mandouze, *Prosopographie Chrétienne du Bas Empire, 1, Afrique*, article "Petilianus," pp. 855–868

9. *Against the Epistle of Parmenianus*, see *Revisions* 2.17. Concerning the works of Parmenianus, see the work of Optat of Mileve in seven books, circa 366.

10. *Sermo Arianorum* and *Contra sermonem Arianorum*, see *Revisions* 2.52 and *Letter 23A* (Divjak, *CSEL* 88, p. 122).

11. Roger Gryson, "Les citations scripturaires des oeuvres attribuées à l'évêque Arien Maximinus" in *RBen* 88 (1978); "Littérature arienne latine, 1: Debat de Maximinus avec Augustin, Scolies ariennes dans le concile d'Aquilée," *CETEDOC*, Louvain–la–Neuve.

12. *Ad Orosium presbyterum contra Priscillianistas et Origenistas*, see *Revisions* 2.44. Augustine carefully notes that: "The consultation itself had been added to the beginning of my answer."

13. *Letter 237*, written to Certius. See the study of this letter in Eric Junod and Jean–Daniel Kaestli, "L'histoire des Actes de Jean" in *Cahiers de la Revue de Théologie et de Philosophie*, 7, 1982, pp. 90–94: "Augustin et sa lettre 237."

14. *Letter 2 of Consentius* (Divjak, CSEL 88). See A.–M. la Bonnardière, "De Nouveau sur le Prescillianisme," dans J. Divjak, *Lettre Aug., Et. Aug.*, 1983, pp.205–215.

15. *De perfectione justitiae hominis*, in *CSEL* 42; Augustine does not list this work in his *Revisions*.

16. For *On Nature* see *On Nature and Grace* and its presentation in *Revisions* 2.42; Pelagius' book was communicated to Augustine by Timase and John. For *On the Proceedings of Pelagius*, see *Revisions* 2.47. Bishop Aurelius of Carthage had asked Augustine for a copy of this work.

17. *Against Julianus*, see *Revisions* 2.62. Augustine had already responded to several extracts of *Ad Turbantium* in *On Marriage and Concupiscence* 2 written in 420–421.

18. See note 8.

19. See note 15.

20. We have attempted, using another method, a study of the text of the Book of Proverbs, in *Biblia Augustiniana*, "Le Livre des Proverbes," chap. 1; Le texte, *Etudes Augustiniennes*, Paris, 1975, pp. 13–31. One can also consult in *Biblia Augustiniana*, "Le Livre de Jérémie," chap. 4: Le Prophète Jérémie dans les controverse, *Etudes Augustiniennes*, Paris, 1972, pp. 25–39.

21. Institut de la Vetus Latina, Die Reste de Altlateinischen Bible, Beuron.

22. P. Maurice Bogaert, "Bulletin de la Bible latine," *RBen*.

23. *On Baptism* 6.34.65: Quietus of Buruc was a Bishop at the Council of 256 who had been consulted by Cyprian on the subject of the re–baptizing of heretics during 256.

24. Cyprian, *Letter* 71.1.1.

25. Augustine suggests to Cresconius the grammarian that he consult the old Greek manuscripts (*maxime graecos*) in order to discover the true meaning of Eccl. 34:25. See *Against Cresconius* 2.27.33.

26. *Questions on the Heptateuch* 4, qu. 33.10: Augustine cites: "He who touches a cadaver, no matter what the manner of death, will be impure for seven days. He will purify himself with water the third and seventh day and he will be pure." Numbers 19:11–12.

27. We should point out that this work has been finished and is found in volumes of *Biblia Augustiniana*, for the following biblical books: Job, Joshua, Judges, Kingdoms (Samuel and Kings), Deuteronomy, the twelve minor prophets, Jeremiah, Wisdom, Proverbs, Esther, Maccabees, Books 2, 1a and 2a of the Epistles to the Thessalonians, the Epistle of Titus, the Epistle of Philemon (see the Bibliography).

28. 1Macc. 2:62 is cited by Crispinus: see *Against Cresconius* 3.46.50; 1Macc. 2:69 is cited in *On Original Sin* 2.30.35; Es. 1:10–11 (this is Esdras' order to the Hebrew commanding them to send away their foreign wives) which had been criticized by Pollentius in *De conjugiis adulterinis* 1.18.20; Esd. 3:8 (apocryphal book) is cited in *Against the Two Letters of the Pelagians* 4.6.14 and in an anti–Pelagian volley. Citations and allusions to Esther all come from the Greek version of the book. They are found in *On Nature and Grace* 36.42; *On the Grace of Christ* 1.24.25; *Against Two Letters of the Pelagians* 1.20.38; *On Grace and Free Choice* 21.42; *Opus imperfectum c. Julianum* 3.114.A, 3.163.A. Outside of the anti–Pelagian treatises, allusions to Esther are sporadic: The following citations affirm Esther's canonicity: *On Christian Doctrine* 2.8.13; *City of God* 18.36. The prayer of Esther is cited in the following: *Commentaries on the Psalms* 52.6 and 53.3; *Letter* 262.10; *Against Two Letters of the Pelagians* 1.20.38; *Commentaries on the Psalms* 118.1– 29.8; *On Christian Doctrine* 4.30.63; *On Grace and Free Choice* 21.42; *Revisions* 1.5.2. It should be noted that few of these citations predate 418.

29. See *Biblia Augustiniana*, historic books, *Paralipommenon* (Chronicles).

30. *On Grace and Free Choice* 21.42: None of this cluster is found in Speculum quis ignorat except for the Pauline text, Rom. 1:24–26–28.

31. *The Fathers of the Church: A New Translation*, Ed. Roy Joseph Deferrari, "Saint Augustine, The *Retractations.*"

32. See A.–M. la Bonnardière, "Quelques remarques sur les citations scripturaires du *De gratia et libero arbitrio*" in *REAug.*, 1963, pp. 77–85. We study in the article the rare citations which are found in *On Grace and Free Choice* belonging to Proverbs, Esther, Chronicles, Kings, Ecclesiasticus, Ezekiel and Deuteronomy. One will also find included a table of citations of Eccl. 15:11–17 throughout Augustine's polemical work. This contains the various biblical versions of these citations.

33. See note 27.

34. See *Traduction oecuménique de la Bible* (TOB), NT, p. 766, n.p: "Enoch is traditionally the seventh patriarch in the genealogy since Adam: Gen. 5:3–18; 1 Chron. 1:1–3; Luke 3:37–38. The explanation of the seventh since Adam is found textually in Enoch 60:8." Jude cites this proof in verses 14–15.

35. *De fide et operibus* 25.46. It is interesting to see Augustine commenting simultaneously on 2 Peter and Jude wherein he had noticed a correspondence.

36. Pierre–Patrick Verbraken, *Etudes critiques sur les sermons authentiques de saint Augustin*, 1976: see the notes concerning *Sermons* 269, 8, 265 and 71.

37. See A.–M. la Bonnardière, *REAug.*

38. *On Baptism* 7.45.88–89. See *TOB*, p. 760, n. *m* : "This rigor, which one also finds in Paul (1 Cor. 5:6–9) is explained by the necessity of preserving a pure Christian faith which is protected from the contagion of heresies."

39. *On Grace and Free Choice* 17.35. All the citations from this paragraph are found in the *Speculum.*

40. *On the Perfection of Human Justice* 19–40: Celestius cites 1 Cor. 7:36; Phil. 13–14; Deut. 30:15, 19; Eccl. 15:14–17 and Is. 1:19–20.

41. Ibid., 19.41.

42. *On Grace and Free Will* 2.4: This is a remarkable series of texts wherein the first word of each scriptural citation is either *Noli* or *Ne.*

43. See *BA* 16, p. 675, which indicates twenty instances of this verse being used.

44. *CSEL* 25, pp. 251–797.

45. Chap. 19–25 (*BA* 11, pp. 94–131).

46. 3, 4.11, 12.20, etc., (*BA* 11, pp. 352–354 and 366).

47. See the debate with Julian of Eclanum in *Against Two Letters of the Pelagians* 3, 4.6–13, *BA* 23, pp.477–500 and the accompanying note on this text by A. C. de Veer, *Les deux testaments selon Augustin*, n. 37, pp. 800–803.

48. Around 400 (see *BA* 29).

49. Undoubtedly from 411 (*BA* 31).

50. One should take note of volumes 21, 23 and 24 of *BA*. Aside from a detailed bibliography, these works provide very complete scriptural indexes and the accompanying notes are often very helpful. I would

like to particularly point out the following: *On Nature and Grace* (*BA* 21, pp. 223–413), *On Marriage and Concupiscence* (*BA* 23, pp. 42–289; note 20 by A. C. de Veer, *Le sens de Rom. 5:12 dans son contexte*, pp. 734–739), *Against Two Letters of the Pelagians* (*BA*, pp.293–657 and notes 26 and 27 by A. C. de Veer, *Le sens de Rom. 14:23b*, pp. 764–770 and *L'exégèse de Rom. 7 et ses variations*, pp.770–778).

51. See *Letter 167* to Hillary 1.2 and 11.5 (*BA* 21, pp.36–111); *On the Perfection of Human Justice*: sixteen citations (*BA* 21, pp. 126–219); and *On Nature and Grace*, seven citations (*BA* 21, pp. 223–413) etc.

52. Initiated by the attacks of Julian against *On Marriage and Concupiscence* and his reply to Augustine's *Against Two Letters of the Pelagians* which was based upon two letters inspired by Julian, the debate was developed in *Against Julianus* (*PL* 44) and *Opus Imperfectum contra Julianum* from 428–430 (*PL* 45).

53. Circumstances have constrained to suspend this research.

13

Augustine, the Manichees and the Bible

ROLAND J. TESKE, S.J.

Augustine engaged in polemics with many heretical groups such as the Donatists, the Pelagians, and the Arians, but his confrontation with the Manichees is unique insofar as he himself had been a member of that sect for some nine years as a "hearer" or layman, as opposed to one of the "elect," or priestly class.[1] This essay will deal with the role the Bible played in Augustine's conversion to Manichaeism, with the Bible he knew as a Manichee, and with his use of the Bible against the Manichees after his baptism.

1. The Bible and Augustine's Conversion to Manichaeism

In his nineteenth year Augustine read the *Hortensius* of Cicero, a work now lost save for some fragments. This work contained an exhortation to the life of philosophy and set the young Augustine aflame with the love for wisdom.[2] One thing, he tells us, held him back: "the name of Christ was absent...and whatever was without that name, no matter how literary and polished and true, could not completely carry me off."[3] Hence, Augustine turned to a study of the Scriptures, but he found them unworthy of comparison with the lofty style of Cicero. The style of the Old Latin version was indeed barbarous, but Augustine found the content objectionable as well.[4] For this reason Augustine fell in with the Manichees, from whose lips the names of the Father "and of the Lord, Jesus Christ, and of the Paraclete, our comforter, the Holy Spirit," were never absent.[5] The *Hortensius* set Augustine aflame with the love of truth, and the Manichees unceasingly spoke of the Truth which they promised to teach without first imposing the burden of believing. In *The Usefulness of Belief*

Augustine writes to his friend, Honoratus, whom he had converted to Manichaeism and would now draw back to Catholicism, that

> we fell in with such men for no other reason than that they kept saying that, apart from the terror of authority, they would, by pure and simple reason, lead to God and free from all error those who were willing to be their hearers.[6]

The African Church seems to have preserved the anti–intellectual spirit of Tertullian who was famous for his claim to believe precisely because it is absurd.[7] Reflections of such anti–intellectualism are found in Augustine's warning that there were within the Church bishops and priests who, "content with simple faith, have no concern for a deeper knowledge."[8] Similarly, Augustine mentions, in dealing with the Manichaean question about what God was doing before he created the world, that he will not give the answer that some give that God was preparing hell for those who ask such profound questions.[9]

The heart of Augustine's intellectual problems centered, as he later realized, around his inability to conceive of God and the soul as incorporeal.[10] Like the rest of the Western world apart from a few Neo–platonists, Augustine shared the implicit materialist metaphysics typified by Tertullian's insistence that, if it is not a body, it is not real.[11] Such a materialism resulted in serious metaphysical problems.[12] But such a materialism also resulted in serious problems for a literal interpretation of the Bible. For example, given such a materialism, God and the soul must be bodily, and the Manichees, themselves materialists in this sense, could use the claim in Genesis that man was made in God's image to argue that the Catholics thought of God as having human form and bodily parts.[13] If, after all, God is bodily, as humans obviously are, then human beings can hardly be the image of God unless God has a human body with hair and nails. In *On Genesis against the Manichees* Augustine points out that it was this question in particular that the Manichees used to raise against us:

> ...because we believe that man was made to the image and likeness of God. For they attend to the shape of our body and ask in their unfortunate way whether God has a nose, teeth, a beard, interior organs and the other things we need.[14]

Another serious problem with the Old Testament for the young Augustine of 373 was the immoral lives of the Patriarchs. Augustine has preserved for us the objections raised by Faustus, the Manichaean bishop. Faustus accuses Abraham of "burning with an insane desire for offspring,

209

not believing God who had promised him a child from Sarah, and having intercourse with a servant with — what is more shameful — his wife's knowledge." He accuses Abraham of lying to Abimelech and Pharaoh, claiming that Sarah was his sister and selling her into concubinage. He mentions Lot's incest with his daughters. And he becomes most indignant over Jacob's bigamous marriages to Rachel and Leah along with his relations with two servants, claiming that, "as the husband of four wives, he wandered among them like a goat," while they fought over who would have him each day as he returned from the field.[15] Secundinus, the Manichee, in writing to Augustine and inviting him to return to Manichaeism, lists such contents of the Old Testament and adds, "I know you always hated these things; I know you always loved great things that would leave the earth behind and seek the heavens, that would put the body to death and bring life to souls."[16] Even the Gospels presented serious problems. For example, the genealogies of Christ in Matthew and Luke seem to contradict each other. Hence, both cannot be true. In fact, Augustine suggests that it was precisely the contradictions between the two genealogies that led him to abandon the Catholics for the Manichees.[17]

2. The Bible Augustine Knew as a Manichee

The Manichees not merely claimed to be Christian, but regarded the Catholics as only semi–Christian, largely because the Catholics retained the Jewish Scriptures.[18] In becoming a Manichee, Augustine would not have thought of himself as abandoning Christianity, but as becoming a member of Christianity's intellectual elite. Peter Brown compares Manichaeism to British Communism during the 30s and claims that the Manichaeism of Augustine was that "of the cultivated intelligentsia."[19] Though we now think of Manichaeism as a distinct world religion, like Islam, Augustine viewed it, after his baptism in the Catholic Church, as a Christian heresy.[20] But as a Manichee, Augustine would have thought of Manichaeism as the true and full Christianity, and he would have read or heard the Gospels and St. Paul.[21] Johannes Van Oort claims that "Manichaeism was so much imbued with Christianity and specifically with Pauline teachings that O'Meara could write...: "In a sense it might seem that to become a Manichee was to depart little, if at all, from being a Christian."[22] Within the Manichaean community the New Testament held a place roughly analogous to that of the Old Testament within the Catholic Church, while the Manichaean scriptures held a position like that of the New Testament in the Catholic community.[23] The Manichees rejected

210

the Old Testament almost in its entirety, but they certainly were familiar with it and used it to undermine the faith of the uneducated Catholics and to lure them into their communion.[24]

François Decret has summed up the Manichaean arguments against the Old Testament under three headings: 1) The Manichees argue that the Old Testament is its own undoing, since its prophecies have not been fulfilled, its Law is immoral and grotesque, and its principal personages led immoral and disgusting lives. 2) They argue that Christ himself rejected the Old Testament, and 3) They argue that, in the name of the New Testament, Christians reject the Law, and they point out that even the Catholics, who claim to retain the Old Testament, do not observe its Law.[25]

Moreover, the Manichees rejected from the New Testament the Acts of the Apostles. In fact, they were reluctant even to mention it, because this book reported the coming of the Paraclete, whom the Manicheans held to be Mani himself.[26] They even rejected parts of the Gospels and of the Letters of Paul, claiming that they had been interpolated by someone else who introduced Jewish elements into the Christian Bible. Hence, for all practical purposes the Bible for the Manichees was the Gospel and the Apostle, though without the passages they rejected as interpolations.[27]

For the Manichees the Gospel meant, in essence, the moral teaching of Christ. When asked whether he accepts the Gospel, Faustus replies that he certainly does, but insists that "the Gospel began to be and received its name from the preaching of Christ."[28] Faustus thus excludes the genealogies and infancy narratives from the Gospel, rejecting the claim that Christ was the son of David and born of a human mother. "The Gospel is not genealogy," he tells us; it is rather "the preaching of Christ" or "of the Son of God."[29] Again asked whether he accepts the Gospel, Faustus insists that he does accept it, namely, "the preaching and command of Christ."[30] He points to the life of the beatitudes he himself is living and to the fact that Christ promised the kingdom of heaven to those who do his Father's will and who keep his commands. He adds, "Nowhere did he say, 'Blessed are those who confess that I was born.'"[31] Given their rejection of the genealogies and the birth of Christ from Mary, the Manichees had to deny the reality of Christ's death and His Resurrection. The wounds he showed to the doubting Thomas had, accordingly, to be merely simulated.[32]

Even in the Letters of Paul there are passages that Faustus has to reject as falsified, for example, that "the Son of God was born according to the flesh of the seed of David" (Rom 1:3). He claims this reflects "an old and former opinion of Paul concerning Jesus, when he considered him the son of David, as the rest did." As proof of his claim, he invokes the text, "If we once knew Christ according to the flesh, we do not now know him," (2 Cor. 5:16), to show that Paul later corrected his earlier belief.[33] On the other hand the Manichees accepted various apocryphal books, such as The Acts of Thomas, as well as those of Peter, John, Andrew and those written by a certain Leutius.[34]

Augustine later recounts how he used to enjoy his victories over the uneducated Catholics, which suggests that he had once used against them some of the same arguments from the Old Testament that he later answered in his writings against the Manichees.[35] Moreover, he mentions that the Manichees praised Mani, especially because "he spoke the bare and proper truth with all the wrappings of figures removed."[36] Later Augustine would hold them in turn to a literal interpretation of one of their own writings that described God as "a scepter–bearing king crowned with garlands of flowers."[37] But the Manichaean boast about their books presenting the bare and proper truth without figures also indicated the typically Manichaean demand for the literal interpretation of the Catholic Scriptures. Augustine would come to learn that such a literal interpretation was fatal: "The letter kills"(2 Cor. 3:6).

3. The Use of the Bible against the Manichees

Augustine's use of the Bible in controversy with the Manichees can be conveniently examined under three headings: a) the canon of the Scriptures, b) the proper approach to the Bible, and c) the interpretation of the biblical text.

a) The Canonical Scriptures

The Manichees, as we have seen, rejected the Old Testament, as well as the Acts of the Apostles and various passages from the Gospels and Paul which they claimed had been added later. Augustine, on the other hand, insisted upon the canonical Scriptures, appealing to the authority of those books.[38] Thus Augustine holds the authority of those Scriptures are preeminent, which from the time of Christ's presence have come down to our times, preserved, recommended and rendered illustrious in the whole world through the ministry of the Apostles and the certain succession of bishops in their sees.[39]

Similarly, he tells the Manichees "that the authority of our books, strengthened by the assent of so many nations through the successions of apostles, bishops, and councils, is against you."[40] The credibility even of the Gospel rests upon the authority of the Church. In his *Reply to the Letter called Fundamental*, Augustine states, "I would not believe the Gospel, if the authority of the Catholic Church did not move me."[41]

Against the Manichaean claims that the New Testament contains passages added by later writers who interjected elements from the Jewish Scriptures, Augustine insists upon the integrity of the Scriptures handed down in the Church. He mentions that, even while he was a Manichee, he had regarded as feeble the Manichaean claim "that the New Testament writings were falsified by some unknown persons who wished to implant the law of the Jews in the Christian faith."[42] Augustine points out that, though the Manichees accept the authority of Paul's Letters as the work of a holy man who speaks the truth, they claim that certain passages are not his. When challenged, they cannot produce better exemplars from more, or more ancient, manuscripts or from those in the original language. Rather, they accept one passage as Paul's because it supports them and reject another because it is against them. To this Augustine retorts, "Are you then the standard of truth (*regula ueritatis*)?"[43] The Manichaean selectivity amounts to the destruction of all the authority of Scripture and makes each one his own authority.[44] But this means that the Manichee "is not subject to the authority of the Scriptures in faith, but subjects the Scriptures to himself...so that he views something in Scripture as correct, because he finds it congenial."[45] Hence, Augustine insists upon the canonical Scriptures handed down in the Church from apostolic times and insists that whatever is stated in the Bible is true, though one may very well not understand how it is true.

b) Humble belief before understanding

In approaching the Bible Augustine insists, first of all, that one accept as true what is stated there. It is this humble act of believing before understanding that is the key to the Catholic Augustine's approach to the Bible. Whereas the Manichees constantly repeated Mt. 7:7 "Ask and you shall receive, seek and you shall find, knock and it will be opened," and Mt. 10:26, "There is nothing hidden that will not be revealed," they refused to believe, that is , to accept as true, any passage of the Bible before they understood it.[46] From Is. 7:9, which in Augustine's Old Latin read, "Unless you believe, you will not understand," Augustine argued for the need for humble intellectual submission to the Word of God as the first step toward understanding. He tells Faustus, "The Catholic discipline teaches that the Christian mind should first be nourished by simple faith so that such faith may render it able to understand lofty and eternal things."[47] Thus when confronted with the apparent contradiction between the two genealogies, one must read the Gospels with piety and investigate diligently rather than condemn them rashly.[48] In preaching to his own flock Augustine presented the Manichaean argument and insisted upon the need for "simple and certain faith" until the Lord grants understanding.[49] When Augustine first confronted the difficulties with the Bible that lead him into the company of the Manichees, he had, he later reports, "disdained to be a little beginner. Puffed up with pride" he considered himself "a mature adult." He had not realized that "the Bible was composed in such a way that as beginners mature, its meaning grows with them."[50]

c) The interpretation of Scripture

It is sometimes assumed that Augustine set aside the Bible in 373 when he became a Manichee and did not return to it until after his ordination in 391 when he asked his bishop, Valerius, for time to study the Scriptures.[51] Augustine did ask Valerius for time to study the Scriptures.[52] But it was not that Augustine was unfamiliar with the Bible; he had, after all, been acquainted with the Gospel and the Apostle during his Manichaean years. He certainly knew the Manichaean complaints about the Old Testament. Indeed, he had already by 388 or 389 written his first commentary on the Bible, *On Genesis against the Manichees*.

At this point Augustine accepted the whole of the canonical Scriptures. He needed time, not for a better acquaintance with the Bible, but for the diligent and pious study that would lead to a Catholic understanding of what he now believed to be true. In other words, having come to a Manichaean understanding of the Bible during his nine years as a "hearer," Augustine now needed time to come to a new understanding of the Bible in accord with the rule of faith in the Catholic Church.

Well before his baptism, Augustine was influenced by the preaching of Ambrose who interpreted the Bible spiritually. As a result of first hearing Ambrose preach, probably late in 384, Augustine began to think that the Catholic faith could be defended against the Manichaean attacks:

> ...especially after I had often heard [Ambrose] resolve one or another puzzle [*aenigmate*] from the Old Testament, where I was being killed, when I understood it literally.[53]

Ambrose gave a spiritual interpretation of many passages from those books, and Augustine came to see that the Law and the Prophets could be defended. The *Confessions* record a second influence of Ambrose's preaching, which probably dates from late in 385. At this point Augustine discovered that the spiritual sons of God did not interpret man's being made in God's image and likeness so that it implied that God himself had the shape and members of a human body, though Augustine still had no idea of what a spiritual substance was. In his sermons Ambrose taught that:

> ..."the letter kills, but that the spirit gives life," when he removed the mystical veil and uncovered the spiritual sense of those things which in their literal meaning seemed to contain a perverse doctrine.[54]

Augustine was then no longer offended by what Ambrose said, but he still did not know whether what he said was true.

What Augustine still needed was the philosophical concept of a non–bodily or spiritual substance which he was to get from "the books of the Platonists," which he read in late spring or summer of 386.[55] Ambrose himself was a student of Neo–platonic thought, along with a group of Milanese intellectuals, so that the sermons of Ambrose that Augustine heard were deeply imbued with Neo–platonic spiritualism.[56] As long as Augustine was unable to conceive of an incorporeal substance, he was unable to interpret the anthropomorphic descriptions of God in the Bible as metaphors for a spiritual reality. That is, what Augustine needed was precisely the philosophical concept of a non–bodily reality, and that he got from the books of the Platonists.[57]

Thus in *On Genesis Against the Manichees*, Augustine's first attempt at biblical interpretation, he speaks of literal interpretation as taking the text "just as the letter sounds."[58] On the other hand, he illustrates what he means by spiritual interpretation when he says:

> ...all those who understand the Scriptures spiritually have learned to understand by those terms [God's eyes, ears, feet, and other parts] not bodily members, but spiritual powers..."[59]

Thus "spiritual interpretation" presupposes some grasp of a spiritualist metaphysics, for unless one can conceive of incorporeal realities, one cannot interpret a text that uses bodily images as referring to non–bodily realities.

In two of his early attempts at biblical exegesis, Augustine mentions four ways of interpreting the Old Testament for those who diligently desire to know it: as history, as etiology, as analogy, and as allegory.[60] In *The Usefulness of Belief*, Augustine explains that a text is presented "as history, when it teaches what was written or what was done, or what was not done, but is only written as if it were done." Thus something is presented as history as long as it is in narrative form, whether the events occurred or not. The text is presented "as etiology, when we are shown the reason why something was said or done," and the text is presented "as analogy, when it is shown that the two Testaments, the New and the Old, are not opposed to each other." Finally, the text is presented "as allegory, when one is taught that certain things which are written there are not to be interpreted literally, but should be understood as figurative."[61] Augustine shows that Christ and the Apostles used these ways of understanding the Law and the Prophets. For example, Jesus recalled as history how David and his men had eaten loaves from the Temple (Mt. 12:3–4) and explained as etiology why Moses had permitted divorce (Mt. 19:8).[62] Augustine does not give here a concrete example of understanding the text by analogy, but Augustine's work, *Against Adimantus*, written in 393 or 394 against a disciple of Mani, a man regarded as a great teacher in that sect and as second in learning only to Mani himself, provides twenty–nine cases of alleged conflict between the two Testaments and Augustine's replies.[63] With regard to allegory Augustine points out that "our Liberator" used it in appealing to the sign of Jonah (Mt. 12:39–40) and that Paul used it in 1 Cor.10:1–10, where Paul says, "These things were figures of us" and "All these things happened to [the fathers in the desert] in figures." So too, he appeals to Gal. 4:22–26, where Paul, speaking of the two sons of Abraham, says, "These things were said in allegory."[64]

The thirty-three books of Augustine's *Against Faustus* provide a wealth of examples of Augustine's interpretation of Scripture in controversy with the Manichees. Augustine states several general principles that he invokes in answering Faustus. For instance, when Faustus is asked whether he accepts the Old Testament, he answers, "How can I, when I do not observe its commandments?" and adds, "I don't think you do either."[65] He is referring to the Sabbath, circumcision, the sacrifices, abstinence from pork, and the observances of feasts, for he regards the moral precepts of the Decalogue as the law of the nations.[66] Augustine distinguishes between "commandments for living life" and "commandments for signifying life" and claims that "You shall not covet" is a commandment for living life, while the commandment to circumcise the male child is a commandment signifying life. The Manichees, he argues, fail to see that the practice of latter commandments were signs or shadows of what was to come about and that, once the reality foreshadowed has come about, the signs signifying its coming need no longer be observed.[67] The Catholics observe everything in the Old Testament, "not now in figures, but in the reality which those figures foretold by what they signified."[68] Thus Augustine can maintain that the Catholics hold that "everything written in the Old Testament is true and commanded by God and adapted to those times."[69] The teaching of both Testaments is found in both the Old and the New, "there in figures, here revealed, there in prophecy, here rendered present."[70]

Secondly, the Manichees denied that the Old Testament spoke of Christ at all, whether by foreshadowing him or by prophesying about him. Augustine, on the other hand, makes the rather bold claim that:

> ...everything that Moses wrote is about Christ, that is, pertains to Christ completely, either because it foretells him by figures of things done or said, or because it recommends his grace and glory.[71]

Or, still more generally, he says, "The Old Testament is, for those who understand correctly, a prophecy of the New Testament."[72] Speaking of the Prophets, Augustine says "everything contained in those books was said about [Christ] or on account of him. But in order to incite the seeker and to delight the finder, many more things are taught there in allegories. and enigmas, in part by words alone, in part by the narration of events."[73] Hence, Augustine charges the Manichees with abusing the marvellous work of the Holy Spirit in those books, in which:

> ...many things are stated simply and in a way suited to those souls that creep on the ground so that they may rise up through human things to things divine, and many things are stated there in figures so that the studious mind may be more profitably exercised in its inquiries and may rejoice more richly in its discoveries.[74]

NOTES

1. Cf. *Against Faustus* 30.1, *CSEL* 25/1, 748, where Faustus speaks of the Elect as a sacerdotal rank as opposed to the Hearers; cf. also *Against Faustus* 30.5: *CSEL* 25/1, 753.
2. Cf. *Confessions* 3.4.7–8: *CC* 27, 29–30.
3. *Confessions* 3.4.8: *CC* 27.30.
4. Cf. H. Chadwick, *Augustine* (Oxford and New York: Oxford University Press, 1986), p. 11.
5. Cf. *Confessions* 3.6.10: *CC* 27.31.
6. *On the Usefulness of Belief* 1.2: *CSEL* 25/1, 4.
7. Tertullian asked, in *De praescription haereticorum* 7.9: *CC* 1.193, what Athens has to do with Jerusalem and what the Academy has to do with the Church. In *De carne Christi* 5.4: *CC* 2.81, he stated that he believed in the death of the Son of God because it is absurd (*ineptum*) and in His Resurrection because it is impossible.

8. *On the Morals of the Catholic Church and On the Morals of the Manichaeans* 1.1.1: *PL* 32.1311; cf. also the Manichaean claim that Catholics say that "one should not inquire into anything with curiosity, because Christian belief is simple and absolute" (*Against Faustus* 12.1: *CSEL* 25/1, 329) which echoes Tertullian's claim that "we have no need for curiosity after Christ Jesus, of inquiry after the Gospel" (*De praesciptione haereticorum* 7.12: CC 2.193.)

9. Cf. *Confessions* 9.7.14: CC 27.201. Cf. E. Peters, "What was God doing before he created the Heavens and the Earth?" *Augustiniana* 34 (1984) 53–74; Peters traces the question back to the Epicureans, who suggested that the gods were sleeping, and to the Gnostics who gave the question the above formulation.

10. Cf. *Confessions* 5.10.19–20: CC 27.68.

11. For example, in *De carne Christi* 11.4: CC 2.895, he says, "*Omne, quod est, corpus est sui generis. Nihil incorporale nisi quod non est,*" and in *De anima* 7.3: CC 2.790, he says, "*Nihil enim, si non corpus.*" On the Stoic position that whatever is is a body, cf. E. Weil, "Remarques sur le 'matérialisme' des Stoïciens," in *Mélanges Alexandre Koyré. II. L'aventure de l'esprit* (Paris: Hermann, 1964), pp. 556–572. Cf. *Confessions* 5.10.19: CC 27.68–69: "*cogitare nisi moles corporum non noveram—neque enim uidebatur mihi esse quicquam quod tale non esset.*"

12. For some of the metaphysical implications, cf. my "The Aim of Augustine's Proof that God Truly Is," *International Philosophical Quarterly* 26 (1986) 253–268.

13. Cf. *Confessions* 3.7.12: CC 27.33.

14. Cf. *Confessions* 5.10.19 and 6.11.18: CC 27.68–69 and 86, where Augustine obviously finds such an anthropomorphic view of God quite disgusting. He had, nonetheless, been convinced that the Catholic Church held such a view. Cf. *Confessions* 6.4.5 and 6.11.18: CC 27.76–77 and 86, for his joy at finding that the spiritual believers in the Catholic Church did not hold such a view.

15. Cf. *Against Faustus* 22.5: *CSEL* 25/1:594.

16. *Secundini Manichaei ad sanctum Augustinum epistula* 3: *CSEL* 25/2, 897.

17. Cf. *Sermon* 51.6: *PL* 38.336–337.

18. *Against Faustus* 1.2: *CSEL* 25/1, 251.

19. Peter Brown, *Augustine of Hippo: A Biography* (Berkeley: University of California Press, 1969), p.54.

20. Cf. his *De haeresibus* 46.1–19: CC 46.312–320.

21. Cf. P. Brown, *Augustine of Hippo*, pp. 370–371, where he discusses the "Letter to Menoch," attributed to Mani by some scholars, which contains a fragment of a Manichaean commentary on Paul.

22. J. Van Oort, *Jerusalem and Babylon. A Study of St. Augustine's City of God and the Sources of His Doctrine of the Two Cities* (Leiden: E. J. Brill, 1991), p. 208. Van Oort cites J. O'Meara's *The Young Augustine. The Growth of St.*

Augustine's Mind up to his Conversion (New York: Longmans, 1954), p. 79, where O'Meara is speaking specifically of one becoming a Hearer.

23. Van Oort and other recent scholars argue that the Christian elements in Manichaeism were present from the beginning and not simply syncretistic additions to African Manichaeism, as had previously been thought. Cf. Van Oort, *Jerusalem and Babylon,*pp. 229–231. Cf. also F. Decret, *Aspects du Manichéisme dans l'Afrique romaine* (Paris: Etudes Augustiniennes, 1970), pp. 11–12.

24. Cf. *On Genesis Against the Manichaeans* 1.1.2: *PL* 34.73. Van Oort claims that Manichees did not reject the Old Testament completely, since there is some good mixed with the bad; cf. *Jerusalem and Babylon*, p. 35, n. 104.

25. Cf. F. Decret, *Aspects du Manichéisme*, pp. 146–149.

26. For the rejection of Acts, cf. *Against Adimantus* 17.5, *CSEL* 25/1, 169–170; *Against the Letter called Fundamental* 5: *CSEL* 25/1, 198–199; *On the Usefulness of Belief* 3.7: *CSEL* 25/1, 9–10; *Against Faustus* 19.31 and 32.15: *CSEL* 25/1:534–535 and 774–775.

27. F. Decret's study of Augustine's works, *Against Fortunatus Against Faustus*, and *Against Felix*, has shown that these Manichees referred most frequently to Matthew (58 references to 42 passages). Next came John's Gospel with 30 references to 23 passages, followed by the Pauline Letters. Cf. F. Decret, *Aspects du Manichéisme*, pp. 169–173.

28. *Against Faustus* 2.1: *CSEL* 25/1, 253.

29. Cf.*Against Faustus* II,1: *CSEL* 25/1, 254.

30. *Against Faustus* 5.1: *CSEL* 25/1, 271.

31. *Against Faustus* 5.3: *CSEL* 25/1, 273.

32. Cf. *Against Faustus* 15.10 and 16.11: *CSEL* 25/1, 437 and 450, where Augustine accuses Faustus of preaching a Christ with false or pretended wounds.

33. *Against Faustus* 11.1: *CSEL* 25/1, 313.

34. Cf. *Against Adimantus* 17.2 and 5: *CSEL* 25/1, 166 and 170. *Against Faustus* 22.79 and 30.4: *CSEL* 25/1, 681 and 751–752. *Against Felix* 2.6: *CSEL* 25/2, 833.

35. Cf. *On Two Souls* 11: *CSEL* 25/1, 65–66.

36. *Against Faustus* 15.5: *CSEL* 25/1, 425.

37. *Against Faustus* 15.5–6: *CSEL* 25/1, 425–426.

38. One must bear in mind that there was not at this time an official Catholic canon of Scripture and that Augustine himself contributed to its formation at the first Council of Hippo in 393. Cf. *Breviarium Hipponense* 36: *CC* 149.43.

39. *Against Faustus* 33.9: *CSEL* 25/1, 796.

40. *Against Faustus* 8.5: *CSEL* 25/1, 382.

41. *Against the Letter called Fundamental* 5: *CSEL* 25/1, 197.

42. *Confessions* 5.6.21: *CC* 27.69; cf. also *On the Usefulness of Belief* 3.7: *CSEL* 25/1, 9–10.

43 *Against Faustus* 11.2: *CSEL* 25/1, 315.

44. Cf. *Against Faustus* 32.19: *CSEL* 25, 780: "You see, then, that your action removes all authority and each mind becomes an authority unto itself for what it approves or disapproves in any Scripture." So too, he claims, "You who believe what you will and do not believe what you will in the Gospel believe yourselves rather than the Gospel" (*Against Faustus* 17.3: *CSEL* 25/1, 486).

45. *Against Faustus* 32.19: *CSEL* 25/1, 780.

46 Cf. *On the Morals of the Catholic Church and On the Morals of the Manichaeans* 1.17.31: *PL* 32, 1324

47. *Against Faustus* 12.46: *CSEL* 25/1, 374–375.

48. *Against Faustus* 3.2: *CSEL* 25/1, 262.

49. Cf. *Sermon 51.5: PL* 38.336. In *Against Faustus* 3.3: *CSEL* 25/1, 263, Augustine argues that the two fathers of Joseph can be readily explained by one being his natural father and the other his father by adoption.

50. *Confessions* 3.5.9: *CC* 27.31. I have here followed H. Chadwick's new translation (Oxford: Oxford University Press, 1991). For the role of the little ones or beginners as opposed to the adults or spirituals, cf. my "A Decisive Admonition for Augustine," *Augustinian Studies* 19 (1988) 85–92.

51. Cf. V. Bourke, *Augustine's Quest for Wisdom. Life and Philosophy of the Bishop of Hippo.* (Milwaukee: Bruce, 1944), p. 125, where Bourke says that "he simply had not had time since his conversion to become well acquainted with the Bible."

52. *Letter* 21.3–4 (ad Valerium): *CSEL* XXIV, 49–54.

53. *Confessions* 5.16.24: *CC* 27.71.

54. *Confessions* 6.4.6: *CC* 27.77.

55. Cf. *Confessions* 7.4.13: *CC* 27.101. The Platonists in question were certainly Plotinus and possibly Porphyry, Plotinus's student and editor. Precisely which of Plotinus's *Enneads* and which works of Porphyry Augustine read is debated. As an example of this debate, cf. the articles by Frederick Van Fleteren and Robert O'Connel in *Augustinian Studies* 21 (1990) 83–152.

56. Cf. the studies by Courcelle which have shown that Augustine's conversion to Neo–platonism was not a conversion to a non–Christian philosophy. Rather he learned his Platonism within the Church of Milan; cf. P. Courcelle's *Recherches sur les Confessions de saint Augustin* (Paris: de Boccard, 1950), especially chapter 3.

57. Cf. my "Spirituals and Spiritual Interpretation in Augustine," *Augustinian Studies* 15 (1984) 65–81.

58. *On Genesis against the Manichaeans* 2.2.3: *PL* 32. 197. Here literal interpretation excludes even such common figures of speech as metaphor and metonymy; it is not coincident with what the human author intended.

59. *On Genesis against the Manichaeans* 1.17.27: *PL* 34.186.

60. Cf. *On the Profit of Belief* 3.5: *CSEL* 25/1, 7–8 and *Literal Interpretation of Genesis, An Unfinished Book* 2.5: *CSEL* 28/1, 461.
61. *On the Usefulness of Belief* 3.5: *CSEL* 25/1, 8.
62. *On the Usefulness of Belief* 3.6: *CSEL* 25/1, 8.
63. On Adimantus, cf. *Against Faustus* 1.2: *CSEL* 25/1, 252 and *Against Adimantus* 7.2: *CSEL* 25/1, 139.
64. *On the Usefulness of Belief* 3.6–8: *CSEL* 25/1, 10–12.
65. *Against Faustus* 6.1: *CSEL* 25/1, 284.
66. In *Against Faustus* 19.2: *CSEL* 25/1, 497, Faustus distinguished "three kinds of law: one is that of the Hebrews which Paul calls the law of sin and death, the second is that of the nations, which he calls natural...and the third kind of law is the truth..."
67. *Against Faustus* 6.2: *CSEL* 25/1, 285–286.
68. *Against Faustus* 16.32: *CSEL* 25/1, 481.
69. *Against Faustus* 10.3: *CSEL* 25/1, 311.
70. *Against Faustus* 16.32: *CSEL* 25/1, 481.
71. *Against Faustus* 16.9: *CSEL* 25/1, 447.
72. *Against Faustus* 15.2: *CSEL* 25/1, 419.
73. *Against Faustus* 12.7: *CSEL* 25/1, 335–336.
74. *On the Morals of the Catholic Church and On the Morals of the Manichaeans* 1.17.30: *PL* 32.1324.

14

Augustine, Sermon 50,
Against the Manichees

ON WHAT IS WRITTEN IN THE PROPHET HAGGAI:
"MINE IS THE GOLD AND MINE IS THE SILVER"

Edmund Hill O.P. *The Works of Saint Augustine–A Translation for the 21st Century:*
Sermons II (20–50) (New York Press, N.Y.: 1990, pages 345; 349-351).

—DATE: before 396

1. The Manichees cast a slur on the prophet Haggai, and blame him unfairly for what he said, with God speaking in person, Mine is the gold and mine is the silver (Hg 2:8). They are always eager to make contentious comparisons between the gospel and the old law, to show up each part of scripture as contradicting and disagreeing with the other, and so they put the question like this: "In the prophet Haggai," they say, "it's written, Mine is the gold and mine is the silver; but in the gospel our savior called this kind of iniquity mammon (Lk 16:9), and the blessed apostle wrote about its use to Timothy with the words, But the root of all evils is avarice, which some people, setting their hearts on, have turned away from the faith and involved themselves in many sorrows (1 Tm 6:10)."

That's how they set the question; or rather it's how they bring a charge against the old scriptures, through which the gospel was foretold, from the gospel which was foretold through them. If they had really set a question, they might have done some questioning perhaps, and if they had done some questioning, they might perhaps have found a solution.

2. Why do the poor wretches not understand the reason why the Lord, speaking in Haggai, said Mine is the gold and mine is the silver? It's in order that those who don't want to share what they have with the poor should understand when they hear the commandments about show-

ing pity that God is not ordering them to give away their own property but his; and that those who do make handouts to the poor should not assume they are doing it with what belongs to them, or else instead of being confirmed in the role of mercy, they would perhaps be puffed up with the hot air of pride. Mine, he says, is the gold and mine is the silver, not yours, you wealthy ones of the earth. So why do you shy away from giving from what is mine to the poor, or why, when you do give from what is mine, do you think so highly of yourselves?

3. And do you want to see how just a judge gold and silver are the property of? They bring torment to the soul of the miser, they are a great help to the plans of the kindhearted. As the divine justice distributes its property, good deeds are thereby publicized and sins are thereby punished. Gold and silver, you see, and every kind of earthly possession are both a means of exercising humanity and of punishing greed. When God bestows such things on good people, he shows by their example how many things are thought lightly of by the mind whose real wealth is the one who bestowed them. After all, it can only be obvious that you think lightly of something if it has come into your possession. Of course, even people who don't have such things can think lightly of them. But whether they are pretending, or really are uninterested, only God, who is the inspector of hearts, can see. People, on the other hand, if they are to imitate such virtue, can only observe the spirit of genuine indifference to wealth in the hands that are giving it away.

When, on the other hand, God concedes such things to bad people, he shows by their example how even the actual good things that God lavishes on us may cause agonies to the mind, to which the giver of such largesse has grown cheap. The good he provides with opportunities to do good; the bad he torments with fear of possible losses. And that's why, if either sort lose their gold and silver, the first will retain their heavenly wealth with a light heart, while the latter will find both their houses empty of temporal goods, and of eternal goods their consciences emptier still....

9. It should, though, be obvious that the Manichees are in their usual way misrepresenting what the prophet says. Anyone who gives even a cursory glance at the context of this passage will discover that the prophet was not talking about this silver or gold which puts silly Avarice in a frenzy, but rather about the sort which the apostle mentions when he says, But if anyone builds on the foundation of gold and silver, precious stones ... (1 Cor 3:12). This gold and silver constitutes that rich treasure which the Lord himself assures us was found in a field by a marvellously

and admirably avaricious man, who sold everything he had to buy it. The prophet, you see, is in his accustomed figurative way foretelling the Lord himself and the times of the new age, that is of the Church, when he says, There is still one little while, and I will shake heaven and earth, and sea and dry land, and I will set all the nations quaking. And there shall come the one desired by all the nations, and I will fill this house with glory, says the Lord of hosts. Mine is the gold and mine is the silver, says the Lord of hosts. Great shall be the glory of this latest house, more than of the first, says the Lord of hosts. And in this place I will give peace, says the Lord of hosts (Hg 2:6–9).

10. If these people were willing not to be dogs to whom we are told not to give what is holy, or pigs before whom we are forbidden to cast pearls, but instead really desired to ask and receive, to seek and find, to knock and be opened to, how soon they would be able to perceive, perhaps even without the help of any commentator and under the guidance of the Holy Spirit himself, that all this refers without any obscurity to the new people's, that is the Christian people's, whose high priest is Jesus the Son of God at the very least in the place where it says, There is still one little while, and I will shake heaven and earth, and sea and dry land, and I will set all the nations quaking. And there shall come the one desired by all the nations.

Clearly it is about the latest, that is to say the second, coming of the Lord, when he is going to come in glory, that this verse is uttered when the prophet says, And there shall come the one desired by all the nations. After all, when he first came in mortal flesh by the virgin Mary, he was not yet desired by all the nations, because they had not yet believed. But now that the gospel seed has been scattered abroad through all the nations, the desire of him is kindled among all nations. Throughout all the nations, you see, there are and there will be his elect, who say with all their heart in prayer, Your kingdom come (Mt 6:10). But his first coming sowed the seed of mercy before that of judgment, while it is in judgment that the glory of his second coming will be conspicuously revealed.

First, therefore, it was necessary for the heavens to be shaken, when the angel announced to the virgin that she would conceive him, when a star led the magi to worship him, when angels yet again told the shepherds where he was born; for the earth to be shaken, when it was disturbed by his miracles; for the sea to be shaken, when this world roared and raged with persecutions; for the dry land to be shaken when those who believed in him hungered and thirsted for justice; finally, "for all the nations to be shaken" when his gospel ran everywhere to and fro. Then at last would come the one desired by all the nations, as indeed according to the prophecy he is going to come. And "this house shall be filled with glory," that is the Church.

11. And so it was only after that he added, Mine is the silver and gold. All wisdom, you see, which is metaphorically signified by the name of gold, and the sayings of the Lord, sayings that are chaste, silver assayed in the fire of the earth, seven times refined (Ps 12:6), so all such silver and gold is not men's but the Lord's, in order that whoever glories (since the house shall be filled with glory) may glory in the Lord (2 Cor 10:17). That high priest, you see, who dwells in this house, our Lord Jesus Christ, was pleased to offer himself as an example of humility, to ensure the return of man who had gone out from paradise through pride, as he declares in the gospel when he cries out, Learn of me, for I am meek and humble of heart (Mt 11:29). Therefore, to prevent anyone in his house, that is in the Church, from getting a swollen head if he managed to think or say anything rather wise and wanted it to look as if it were his very own, just notice what an excellent cure he is told of by the Lord God: Mine is the gold and mine is the silver. In this way, you see, what follows will come to pass, that great shall be the glory of this latest house more than of the first.

The first house, that is the citizens of the earthly Jerusalem, being ignorant, as the apostle says, of the justice of God and seeking to establish their own justice, did not submit themselves to the justice of God (Rom 10:3). Just see whether it is not these people who have been unable, as long as they call the gold and the silver their own, to attain to the eternal glory of the latest house. And yet when the prophet says Great shall be the glory of this latest house more than of the first, he indicates that even the first one itself was not without some glory. The apostle also talked about it when he said, For if what is being nullified comes through glory, much more will that which remains come in glory (2 Cor 3:11).

12. Now the last verse, which concludes this oracle of the prophet's: *And in this place*, it goes, *I will give peace, says the Lord of hosts*. What can *in this place* signify, if not that he is possibly pointing out something earthly, almost you might say with his finger? After all, what but a body can be contained in a place? So it would not be far–fetched for us to understand here the ultimate resurrection of the body, in which the most

perfect bliss will find its term, when no more does the flesh lust against the spirit, nor the spirit against the flesh (Gal 5:17). For this perishable thing will put on imperishability, and this mortal thing will put on immortality (1 Cor 15:53). There will not be another law in our members fighting against the law of our minds, because in this place I will give peace, says the Lord of hosts.

13. Can anyone, I ask you, be so deaf to the divine words that they do not know what the prophets say about thinking lightly of earthly gold and silver? These fellows, you see, in order to take people in, trot out this text from the apostle where he says, Avarice is the root of all evils, and some people setting their course by it have strayed from the faith, and involved themselves in many sorrows (1 Tm 6:10); and they do it in such a way as to suggest that you can easily find some book of the old scriptures where avarice is not treated as culpable, and properly execrated and condemned. But because we are now discussing gold and silver, why do they not listen to the prophet when he says, But their silver and their gold will not be able to deliver them in the day of the wrath of the Lord (Ez 7:19)? Any who are thirsty only have to listen to this text and let it sink into the marrow of their souls, and they will surely turn their backs totally on the allurements of false felicity and throw themselves into the arms of God, putting off the old man in order to clothe themselves with immortality.

But why should we spend any longer dealing with this question? I am sure it is perfectly clear to your graces that the sect of the Manichees uses fraudulent, not honest, means with the unlearned to get them to set parts of the scriptures above the whole, the new above the old; they pick out sentences which they try to show contradict each other, in order to take in the unlearned. But just in the New Testament itself there is no letter of the apostle or even book of the gospel in which that sort of thing cannot be done, so that any one book may be made to look as if it contradicted itself in various places, unless the reader pays very careful attention to its whole composition and design.

15

Augustine, the Bible and the Pelagians

GERALD BONNER

As in his other controversies — with the Manichees, with the Donatists, and with the Arians — Augustine's debate with the Pelagians can be seen as turning on scriptural exegesis: What do certain texts mean? With an unacknowledged rider on both sides that neither party had any intention of modifying its own opinion in response to the arguments of the other, Augustine and the African bishops believed in Original Sin and held it to be the doctrine of the universal Church; the Pelagians denied this and saw such belief as, at best, a personal option. Such was the argument of Celestius at his trial at Carthage in 411, at the outbreak of the Controversy: "I have told you that as regards the transmission of sin, I have heard various people within the Catholic Church deny it and others assert it. It therefore follows that the affair is a matter of opinion, not of heresy."[1] This was not the view of the diocesan synod before which he was arraigned, and Celestius was duly condemned. Seven years later the doctrine of Original Sin was enunciated by the Emperor Honorius, in the law of 30 April 418, which condemned Pelagianism;[2] pronounced by the African General Council of Carthage on 1 May;[3] and subsequently, if reluctantly, confirmed by Pope Zosimus in his *Epistula Tractoria*.[4] For Augustine such witness, though welcome, made no difference. He had, from the first, assumed that Original Sin was part of Catholic belief. Julian of Eclane accused Augustine's theology of being, in fact, Manichaeism under a new name.[5] While a good debating tactic, it came too late to be effective. And in any case, the African episcopate would never have accepted that its theology, derived from St. Cyprian, had anything in common with the teaching of Mani, which had not reached Africa when Cyprian was martyred in 258.

It was, then, their underlying theological preconceptions which determined the exegesis of Scripture by the disputants in the Pelagian Controversy. Their actual methodology was the same. Thus, Augustine could deny any interpretation other than his own of 1 Timothy 2:3: "God wills all men to be saved and to come to a knowledge of the truth," by claiming that the words mean "that no man is saved unless God wills his salvation" or that "all" must here be understood as meaning "humanity in all its manifestations — kings and subjects, nobles and commoners, high and low," so that by "all men" is meant "every sort and condition of man," for not all are saved. Indeed, many more are lost, "but who in his madness reaches such a degree of impiety as to say that God cannot turn the evil wills of men, as He wills, to good, when and where He wills?"[6] This reads like a mere quibble on Augustine's part, designed to safeguard his conviction of the overriding power of God. But an exactly similar technique is employed by Julian of Eclane, faced by Romans 5:18: "Then as one man's trespass led to condemnation for all men, so one man's act of righteousness leads to acquittal and life for all." Julian no more believed in universal salvation than did Augustine. Accordingly, he declared that, in accordance with scriptural usage, we must understand "all" to mean "many," just as Augustine had done.[7] Each disputant had a predetermined theology to which the plain wording of the text had to be accommodated, and each claimed to uphold the tradition of the Catholic Church. This explains why Augustine, in the later stages of the Pelagian Controversy, was concerned to appeal to a long succession of Catholic teachers, and especially to St. Cyprian, the hero of Christian Africa, and to St. Ambrose, the champion of Nicene orthodoxy and his original instructor in the Catholic faith, as witnesses to his own teaching.[8] It was not that he put such witnesses on a level with the Bible. However great their authority, it could never approach that of the sacred text, but they provided evidence of the catholicity of his own understanding.

It was therefore the fundamental theological disagreement between Augustine and the Pelagians which determined their exegetical disagreement. From the outset the two parties differed totally in their respective doctrines of Adam and the Fall. "I say," said Bishop Aurelius of Carthage, "that Adam was placed in Paradise and is said to have been originally created immortal, but afterwards through the Fall was made corruptible."[9] Thus spoke Catholic Africa. The Pelagian position was otherwise: Adam was created mortal, and his sin injured only himself and not the human race. Neither of these positions exactly follows from the text of Genesis, and both parties accordingly set out from different assumptions. For Augustine, Adam was intellectually far superior to his descendants, as was demonstrated by his ability to name the animals.[10] Julian of Eclane thought differently: "Raw, inexperienced, rash, without experience of fear or example of virtue, he stole the food whose sweetness and beauty ensnared him at the suggestion of the woman."[11] Between such mutually opposed first principles there could be no fruitful dialogue, and Augustine and his African colleagues, unlike Celestius, were not prepared to differ.

The Pelagian Controversy gives the appearance of having suddenly erupted in 411, when Celestius was condemned at Carthage in terms which were to be repeated, even more forcefully, in 418. It can, however, be seen as the delayed result of a flowering of Latin Pauline exegesis which had taken place at Rome a decade or so earlier, which came into collision with African tradition as the result of an apparently fortuitous clash between Celestius and the Milanese deacon, Paulinus, who agreed with the African tradition. The Roman Pauline exegetes included Rufinus the Syrian, a shadowy but decisive influence in the controversy; Ambrosiaster, whom Augustine identified, wrongly, with St. Hilary of Poitiers, and who is supposed by some to have influenced Augustine's interpretation of the famous phrase of Romans 5:12: *in quo omnes peccaverunt* as referring to Adam, and Pelagius himself.[12] What brought about this sudden enthusiasm for St. Paul's writings at Rome at the end of the fourth century is not clear. A possible explanation would be the challenge of Manichaeism, which we know from Augustine to have been prevalent at Rome in the 380s, and which could appeal to St. Paul as a witness for its own theology, which identified evil with the material world. Among these Roman exegetes, Rufinus of Syria stands out for his absolute rejection of Traducianism – the belief that Original Sin passed from Adam to his descendants by sexual reproduction and caused infants to be born in sin.[13] It was Rufinus of Syria, according to Marius Mercator, who corrupted Pelagius and then employed him to disseminate his own heretical views. Whether Rufinus corrupted Pelagius or not, he certainly inspired Celestius, with the result that throughout the course of the Pelagian Controversy, whatever other issues might be raised, traducian doctrine and infant baptism were always at the back of the arguments of the debate.

While Rufinus and his fellow exegetes were at work at Rome, on the other side of the Mediterranean, Augustine, following upon his unexpected and undesired ordination in 391, was pursuing a self–directed course of biblical study, in which the Epistle to the Romans figures prominently. It was probably during his years as presbyter of Hippo, perhaps in 394, that he wrote the reply to Question 68 of the collection of queries and answers which he published soon after becoming a bishop, under the title of *83 Diverse Questions*: What is the meaning of the text of Romans 9:2: "O man, who art thou that repliest unto God?" Augustine's answer amounted to a paradigm of his later anti–Pelagian arguments, for here are found the doctrine of the *massa luti*, the lump of clay which is the *massa peccati*, the lump of sin,[14] the statement that we are called to faith, not by any merit of our own but by grace,[15] the quotation from Romans 9:18–19, that God has mercy on whom He wills,[16] and the assertion that "from the same mass of sins, God brought forth vessels of mercy whom He would succour when they called upon Him, and vessels of wrath who, by their punishment, would teach a lesson to the Israelites."[17] All that is different from Augustine's later position (an error which he would duly note in the *Revisions* in 426)[18] is the suggestion that a sinner might, by grief and penitence, become worthy of the divine mercy — though even in 394 Augustine qualified the suggestion by declaring that the penitent's good will is produced in him by God.[19] There is, therefore, in these otherwise completely anti–Pelagian sentiments, a hint of Semi–Pelagian doctrine: in certain cases an individual's good will may anticipate the grace of God, even though that will has been prepared by God.[20] That such a sentiment probably still lingered in Augustine's mind in the period 394–395 is confirmed by a passage in his *Expositio quarundam propositionum ex Epistula ad Romanos*, composed about that time. For in this Augustine would maintain that God loved Jacob and rejected Esau because He foresaw Jacob's future faith, and declared that "it is ours to believe, ours to will, but God's to give to those who believe and will the power of doing good by the Holy Spirit, by whom charity is poured into our hearts (Rom.5:5)."[21] Another statement carefully explained in the *Revisions* as meaning that "both are His, because He Himself prepared the will (Proverbs 8:35), and ours also, because we only do what we will."[22]

Upon this concession to human free will, which left some degree of initiative, however small, to the individual, the illumination regarding the significance of 1 Corinthians 4:7: "What have you that you did not receive? If then you received it, why do you boast as if it were not a gift?"[23] experienced by Augustine in 396, when he was replying to the questions of his old pastor, Simplicianus of Milan, would seem, from Augustine's account in the *Revisions*, to have come upon him with an effect comparable with that following the recognition of the immaterial character of evil which had resulted from his reading of the Neo–platonists a decade earlier.[24] That Augustine regarded this later illumination as having constituted a major step in his theological development is made clear by his assertion in the *Revisions* that he long struggled for the free choice of the human will, "but the grace of God conquered,"[25] and by references to *To Simplicianus* in the *De Praedestinatione Sanctorum* and the *De Dono Perseverantiae*, both written in 429 — the year before Augustine's death.[26] Augustine's key to understanding the message of the Bible was accordingly found by 396, and was understood with a conviction and subsequently asserted with a rigor which suggests that this theological conviction was not established by a process of exegetical reasoning but suddenly apprehended by a flash of intuitive apprehension. For it is clear that throughout the Pelagian Controversy Augustine never questioned the rightness of his position, even in the period 411–415, when he was still inclined to regard the Pelagians as erring brethren rather than as heretics.[27]

Nevertheless, despite the vigor of the study of Pauline theology in the last decade of the fourth century, both by the Roman commentators and by Augustine in Africa, more than ten years elapsed before the outbreak of the Pelagian Controversy was initiated by Celestius at Carthage in 411. Since Augustine only came to read Pelagius' commentary on Romans in 412 while he was already writing his first anti–Pelagian treatise, *On the Merits and Remission of Sin*[28] it seems reasonable to suppose that until Celestius began his propaganda in Africa, Augustine knew very little of the activity of the Roman exegetes. Furthermore, although Caelestius is traditionally regarded as a disciple of Pelagius, he appears to have been equally, or even more, a student of Rufinus of Syria, and the main thrust of his theology seems to have been a denial of the doctrine of Original Sin, following the lines laid down by Rufinus in his *Liber de Fide*.[29] It was against this theology that Augustine directed *On the Merits and Remission of Sins* and it was to remain a dominant issue throughout the Pelagian Controversy, subsequently to be joined by another, in which belief or denial of Original Sin was to be of vital importance: the nature of human freedom.

It has been remarked that the number of texts to which Augustine appealed to establish this doctrine of Original Sin is remarkably limited: Ps.50:7 [51:5 EVV]: "Behold, I was shapen in wickedness and in sin hath my mother conceived me"; Job 14:4–5 in the Greek Septuagint version: "Who shall be free from defilement? not one, even though his life be but a day upon the earth"; John 3:5: "Unless one is born of water and the Spirit, he cannot enter the kingdom of God"; Ephesians 2:3: "We are by nature children of wrath, like the rest of mankind"; and, notoriously, Romans 5:12: "in whom all sinned."[30] Here, Augustine tried to read into the Latin translation: *in quo omnes peccaverunt* — "in whom [Adam] all sinned" — a meaning that the Greek original *Eph hoi* will not bear. Julian of Eclane understood the meaning of the passage better: "For after [the Apostle] had said: "[and thus sin] passed into all men," he immediately added: *in quo omnes peccaverunt*. This *in quo omnes peccaverunt* means nothing other than that all have sinned, like that phrase of David's: *in quo corrigit adulescens viam suam?* that is, "in what manner does a young man correct his way? By keeping thy words" (Ps.118 [119]:9).[31] Julian was right. In this context *in quo* meant "in that" or "in what way?" Augustine, however, remained completely self–confident, telling Julian "to open his eyes":

> All die in Adam. If infants are not dead in him, neither are they made alive in Christ. Why, then, do you hurry with them to the baptism of the lifegiving Saviour with a damnable pretence, when you do not want them to be made alive and healed, by claiming that they are already alive and healed?[32]

Augustine's exegesis was inspired by the doctrine of the African Church and confirmed by liturgical practice: infants inherit Adam's primal sin, so that we are either in him by our natural birth or in Christ, the Second Adam, by a sacramental rebirth through baptism. This belief validated Augustine's understanding of the Pauline text, and he expressed this very clearly in a letter to his supporter, Hilary of Syracuse, written in 414.

> With regard to what the Pelagians say, that an unbaptized infant, cut off by death, cannot perish eternally because it is born without sin,[33] the Apostle does not say this, and I think it better for us to believe the Apostle than those objectors. For the teacher of the Gentiles, in whom Christ speaks, says: "By one man sin entered into the world, and by sin death, and so death passed into all men, in whom all sinned" (Rom.5:12)...Thus, just as man cannot be found who is born of the flesh apart from Adam's line, so no one is found spiritually reborn apart from Christ's grace.[34]

Julian of Eclane flatly rejected any such interpretation. According to him, sin entered the world, not by generation from one individual — for generation requires two, Adam and Eve — but by the imitation of one — Adam.

> "By one man," says the Apostle, "sin entered the world." But here *"one"* adequately provides an example for imitation, but not for effecting generation. Sin has entered, but by one alone. It is clear that imitation is here implied, not generation, which cannot be except by two.[35]

Augustine would counter this by referring Julian to the verse of Ecclesiasticus: "The beginning of sin was made by a woman and on account of her we all die" (25:33 [EVV 24]); but he argued that, while the beginning of "sin" is said to be by a woman, the beginning of *generation* came from a man:

> ...for the man first sowed the seed that the woman might bear. Therefore "by one man sin entered the world," because it entered by the generative seed through which the woman conceived, receiving it from the man. Hence, he did not will to be born in this fashion, who alone was born of a woman without sin.[36]

Augustine here refers to his theory that Original Sin is passed from parent to child in the sexual concupiscence which the act of generation involves, and he would later illustrate this notion by a medical analogy: if a man contracts gout through intemperance and passes it on to his sons, do we not rightly say that the infection has passed into them from the parent, and that the sons contracted the infection in the parent, since when that happened they were in him?[37] The foundation of Augustine's conception was not, however, medical analogy but the doctrine expressed in the condemnation of Celestius in 411. Children inherited the guilt of the Fall, and unless they were freed from that guilt by baptism, they were damned. Augustine had taken no part in the Carthaginian council which condemned Celestius, and it was only afterwards that he began writing and speaking against Pelagianism. The Pelagian Controversy, begun with a dispute over Original Sin and infant baptism, was juridically concluded, so far as the African Church was concerned, by the promulgation of nine canons by the Pan–African council assembled at Carthage on 1 May 418, which declared that human mortality was a consequence of the sin of Adam; that infants needed to receive baptism as a remedy for Original Sin; that without baptism there was no salvation; that Grace was more than forgiveness of sins or illumination; and that even the holiest person has sins for which they needed to ask God's forgiveness.[38] These canons were diametrically opposed to the opinions for which Celestius had been condemned and effectively comprehended the issues for which Augustine had been campaigning and would go on campaigning until his death in 430; but the theology underlying them had either been explicitly stated, or at least implied, by Augustine in Question 68 of *On Diverse Questions*, written before 395, and in *To Simplicianus*, written about 396.

The principles of this theology are perfectly clear. All human beings come into this world under condemnation for Adam's primal sin, and the vast majority are left to damnation, including those infants who die unbaptized. Such a view could only revolt any self–respecting Pelagian. Julian of Eclane, characteristically, accused Augustine of worshipping a god who was a "tormentor of neonates" (*persecutor infantium*), a god who, for their alleged evil will, hands over little children to eternal fires, when He knows that they are not able to have either a good or an evil will.[39] But the matter went deeper, for it raised the whole issue of human free will, which Augustine had defended in his earlier writings against the Manichees. Julian gleefully seized upon Augustine's definition of sin, given in his anti–Manichaean work *On Two Souls*, 15, composed in 392: "Sin is the will to permit or to hinder what justice forbids to permit or to hinder and from which one is free to abstain."[40] Since Julian denied the existence of Original Sin, and declared that free will, "by which man is emancipated from God,"[41] remained as full after the commission of sin as it was before,[42] he was faced by none of the moral problems raised for Augustine by the implications of the theology of Original Sin and divine Grace. For Augustine, however, these problems were very real. In the third book of his *On Free Choice* (c.395), he had asserted that the Fall was a voluntary sin, and therefore culpable, and had further asserted that there can be no sin where the will is unable to avoid sinning.[43] This passage was subsequently quoted by Pelagius, in support of his own doctrine of human free will. Augustine, in his reply, *On Nature and Grace*, written in 414, was careful to explain that in *On Free Choice* he had been concerned with human nature in Paradise, but the problem remained: to what extent, if any, did human freedom continue after the Fall? Can there be any merit in a good action by a human being? Pelagius had said that there were three elements in any good action: the possibility of performing it, the will to perform it, and the performance. God gives the power, but the will and the performance pertain to man.[44] Julian of Eclane, for his part, observed that Augustine, in his *Against Two Letters of the Pelagians*,[45] had asserted that free will exists in the wicked, but not in the good,[46] and declared repeatedly that Augustine had remained at heart a Manichee, regarding sin as inevitable, despite the goodness of the omnipotent Creator.[47]

234

The accusation of Manichaeism levelled by the Pelagians against Augustine, although made plausible by his emphasis on *concupiscentia* in its aspect as a disordered sexual appetite brought about by the Fall,[48] was a slander. Augustine's anti–Manichaean polemic had been devoted to asserting the sovereignty of God and creation from nothing, which meant that humanity, as God's creation, was essentially good and endowed by God with freedom of choice, but at the same time, Augustine emphasized that human nature has been vitiated by the Fall, so that without a special divine grace, greater than that which Adam had enjoyed in Paradise, man could only do wrong.[49] The vital question was: how was this grace bestowed? Here Augustine was faced with the problem of the criterion by which God gives grace to one individual and not another.

As has already been described, in the course of his biblical studies during his presbyterate and in his early years as a bishop, Augustine devoted much attention to the theology of the Epistle to the Romans. One problem in particular was raised by the case of Esau and Jacob (Rom.9: 11–13): why was Jacob loved and Esau hated, even before they were born? Could there be any injustice in God, when He chooses some and rejects others in an apparently arbitrary fashion? In *83 Diverse Questions*, q.68, written before 395, Augustine raised the matter but declined to answer it. It was a mystery, to be discussed only by holy souls.[50] In the *Expositio quarundam propositionum ex Epistula ad Romanos*, written about the same time as *On Diverse Questions* q.68, he suggested that God's love of Jacob was due to a foreknowledge, not of Jacob's works, which would imply election based on merit, but upon Jacob's future faith, since faith is a free response to a divine call.[51] Thus, although merit is here ruled out, man still retains some freedom of action, he can accept or reject an entirely gratuitous offer of salvation.

Thus, as late as 394, Augustine still believed in a certain initiative being left to the individual, in a manner analogous to, though not precisely identical with, the views of the Massilian divines in the final stages of the Pelagian Controversy. Augustine's outlook has been characterized as being, in some degree at this time, Semi–Pelagian. Speaking of the choice of Jacob and the rejection of Esau (Malachi 1: 2–3; Rom. 9:13), he would write:

> God did not therefore make His choice in the foreknowledge of anyone's works, which He Himself would give; but He chose faith in His foreknowledge, so that He would choose him who, He knew, would believe, to whom He would give the Holy Spirit, so that by working good works, the recipient would also obtain eternal life.[52]

This persuasion did not last. In 396, in *To Simplicianus*, Augustine flatly rejected the notion that Jacob was chosen because of his foreseen faith. The message of 1 Cor. 4:7 wholly altered Augustine's outlook and revealed to him that faith, no less than works, is the gift of God. In the *De Praedestinatione Sanctorum*, one of his last writings, composed in 429, Augustine commented upon his earlier view.

> I had not sufficiently enquired, nor had I then found, what election by grace might be, about which the same Apostle says: "There is a remnant, chosen by grace" (Rom.11:5), which indeed is not grace, if any merits precede it; for what is given, not by grace but according to what is due, is a reward for merits rather than a gift.[53]

It was this conviction that grace is gratuitous which conditioned Augustine's anti–Pelagian theology. As he saw it (and in the last resort saw rightly), Pelagian doctrine assumed the power of the individual, once freed from sin by baptism, to work out his own salvation.[54] But where did Augustine himself stand in relation to human freedom of choice, given his conviction that all good actions are due to grace and not to the will of the individual? And if this is the case, where is the justice of God, who gives grace to one, wholly undeserving, and leaves another, equally undeserving, in the mass of sin?

Augustine was concerned, as far as possible, to explain and defend the apparent injustice of God, as revealed in His predestinating decrees. In *To Simplicianus* he suggested that Esau, no less than Jacob, received a call from God, but so formed that he did not respond to it. The same was true of the tyrant Pharaoh.[55] Esau did not respond because God willed otherwise, with a secret justice beyond human comprehension. This notion seems to have remained with Augustine for the rest of his life. In the *De Dono Perseverantiae* he expressed his opinion with brutal clarity but absolute conviction, citing *To Simplicianus* and the *Confessions* as works in which he had already opposed Pelagianism in anticipation, before it arose.

> Likewise, as the Apostle says, "Not of him who wills nor of him who runs, but of God showing mercy" (Rom.9:16). He comes to the aid of some infants, although they do not yet even will or run, when He wishes to aid them, whom He chose in Christ before the foundation of the world. To these He gives grace gratuitously, that is with no preceding merits on their part, either of faith or of good works. But He did not come to the assistance of those adults whom He did not will to aid, even when He foresaw that they would have believed His miracles, if they had been worked among them [like the inhabitants of Tyre and Sidon]. In His foreknowledge He judged otherwise about them, secretly indeed, but justly,

because there is no injustice in God, for "inscrutable are his judgments and his way past finding out" (Rom.11:33) and "all the ways of the Lord are mercy and truth" (Ps.24, 25:10).[56]

There is, therefore, a remarkable doctrinal continuity in Augustine's writing from *To Simplicianus*, composed in 396, through *On the Merits and Remission of Sin*, written in 411–412, and the *De Praedestinatione Sanctorum* and the *De Dono Perseverantiae* of 429, to the *Opus Imperfectum adversus Iulianum*, upon which Augustine was engaged at the time of his death in 430. There was, however, a development in his outlook. In the first place, Augustine increasingly laid emphasis upon the saving work of Christ, as, for example, in his treatise *On Nature and Grace*, written in 415 in answer to Pelagius's *De Natura*. Pelagius's theology was certainly not "godless," as Harnack claimed; but precisely because of his denial of any transmission of Original Sin, Pelagius was constrained to see a natural power in human nature to avoid committing any further sins, once the guilt of existing sin has been washed away by baptism. A similar view was held by Julian of Eclane: "Free choice is as full after sins as it was before sins."[57] Such a view leads naturally to the Pelagian conception of divine grace as consisting essentially in our God–given human nature, in the Law, and in the remission of sins in baptism. It was expressed by Pelagius in his *Defence of Free Will* (418), which Augustine subsequently attacked in his *On the Grace of Christ and Original Sin* (418).[58] For Augustine, prevenient grace, by which we are enabled to do good, can only be the gift of Christ, through the indwelling of the Holy Spirit. It was this conviction which led him increasingly to urge the mediation of Jesus Christ the God–man, apart from whom there can be no salvation.[59]

Secondly, Augustine's recognition of the continuing effects of Original Sin in the baptized led him increasingly to develop his notion of concupiscence (*concupiscentia carnis* or *libido carnalis*) in his writings against Pelagianism.[60] Here we have another example of how Augustine's interpretation of Scripture was conditioned by his theological presuppositions. He was aware that, in the Latin Bible, *concupiscentia* could have a good sense (e.g. Wisdom 6:21: *concupiscentia itaque sapientiae deducit ad regnum* and Gal. 5:17: *caro concupiscit adversus spiritum, spiritus adversus carnem*) but that its general connotation is pejorative (Ex. 20:17; Eccl. 18:30; Rom. 1:24; 7:7; Gal. 5:24; Eph. 4:22; and 1 Joh. 2:16). Such an understanding admirably agreed with his theory of the deterioration of the human body since the Fall, so that we now see "another law in our members" (Rom. 7:23), namely, concupiscence, and further helped to explain how the guilt of Adam's primal sin is passed to his descendants.[61] Augustine's elaborate theological conception, which ultimately derived from African tradition, could hardly be directly constructed from the Bible, even though it might be defended by biblical citation. Julian of Eclane, who denied Original Sin and, as a natural consequence, any transmission of it, was able to regard concupiscence as a natural and innocent appetite,[62] which could have existed in Christ's human body, an idea which horrified Augustine.[63] It is not necessary to endorse Pelagian theology as a whole to feel that Julian's understanding was, in this instance, more reasonable than Augustine's, but it is clear that Julian was less concerned to establish the biblical meaning of concupiscence than to advance his own argument that Augustine's doctrine was, in fact, an expression of the Manichaeism which Augustine claimed to have renounced. Julian's approach was that of a controversialist anxious to win, and not of an exegete, trying to understand.

If Augustine's treatment of the meaning of *concupiscentia* was a very personal one, his doctrine of predestination was equally so. Its roots lay in the revelation of the gratuity of divine grace, which came upon him when answering Simplicianus in 396. This illumination regarding God's absolute sovereignty and man's utter dependency was enhanced by Augustine's steadily increasing Christocentricity, with its emphasis on Christ as the only Mediator between God and man, and on the need for the indwelling of the Holy Spirit, which is made possible after the Incarnation only through baptism. But the reception of baptism and its subsequent effect did not, for Augustine, rest with the decision of the individual but with the will of God, which takes no account of human merit. It was Augustine's insistence upon human helplessness which led to his debate with the so–called Semi–Pelagians. While entirely accepting the need for a grace which went beyond man's natural endowments, they held that in certain cases the beginning of faith might come, not from a sudden conversion experience, as in the case of Paul, but as God's reward for an individual in whom there already existed a good disposition. They could point to such biblical examples as Zacchaeus the publican, the Penitent Thief, Abraham, and Cornelius the centurion.[64] They accused Augustine of teaching new doctrine,[65] an accusation which he naturally denied. As with the Pelagians, so with the more orthodox theologians of Marseilles: Augustine would admit no other understanding of the meaning of Scripture than his own. A single passage from the *De Dono Perseverantiae*, the last of his completed works, composed in 429, admirably epitomises his position.

This is the predestination of the saints and nothing else: the prescience and preparation of the benefits of God, whereby whoever are set free are most certainly set free. And where are the rest left by the just judgment of God, save in that mass of perdition, where were left the men of Tyre and the Sidonians, who were also capable of belief had they but seen those wonderful works of Christ?[66]

John Calvin claimed that, if he had so desired, he could have composed a whole book out of Augustine alone to support his own theology but feared to burden the reader with prolixity.[67] It would certainly seem that, in his use of the Bible against the Pelagians, Augustine deliberately refused to consider any interpretation of a disputed text other than his own and in so doing affected the course of Western biblical exegesis for fifteen centuries and more.

NOTES

1. *On the Grace of Christ* 2.3–4.3; *CSEL* 42, 169.
2. *PL* 45, 1726–8; 48, 379–86.
3. *PL* 45, 1728–30; *CCSL* 149, 69–73; 74–77.
4. Marius Mercator, *Commonitorium* 1.5; 3.1. *PL* 48, 77–83; 90–95. Fragments in Augustine, *Letter* 190.6.23. *CSEL* 57, 159; Prosper, *Contra Collatorem* 5 (9). *PL* 51, 228; Celestinus, *Ep. ad Galliarum Episcopos* 8, 9 *PL* 45, 1758.
5. e.g *Opus Imperfectum adversus Iulianum* 3.123: "*Huius autem veritatem catholici confitentur, Traduciani autem cum Manicheis, magistris suis, negant.*" *CSEL* 85, 440.
6. *Enchiridion to Laurentius* 27, 103. *CCSL* 46, 104–6; cf. *Against Julian* 4.8.44: "*Omnes* positos esse pro *Multis*, quos ad istam gratiam vult venire." *PL* 44, 760; *On Rebuke and Grace* 15, 47. *PL* 44, 945.
7. *Op.imp.* 2, 135. *CSEL* 85, 260; cf. 2,68 [on Romans 5:12]: "*quo verbo, id est 'omnes', scripturarum more 'multitudo', non universitas, indicatur.*" *CSEL* 85.212.
8. *Op.imp.* 6, 21. *PL* 45, 1548–9. On Augustine's view of the Canon of Scripture, see *The Cambridge History of the Bible* Vol.I (Cambridge, England: Cambridge University Press, 1970), 544.
9. *On the Grace of Christ.* 2.3–4.4. *CSEL* 42.169.
10. *Op.imp.* 5.1. *PL* 45, 1432.
11. Ibid. 6.23. *PL* 45, 1554.
12. See Jean–Michel Girard, *La mort chez Saint Augustin. Grandes lignes de l'évolution de sa pensée telle qu'elle apparaît dans ses traités* (Fribourg Suisse: Éditions Universitaires 1992), 129–46. On Augustine's Pauline studies, see William S. Babcock, "Augustine's Interpretation of Romans (A.D. 394–396)," *Augustinian Studies* 10 (1979), 55–74; J. Patout Burns, "The Interpretation of Romans in the Pelagian Controversy," *Augustinian Studies* 10 (1979), 43–54; M.–F.Berrouard, "L'exégèse augustinienne de

Rom.7:7–25 entre 396 et 418, avec des remarques sur les deux premières périodes de la crise 'pélagienne,'" *Recherches Augustiniennes* 16 (1981), 101–95; Paula Fredriksen, *Augustine on Romans. Propositions from the Epistle to the Romans, Unfinished Commentary on The Epistle to the Romans* (Texts and Translations 23. Early Christian Literature Series 6) (Chico, California 1982); Stanislas Lyonnet, "Rom.V, 12 chez Saint Augustin. Note sur l'élaboration de la doctrine Augustinienne du péché originel" in *L'Homme devant Dieu. Mélanges offerts au Père Henri de Lubac* (*Théologie* 56), 1 (Paris 1963), 327–39; "A propos de Romains 5:12 dans l'oeuvre de Saint Augustin. Note complémentaire," *Biblica* 45 (1964), 541–2; "Augustin et Rom. 5:12 avant la controverse pélagienne. A propos d'un texte de Saint Augustin sur le baptême des enfants," *Nouvelle Revue Théologique* 89 (1967), 842–9.

13. See Gerald Bonner, "Rufinus of Syria and African Pelagianism," *Augustinian Studies* 1 (1970), 31–47; *Saint Augustine and Modern Research on Pelagianism* (Saint Augustine Lecture for 1970) (Villanova, PA.: Villanova University Press, 1972), 26–7.

14. *83 Diverse Questions*, qu. 68.3. *CCSL* 44A.177.

15. Ibid., *CCSL* 44A.177–8.

16. Ibid., 1. *CCSL* 44A.175.

17. Ibid., 4. *CCSL* 44A.179.

18. *Revision Book* 1.25.24. *CCSL* 57.85.

19. *83 Diverse Questions*, qu. 68.5, *CCSL* 44A.180–81.

20. cf.*On Grace and Free Choice* 7.17. *PL* 44, 891.

21. *Expositio quarundarum propositionum ex Epistula ad Romanos* 52.60.9; 53.61.7. *CCSL* 84.34; 36.

22. *Revisions* 1.22.23, 3. *CCSL* 57.69.

23. *To Simplicianus* 1, q.2.9. *CCSL* 44.34 (the only direct citation in the treatise); cf. 1, q.2.17: "*illud tantummodo inconcussa fide teneatur, quod non sit iniquitas apud deum, qui sive donet sive exigat debitum, nec ille a quo exigit recte potest de iniquitate eius conqueri, nec ille cui donat debet de suis meritis gloriari. Et ille enim nisi quod debetur non reddit, et ille non habet nisi quod accepit.*" *CCSL* 44.44.

24. *Confessions* 7.10, 15–16, 21. *CCSL* 27.103–6.

25. *Revisions* 2.1.27: "*In cuius quaestionis solutione laboratum est quidem pro libero arbitrio voluntatis humanae, sed vicit dei gratia; nec nisi ad illud potuit perveniri, ut liquidissima veritate dixisse intellegatur apostolus: Quis enim te discernit? Quid autem habes quod non accepisti? Si autem accepisti, quid gloriaris quasi non acceperis? Quod volens etiam martyr Cyprianus ostendere, hoc totum ipso titulo definivit, dicens: 'In nullo gloriandum, quando nostrorum nihil sit'*" (Cyprian, *Testimonia* 3, 4. *CSEL* 3.1.116. *CCSL* 57.89–90.

26. *De Praedestinatione Sanctorum* 3.7; 4.8. *PL* 44, 964; 965–6; *De Dono Perseverantiae* 20.52; 21.55. *PL* 1025–6; 1027.

27. See his letter to Hilary, *Letter* 157. *CCEL* 44.449–88 and to Honoratus,

Letter 140 (*De Gratia Novi Testamenti*). *CSEL* 44.155–234. Augustine was certainly concerned in 416, when it seemed as though the Synods of Jerusalem and Diospolis had vindicated Pelagius; but this did not cause him to doubt his own theology.

28. *On the Merits and Remission of Sin* 3.1.1; *CSEL* 60.129.

29. See Girard, op.cit. note 12 above, pp.140–42, following the arguments of Eugene TeSelle, "Rufinus the Syrian, Celestius, Pelagius: Explorations in the Prehistory of the Pelagian Controversy," *Augustinian Studies* 3 (1972), 61–95.

30. See Norman Powell Williams, *The Ideas of the Fall and of Original Sin* (London/New York/Toronto: Longmans, Green & Co., 1927), 378–9.31. *Op.imp.* 2.174. *CSEL* 85.294; cf. 2.197. *CSEL* 8.310–11.

32. Ibid.

33. *Letter* 156. *CSEL* 44.448.

34. *Letter* 15. 3.11. *CSEL* 44.457, 458. My translation.

35. *Op.imp.* 2.56.1. *CSEL* 85.203. My translation.

36. Ibid. (Augustine). *CSEL* 85.204–5. My translation.

37. Ibid. 2.177. *CSEL* 85.296–7.

38. Text in *PL* 45.1728–30; *CSEL* 149.69–73; 74–77.

39. *Op.imp.* 1.48.4. *CSEL* 85.38.

40. *Op.imp.* 1.4, 82, 104; 2.38, 187. *CSEL* 85.31, 96, 121, 190, 304.

41. Ibid. 1.78. *CSEL* 85.93.

42. Ibid. 1.91. *CSEL* 85.104.

43. *On Free Choice* 3.1.2, 3.18.50. *CCSL* 29.276, 304. *On Nature and Grace* 67.80–81. *CSEL* 60.293–6.

44. *Grat. Christ.* 1.4.5. *CSEL* 42.127–8.

45. *Against Two Letters of the Pelagians* 1.3.7. *CSEL* 60.428–9.

46. *Op.imp.* 3.118. *CSEL* 85.436.

47. Ibid. 3.123–6, 136, 154.1. *CSEL* 85.440–41, 443, 457.

48. *City of God* 14.16. *CCSL* 48.438–9.

49. *On Rebuke and Grace* 11.29, 31: "*Quid ergo? Adam non habuit Dei gratiam? Imo vero habuit magnam, sed disparem. Ille in bonis erat, quae de bonitate sui Conditoris acceperat: neque enim ea bona et ille suis meritis comparaverat, in quibus prorsus nullum patiebatur malum. Sancti vero in hac vita, ad quos pertinet liberationis haec gratia, in malis sunt, ex quibus clamant ad Deum: 'Libera nos a malo'* (Matt.6:13). . . .*Istam gratiam non habuit homo prius, qua numquam vellet esse malus: sed sane habuit, in qua si permanere vellet, numquam malus erit.*" *PL* 44.933, 935.

50. *83 Diverse Questions* q.68.6. *CCSL* 44a.182–3.

51. *Exp.quarundam prop.* 52.60.9. *CSEL* 84.34. See Babcock, art. cit. note 12 above, p.64.

52. Ibid. My translation.

53. *Praed. Sanct.* 3.7. *PL* 45. My translation.

54. *On Grace and Free Choice* 6.15. *PL* 44.890. See the remarks of Jean Chéné in *Oeuvres de Saint Augustin: Aux moines d'Adrumète et de Provence* (Bibliothèque Augustinienne 24) (Paris: Desclée de Brouwer 1962), 771–3.

55. *To Simplicianus* 1, q.2.13–15. *CCSL* 44.37–41.

56. *De Dono Pers.* 11.25. *PL* 45.1007. My translation.

57. *Op.imp.* 1.91. *CSEL* 85.104.

58. *Grat.Christ.* 1.7.8. *CSEL* 42.130–31. See Gerald Bonner, *St. Augustine of Hippo. Life and Controversies* 2 (Norwich, England: The Canterbury Press, 1986), 361–4.

59. See Burns, art.cit. note12, p.54 and Babcock, art.cit. note12, p.61.

60. See *Augustinus–Lexikon*, art. "Concupiscentia."

61. *City of God* 14.16. *CCSL* 48.438–9; *Grat.Christ.* 2.33.38. *CSEL* 42.196–7.

62. *Op.imp.* 5.11. *PL* 45.1140.

63. Ibid. 4.48–54. *PL* 45.1366–71.

64. Cassian, *Liber Collationum* 13.11, 14–15. *CSEL* 13.375–8, 384–90.

65. *Letter* 225.2. *CSEL* 57.455.

66. *Dono Pers.* 13.35. *PL* 45.1014. My translation.

67. *Institutio Christianae Religionis*, ed. P. Barth & W. Wiesel, *Iohannis Calvini Opera Selecta* 3 (Munich 1931), 389.

PART IV

Augustine:

Minister of the Word

16

Augustine, Minister of the Word of God

ANNE-MARIE LA BONNARDIÈRE

On the day of his ordination by Bishop Valerius of Hippo, Augustine understood that the voice which he had so long employed in secular instruction from this time forward would be dedicated to the service of the Word of God. To anyone who is familiar with Augustine's work it seems with some justification that for Augustine his Bible is primarily the Bible of a preacher. Paradoxically his work has been transmitted to us in writing. However, from these written works emerge the homilies, the discourses, the sermons, the debates, and the prayers, all of which were primarily spoken and listened to. In 404 Augustine wrote to Jerome:

> I neither have nor ever will possess a science of sacred Scriptures which is comparable to that which I recognize in you. If I have some small capacity in this field I use it in the service of the people of God. Whenever I attempt to study scripture more diligently than the instruction of the people who listen to me demands, my ecclesial duties prevent me." (*Letter 73.5*)

Augustine could not have expressed better his intention of studying the scriptures within the functioning of his ministry of the word of God. It is not accidental that he loved to cite the following words "Preach the word, be urgent in season and out (2 Tim. 4:2)," written by his master Paul. Liturgy was most appropriate for that announcement and insistence. Valerius knew this well and he also knew to whom he was trusting the ministry of the liturgy at Hippo when he ordained Augustine.

"Liturgy" wrote François Dreyfus, "has always been a privileged place for the actualization of Scripture... In Christian tradition, throughout the patristic period the liturgical homily constituted by far the most important form of exegetical literature. Certainly the Fathers also explained Scripture in their treatises outside of the liturgical context, but this latter form is less frequent than the homily. The study of the characteristics of this contextualization of Scripture in the liturgical homily by the Fathers constitutes an exciting and difficult subject..."[1]

These words seem to describe marvelously well the liturgical Bible of Augustine and express one of its major characteristics. The best way to appreciate this is through the striking example of the Paschal Vigil and Easter morning liturgy of the period.

The opening theme of the Paschal liturgy is provided by the Pauline verses, Romans 6: 8–11:

> But if we have died with Christ, we believe that we shall also live with Him. For we know that Christ being raised from the dead will never die again; death no longer has dominion over Him. The death He died He died to sin, once for all, but the life He lives He lives to God. So you also must consider yourselves dead to sin and alive to God in Christ Jesus."[2]

The tone has been set. The teachings and the rites of the Vigil continue with the reading of the great prophecies and the singing of Psalms. Three events are celebrated and lived by the people of God.

1. The Celebration of the Miracles of God

God's miracles, accomplished in the past and evoked by the following prophecies, manifested the power of God's activity in saving his people from peril. The stories of the crossing of the Red Sea (Ex. 14),[3] the saving of the three children from the furnace (Dan. 3),[4] Jonah and the conversion of the Ninevites, were read. The reading was accompanied by the singing of the Hymns of Miriam[5] and the youths in the fiery furnace. These prophecies attested to the deliverance from sin which awaited the candidates for baptism. They approached the baptismal font singing Psalm 42; "As the deer longs for living waters..."[6]

2. Celebration of the Resurrection of the Lord Jesus Christ

The sermons of the Paschal Vigil attest to the reading of several such prophecies such as Is.2:2–3: "It will happen at the end of days that the mountain where the Lord lives will appear established at the top of all mountains..."[7] The mountain in this case is Christ. Another prophecy

246

frequently cited by the Fathers[8] was also called to mind during the Pascal Vigil at Hippo. It was the announcement of the awakening of the lion of Judah which was part of Judah's blessing. The Genesis 49:9 passage reads: "Judah is a young lion, my son, from your prey you got up; like a lion he crouches and lies down, ...who dare rouse him?"[9]

These prophecies had become realities. They had been accomplished by the Resurrection of Christ as attested to by Matthew (Mt. 28),[10] Paul (Romans 4:25, 6:9–11),[11] and Revelation 5:5 (The lion of Judah has conquered).[12] The linking of Gen. 49:9 and Rev. 5:5 proclaimed the sleep and awakening of the lion of Judah, or in other words, the death of Jesus on the cross and his Resurrection. These two texts were accompanied by John 10:18: "No one takes my life from me; I lay it down of my own free will, and as it is in my power to lay it down, so it is in my power to take it up again; and this is the command I have been given by my Father."[13] The celebration of the victory of Christ over death, his freedom in his Resurrection realized once for all, exploded in joy with the singing of an anthology of psalmic fragments. These included: "I lie down and sleep; I wake again, for the Lord sustains me" (Ps.3:5), "Lo, He who preserves Israel rests not, neither sleeps" (Ps. 102:4), "I kept vigil, a lonely sparrow on the roof" (Ps.101:8), and "Would he who sleeps not succeed in waking himself?" (Ps. 40:9b). In these multiple ways the Resurrection of the Lord, which is the unique essence of Christian faith, was affirmed, contemplated and sung.

3. The Celebration of the Day of Creation

To this celebration all the choristers of the Light were invited, particularly the author of the first chapter of Genesis. Even if this chapter was proclaimed in its entirety, the surviving sermons of the Paschal Vigil contain only the first five verses of Genesis. These words were read:

> In the beginning God created the heavens and the earth. Now the earth was a formless void, there was darkness over the deep, and God's spirit hovered over the water. God said, 'Let there be light,' and there was light. God saw that light was good and God divided light from darkness. God called light 'day' and darkness he called 'night' (Gen. 1:1–5a).[14]

Augustine's sermons comment upon the creative role of the Father who makes the Son equal to Himself and they celebrate the creation of the primordial light.

The commentaries, always kept brief, bring the theme of Genesis close to verses borrowed from Paul and Peter. They were:

a. Ephesians 5:8: "For once you were darkness, but now you are light in the Lord."

b. Romans 13:12–13a: "The night is far gone, the day is at hand. Let us then cast off the works of darkness and put on the armor of light; let us conduct ourselves becomingly as in the day."

c. 1 Thess. 5:2–8a reinforced the affirmation, particularly 1 Thess. 5:5: "For you are all sons of light and sons of the day; we are not of the night or of darkness."

d. 2 Peter 1:19: "And we have the prophetic word made more sure. You will do well to pay attention to this as to a lamp shining in a dark place, until the day dawns and the morning star rises in your hearts."

This celebration of the "Day" provided the orchestration during the night for the sacred rites of baptism and confirmation. We can see that these texts were addressed particularly to the newly baptized as they climbed up from the baptismal font to be henceforth called neophytes. They were the newborn of the Mother Church. In their honor were sung the words of Psalm 117:24a: "*Hic est dies quem fecit Dominus* (This is the day that the Lord has made)." These fragments of psalm accompanied Gen. 12:5 and Ephesians 5:8 and this song of triumph resounded throughout the Paschal Week.

After a brief rest, all the people of God from the Church in Hippo were back in the Basilica for Easter morning. The "Prologue" of John's Gospel and the story of Pentecost from Acts were solemnly proclaimed.

Such was the contextualization of the Word of God in the Paschal Vigil and Easter morning at Hippo during Augustine's episcopate: Three series of passages with biblical songs were linked by plays upon key terms, which celebrated the escape from perils *eruere*, the awakening from death *exsurgere*, and the day *dies* emerging from the shadows. One after the other all the births were exalted: the creation of the world (Gen. 1), the birth of the people of Israel (Ex. 14 and 15), the eternal generation of the Word in the Trinity (John 1), the birth of the Church (Acts 2), and the initiation of the baptized by the Mother Church into the life of Jesus Christ (the sacrament of Baptism). Easter was the celebration of new beginnings. It was the celebration of passages (*pascha = transitus*). It was the passage from Egypt to the promised land, the passage from shadow to light, the passage from death to life, from sin to life in Jesus Christ, from prophecy to fulfillment. The Christ event tore away the veil and illuminated the meaning of the Psalms. It is this Christ who sang his

Resurrection. Each birth, each passage, each beginning, creation, resurrection and sanctification were the works of the Trinity. This was how, while awaiting the dawn in the depth of the night, the Word of God was actualized, sung, proclaimed and lived. Augustine knew that a theological explanation was hardly necessary. His homilies were short. Augustine and his congregation lived intensely the ancient anticipation of the Messiah, the event of Christ and the new hope of Christ's return. It was written in 2 Peter 1:19: "We have the prophetic word made more sure. You will do well to pay attention to this as to a lamp shining in a dark place, until the day dawns and the morning star rises in your hearts." The baptized were the 'day' but they continued to need the prophetic lamp until the great morning of the Resurrection.

If Easter was the summit of the liturgical year, other high points existed. These included the Ascension, Pentecost, Christmas, Epiphany, Lent, the Feast of the Martyrs of the Universal Church and Africa, the dedication of churches, episcopal ordinations and celebrations for the dead. It is impossible to detail for each of these how Augustine's charism for actualizing the Word of God throws into relief the theological importance of harmonious associations of biblical readings and songs. Augustine professed that scripture was explained by scripture. No one understood this better than Pascal who wrote: "Whoever wishes to give meaning to scripture and does not take it from scripture is the enemy of scripture." The same liturgical moment each year uses the same biblical anthology. It is not always expressed in an integrated way, however its significance is that it allows for an actualization adapted to the moment and to the listeners. The contribution by Michel Alberic illustrates this in a eucharistic catechesis.

Biblical citations referring to liturgy are not contained solely in liturgy itself. Biblical readings, prophecies, and hymns surface abundantly in circumstances other than liturgical ones. All Augustinian students are aware of the frequency with which Augustine took up the meditation, exegesis, and grammatical explanation, of the first chapter of Genesis and in particular Gen. 1:1–5. The creation of the Light, the creation of angels and the fall of Satan, the origin of the City of God which was represented by the faithful angels, the mysterious revelation of the Trinity, the prologue of John, are such a frequent leitmotif that the citation of these verses exceeds a thousand references. The Gospel of Matthew, read throughout the liturgical year, is found constantly in Augustine's letters, the polemical writings and the *City of God*. It should be noted that the four gospels in and of themselves constitute a third of Augustine's biblical citations. To the enumeration of these key Augustinian themes must be joined the citations of ten principal liturgical Psalms (18, 21, 33, 40, 41, 50, 100, 115, 117, 140) which on their own make up 1,750 references. One must also note the great importance of the repetition of the liturgical pericopes extracted from Paul's Epistles. Here we cannot help but call to mind the texts of the Paschal Vigil cited above. Finally, albeit more rarely, the great liturgical passages from the Old Testament are equally present elsewhere. They are, on occasion, the theme of Augustine's polemical works.

In fact, it is in polemical writings that liturgical pericopes resurface. This is particularly true of Donatist documents. Above all, in his commentaries on the Psalms, Augustine explains obscure passages, in reference to the clearer texts of Paul and the Gospels.

These few examples allow one to appreciate the diffusion of the liturgical Bible throughout all of Augustine's work. It alone constitutes half of the biblical citations found in Augustine.

This Bible, solemnly read or sung each year, was recalled incessantly on numerous occasions. Because of the oral transmission normative for this period, it was obviously a memorized Bible. Augustine and his congregation knew the liturgical lessons and their related Psalms by heart. This explains the biblical memory of Augustine. It was not a knowledge of the entire Bible but rather of the Pauline Epistles. He had been imbued with these epistles at the time of his conversion. They were the part of the liturgical life for which Augustine was responsible during the thirty–five years of his episcopate. The "memory" of the baptized was such that they would not accept modification of the readings by their bishop. Augustine, on the day of the Passion, could read no other version than that of Matthew. Frequently Augustine's listeners could finish a scriptural text which he had started. This type of memory is limited. Augustine himself states that he did not know the entire Psalter by heart. A large portion of the Old Testament is absent in Augustine's work. Can it be inferred that Augustine did not know it by heart? We have no proof that the absent texts were not liturgical or even disputed in Africa since Augustine did not, like Jerome, have the occasion to comment systematically upon the great books of the prophets, etc. Regardless, the mnemonic learning of the Bible by the people of Hippo is an example of the oral tradition that the Creed and the Our Father had to be learned by heart and never written.

NOTES

1. F. Dreyfus, "L'actualisation de l'Ecriture, 1: Du texte à la Vie," *Revue Biblique* (Jan., 1979) : 23 see "Le témoignage de l'histoire."

2. Sermons de la Vigile: Guelferbytanus 4.1; Guelf. 5.4; Guelf. 6.1.

3. *Sermo* Wilmart 5.2; *Commentaries on the Psalms* 2. s.1.1; *Commentaries on the Psalms* 105.12.

4. Answer to Letters of Petilianus 2.92.211; *Homilies on the Gospel of John* 3.9.

5. *Sermo* Wilmart 5.2; *Sermon 363*; *Commentaries on the Psalms* 105.12.

6. *Sermo* Denis 2.4; *Commentaries on the Psalms* 117.1.14.22; *Commentaries on the Psalms* 41.1.2.4.12

7. *Homilies on the Gospel of John* 1.12; *Sermo* Denis 12.4; *Sermo* Wilmart 14.

8. See Manlio Simonetti, "Rufin d'Aquilée, Les Bénédictions des Patriarches" *SC* 140 (1968): pp. 11–21: Jalons pour l'Interpretation Patristique du chapitre 49 de la Genèse (Study of the blessing of Judah, Gen. 49:8–12). See also M. Audineau, *SC* 187, pp. 385 and 464–465.

9. *Sermo* Wilmart 6; *Sermo* Guelf. 6; *Sermo* Denis 4.1, 218.12.12; *Commentaries on the Psalms* 88.s.2.7; *City of God* 16.41–42.

10. This is Matthew's account of the Resurrection.

11. Note that Romans 4:25 confirms the deliverance from sin with its statement: "Jesus who was put to death for our sins and raised to life to justify us." See Romans 4:25; *Sermo* Guelf. 5.1; *Sermo* Wilmart 4.1; *Sermo* Guelf. 4.

12. Revelations 5:5; *Sermo* Wilmart 6.2; *Sermo* Guelf.6; *Sermo* Guelf. 4.

13. *Sermo* Guelf. 6, 218.12.12; *City of God* 16.41–42.

14. *Sermons des Vigiles*: Guelf. 5.4 (Gen. 1:2–4); Denis 2 (Gen. 1:1–2). *Sermons du jour de Pâques*: 118.1 (Gen. 1:1); 230 (Gen. 1:2–3); 225 (Gen. 1:1); 226 (Gen. 1:2–5a); 119.2 (Gen. 1:1). *Sermons du jour de l'Octave*: Guelf. 18.1 (Gen. 1); 258 (Gen. 1:1–4); 223 (Gen. 1:4–5). Also see Cyrille Lambot, "Une Série pascale de sermons sur les jours de la Création," *Mélanges Ch. Mohrmann*, (1913) pp. 213–220. It would have been on the afternoon of Easter Sunday of that year that Augustine commented upon the Gen. 1:1–5 passage.

17

"He Pitched His Tent in the Sun"
PS. 18:6 (LXX)

JOSEPH WOLINSKI

How does Augustine use the Bible? I would like to approach this question by taking a concrete example. I will look at how Augustine uses a phrase from Psalm 18 (Psalm 19) which says: "He pitched his tent in the sun" *in sole posuit tabernaculum suum* (Ps.18:6a [Ps. 19]).

The General Problematic

My research is animated by three convictions which motivate the study of the Church Fathers in general and Augustine in particular:

1. The faithful reading of the Bible was the privileged source of inspiration and spiritual nourishment for the discourse of the Church Fathers.

2. Reference to the Bible allowed the earliest commentators to present the Christian mystery globally, in a synthetic way. What was later to be broken up into distinct treatises is presented in small organic units. If a theme is recurrent, it is constantly reworked. One of the expressions of this creativity is the phenomenon of 'constellations' of scriptural citations. These constellations revolve around a given nucleus, expanding, diminishing and, on occasion, dissolving themselves only to regroup around another nucleus.

3. In Augustine's actual day–to–day teaching, he was able to avoid the inconveniences of what is sometimes known as "Augustine's trinitarian scheme." By "Augustinian trinitarian scheme," we mean a way of presenting the data of faith which disassociates the mystery of God considered in itself *ad intra*, from the work of God, considered as being exterior to God *ad extra*. Consequently, one envisions the trinitarian relationships *ad intra* and

the trinitarian operations *ad extra* separately or, in the words of Karl Rahner, the immanent Trinity and the economic Trinity as treated separately. Augustine is traditionally held responsible for the disassociation of the immanent and economic Trinity. It is true that in Augustine we find forcefully defined the principle of *insparabiliter operari* (operating without separation) which leads, if one is not careful, to this disjunction. Since the Father, the Son and the Holy Spirit are "of the same unique substance" and these three are "one unique God" (*On the Trinity* 1.2.4, 1.4.7), the Trinity "is said to act inseparably *inseparabiliter operari* in what it does"(1.5.8).

Inseparabiliter operari flows from a fundamental given of faith defined at the Council of Nicaea. If the Son is "consubstantial with the Father" (Nicaea); if the Father, Son and Holy Spirit are not formed of three heterogeneous substances as Eunomius postulated, but of one and the same substance, then the Three are not three separate gods, but "one unique God." This unity is obviously translated in a unity of operation wherein the three are inseparably manifest.

The danger of such a way of speaking, which was elaborated in reaction to Arianism, is that one can formulate one's discussion on the Persons of the Trinity and their mutual relationship (*On the Trinity* Book. 5) in making an abstraction from all relations to creatures. This step is certainly legitimate. Athanasius saw, when he dared to write in his celebrated passage from *Against Arianos* (2.31): "Even if God had judged it good not to create, He would nonetheless have had His Word." Thus is the absolute independence of the Father and the Word from creation and the absolute gratuity of the act of creation magnificently affirmed. But legitimate though it may hypothetically be, this statement should be paired with the consideration of the situation as it exists. God could have created nothing, but, in fact, it pleased Him to freely decide for all eternity to create man and bind Himself to his creation in a definitive and irrevocable manner. K. Barth magnificently expressed this mystery when he wrote: "Once and for all, it was decided in Him (Christ) that God does not exist without humanity..." [1]

If it is true that Augustine formulated the principle which eventually led to one part of the trinitarian mystery being *ad intra* and the work of salvation being *ad extra*; if it is true that he attached trinitarian operation not to the Divine Persons, but to their unique substance (*On the Trinity* 1.12.25); then his contention must be completed with two other affirmations:

1. By affirming unity of substance in the Trinity and unity of operation *ad extra*, Augustine is not being innovative but merely passing on a heri-

tage which he received from his predecessors. Augustine says this himself in *On the Trinity* 1.4.7. He does this by being compelled to answer questions which were being asked around him on precisely the subject of *inseparabiliter operari* (1.5.6)! His discourse falls into the narrow parameters of the Council of Nicea, even though he does not mention this in his *On the Trinity*.

2. Regardless of the importance which this discourse has for the history of theology, the development of *insparabiliter operari* takes up only a small portion of Augustine's work. It is the result of a late confrontation with anomoeanism (Father and Son unlike in essense). When considered as a whole, Augustine's thought does not introduce a disjunction between God and man. In this sense, Augustine is not "Augustinian." Being faithful to scripture and older patristic tradition, he ordinarily envisages the whole of the Christian mystery in which God is not thought of without humanity, nor humanity without God. We will find a confirmation of this, particularly at the end of our study.

General Presentation of the Biblical Documentation

The documentaion related to Ps. 18:6a (Ps. 19) includes thirteen texts, in which the phrase is cited once or several times, making eighteen citations in total. Some of the texts can be dated and others cannot. Here is the list:[2]

No.	Date	Text	Reference
1	394–395	*En. in Ps.* 18.s.1.6	*CCL* 38, pp. 102–103.
2	401–402	*C. litt. Petil.* 2.32.74	*BA* 30, p.321.
3	Sept. 2, 403	*En. in Ps.* 44.3	*CCL* 38, pp. 494–495.
4	405–406	*De consensu Evang.*1.30.46	*CSEL* 43, pp. 46–47.
5	Easter 407	*Tract. in Io. Ep.*1.2	*SC* 75, pp. 114–116.
6	Easter Mon. 407	*Tract. in Io. Ep.*2.3	*SC* 75, p. 160.
7	June 29, 409–410	*Sermo Denis* 12.3	*Misc.Agost.*1, p. 52.
8	409–410	*Ep.*105.4.14	*CSEL* 32.2,pp.605–6.
9	Christmas	*Sermo* 194.4.4	*PL* 38.1017.
10	Christmas	*Sermo* 372.1.4	*PL* 39.1661.
11	(no date?)	*En. in Ps.*18.s.2.6	*CCL* 38, pp. 109–110.
12	(no date?)	*En. in Ps.* 90.s.2.5	*CCL* 39, pp. 1270–71.
13	428	*De haeresibus* 59	*CCL* 46, p. 238.

If we set aside text 4 where Ps. 18:6a (Ps. 19) is used to criticize Lucanus, a pagan poet, and text 13 which deals with sects which quote the passage, we can state that Augustine uses the phrase in three main instances:

    a) in his *Commentaries on the Psalms* (texts 1, 3, 11 and 12);

    b) in his *Sermons on the Nativity* (texts 9 and 10);

    c) in his anti–Donatist works (texts 2, 5, 7, and 8).

Furthermore, when one observes that texts 3 and 4 date from the anti–Donatist period, that text 4 against Lacunas uses an anti–Donatist argument, that text 11 has an anti–Donatist character, we are left with eight texts out of thirteen which are influenced by this famous controversy. Text 1 from 394–395 shows elsewhere that Augustine uses his interpretation of Ps. 18:6 (Ps. 19) to get into the question. It is an interpretation which he will take up continually in his latter work wherein Ps. 18:6 (Ps. 19) is simultaneously applied to Christ and the Church in a trinitarian context.

Ps.18:6a (Ps. 19) according to the Septuagint

In the thirteen cases cited above, Augustine invariably quotes the same version of Ps. 18:6a: *In sole posuit tabernaculum suum*, "He pitched his tent in the sun."

This text coincides with the Verona Psalter in which A. Vaccari[3] has distinguished an ancient Roman source and various revisions, some prior to Augustine, and others from Augustine himself. Ps. 18:6a (Ps.19) has not been revised. It corresponds exactly to the Latin of the Vulgate and the Greek Septuagint:

In sole posuit tabernaculum suum (Vulgate: Ps. 18:6a)

ἐν τῷ ἡλίῳ ἔδετο τὸ σκήνωμα αὐτοῦ (LXX: Ps. 18:5c).

It differs from the received Hebrew text. The three Hebrew words corresponding to this phrase are added to the end of verse 5 (as in the Septuagint). They are translated in several ways: "From (heaven, God) made a tent for the sun" (Clamer–Pirot) or "For the sun, (God) pitched a tent on high." This may be translated as "on the ocean," or "in the ocean," or " in the abyss" with the modification of *bâhem*, "in them" (the heavens), in *bayem*, "in the ocean" or in *bitehôm*, "in the abyss" (Clamer–Pirot, 1950, p. 133).

The general sense of the Hebrew is easily understood. God pitched a tent for the sun by which He affirmed his sovereignty. The Septuagint version is more enigmatic. It appears that God made his dwelling in the sun! E. Pannier (Clamer–Pirot) sees this as a mistranslation. However, the Hebrew meaning is too clear for such a gross mistranslation not to cause

problems. One could wonder if this is not a clue, among others, support-
ing the contention that the authors of the Septuagint worked with a Hebrew text which is different from the one we know. In any case the Greek
Fathers comment upon the Septuagint version, even though Origen (*PG*,
16.1.665–666) and Eusebius of Caesarea (*PG* 23.191 C; see *DSp*, 4. col. 1689)
knew the Hebrew meaning. The Septuagint version is found again in
Aquila, Symmachus, Theodotion and the "fifth column" mentioned by
Eusebius (*PG* 23.191 C as previously cited). The Septuagint text will be
used, more paradoxically and suggestively, by certain heterodox currents
and also, in a different way, by the writers of the Great Church.

Heterodox Readings of Ps. 18:6a (Ps. 19)

In *De haeresibus* 59, Augustine names two heretical groups, the
Seleucians and the Hermianians. Both, in their dualistic vision of the world,
refuse to accept the definitive character of the Incarnation and Christ's
return to the Father in the flesh:

> ...They say that the Savior is not seated at the right hand of God in the
> flesh, but rather that he has disposed of it and that he left it in the sun,
> taking as a pretext for that the Psalm which reads: "He pitched his tent
> in the sun..."(*De haer.* 59, 60).

Augustine has taken Philasterius almost word for word (*De
diuersis haeresibus* 55). We are dealing with gnostic sects of the second and
third centuries, whose thinking is very close to Hermogenes of Carthage.
Tertullian, Clement of Alexandria (*Eclogae propheticae* 56) and Hippolytus
(*Elenchos* 8.71.3) refer to Hermogenes. Origen, who is also familiar with
this christology, attributes the error to one of scriptural exegesis. These
heretics are mistaken because they do not recognize the "allegorical meaning" of the passage cited (from Pamphilus, *Apologia pro Origene* 7).

Some Traditional Readings of Ps. 18:6a (Ps. 19)
Prior to Augustine:

It was through allegorical interpretation of Ps. 18:4–7, that the
Church Fathers, prior to Augustine, could admit the Septuagint version
of the Ps. 18:6a, without difficulty.

In identifying Christ with the sun, the first Christian authors could
give a christological slant to this portion of the verse. This is witnessed to
by Justin (*Dialogue with Tryphon* 64.7), Irenaeus (*Adversus haereses* 4.33.13)
and Tertullian (*Adversus Marcionem* 4.11.7). They saw in this text and par-

ticularly in verse 7, the encapsulation of Christ's mission: His descent from heaven, His passage on earth and His return to heaven. In this context, however, Ps. 18:6a posed a problem. How was one to understand the Christ/sun pitching his tent "in the sun"? Origen (or rather Evagarius of Pontus[4]) answers that "he" concerns the Father who has made Christ his dwelling place. However, if one agrees that the subject of the phrase in verse 6 is Christ, how does one interpret the beginning of the verse?

According to F. Doelger[5] the christological interpretation of this passage led to two allegorical readings. The first one identifies the "tent" of the psalm with the body of Christ. Such is the case with the Gnostic sects about which we have already spoken. The second identifies the "tent" as the Church, which itself is considered as the body of Christ. Consequently Origen wrote (if one accepts the testimony of Pamphilus in his *Apologia pro Origene*):

> "He pitched his tent in the sun." What is this tent of Christ, and the place in which Christ's tent is pitched? By "tent" of Christ, I understand the Church, and by "sun", what could I understand but this true light which enlightens all men coming into this world? (Jn. 1:9)... Therefore he pitched his tent in the sun which is to say he pitched his Church in the "Sun of Justice" (Mal. 3:20)...(cited by Pamphilus in *Apologia pro Origene* 7).

Aside from the identification of the "tent" with either the personal or ecclesial body of Christ, Christian tradition prior to Augustine, retained other elements of interpretation. In particular, it retained the image of Christ as a giant who surpassed Hercules (Justin) or the vision of Christ as being like this sun which extended its influence throughout creation so that nothing escaped its heat. However, the nuptial character clearly expressed in verse 6b (like a bridegroom leaving his nuptial chamber...) attracted most attention. Cyprian (*Ad Quirinum* 2, 19), Novatian (*On the Trinity* 13.68.5), Origen or Evagrius (*PG* 12.1243 A) and Eusebius of Caesarea (*PG* 22.1106 B) bear witness to this.

Commentary *1 on Ps. 18 (Ps. 19) and* Sermons *194 and 372 on the Nativity*

There existed, therefore, a strand of Christian tradition which applied Ps. 18:6–7 to Christ and the Church. How did Augustine tap into this tradition? Direct contact with the Greek Fathers has yet to be proven. Jerome's letter 75, to the young Augustine, would lead one to believe that Augustine explained the Psalms in a personal manner, independent of the great Latin or Greek authors (*CSEL* 34.2, p. 318.4 to p. 319.1). Two things are certain. On the one hand, Cyprian cites Ps. 18:6–7 to prove that "Christ takes the Church as His bride" (*Ad Quirinum* 2.19). On the other hand, the church in North Africa used Ps. 18:6 in its Christmas celebrations. This is proved by the six Christmas sermons which commented upon the whole verse (*Sermons* 187.4; 191.2; 194.4; 195.3 and 372.1).

Augustine takes an interest in Ps. 18:6a for the first time in *Commentary* 1 dating from 394–395 and devoted to Psalm 18 (Ps. 19).

> "He planted his tent in the sun" (Ps. 18:6a). In order to fight against the power of temporal errors, the Lord Who needed to bring on earth the sword (Mt. 10:34) and not peace, brought to evidence in the temporal dispensation a habitation for himself of a military type ("tent"), which is the disposition of his incarnation. He himself is like the "Bridegroom coming out of the nuptial chamber" (6b) as He himself comes out of the virginal womb in which God united with human nature as the Bridegroom became one with the Bride. "He leapt like a giant to enter into his course" (6c). He leapt like the strong one *par excellence* who surpasses other men with his incomparable strength in order to run through his life, not to stay in it. For he did not "stop in the way of sinners" (Ps. 1:1). "From heaven above he comes out" (7a). He comes from the Father by an exit which is not temporal but eternal, the one by which he was born from the Father. "And his course goes up to the highest heaven"; (7b). He raises himself through the fullness of his divinity to be equal with the Father "and nobody can avoid his heat" (7c). When the Word became flesh and dwelt with us (John 1:14) taking on himself our mortality, He did not allow any mortal to find refuge in the shadow of death, for death also had been penetrated by the heat of the Word. (*Commentaries on the Psalms* 18.s.1 *text 1*)

For Origen, "to pitch his tent in the sun" meant "to establish the Church in the light of Christ, the Sun of Justice." The expression here in Augustine means to found the economy of the incarnation in broad daylight (*in manifestatione*). It takes on a militaristic patina in accordance with the current meaning of *tabernaculum* as a soldier's or commander's tent. The Lord's marriage with human nature is only mentioned in reference to verse 6b. Verse 7 provides the dimension of the Son's mission, all the while conforming to earlier theological tradition. He who is united with us originated eternally with the Father. He returned to his original equal status with the Father after the Resurrection and the Ascension. His kenosis and his departure to heaven do not impede his influence from reaching all humanity (V.7c).

For Augustine, the association of Ps. 18:6a with the economy of the incarnation is taken up again in *Sermon* 194 written for Christmas day.

> ...as we are walking in faith, still at a long distance from Him, as we are hungry and thirsty for justice and wish with unspeakable desire to contemplate the beauty of the form of God, let us celebrate with humble devotion the birthday of his form as a slave. We cannot yet contemplate what is born from the Father before the dawning; let us celebrate in the night what is born from the virgin. We do not yet realize that "His name remains before the sun" (Ps. 71(72):17). Let us recognize "his tent pitched in the sun" (Ps. 18:6). We do not yet see the only Son living in the bosom of the Father, but let us remember "the Bridegroom coming out of the nuptial bed" (Ps. 18:6). We are not yet able to sit at the table of the Father, but let us discover the crib of our Lord Jesus Christ. (*Sermon* 194.4.4) *text 9*

Sermon 372, also written for Christmas day, cites all of verse six. In this way the theme of the incarnation is linked with that of Christ, Husband of the Church:

> The holy King David speaking of Christ declares in the Psalms: "He pitched his tent in the sun; like a bridegroom coming out of the nuptial bed, he leaps like a giant..." (Ps. 18:6). Today indeed he came out of the sacred bed, which means the inaccessible and incorruptible recesses of the bosom of the virgin. From there he has come out Son of the virgin, Spouse of the virgin, which means Son of Mary, Spouse of the Church. (*Sermon* 372.1.2) *text 10.*

The subsequent portion of *Sermon* 372, (we will return to this later), develops the theme of the marriage of the Lamb with the Church (Ps. 18: 6b, c). This is prepared for by Christ's death, celebrated in His Resurrection, and consolidated in the eternal marriage of the Ascension, to which we owe the gift of the Holy Spirit. As with *Sermon* 194, this treatise also ends with a vibrant appeal to wish for the invisible and to enflame hope.

Ps. 18:6a in the Anti–Donatist Texts

The few texts, which I have called to mind, already show the way in which Ps. 18:6 allows Augustine to offer a global vision of the Christian mystery, a link to Christ and the Church. The same theology is at work in the Donatist controversy.

Augustine unceasingly reproaches the Donatist party for the particularism which claims that the Church is confined to Africa, while on the other hand he himself never stops affirming the universality of the Church. In the service of this theme he plays with Ps.18:6a (Ps. 19:6) and the traditional image of the sun crossing the sky from one extreme to the other. This is seen in the earliest anti–Donatist text, which is presented in a passage of *Answer to Letters of Petilianus* 2. After citing Ps. 18:4–5, where he explains prophecies that the gospel "would offer itself to all the languages of the nations, and that the Body of Christ would make it sound throughout the universe in all languages" Augustine continues:

> Hence it is that the true church is hidden from no one. And hence comes that which the Lord himself says in the Gospel: "A city that is set on a hill cannot be hid." And therefore David continues in the same Psalm: "He has placed his tabernacle in the sun," that is in the open light of day; as we read in the Book of Kings, "For you did it secretly but I will do this thing before all Israel, and before the sun." (2 Kings 12:12); and He Himself is as "the Bridegroom coming out of his chamber, and rejoicing as a giant to run his race. His going forth is from the end of heaven." Here you see the coming of the Lord in the flesh. "And his circuit to the ends of it." Here you have his Resurrection and Ascension. "And there is nothing hidden from the heat thereof." Here you have the coming of the Holy Spirit, whom He sent in tongues of fire that He might made known the glowing heat of charity, which he certainly cannot have who does not keep the bond of peace with the Church which is spread throughout all languages. (*Against the Letters of Petilianus* 2.32.74: BA 30, p. 321, *NPNF* 4, p. 548) *text 2*

The general tone of this passage calls to mind other anti–Donatist writings, in particular certain homilies from *Homilies on Saint John* and *Homilies on the First Letter of Saint John*. Both insist upon charity and unity as gifts of the Holy Spirit. In this context, two themes are developed: a) the theme of the Body of Christ, or the Church which will make the Gospels sound throughout the universe, and b) the theme of the city built on the mountain which cannot escape anyone's notice. Elsewhere (texts 5 and 6) the mountain itself is seen by everyone. In this case the second theme is an illustration of the first. The first and principal theme is the appearance of Christ *in sole*, "under the sun (in sunlight)."

The Meaning of In Sole

The expression *in sole* is ambiguous. It can be translated by "in the sun," meaning that the sun is the site where the tent is pitched. This is what the Gnostics, denounced by Augustine (text 13), did. It can also be translated as " under the sun." In this case it is understood as in the sunlight or, in other words, the tent is pitched in the light of the sun. The theme of the city or mountain which is visible to the whole world uses this interpretation. This is the meaning which Augustine adopts, which is illustrated by the over twenty equivalent expressions he uses for it. Christ pitched his tent "conspicuously" (*in manifestatione* is the formulation which is most frequently used) in the sense that it was visible in the light of the sun to all humanity, unto the ends of the earth (text 8). However, the first meaning, which Augustine does not employ, could also feed into Augustine's thinking in a circuitous manner. Let us suppose that Christ had pitched his tent in the sun which is identified in some way with Him. It follows that Christ, while crossing the sky, would contact in his humanity, the whole world lit by the sun (See Ps. 18:7). During his earthly life, Christ's human presence was limited to a small corner of the world, and after His Ascension his physical presence was removed altogether. How could he exercise an influence as universal as the sun's by his humanity? This is where the Church comes in. The Church, Christ's Body, is spread over the entire surface of the earth. Christ is visibly and perceptibly present everywhere. We find here again the great anti-Donatist theme of the universality of the Church in reference to the "tent" in which the Word becomes visible. The "tent" symbolizes the Word made flesh which refers inseparably to Christ and to the Church.

"In the Sun" One Flesh: Christ and the Church (Homily on the First Epistle of John 1.2)

Ps.18:6a makes its entrance shortly after the beginning of *Homily* 1 on the First Epistle of John, as an illustration for the first verse of the epistle. It solemnly affirms that the Word of Life is given to be seen and touched. Augustine writes: "Life itself is seen in the flesh: it has been set in full view so that a reality which was only visible to the heart has become visible to the eye, in order to heal the heart"(*Homily on 1 John.* 1.1). The expression "set in plain view" *in manifestatione posuit* announced the *in sole posuit* of the Psalm which appears in the following text:

> "We have seen and are the witnesses."(1 John 1:1) What have they seen? In the manifestation. What does this mean? In the sun, that is, in this light of day. And how should He be seen in the sun who made the sun, except as "in the sun He has set forth his tabernacle; and Himself as a bridegroom going forth out of his chamber, exulted as a giant to run his course?" (Ps. 18:6)...that He might be seen by eyes of flesh which see the sun, set His very tabernacle in the sun, that is showed His flesh in mani-

festation of this light of day. (*Homily on 1 John*. 1.2: SC 75, pp. 115–117; *NPNF* 7 p. 461) *text 5*.

Remembering that the bosom of the Virgin united the Word of the Husband and the flesh of the bride, Augustine cites Gen. 1:24 (They will be two in one flesh), Mat. 19:6 which takes up Gen. 2:24 and Is. 61:10:

> And Isaiah remembers right well that they are two, for speaking in the person of Christ he says: "He has set a mitre upon me as upon a bridegroom, and adorned me with an ornament as a bride." (Is. 61:10) One seems to speak, yet makes himself at once bridegroom and bride, because "not two but one flesh:" because "the Word was made flesh and dwelt among us." (John 1:14) To that flesh the Church is joined, and so there is made the whole Christ, Head and body. (*Homilies on the Gospel of John*. 1.2, trans. SC, p.117; *NPNF* 7, p. 461) *text 5*

The Church "is joined to the flesh of Christ" and prolongs it in a certain way. Augustine goes on to say: "The whole Church is the Spouse of Christ; from his flesh it receives its origin and foundations." The Church, however, prolongs the flesh of Christ without fusing with it. Unity does not eliminate the distinction. Augustine makes this important point in his thinking, by using at the same time, two comparisons which are mutually self-correcting. The body illustrates the unity while the spouse safeguards distinction in unity. This is what is expressed in Gen. 2:24 and taken up again in Mat. 19:6. "They will be two in one flesh." It is also seen in Is. 61:10 when Augustine reads it using an exegesis based upon the *First Rule* of Tyconius, the Donatist (*On Christian Doctrine* 31.44; R. P. H. Green 98). "The one" means one voice which both the Husband Christ and the Spouse Church use to express themselves.

Anne–Marie la Bonnardière[5] has shown that this is a frequent teaching of Augustine. It concerns making known the "great mystery" *magnum sacramentum* spoken of in Eph. 5:31–32, the whole mystery of Christ, the "one man" of which the Head is Christ and the Body, the Church. This touches on the main points of Augustine's theology. Before we return to it, we will glance at the second passage in the *Homily on 1 John* which makes reference to Ps. 18:6a (*Homily* 2.3). "The omnipresent mountain, whose extension is throughout the universe of the paschal mystery" (*Homily on 1 John*. 2.3).

> On first reading, this second reference to Ps. 18:6a does not seem important. "Into all the earth is their sound gone forth, and to the end of the earth their words." (Ps. 18:5) Why is this? Because "he has set his tabernacle in the sun" that is, in the open light. (Ps. 18:6) His tabernacle, His

flesh, His tabernacle, His Church: "in the sun" it is set; not in the night but in the day. But why do those not acknowledge it? Return to the lesson at the place where it ended yesterday, and see why they do not acknowledge it: "He that hates his brother, walks in the darkness and knows not where he goes, because the darkness has blinded his eyes." (1 John 2:9)...How shall we not be in darkness? If we love our brothers. (*Homily 1 John*. 2.3, SC 75, p. 161, NPNF 7 p. 471) *text 6*

This passage virtually concludes a long digression of the gospel reading of the day (Lk. 24) with which Augustine opened *Homily* 2. He relies upon two previously developed themes which correspond with each other. The first is the theme explored at the end of *Homily* 1 (1.13), of the mountain which is visible to all. The second is that of Christ explaining scripture to the disciples on the road to Emmaus, which is the focus of the digression at the beginning of *Homily* 2 (2.1–3).

a) The theme of the mountain which is present throughout the world presents an occasion to castigate the blindness of the Donatists who do not see it. They haven't eyes for the Mountain–Church because they have no charity and they don't love unity. However, chapter 1.13, which develops this theme, explains that the Mountain–Church originated from the mysterious rock which had been broken from it without human intervention (Dan. 2:34–35). This rock had grown until it became the mountain which filled the entire universe. One recognizes here, aside from the affirmation of the universality of the Church, the theme of an organic and living link which anchors the Church in the mystery of the Incarnation.

b) We pick up the same theme in the digression at the beginning of *Homily* 2 regarding the disciples on the road to Emmaus (2:1–3). Here Augustine presents the exegesis which Christ himself gave from the entire Old Testament. The main point is that his explanation is not limited to the proclamation of the Paschal mystery. According to Lk. 24:47, it includes equally, the extension of this mystery to all of humanity by preaching, conversion (penitence) and baptism ("for the remission of sins"). Augustine writes:

> But what did the Lord show to be written of Him in the Law and the Prophets? What did He show us?...Why did it behoove Christ to suffer and to rise again? For this reason: "All the ends of the earth shall be reminded and converted to the Lord, and all the kindreds of the nations shall worship before Him." (Ps. 21:28/ Ps. 22:27; cf. Luke 24:47) For that you may know it behooved Christ to suffer and to rise again, in this place also He added, that after setting forth the Bridegroom He might also set forth the Bride? "And that there be preached in His name, repentance and remission of sins throughout all the nations, beginning at

Jerusalem" (Luke 24:27)...It is manifest that Christ has suffered, is risen again, and is ascended into heaven. The Church is also made manifest, because there is preached in His name "repentance and remission of sins throughout all the nations" Where did it begin? "Beginning at Jerusalem." A man hears this; foolish and vain (how shall I express it?) worse than blind! So great a mountain, and he does not see it; a candle is set upon a candlestick, and he shuts his eyes against it. (*Homily on 1 John.* 2.2, *SC* 75, pp. 155–57; *NPNF* 7 p. 469.70).

In the modern Church this same dynamism is seen. It is the dynamism of Christ who entered into time to save humanity and bring it the eternal life which transcends time. It is the presence of the resurrected Christ which continues in the Church through its history, preaching, liturgy and sacraments. In the words of a modern theologian, the Church is truly "the resurrected Christ made visible to the world" (J. Doré).

"One man, one God": Some Aspects of the God–Man, Man–God Relationship according to Augustine's rereading Ps. 18:6a (Ps. 19:6)

"One man, one God": Ps. 18:6a in
Commentaries on the Psalms 90

The meaning of this phrase appears simple: Christ "pitched his tent in the sun" meaning that he manifests "his flesh" in full light to everyone. However, this manifestation needs no less of an explanation in Augustine's estimation. Manifest to all, this flesh is not recognized by all. Augustine resolves this first difficulty by saying to see what is shown, one must have the Holy Spirit and charity. Shown to all, this flesh is not only the personal body of Christ but the whole reality of the Church spread throughout the universe. The explanation of this second difficulty requires closer attention.

It is not sufficient to say that the flesh of Christ spreads itself horizontally across the earth (and across the centuries) because of the Church. Another sort of vertical dimension gives the horizontal one its value. If Christ formed with the Church "one man," mysteriously he is also in some way "one God." The two expressions, "one man , one god" are juxtaposed in a passage of sermon 2 from the *Commentary on Ps. 90*, which also mentions Ps. 18:6a:

> Because He manifests His own flesh in the sight of all, the psalm says: "He pitched his tent in the sun"...But how could He have pitched His tent there, had He not "like a Bridegroom come out of the nuptial bed?"...The "tent" is the same as the bride. The Word is the Bridegroom, the flesh the bride,

and the nuptial bed is the womb of the virgin. And what does the apostle say? "They will be both in one flesh; this is a great mystery; I am applying it to Christ and the Church" (Eph 5:32). And what does the Lord say Himself in the gospel? "Hence they are no longer two but one flesh" (Mat. 19:6). From two, one single man, one single God, *ex duobus unum, ex Verbo et carne unus homo, unus Deus*. (*Commentaries on the Psalms* 90.s.2.5.) How is one to understand the expression *unus homo, unus Deus*?

The formulation continues with *ex Verbo et carne*, which could lead one to believe that Augustine had only the mystery of the Incarnation and hypostic union in mind. The union of the Word and the flesh constituted Christ at the same time man and God. The Péronne–Ecalle edition translates it in the following way: "The Word and the Flesh make one Man–God" (Trans. M. Vincent, t. 13, Paris, 1871, p. 682). But we know that the expression "one man" includes for Augustine, the human Jesus and all the humans in the Church who make up the "flesh" of the Word. He writes: "Today, one man speaks in the middle of all people, in everyone's language; one man, in other words, the Head and the Body; one man, Christ and the Church, he the perfect man, the Husband, she, the Wife. But they will be, it says 'Two in one flesh' (Gen. 2:4)" (*Commentaries on the Psalms* 18.s.2.10). It is this man who constitutes paradoxically, "one God." Now the expression "one God" also takes on expanded meaning, which is not limited to the Word! How can the Word be declared good, Augustine wonders, when Jesus said that "God alone is good"(Mt.19:17)? He answers by saying the Word is also "God," one God *with the Father*:

> How is He good, if not because He is God? For He is not just God. He is "one single God" with the Father. In saying "nobody is good but God alone" He did not separate (from the Father). He united (with Him). (*Commentaries on the Psalms* 44:4/45)

The goodness of God is the goodness of the Father which shines forth in the Son, by the Son and is communicated in some manner to man. Augustine writes: "God says this (Ps.44:2) of His good Word and source of goodness for us, him the only goodness by which we can be good" (ibid.).

Two equally admirable births because both are divine...

The expression *unus homo, unus Deus* brings us back to the principle enunciated at the beginning of the paper. Far from separating the mystery of God *ad intra* and the work of salvation *ad extra*, Augustine holds both together. He envisages the whole in his unity of being. This appears in our first text (*Commentaries on the Psalms* 18.s.1). It is confirmed by the two Christmas sermons (texts 9 and 10). *Sermon* 372 provides a further example. Because the divinity engaged itself into human existence, the birth of Christ is as indescribable as the eternal birth from the Father, and as admirable since it is also divine. Augustine writes:

> The two births *utraque nativitas* are unspeakable, both are marvellous, are admirable, because both are divine *quia divina est* (*Homily* 372.1.1).

In the poverty of the flesh, Christ is both the hiddeness and the manifestation of God Himself. This is why the Christmas sermons can invite the faithful to invest in their contemplation of the crib, the inexplicable and burning desire which moves them to contemplate the divine nature and the person of he who is begotten of the Father (*Homily* 194.4.4). Even the humbling of the Son is impregnated with beauty for the believer:

> Why did He have beauty up to the Cross? Because what is folly for God is more wise than human wisdom. What is weakness for God is much stronger than men (1 Cor 1:25). So may He come to us who believe in Him, the Bridegroom ever beautiful...He is beautiful in heaven and beautiful on earth, beautiful in the womb of His mother, beautiful in the arms of His parents...beautiful on the wood, beautiful in the tomb, beautiful in Heaven. Listen to this Song (Ps. 44) with intelligence and may the weakness of the flesh not take your eyes away from the splendor of His beauty (*Commentaries on the Psalms* 44.3, Péronne–Ecalle, t. 12, pp. 355–356).

God is united with humanity in such a way that humanity can unite with God. This is not union with a faceless God but union in relationship with the God who presented himself in Christ's face and entered with him into history.

The wedding "under the Sun" of Him who was "before the sun"...

The relationship between God and man which is seen "in the sunlight" is presented in our texts under the motif of marriage. This marriage illustrates the "vertical" relationship with Him whose "name was before the sun" since He "made the sun" (*Homily* 194.4.4; *Homily on 1 John* 1.2).

From Christ's perspective, the "marriage with flesh" occurs in the bosom of the Virgin, but continues throughout His life, in order to be fully realized in the Resurrection. Paradoxically, the "distance" with regard to the Church, which is introduced by the Resurrection and the Ascension, accords with the growing union of the Church and its Bridegroom thanks to the gift of the Holy Spirit. Augustine writes:

In the bosom of the virgin, He received human flesh as an earnest; on the Cross He shed His blood as a very precious dowry; in the Resurrection and Ascension He sealed the bonds of His eternal marriage...He has gone up to heaven; He has taken captivity captive; He has given presents to humankind (Ps. 67:19 /Ps. 68:18).Which presents? The Holy Spirit through whom charity has been shed into the minds of people; the Church has been united with Christ her Spouse without possibility of separation. (*Homily* 372.2) *text 10*

From the Church's perspective all reality is placed under the sign of the Resurrection. A passage from the *Commentary* on Psalm 90 (in which Ps.18:6a occurs) illustrates how the Paschal Mystery inaugurated the setting in which the Church's relationship to Christ is established. By His Resurrection and Ascension, Christ *placed his refuge in a very high place* (Ps.90:9/ Ps. 91:9), but His "tent" (Ps. 90:10; Ps. 18:6a) remains exposed to blows and persecution (Mt. 27:26; Act. 9:4). "He is raised above all the heavens, but His feet are still on earth; the Head is in heaven but the Body is on the earth..." Therefore the "flesh of Christ" knows two very different states, but these may not be separated. The incommensurate distance which exists between the Head and the Body opens a space of tension and upward movement which mobilizes the Church to a life of progress and transformation (*Homily*, 91.7–9). The time of the Church makes possible an exterior change, visible throughout the earth. The new exterior should correspond to an interior change: "the casting aside of the old man and the changing to the new man" (*Commentaries on the Psalms* 44.2). Here we find the "conversion" which constitutes for humanity the path of the Paschal Mystery. Augustine alludes to this path in his commentary on Luke 14:47 (*Homily on 1 John*. 2.2).

The Body, for the whole of its earthly life, across the centuries, climbs towards the Head, thereby entering progressively into the newness inaugurated by the Resurrection. All of the moral effort proposed by Augustine finds its place here. The transformational union of the Bride to the Bridegroom is celebrated in a special way in the Eucharist. Reminding his listeners that the Husband had to "suffer and be resurrected on the third day," Augustine invites Christians to enter from now on, each in his or her turn, the nuptial mystery:

For every celebration is a celebration of marriage: the Church's nuptials are celebrated. The King's Son is about to marry a wife, and that King's Son is Himself a King; the guests frequenting the marriage are themselves the bride. Not as in a carnal marriage, some are guests, and another is she that is married; in the Church they that come as guests, if they come to good purpose, become the bride. For all the Church is Christ's bride, of which the beginning and the first fruits are the flesh of Christ: there was the bride joined to the bridegroom in the flesh. With good reason when He would betoken that same flesh, He broke bread, and with good reason in the breaking of the bread the eyes of the disciples were opened and they knew Him. (*Homily on 1 John* 1.2; *SC*, p.155 NPNF 7, p. 469)

He, equal to the Father in the form of God, who became like us in the form of a slave, remakes us in the image of God. Becoming the son of man, He, the only Son of God, has made the many sons of men, sons of God. Nourishing the slaves in the form of a slave, he made children see the form of God..." (*Homily* 194.2.3).

This passage, also taken from our list, summarizes the doctrine which Augustine finds hidden in Ps. 18 and in a more general fashion throughout scripture. It is extraordinarily reminiscent of Irenaeus of Lyons and is strongly inscribed in the great Greek patristic tradition. We do not wish to minimize the manner in which Augustine distinguishes himself from this tradition but neither do we wish to exaggerate his difference. For those who are attentive to this question, abundant instances are available demonstrating that Augustine does not separate the work of salvation *ad extra* from the mystery of God *ad intra*. They include in this mystery the reference to the whole mystery of Christ, Word of God, "born, died, resurrected, risen (to heaven)" (*On the Trinity* 4.18.24). One could equally say that it roots God in man because of his "tent" irrevocably glorified in heaven, which is Christ still "pitched" here below "under the sun" which means the Church.

NOTES

1. K. Barth, *L'humanité de Dieu*, 1956, p. 28.
2. The list which we are using was established by A.–M. la Bonnardière.
3. A. Vaccari, "Scritti de erudizione e di filologia," 1.1: *Filologia Biblica e Patristica*, Rome, 1952, pp. 253–254, as cited by Dom R. Weber, *Le Psautier romain et les autres anciens psautiers latins*, Rome, 1953, p. x; see ibid., p. 36.
4. See M.–J. Rondeau, *OCP* 26, 1060, pp. 307–348, particularly pp. 311–312 and 325–328.
5. F. J. Doelger, *Die Sonne der Gerechtigkeit und der Schwarze. Eine religionsgeschichtliche Studie zum Taufgelöbnis*, 2nd edition 1971, (1918) pp. 100–111 and in particular pp. 103–105.
6. A.–M. la Bonnardière, "L'interprétation augustinienne du *magnum sacramentum* de Ephés. 5:31," in *Recherches Augustiniennes* 12, 1977, pp. 3–45, in particular pp. 14.29, 14–15, 22–28 (pp. 27–28: Tyconius).

18

A Eucharistic Catechesis

Michel Albaric, O.P.

During the Paschal night, the catechumens, having been enlightened by their baptism, participated for the first time in the Body and Blood of Christ.[1] While they knew that one portion of Christian liturgy was reserved only for those who had been initiated, the arcane discipline was such that they were unaware as to what this liturgy was.[2]

This discipline explains the fact that throughout Augustine's preaching, there are few sermons about the Lord's Table[3] and only discreet allusions to the Eucharist in his works.

On the day following the baptismal night (ad infantes) the new initiates were able to participate communally in a sacrament which they had previously taken separately. The sermon would be short but dense. *Sermon* 227 is perhaps Augustine's richest eucharistic sermon and provides a useful illustration of how the pastor of Hippo transmitted Christian faith with the sacrament of life.[4]

The Liturgical Context

Preached upon an Easter morning after 411[5] it seems that this catechesis had no ordinary place in the liturgy. The arcane discipline stipulated that it not be addressed to the catechumens. The sermon took place, therefore, after they had been sent out. The text of the exhortation (*exordium*) shows that at the precise moment when Augustine spoke, the recitation of the Institutions had been pronounced. The congregation had heard: "The sacrament which you see now (line 6), This bread, which you see on the altar, sanctified by the word of God, is the body of Christ (lines

10–11)." The sermon which was placed between the consecration and the communion was really an admonition and therefore brief.

The newly baptized initiates had received communion for the first time the preceding night (line 7). In the morning the readings from the Books of Genesis, John and Acts began. Augustine said: "Today starts the book which is called The Acts of the Apostles" (lines 31–32). These three beginnings, or three 'births' (to use an expression of Anne–Marie la Bonnardière's) accompanied both the celebration of the Resurrection and the new birth of the *infantes*.

In his exhortation, Augustine invited the newly baptized initiates to participate at the Lord's Table "which you should receive each day" (lines 8–9). This was in keeping with the tradition of daily celebration of the Eucharist[6] at Hippo.

The Order of the Liturgy

"You know the order of the sacraments" (line 42)

1. Reading (Acts) (line 31)
2. Prayer for the Exit of the Catechumens (line 42)
3. Recitation of the Symbol (Creed) (line 47)
4. Dialogue of the Preface (line 49)
5. Sanctificatio Consecration (line 60)
6. Lord's Prayer (line 165)
7. Exchange of the Peace (line 165)
8. Communion (line 71)

Even if this description does not provide new insight into the liturgy, it should be noted that the thread of the liturgy is that of the sermon itself. Augustine's eucharistic catechesis is also a liturgical catechesis.

In this case, the Eucharist is not being examined from the moment following the consecration, *sanctificatio*, but rather from the perspective of the entire movement of the celebration. The movement begins with the comment in the Preface dialogue; "Let us raise our hearts." It is the spiritual movement of the assembly which is united in its progression to its climax. Each element, each moment of the order of the celebration is a *sacramentum: tenetis sacramenta* (the word is in the plural) *ordine suo*. One is far from the precise and rigid meaning of the Sunday sacramentality of later theology. Furthermore, this phrase (line 42) forms an inclusion with the words spoken by Augustine on line 70: "They are great, very great sacraments." Consequently each of these sentences, enumerated from line 42 to line 70, is a *sacramentum*.

It seems that the accomplishment of the Eucharist (the Body of Christ, the ecclesial body, the sacramental body) is linked to the entire movement of the Mass. This is certainly true for the ecclesial body, even if the central moment, for the body of Christ and the sacramental body is the *sanctificatio*. It is not easy for modern Christians, used to mediaeval and Tridentine formulations, to preserve the meaning of this movement.

The Scriptural Citations Found in Sermon 227

1. Explicit Biblical Citations: 1 Cor 10:17a and 1 Cor. 11:27

1 Cor. 10:17a *Unus panis, unum corpus multi sumus.*

"The apostle says: 'We are many, but one bread, one body.' This is how he explains the sacrament of the Lord's Table: 'We are many, but one bread, one body.' (lines 16–18)"

The context of this Pauline verse indicates that to be a communicant of the sacrifice which is on the altar is to be a communicant of the altar, whether it be the altar of God or the altar of demons. Augustine never cites the rest of the 1 Cor. 10:14–17b passage. On the other hand, he cites, 1 Cor. 10:17a sixteen times in various works.[7]

Text 1: after 404 (405–6)	*De consensu Evang.* 3.25.72
Text 2: Dec. 409 in Carthage	*En. in Ps.* 147.7 (preached)
Text 3:	*En. in Ps.* 147.25 (preached)
Text 4: 410–12, Easter Day	*Sermo* Guelf. 7 (preached)
Text 5: after 411, Easter morning	*Sermo* 227 (preached)
Text 6: (date uncertain), Easter Day	*Sermo* 272 (preached)
Text 7: 414?, at Thagaste	*En. in Ps.* 68.s.2.6 (preached)
Text 8: 412	*Ep.* 140.6.63, to Honorarius
Text 9: 415–16	*Ep.* 149.16 to Paulus of Nole
Text 10:417	*Ep.* 185.50 to Count Boniface
Text 11: 417	*Ep.* 18.20 to Dardanus
Text 12: after 420	*De civ. Dei.* 17.5.5
Text 13: (date uncertain)	*Tract. in Io.* 26.13
Text 14: 420–26	*De civ. Dei.* 21.20
Text 15:	*De civ. Dei.* 21.25.2
Text 16:	*De civ. Dei.* 22.18

Text 1: In questioning the blindness of the pilgrims on the road to Emmaus, Augustine states that their eyes were opened by the breaking of the bread. He comments upon the event in the following manner: "No one can hope to know Jesus Christ if he is not a participant in His Body, or in other words, in the Church, the unity of which is shown to us by the Apostle in the sacrament of bread when he says '1 Cor. 10:17a' and when he showed them the bread he had blessed their eyes were opened." In a discreet and rare allusion to the context of the Corinthians verse, it is noted that a demon had blinded the pilgrims. Their eyes were opened when Jesus gave them the sacrament of bread. "Participating in the unity of His Body," the Apostle could recognize Christ since the obstacles of the enemy had been destroyed.

As the meaning of the verse invites, the sixteen citations are based upon the same theme. The bread is the sacrament of unity, a unity of members of which Christ is the head.

Text 2: Because in Him we are one, always one.

Text 3: If therefore the body of Christ is a whole loaf of bread, the members are the pieces.

Text 4: That which you see is the sacrament of unity.

Text 5: (see *Sermon 227*)

Text 6: He has consecrated on His table the mystery of our peace and our unity.

Text 7: In this so sweet food, the so sweet unity of Christ.

Text 8: These words show the communion of a divine republic.

Text 9: The offering of the sacred altar: the sacrament by which is expressed the greatest of our vows....to be in 'the company' of the body of Christ.

Text 10: One loaf, the sacrament of unity.

Text 11: By our Head we are reconciled with God, because in Him the divinity of the only Son participated in our mortality in order that we might participate in His immortality.

Text 12: To eat the bread is the sacrifice of the Christian in the new covenant.

Text 13: Be in the Body of Christ....O sacrament of piety, O sign of unity, O link of love.

Text 14–15: (argument of the "Compassionists" — those who advocated acceptance for baptism of those in adulterous unions — and its refutation)... when a heretic has participated in the body of Christ, he can no longer die eternally. No, says Augustine, he is separated from the Body of Christ because he is not in the relation of peace expressed by this sacrament.[8]

Text 16: Each day members add themselves to this same body.

1 Cor. 11:27: *Qui manducat corpus Christi aut bibit calicem domini indigne, reus est corporis et sanguinis domini.*

"Do you wish to know by what manner the sacraments are given to us? The Apostle says: 'Whoever eats the body of Christ and drinks the chalice of the Lord unworthily is guilty against the body and blood of the Lord.' What is it to take unworthily? To take with distrust, to take with derision. Would that this not appear vile because you see it" (lines 70–75).

Elsewhere in his works, Augustine cites verse 27 only four times. This should not be confused with verse 29 which resembles 27 at the beginning.

Text 1:428?	*Speculum*, 1 Cor. 2:27
Text 2: 405–6	*Contra Cresconium* 1.25.30
Text 3: after 411	*Sermo* 227
Text 4: after 418	*Tract. in Io.* 62.1.

If we ignore the *Speculum* citation, which is merely a scriptural flourish, we find in *Against Cresconius* and the *Homilies on Saint John* that Augustine insists upon the conditions for receiving the sacrament. He writes, "The flesh and blood of Christ is pernicious to those who use it badly" (*Against Cres.*): In Judas (the traitor) the good (the piece of bread given by Christ) produces evil (the entrance of Satan into Judas) because the good is badly received (*Homilies on St. John*). To receive unworthily is "to take with distrust, with derision" (*Sermon 227*); it is to take "without discernment and negligently" (*Homilies on St. John*).

In the texts considered here, it should be noted that the unworthiness about which the Apostle and his commentator speak, is not moral unworthiness or the unworthiness of imperfection of the believer engendered by sin in general, but rather unworthiness provoked by lack of adhesion to the faith. It is also the unworthiness of the nonrecognition of the mystery of the unity of Christ which is made by those who receive the bread and the wine without recognizing Christ's body.

2. Implicit Biblical Citations in *Sermon 227*

Augustine's meditation on the Scriptures is constant, to the point that his preaching is woven through and through with scriptural expressions which seem to spring naturally to his lips. Researching the context of these numerous scriptural allusions will permit us to understand better the biblical background of Augustine's thinking. It will also illustrate that Augustine's theology is, above all else, scriptural.

Lines 5–7	*mensae dominicae...participes factis estis.*
(See 1 Cor. 10:21)	*mensae domini participes esse.*

Saint Paul explains that in participating at the sacrificial table, one is in communion with him, who offered the sacrifice. Participation at the Lord's table in order to realize the unity of the body of Christ will be the whole theme of this preaching.

Line 8	*accipere* (the word is used 10 times)
(See Mt. 26:26)	*Accipite, et comedite: hoc est corpus meum.*
Line 14	*corpus et sanguinem suum quem pro nobis fudit in remissionem peccatorum.*
Line 10	*sanctificatus per verbum dei.*
(See 1 Tim. 4:5)	*sancificatur enim per verbum dei, et orationem.*

Saint Paul vilifies the false doctors who forbid the "use of the food which God created to be used with thanksgiving by believers...The Word of God and prayer which sanctify." Paul did not have the eucharistic meal in mind here. Augustine's rare citation of this verse does not occur in reference to the Eucharist either. They are found in three anti–Manichean treatises.[9]

Line15	*si bene accepistis*
(See 1 Cor. 2:27)	*manducaverit panem...indigne.*

Having explicitly cited 1 Cor. 2:27 earlier, *bene* could in this instance be placed in opposition with *indigne*.

Line 19	*unitatem amare debeatis*
(See Ephesians 4:3)	*sollicite servare unitatem Spiritus in vinculo pacis.*

Only the word *unitas* holds the allusion together, but the context of the Letter to the Ephesians, which calls for unity, is such that it does not seem rash to think that Augustine had it in mind. He writes "There is only one body...one hope... one faith (line 83), one baptism; only one God... who is *above* all ... (*above*: see the commentary of Augustine line 49 from the words *Sursum cor*)."

Lines 42 to 59   surrounding the *ascendit in caelum* of the Symbol.

(See Ephesians 4:9–16)   *qui ascendit super omnes caelos.*

The continuation of the Eph. 4:9–16 pericope concerns the construction of the unity of the body of Christ in the movement of the Ascension. We have already mentioned the *plus haut* movement of the liturgy. It seems that this movement is inscribed in the economy of salvation. The blood is poured for us, followed by the Ascension, and Pentecost where the fire of the Holy Spirit comes to bake the bread of unity (lines 35–41). Augustine concludes with "Thus, in a certain way, is signified unity (line 41)."

Lines 83–84   *spes vestra…in caelo; fides vestra… sit in deum.*

(See 1 Peter 1:21)   *ut fides vestra, et spes esset in Deo.*

The context of 1 Peter 1:17–25 is the fraternal unity which endures, while all that is corruptible passes and that which endures is incorruptible. This is also the meaning found at the end of *Sermon* 227 from line 75 to the last statement: "All that you see passes, the invisible which it points to does not pass." Lines 37 to 39 occur in the same context. "Our straw is consumed, and our heart purified like gold" could allude at the same time to Is. 40:6–8 as cited in 1 Peter 1:24–25 or a similar citation in 1 Cor. 3:12–13.

Lines 85–86   *videtis et creditis*

(See John 6:36)   *vidistis me, et non creditis*

To see and to believe is one of the major themes in John's Sermon on the Bread of Life. To see and to believe is one of the great axes in Augustinian thinking. At the end of *Sermon* 227, faith in the body of Christ leads the believer to the eternal joy of the vision of the whole Christ.[10]

3. A Non–biblical Allusion:

Lines 85–86   *…nonne multa erant tritici grana?*

This reference to Didache 9.4 (How this broken bread, which was dispersed on the mountains was gathered to become one.) is too obvious and well known to require more than a reference.[11]

4. *Accipere* and *conmendare:*

The verb *accipere* appears ten times in this short sermon. In the eucharistic context it presents difficulties in translation since its first two meanings are: to receive and to take. Present day and official French versions of the canon of the Mass translate the word by "prenez et mangez" (take and eat). Its very grammatical ambiguity is rich in meaning. This verb will be considered is two ways: its intrinsic meaning and its imperative voice.

To receive: In this case Christ gives himself. The communicant is passive. He has only to receive (once more is it necessary to receive).

To take: In this case the communicant instigates the action. The verb is active.

In the Latin text of the Gospel (Mt. 26:26) the verb is imperative. Jesus gives the order 'to take' or 'to receive.' He is therefore the master of His body or, in other words, of the sacrament.

Augustine writes: "*Per ista* (bread and cup) *voluit dominus Christus conmendare corpus et sanguinem* (lines 13–14)" and at the end of the sermon (lines 70–71) he continues: "*Magna ergo sacramenta...Vultis nosse quomodo conmendentur.* (With *conmendare* we note the same type of construction in the form of an inclusion as found with *sacramenta*).

Conmendare: Does it mean to commend, to confer, to prove, or to manifest? When used first in the sermon it is active and in the second instance it is passive. Does Jesus commend His body to the hands of the communicants in the same way that He commended His spirit into the hands of his Father? (see Luke 23:46 "Into your hands I commend (*conmendo*) my spirit.")

The Theology of the Three Bodies

1. The Personal Body of Christ

The sanctified bread and wine are the body and blood of Christ (lines 10–12) ...(Sermon 272).

One could hardly be more realistic in the description of the nature of the elements after sanctification. However, the bread and wine are not human flesh and blood but rather the flesh and blood of the resurrected Christ, risen to heaven, seated at the right hand of the Father. They are the mysterious reality of a celestial body. The visible manifestation of this is the bread and the wine which is given and received as a sign of a spiritual fruit. One listens to the word of the apostle: "For not all flesh is alike, but there is one kind for men, ... another for fish. There are celestial bodies and there are terrestrial bodies..."(1 Cor. 15:39–40). The human

276

body and blood of Christ, delivered for the remission of sins (lines 14–15), are at the same time the cornerstone of a happy life "where you will rejoice without end" (line 86, to the end).

Here again the literary structure of the sermon should be noted along with another inclusion. Sins are forgiven in the first lines of the text and the text concludes with the beatific vision.

2. The Ecclesial Body

Without any transition, Augustine moves from the "physico–spiritual" realism of Christ's body to the realism of the ecclesial body of which Christ is the head. He cites 1 Cor. 10–17: "one bread, one body, we are many." Addressing the congregation, Augustine affirms: "you are what you receive (line 15)."[12] This strong expression is not a hapax (an isolated instance) for Augustine writes: "Your mystery is placed on the Lord's table, receive your mystery, be what you see and receive what you are" (*Sermon 272*), "that which we receive we are" (*Sermon 229*) "what you receive you are by the grace of Christ" (*Guelf. 7*).

Taking up the steps of baptism, the preacher develops the analogy between the making of bread and the constitution of the ecclesial body. The multitude of grain becomes the multitude of people. Ground grain are people become humble by fasting and exorcism. The flour soaked in water are people baptized in water. Bread baked in the fire are people receiving the fire of the Spirit which is symbolized by holy oil.

"Weigh the words, don't count them" (*Guelf. 7*) says Augustine regarding the Pauline citation. In effect, this very short verse (we are many but one bread, one body) assembles with great density the meaning of bread and body. The multitude of grain and the people joined together are both a sign of unity. The theme recurs in almost all the texts wherein this First Corinthian verse is cited. Augustine writes: "what you see is the sacrament of unity" (*Guelf. 7*) and "It is in this way, in some manner, that unity is signified (line 41)" etc.

'Sacrament of unity' is a very strong expression. It is more than an analogy, more than a symbol. It is a gift of God Himself for which He should be thanked (line 55).

Commenting upon the dialogue of the Preface, "Raise our hearts," Augustine insists upon the fact that the members of the body must be joined to the Head in order to constitute the whole Christ since it is the head which animates the members. This juncture, this "participation" (and the word recurs frequently), is the work of God for which we owe him thanks. Christians, while participating at the eucharistic table, are united by the Lord into His body.

3. The Sacramental Body

The personal body of Christ, the ecclesial body of Christ and the sacramental body "are great, very great sacraments" (line 70).

The sacramental reality of the consecrated bread and wine is inseparable for the sacramental reality of the Church constituted in the body of Christ by the baptism of its members. Two visible realities are joined. Eucharist is the sacrament of unity; unity in faith, and unity in love which is expressed by the kiss of peace. Augustine writes: "May that which the lips express be realized in the conscience" (line 62). This includes unity in hope shown by the raising of one's heart to the head. He writes: "your hope... is in heaven (lines 83–84)" and "Therefore our head is in heaven" (lines 48–49).

The sacrament is visible in its physical form. To receive it without taking into consideration its meaning would be to receive it unworthily (line 72). Augustine writes: "May that not appear vile to you because you see it. That which you see passes, but that which is invisibly signified does not pass, but remains. Here it is, that we take it, that we consume it, that we eat it "(lines 74–77). Augustine continues with the following questions:

" Is the Body of Christ consumed?

Is the Church of Christ consumed?

Are the members of Christ consumed?

Certainly not..."

The theological approach of *res et signa*, the thing and the sign, is very dear to Augustine. The words, "sign" and "to signify," recur six times. The bread and wine placed on the altar and consecrated are both the sacrifice of God and ourselves (the body of Christ and the ecclesial body). Augustine writes: "*id est signum rei*, (it is the sign of the thing)" (line 63). The sacrament is the mediation between the visible and the invisible. The invisible fruit is unity given by God to Christians as desire for unity. It is found in the desire to participate at the communion table. It recognizes there, both the visible and invisible body of Christ and of the Church in the movement of hearts to the head. This movement is constitutive, in the fullest sense of the word, of unity. Augustine writes: "Receive therefore in order to conform your thinking to it, to preserve the unity of your hearts, to fix you heart on high (lines 82–83)."

The Eucharistic Theology of Augustine in the Vatican II Liturgy

The central theological theme of *Sermon 227* is unity. It is the unity of the body of Christ through the theology of the three bodies. It is unity given by Christ and unity in process, unity becoming that which is illustrated even in the movement of the liturgy. It is unity on the way, *in via*, where the baptized, purchased by Christ's blood, progress towards the blessed vision. As Augustine states: "That which you believe now, you will see on high, where you will rejoice without end" (lines 85–86).

In this way the glorious expression "You are what you have received"(line 15) unites the gift of Christ with the procession of the congregation towards Him.

Two post-communion prayers from the liturgy revision stemming from Vatican II take up this expression. Naturally, one arises from the Feast of Augustine written for the new missal:

"May participation at the Lord's table sanctify us, Lord; so that as members of his body, we will truly become what we have received."[13]

The second occurs in the liturgy of the twenty–seventh Sunday in ordinary time:

"Let us, Lord God, find in this communion our strength and our joy so that we may become what we have received."[14]

Aside from these two explicit citations, we can consider Augustine as the implicit source for a further ten post–communion prayers.

- Eucharist as source of peace (Dec. 20)
- Glorious communion with the Son (Midnight Mass, Christmas)
- Communion as the realization of our unity (Monday, third week of Lent)
- To always be counted as a member of Christ (fifth Sunday of Lent)
- Communion makes us participants in eternal life (Holy Tuesday)
- Communion prefigures the union of the faithful in Christ and serves to unify the Church (eleventh Sunday in ordinary time)
- Eucharist unites us to Christ (twentieth Sunday in ordinary time)
- Do not permit to be separated from you all whom you allow

to participate in the communion of the joy of heaven (thirty-fourth Sunday in ordinary time)
* May our communion realize our unity (post-communion #7)

NOTES

1. N.B. The references indicated in the following manner, (line 6), indicate the line number of the Latin text of *Sermon 227* which was edited by Suzanne Poque in *Augustin d'Hippone*, "Sermons pour la Pâque," Paris, Le Cerf, 1966, pp. 234–243, *SC* 116. The translation of this sermon here provided follows closely that of S. Poque. I have also made great use of her notes and commentaries.

    The steps leading to baptism are described in *De fide et operibus* 6. 8–9. See the note about this text in *Bibliothèque Augustinienne*, 1951, vol. 8, p. 507, n. 17, "Préliminaires au baptême."

2. See *Sermon 132.1* concerning the arcane and ignorance regarding the position of the nonbaptized vis-à-vis the Lord's Table.

3. Sermons definitely attributed to Augustine: 227, 272, *Denis 11, 6 Guelf. 7.*
    Sermons which are contested: *May 129*
    Sermons which are doubtful: 229, *Denis 3, Denis 6.*

4. For the expression "sacrament of life" see *De peccatorum meritis* 1.24.24.

5. See S. Poque, p. 90, n.2. *Sermon 227* can only be a work of great theological maturity. It regroups almost entirely the themes contained in the other sermons about the Eucharist. Therefore it is not a sermon written by a young man. For example, I cite this audacious example of oratory: "We are, (I am) your books" (1.35). The expression: "So that you will not attribute it to your own force (1.50–51)" is perhaps an anti-Pelagian allusion, a heresy which Augustine learns of in 412. See also Pierre–Patrick Verbraken, *Études critiques sur les sermons authentiques de saint Augustin.* The Hague, Nijhoff, 1976. Kunzelmann dates it from 416 or 417 and Fischer dates it from 412 to 413.

6. Regarding the daily celebrations of Eucharist at Hippo, see S. Poque, p. 235, n.2: and Anne–Marie la Bonnardière, "Pénitence et réconciliation des Pénitents d'après saint Augustin," 1st section in *REAug* 1967 (8.1–2), pp. 50–52.

7. The list of these biblical citations was provided to me, with numerous comments, by A.–M. la Bonnardière.

8. The refutation of the Compassionists' argument illustrates that for Augustine eucharist does not imprint 'character' (This word is strange in Augustine) and that communion builds the body of Christ. For Christ unity is given, but to people unity is not acquired once for all, even if baptism makes them definitively capable of such unity. Unity, peace and love are the works of a whole life, symbolized by communion with the only bread, which should be a daily occurrence.

9. *Against Adimantus* 14.2; *Against Felix* 1.7; *Against Secundum* 2.

10. See *De videndo Deo, Letter 147.*

11. Concerning the influence of the Didache see Luigi Clerici, *Einsammlung der Zerstreuten. Liturgie–geschichtliche Untersuchung zur Vor–und Nachgeschichte der Fürbitte für die Kirche in Didache 9, 4 und 10, 5.* Münster, Aschendorffscher Verlag., 1966. *Sermon 227* is not cited here.

12. The reader is perhaps reminded of the aphorism: "Become what you are." It is aphorism 270 in Nietzsche's *Le gai savoir.*

13. *Sanctificet nos, quaesumus, domine, mensae Christi participatio, ut, ejus membra effecti, simus quod accepimus...*

14. *Concede nobis, omnipotens Deus, ut de perceptis sacramentis inebriemur atque pascamur, quatenus in id quod sumimus transeamus.*

19

Augustinian Exegesis and Sexist Canon from the New Testament

CONSTANCE E. MCLEESE

Introduction

Augustine the Sexist?

It is generally conceded that Augustine's attitude towards women is, at the very least, ambiguous. He seems an atypical sexist. In an effort to explain Augustine's atypicality, analysis has been divided between two schools of thought.

The first group of scholars argues more strongly for the contextual mediation of Augustine's writing. They suggest that Augustine is less sexist than is generally assumed. His apparent sexism results from his conceptual and linguistic baggage. Kari Børresen[1] and Margaret Miles[2] have argued that Neo–Platonic metaphysical and anthropological[3] language allowed an unintentional sexism to creep into Augustine's work. From this perspective, Augustine reveals a more positive attitude towards women than that manifested by other patristic writers. Most dramatically Kari Børresen has described Augustine as a patristic feminist.[4]

A second group of scholars assumes a high degree of intentional sexism in Augustine's writing. Any positive attitudes towards women are the result of the historical context of the debates and not genuinely reflective of a non–sexist attitude. Given the overall theory of historical patriarchy, Augustine could no more escape his sexist environment and cosmology than he could develop a theory of quantum mechanics. For example, Susan Schreiner suggests that Augustine's positive description of marriage, and consequently women, is a function of the Manichaean discourse against procreation.[5] She argues that Augustine's truly sexist bias is evident in his description of Adam's ideal companion, who seems closer to Alypius than to Eve.[6] Elizabeth Clark suggests, on the basis of Augustine's descriptions of his relationships with women,[7] that Augustine's less sexist language is not genuinely reflective of a nonsexist attitude.[8]

Consequently the existent analysis of Augustine from within the feminist perspective has proved ambiguous. Augustine may or may not have employed language in an intentionally sexist manner. Augustine may or may not have promoted behaviors and attitudes that are negative to women. Augustine may or may not have proved sexist in his concrete dealings with women.

Purpose

It is this ambiguity which becomes the starting point for the present study. It proposes to look at four key New Testament passages which have been systematically used to argue for female subordination.[9] These are 1 Corinthians 11:3–12, Ephesians 5:22–24, 1 Timothy 2:9–15 and 1 Peter 3:1–7.[10] This project will attempt a depth sounding of Augustinian sexism using these four passages. Therefore the paper will be divided into four sections. Each section will look at Augustine's use of a particular passage. Augustine's subordination of women through these texts will be discussed in a fifth section. The following two questions will be asked: 1. Does Augustine use the passage to argue for the natural inferiority of women? 2. Does Augustine use the citation to promote the social subordination of women?

Section One

1 Corinthians 11:3–12

Of all the passages from the New Testament which have been used to subordinate women this is probably the one people are most familiar with. The passage taken in its entirety is ambiguous and convoluted. Individual pericopes from it have been used to argue against the ordination of women. Parts of it appear to attribute the subordination of women to divine sanction. This subordination appears to accrue from the inferior nature of women. Portions also seem to suggest that women were not created in God's image. Feminist biblical scholars have conceded that the entire passage is contradictory and chaotic in its logic.[11]

1 Corinthians 11:3

Augustine cites some portion of 1 Cor. 11:3–12, forty–three times throughout the corpus of his work. The most frequently quoted is 1 Corinthians 11:3. It occurs twenty–four times and makes up approximately 56% of the references.

Ecclesiology: Out of these twenty–four citations roughly 20% are concerning ecclesiology. Christ is the head of the church. (*On Original Sin* 2.31.27, *On the Psalms* 45:7, *Seven Books of Questions on the Heptateuch* 7.22, *Sermons on the Gospel of John* 57.4.1, *Two Books on Grace of Christ and Original Sin* 2.26.31).

Christology: Five instances, or a further 20%, are christological, dealing with variations upon the theme of Christ's nature. In *On Faith and Symbol* 9.18 this passage is used twice in support of the argument that Christ is the same reality as God. In the same work at 9.20 the personages of Christ, man, and woman become a metaphor for the Trinity. This interpretation is repeated in *On the Trinity* 1.6.2. and 6.9.10. In these instances woman, man, and Christ become an allegory for the relational dynamics of the Trinity. In *Sermon 14.3* Christ's headship is soteriological. It mediates humanity's salvation.

Exegesis: Three times (13%) the passage is used to explain some problem of interpretation in the Old Testament. Twice Christ's headship is prefigured in the Old Testament. Thus the stone of Psalm 45 prefigures Christ's headship (*On the Psalms* 45.18). Similarly the anointing of Jacob's head is proleptic of Christ as the head (*Sermon 39.5*). In *On Marriage and Concupiscence* (1.9.10) Augustine attempts to explain why the patriarchs were allowed multiple wives when such a state of affairs was no longer permissible for Christians by invoking 1 Cor. 11:3. In this case it is part of the natural order for one to rule many.[12] While the text is not expressly used to argue for the subordination of women given the context, implicitly the ruler is the man while the ruled are the women. The gender divisions of the Hellenistic household code are obviously assumed.

Allegory: 46% of 1 Corinthians 11:3 citations follow a similar exegetical pattern. Man and woman are interpreted allegorically. This particular passage does not speak about two distinct genders but rather the anthropology of humans in general. The passage becomes an allegory for the soul without reason in *On the Psalms* 3.10. In *Two Books of Genesis Against the Manichees* 2.12.16 and 2.11.15, Augustine again describes the passage as an allegory about the human mind and body. In the last instance (*Two Books of Genesis Against the Manichees* 2.11.15), having argued elsewhere that woman is created in God's image,[13] Augustine goes on to suggest that Paul included the woman as an illustration quite obviously intended in an allegorical way. To suggest that Paul wanted this verse to be understood literally would countermand Genesis 1:27. Augustine repeats this notion in *Sermon on the Mount* 1.12.34 and *83 Diverse Questions* 67.1. In these instances the wife becomes an allegory for human carnal desire and the man for reason. Consequently, carnal desire is subject to reason which is in turn subject to Christ. The allegorical interpretation occurs once again in *83 Diverse Questions* 57.1 and the *Literal Interpretation of Genesis an Unfinished Book* 3.6. In the former case, the verse is used to illustrate how numbers attributed to the various individuals mentioned in the text can add up to ten. "Ten" mystically signifies God. In the latter instance Augustine suggests that headship refers to the first intellectual creature.

The notion of intellectual headship without reference to Gen. 1:27 is repeated in *83 Diverse Questions* 64.7. In this case the Samaritan woman's five husbands are an allegory for the five senses. "However when each one reaches that age at which he is capable of reason...he will possess a husband, the rational spirit." Continuing, Augustine states that the "divine Word" is "its lawful husband" because Christ is "the Head of the husband (rational soul)."[14] The allegory is repeated in *Homilies on the Gospel of John* 15.19. Once again the Samaritan woman is presented as having had the five senses as her husbands and as lacking the husband of reason which Christ advises her to get.

Finally, the text is cited once as proof of the goodness of Creation. *True Religion* 23.44 stipulates that no part of the created order is evil because Christ is its head.

1 Cor. 11:5–12

This passage includes the famous pericope about the veiling of women. It has been used to argue many things regarding female dress. It was cited to explain the necessity for women of wearing hats in church and to admonish against the cutting of female hair. It is a verse which has plagued interpreters and Augustine is no exception.

In *Letter 245*.1, to Possidius, Augustine interprets Paul's injunction for the veiling of women literally. This is an isolated instance since his natural inclination is to deal with these texts allegorically as shall be seen further on. Discussing the dress of spouses, Augustine comments that husbands should please their wives and wives their husbands, Paul's admonition not withstanding.

285

In *The Work of Monks* 31.39, verses 6–7 are cited in reference to Augustine's argument for male humility. The covering or unveiling of the head when prophesying has become an issue of contention since some monks have argued that long hair is more of an indication of humility than short hair. Augustine resolves the issue by cautioning all to humility. In *The Work of Monks* 32.40 the debate continues. Augustine cites 1 Cor. 11:7 as an example of Paul using a corporeal figure to explain a spiritual reality. Echoing his anthropology from 1 Cor. 11:3, Augustine stipulates that the injunction to veiling is to be carried out in the mind where the true image of God resides.

1 Corinthians 11:7

This verse bears commenting upon before looking at its Augustinian interpretation. Jouette Bassler states that with the framing of the passage Paul implies that woman has a "secondary and derivative status."[15] Ross Shepard Kraemer more bluntly writes: "Paul's distress over the autonomy of Corinthian women...and over an attendant minimization of gender discrimination is clear enough from his otherwise unclear outpouring."[16] Perhaps the most contentious aspect of the verse is the implication that women are not created in God's image.

Imago Dei: Augustine refers to this verse thirteen times. Twelve instances are devoted to the question of *imago Dei*. In four cases Augustine argues that humanity has been created in God's image. They are *Revisions* 1.26, *Literal Interpretation of Genesis an Unfinished Work*, 16.61, *Against Adimantus Disciple of Mani* 5.2 and *The Literal Meaning of Genesis* 11.42.58. Invariably Augustine interprets the biblical *vir* as *homo* in his explanation. In doing so Augustine ignores entirely the second portion of the verse regarding women. While the language is androcentric Augustine quite obviously considers woman to be part of *homo* and therefore in God's image.

On six occasions Augustine attempts to reconcile 1 Cor. 11:7 with Gen. 1:27. In *The Literal Meaning of Genesis* 3.22.34 Augustine resorts to an allegorical interpretation. Paul has a psychological notion in mind wherein the "masculine part (of the mind) is the planner and the feminine the one that obeys."[17] The image of God is found in the part of the mind, regardless of the gender of its owner, which is devoted to "the contemplation of immutable truth."

Again in Book 11 of *The Literal Meaning of Genesis* (11.42.58), Augustine speculates about Paul's meaning in light of Gen. 1:27. This time he develops his thinking at more length. He also attempts to answer the question of the entry of sin into the world. Why did the serpent seduce Eve but not Adam? He suggests that perhaps "the woman was employed on the supposition that she had limited understanding." He goes on to endorse another possibility: "perhaps ...she was living according to the spirit of the flesh and not according to the spirit of the mind." Augustine prefers this version since it serves to explain 1 Cor. 11:7. He writes that Paul did not attribute God's image to her since she had not yet received the "gift of the knowledge of God." Augustine also adds, "This is not to say that the mind of woman is unable to receive the same image." However, the knowledge of God, Augustine speculates, could be acquired under the tutelage of her husband.

Here the reader asks why could the woman not acquire the knowledge directly from God as did her husband? Unfortunately this is not Augustine's question. His deals with the thorny issue of biblical interpretation and an attempt to understand why the woman was seduced and fell into sin and the man apparently just agreed to it with his eyes open. Interestingly Augustine suggests that the man ate because of altruism. He writes: "He (Adam) did not wish to make her unhappy, fearing she would waste away without his support, alienated from his affections, and that this dissension would be her death."

Twice in *Two Books of Genesis Against the Manichees* (2.26.40 & 2.28.42) Augustine merely states that woman was created in the image of God. In the first instance 1 Cor. 1:7–12 is an allegory about human nature. Eve/woman represents human carnal concupiscence. It is a Manichaean misreading of 1 Cor. 11:7 to suggest that all things are not from God. In the second case, the Manichaeans have apparently suggested that woman should not have been created. Augustine cites 1 Cor.11:7–12 as non–technical proof that women are good.

It is in *On the Trinity* 12.7.9 that Augustine most fully develops his reconciliation of Gen. 1:27 and 1 Cor. 11:7. He asks: "Why is not the woman also the image of God? For this is also the reason why she is commanded to cover her head..."[18] Augustine offers the following description of the human mind by way of explanation:

> As we said of the nature of the human mind, that if as a whole it contemplates the truth, it is the image of God: and when its functions are divided and something of it is diverted to the handling of temporal things, nevertheless the part which consults the truth is the image of God, but the part which is directed to the handling of inferior things, is not the image of God. (*On the Trinity* 12.7.10)

He continues: "what the Apostle meant to signify is evident, and it is expressed figuratively and mystically" (*On the Trinity* 12.7.11). The portion of the mind which contemplates God rules or covers the portion which is devoted to temporal things. Otherwise, for Augustine, the veiling of a women's head would be an "empty precept." Consequently, the form of the body is not in the image of God but rather the rational mind which "not only men but also women possess" (*On the Trinity* 12.7.12). Further on (*On the Trinity* 12.13.21) Augustine continues the discussion. He prefers to interpret the women not as the senses of the body (the serpent enjoys that distinction) but as suggested earlier, as a portion of the mind. A full treatment of *imago dei* and Book 12 of *On the Trinity* is found in the published articles of Richard J. McGowan, Mary Cline Horowitz and Kari Børresen.[19]

Finally, Augustine uses 1 Cor. 11:7 ecclesiologically in *Sermon* 262.6. Woman becomes the bride/wife church while Christ functions as the man/husband. In this sense woman becomes the glory of man.

1 Corinthians 11:12

Augustine cites this verse five times. Four instances occur within the context of his polemic concerning the Manichaeans. In *Against Adimantus Disciple of Mani* 3.3, Augustine argues that the union of the two sexes was part of God's plan since all things come from God. *In the Reply to Faustus the Manichaean* 24.2. Augustine makes a similar argument. Augustine rather sarcastically explains that all Catholics know that it is the body not the soul which has gender. In *Continence* 10.24 Augustine again refutes the Manichaean reading of the text which suggests that the two sexes are not from God. Augustine contends that regardless of the order in which they are introduced, Paul intends the reader to understand that everything is truly from God.

The problem of reconciling two biblical passages (1 Cor. 11:12 and John 8:47) is the focus of *On Two Souls Against the Manichaeans* 1.7. How can all things be of God when John writes that "Ye are not of God."? Augustine explains that all of creation is from God which was the intended meaning of 1 Cor. 11:12; however, those who repudiate Christ are not spiritually of God which was John's intended meaning.

Finally, in *The Soul and Its Origin* 1.2.27, Augustine refutes a reading of 1 Cor. 11:12 which argues for a strictly corporeal interpretation of the verse. Augustine contends that, in this instance, the Corinthians passage should not be read literally. Paul intends the reader to understand that both male and female contain a body and soul.

Section Two

Ephesians 5:22–24

This citation echoes the sentiments of 1 Corinthians 11:3. In each of the three verses the analogy is made between the Lordship of Christ and the lordship of a husband. Rhetorically, by linking a wife's subordination to her husband with the Church's subordination to Christ, the Hellenistic household code appears to receive divine sanction.[20] E. Elizabeth Johnson points out that: "the logic of the analogy collapses because husbands do not die for their wives as Christ died for the church..."[21]

Some portion of Ephesians 5:22–24 is cited thirteen times in Augustine's work. Eight of the references exclude the comments about the lordship of men over women. They discuss some aspect of Christ's headship. Six of these are ecclesiological while the remaining two are exegetical. Five times the lordship over women is mentioned. Two instances are prompted by exegetical questions. Of the remaining three, one is pastoral, one is in conjunction with the spiritual attitude of Mary and one concerns the nature of marriage. The section immediately following will deal with the eight occasions when subordination of women is not an issue. The focus is primarily Christ's lordship. Subsequently, the five instances dealing with man's lordship will be discussed.

Christ's Lordship: Following a pattern similar to his treatment of 1 Corinthians 11:3, Augustine uses these Ephesians references to describe an ecclesiological structure. In *On the Psalms* 89.5, Ephesians 5:24 is used adjectivally to describe Christ. In *Letter 142.1*, addressed to the Donatists, Saturnus and Euphratus, who have returned to the Catholic Church, Christ as the head of the Church is used to illustrate the unity of the Church. Eph. 5:24 is used to illustrate to Crecsconius the Donatist that the sacraments, even when administered by sinners, are valid (*Four Books Against Cresconius* 11.21.26). The efficacy of sacraments comes from the headship of Christ. In *Continence* 11.25, Eph. 5:24 leads Augustine to speculate about whether the Church can lust against Christ since Christ as the head of the Church would appear to be analogous to the relationship between a human head and body. He concludes that such lust is possible because the Church has not yet received peace. Eph. 5:23 is combined with 1 Cor. 11:3 in *Seven Books of Questions on the Heptateuch* 7.49.22. Here Augustine makes the ecclesiological statement: *Quoniam caput viri Christus, et ipse est caput corporis Ecclesiae.*[22] With *On Christian Doctrine* 1.16.15 Augustine uses Eph. 5:23 as an introductory statement about the relationship between Christ and the Church.

Twice these passages are used to clear up some exegetical problem. In *Commentaries on the Psalms* 40.5, the God addressed by the psalmist is the same Christ referred to in Ephesians 5:23 as the head and savior of humans. In *83 Diverse Questions* 69.1, Eph. 5:23 refers to the universal Christ. This is the Christ who is formed with the head when the members of the Church are included.

Man's Lordship: The following five passages deal with some aspect of man's lordship over woman. In *Sermon 1*.18.9 Augustine attempts to explain why Mary, in Luke 2:48, describes the child Jesus's father and herself as anxiously looking for him while he sat among the elders at the temple. Obviously the true Father of the boy knew exactly where he was. Augustine suggests that Jesus, who was the incarnation of humility,[23] would never have been born of a proud mother. Mary speaks this way in order to show her humility.

In *Continence* 9.23 Augustine introduces his discussion of Eph. 5:22–23 by stipulating that Paul has drawn attention to three distinct unions. These are "Christ and the Church, husband and wife, and spirit and flesh."[24] He writes: "All are good when, among them, some, excellently as superiors, and others, fittingly as subjects, preserve the beauty of order." Paul has described the social model of human marriage using the Church as an example for women and Christ as the ideal for men. Quite obviously Augustine has understood the rhetorical logic of Eph. 5:24 and he offers a rhetorical explanation for the choice of models. Paul has instructed by higher example. That is why Ephesians 5:25 was written. Paul also uses the *exemplum* of the flesh to man in order to argue from a lower example. However, Augustine is puzzled why the rhetorical logic is not continued. Why does the woman not receive an example from the flesh? Here Augustine suggests that possibly since "the flesh lusts against the spirit, in this mortal life" it was not an appropriate example "of submission for the wife."[25] Augustine stipulates four times during this discussion that Eph. 5:25 ("Husbands love your wives, just as Christ loved the Church and gave himself up for her.") is the appropriate Christian model for the dominion of husbands.

In *Adulterous Marriage* 8.7 Augustine uses Eph. 5:24 to male disad-

290

vantage. Augustine describes male reaction to his admonition against adultery. "They say: We are men; will the dignity of our sex sustain this affront, so that we become like women in paying the penalty for our sins if we have relations with women other than our own wives?"[26] Such men are not pleased that, "in the matter of chastity, there is a single norm for both husband and wife."[27] Furthermore, if men presume they are the leaders and the women the followers in marriage, as Eph. 5:24 suggests, a greater moral rectitude is demanded in their marital conduct. They must refrain from adulterous activity since their wives may follow by imitation.

The final citation is Eph. 5:22. It occurs in *Against Adimantus the Disciple of Mani* 3.3. The issue is one of biblical interpretation. Apparently Adimantus had been mocking the Old Testament by arguing that Eph. 5:22 contradicted Gen. 2:24. Augustine criticizes the Manichaean penchant for playing certain biblical passages off against one another when both Old and New Testament *uno sancto Spiritu conscripta et commendata esse.*[28] While arguing that both are products of the Holy Spirit, he does not attempt to resolve how the two can be harmonized.

Section Three

1 Peter 3:1–7

This particular passage is probably one of the most dangerous for people living in abusive or oppressive situations. Kathleen Corley describes how 27% of American pastors believe that these verses reflect God's will even for women living with abuse.[29] While recognizing its insidious nature, Sharyn Dowd points out that the author of the text does not argue that God has ordained this particular social arrangement. Rather the author accepts it as the conventional wisdom of the time.[30]

Augustine cites some portion of 1 Peter 3:1–7 seven times. Two of these instances are quite obviously not used to argue for female inferiority. On two occasions, in *Sermon* 111.11 (1 Peter 3:3–4) and *Sermon* 50.4.6 (1.Pet. 3:4), ornaments become a metaphor for the virtue of the outer/nonspiritual human and the inner/spiritual man. In the first instance, virgins are admonished that seeking after the ornaments of the outer man diminish the ornaments of the inner man. In the second instance, wise people *justitia* know that the only true ornamentation is the virtue of the interior man.

On three other occasions some portion of the text is used to prove that marriage is good.[31] All of the citations accept implicitly the sociology of ruler and ruled within the marriage relationship. In *The Excellence of Widowhood* 5.7, 1 Peter 3:7 and 1 Peter 3:5–6 are used as proof that marriage itself is good. In *The Good of Marriage* 12:14 the entire passage is used as a model for the goodness of marriage. It is also worth noting that although Augustine does not use this particular citation to describe the marriage of his parents, his elaboration of Monica's relationship with Patricus is eerily reminiscent of the aforementioned passage.[32] On a fourth occasion (*Treatises on the Psalms* 147.2), 1 Peter 3:7 is used to admonish Christian men not to force themselves upon their wives but rather treat them with respect since all are made and saved by Christ.

In the final instance, the issue is again one of biblical interpretation in response to the Manichaean critique. 1 Peter 3:6 is used in conjunction with 1 Cor. 11:3 in *On Marriage and Concupiscence* 1.9.10 in order to explain the principal of unity. The theory stipulates that unity rules over plurality both philosophically and in the natural world. This discussion takes place within the context of attempting to explain the biblical question of why the patriarchs were allowed more than one wife while wives were not allowed more than one husband. Manichaeans frequently argued that the Old Testament was not authoritative because of the sexual immorality of the patriarchs.[33]

Section Four

1 Timothy 2:9–15

Historically this passage has been used to exclude women from the political structure of the Church. Joanna Dewey describes this as the intention of the second-century author and the *raison d'être* for the letter.[34] Augustine, not being privy to latter day exegetical techniques, assumes that the epistle is genuinely Pauline. He cites some extract of the pericope seven times. Interestingly, several of the most ferociously misogynistic of the verses (1 Tim. 2:11–12) are never cited. Augustine never uses these verses to counsel women to submissive silence nor does he suggest that women cannot teach men.[35]

1 Tim. 2:9

On four occasions he quotes 1 Tim. 2:9. Typically, in Sermon 111.11 Augustine argues that value resides in the inner man and not the outward adornment. In *Letter 262* he advises Ecdicia not to use this passage to support her wearing of widow's dress while her husband is still alive.

One suspects that the anonymous husband must have found this somewhat disconcerting. Throughout the letter Augustine outlines the legal situation of a wife which is submissive. In *On the Soul and Its Origin* 1.17.29, while explaining that Eve had been created both spiritually and corporeally, Augustine cites 1 Tim. 2:9 by way of proof. Why, he asks, would the apostle concern himself with the physical appearance of women if this were not true? In *The Good of Marriage* 12.14 Augustine suggests that married women who concern themselves solely with pleasing God are rare. Nevertheless, simplicity in adornment is presented as Christian ideal regardless of marital status.

1 Tim. 2:14

1 Timothy 2:14 presents a theology of sin. Woman is responsible for the entry of sin into the world. For feminists this is an extremely contentious issue since one of the key factors in determining the level of sexism in a religious belief system is the attribution of responsibility for sin.[36] Anyone familiar with Augustine's writings knows that the entry of sin into this world is not explained upon the basis of gender but rather upon the basis of pride.[37] It is within this context that Augustine attempts to reconcile his interpretation of verse 14 with his theology of sin in the *City of God* 14.11. If Adam was not deceived then he obviously sinned with his eyes open. Augustine writes: "In fact, the Apostle was not off the mark when he said, 'It was not Adam but Eve, who was seduced,' for what he meant was that Eve accepted the serpent's statement as the truth, while Adam refused to be separated from his only companion even if it involved sharing her sin. That does not mean that he was less guilty if he sinned knowingly and deliberately."[38] Verse 14 is cited once again in *Two Books to Simplicianus on Diverse Questions* 1.1.4. In this instance it serves as the Apostle's reminder that the sin experienced in the world is the sin of old. Augustine writes: *Non enim potest reviviscere, nisi quod vixit aliquando.*[39]

1 Tim. 2:15

1 Timothy 2:15 appears to suggest that woman can only be saved through childbirth.[40] Augustine refers to the passage once in *On the Trinity* 12.7.10. He argues that it must be meant allegorically since quite obviously it is ludicrous to suggest that widows save themselves through procreation. He writes with a rhetorical flourish: "As if it could possibly harm a good widow if she did not have any children..."[41]

Section Five

Augustine and Subordination

On seventy occasions some portion of these four New Testament passages is cited. In roughly 75% or fifty of the instances the passages are clearly not used to subordinate women. Of these fifty, the issue of ecclesiology accounts for 25% of the citations. Another 25% deals with allegorical interpretation. Approximately 10% of the citations are concerned with some technical problem of exegesis while another 15% deal with the identity of Christ. The remaining 25% are incidental or isolated instances wherein the passages have been cited to promote, for example, the humility of monks. This leaves twenty citations (25%) which are ambiguously or obviously subordinationist.

Evaluating Subordinationist Texts

In order to evaluate Augustinian sexism, the first question which was asked was: Does Augustine use the passage to argue for the natural inferiority of women? In other words does Augustine suggest, based upon these scriptural texts, that women are ontologically inferior to men? The answer is no. If anything, Augustine expends a fair amount of energy arguing precisely the opposite as is evident particularly during the *imago dei* discussions.

The second question was: Does Augustine use the citations to promote the social subordination of women? The twenty aforementioned citations appear to fall into two groups. The first group of seven obviously supports and/or assumes that the subordination of women is normative in some situations. They account for 9% of all the citations. The second group of thirteen is more ambiguous. These account for 16% of the citations.

Passages Assuming Subordination

Augustine does betray a certain patriarchal social bias upon several occasions. He assumes that the natural social or political order requires that the many be ruled by the one.[42] He certainly never questions this assumption and uses it to explain some thorny exegetical questions. It is this argument which is used in *Continence* 9.23 to explain the hierarchical structure of Eph. 5:22–23. Consequently, Augustine counsels Ecdicia to submit to her husband about matters of dress (*Letter* 262). In the *Excellence of Widowhood* 5.7. and the *Good of Marriage* 12.14, the smooth functioning of the marriage is based upon this hierarchical model. There are hints of this in *The Literal Meaning of Genesis* 11.42.58, when Augustine suggests that Paul intended the wife to be taught by the husband. This is the model Augustine appears to have in mind in *Sermon 1*.18.9 where Mary's humility is described. Augustine adroitly uses the model to male disadvantage when men argue for a double standard concerning sexual behavior (*Adulterous Marriage* 8.7). He also appears to believe that husbands within this model will truly function as Christ did for the Church. In other words they will sacrifice everything for love of their wives.

Ambiguous Passages

A second group of passages could be interpreted as promoting the subordination of women by inference. These are the anthropological explanations which occur in the context of Augustine's allegorical exegesis. The purpose of the discussions is generally to repudiate the notion that women are not created in the image of God and that Augustine is frequently trying to reconcile Gen. 1.27 with the passage cited. In *Sermon on the Mount* 1.12.34, *83 Diverse Questions* 64.7, 67.1, *Commentaries on the Psalms* 3.10, *Homilies on the Gospel of John* 15.19, *The Literal Meaning of Genesis* 3.22.34, 11.42.58, *Two Books of Genesis Against the Manichees* 2.11.15, 2.12.16, 2.26.40, 2.28.42, *Literal Interpretation of Genesis an Unfinished Book* 3.6, and *On the Trinity* 12.13.21 the woman becomes an allegory for part of the human mind. She represents carnal concupiscence or the nonrational aspect of the human psyche. As such, the male part of the allegory would appear to have a more desirable role. Furthermore, it does not take a great leap of the imagination to imagine such a model being used to argue for female irrationality. Augustine, however, does not do this. For Augustine all humans regardless of gender contain these two aspects.

Augustine the Sexist or the Exegete?

What is at stake for Augustine with these allegorical texts, is not so much gender but biblical exegesis and foundational theology. To frame debate upon the basis of female subordination, albeit a burning concern for our era, is to do a disservice to the issues which were important to Augustine. One of the fundamental tenets of Christian theology which Augustine attempts to uphold, is the fact that women are created in God's image. He is left with the problem of resolving some apparently contradictory biblical passages. In *On Christian Doctrine*, Augustine explains how the exegete might approach such a dilemma. First of all, Augustine writes: "Now from the places where the sense in which they are used is more manifest we must gather the sense in which they are to be understood in obscure places"[43] to which he adds it is far safer to interpret scripture by applying "the testimonies sought out in every portion of the same Scripture."[44] This is certainly the method Augustine follows in attempting to interpret the New Testament passages which would appear to suggest that woman was not created in God's image. Gen. 1:27 is used as the basis of Augustine's interpretation.

A second approach is also described in *On Christian Doctrine* 3.12.18. Apparently evil or wicked sayings or deeds ascribed to the Saints or God are to be considered as "wholly figurative." They are to be interpreted as "bearing ultimately upon the end of love towards God or our neighbor, or both" (3.12.19). Augustine has interpreted 1 Cor. 11:3–7, Eph. 5:22–24, 1 Peter 3:1–7 and 1 Timothy 2:14 allegorically because to do otherwise would be to attribute to Paul the untenable theology that women were not created in God's image.

In conclusion, Augustine's use of these biblical passages does not bear out the contention that he systematically employed them to argue for female inferiority. In approximately 75% of the cases the issue has nothing to do with women. He does, however, assume a social arrangement within marriage where women are ruled by their husband, which is certainly consonant with Greco–Roman household codes. Furthermore the rulers, perhaps somewhat unrealistically, are to rule like Christ.

NOTES

1. Kari Børresen, *Subordination and Equivalence–Nature and Role of Women in Augustine and Thomas Aquinas,* trans. Charles Talbot, (Washington: University Press of America, Inc. 1981). "Sexual difference belongs only to bodily substance; the rational soul is identical in both sexes, because, since it is spiritual, it is asexual. The soul makes both sexes *homo*, a human being in general; the body makes them differ as *vir* or *femina*, human beings of male or of female sex." (p. 315)

2. Margaret Miles, "The Body and Human Values in Augustine of Hippo," in *Grace, Politics and Desire: Essays on Augustine,* ed. H. A. Meynell (Calgary: University of Calgary Press, 1990), pp. 65–66. "to understand both the intent and the effect of Augustine's thought and teaching on body and sexuality permits us, in the final analysis, to find Augustine not so much a formidable and threatening authority of the history of Christian doctrine, but, as he asked and expected to be seen, in the context of his own struggles, our fellow pilgrim."

3. Kari Børresen, "L'anthropologie théologique d'Augustin et de Thomas d'Aquin," *Recherches de Science Religieuse* 69/3 (1981), pp. 393–406. Describing Augustine's and Aquinas' Neoplatonic anthropology, Børresen writes: "L'intention d'Augustin et de Thomas a été de rendre le message évangélique accessible à la culture de leur temps, en utilisant des systèmes conceptuels humainement déterminés et historiquement donnés." (p. 405)

4. Kari Elisabeth Børresen, "Patristic 'Feminism': The Case of Augustine," *Augustinian Studies* 25 (1994), pp. 139–152. Børresen has nuanced her argument in this article. Only work from Augustine's middle years can be considered feminist in flavor.

5. Elizabeth Clark, "Adam's Only Companion : Augustine and the Early Christian Debate on Marriage," *Recherches Augustiniennes* XXI (1986), p. 139.

6. Susan E. Schreiner, "Eve, The Mother of History; Reaching for the Reality of History in Augustine's Later Exegesis of Genesis," in *Genesis 1–3 in The History of Exegesis: Intrigue in the Garden*, ed. G. A. Robbins, Studies in Women and Religion Vol. 27 (Lewiston/Queenston: The Edwin Mellen Press, 1988), p.153.

7. Elizabeth Clark, "Theory and Practice in Late Ancient Asceticism, Jerome, Chrysostom, and Augustine," *Journal of Feminist Studies in Religion* 5/2 (Fall 1989), p. 44.

8. Ibid., p. 46. "That Augustine for his own reason chose to modify the harsh rhetoric of his predecessors does not mean that he, any more than they, challenged male dominance..."

9. Quite obviously there are passages from the Old Testament which are also potentially extremely damaging for women. Most frequently Genesis 2 and 3 have provided prime fodder for sexist exegesis. Anyone familiar with Augustine knows that the first chapters of Genesis were a favored exegetical exercise for him. He attempted five systematic interpretations on five occasions. (*On Genesis Against the Manichees* 388–89 C.E.; *On the Literal Interpretation of Genesis: An Unfinished Book*, 398 C.E.; *Confessions* Bk. 12–13, 397–398 C.E.; *On Genesis Literally Interpreted: Twelve Books* 404–420 C.E.; *City of God*, Book Eleven, 417–418 C.E.) He also cites Genesis 2 or 3 incidentally over 400 times throughout his work. Genesis 2 is cited 192 times and Genesis 3 is referred to 219 times according to the Benedictine concordances. Consequently, these have been deliberately excluded from this analysis since they entail a far larger work than the present one.

10. Carolyn De Swarte Gifford, "American Women and the Bible: The Nature of Woman as a Hermeneutical Issue" in *Feminist Perspectives on Biblical Scholarship*, ed. Adela Yarbro Collins (Atlanta, Georgia: Scholars Press, 1985), p. 16. There are certainly other New Testament verses which could be used negatively with regard to women; however, given the limited space available, these four have been chosen as generally representative.

11. Jouette M. Bassler, "1 Corinthians" in *The Women's Bible Commentary*, ed. Carol A. Newsom and Sharon H. Ringe (London: SPCK, 1992), p. 327.

12. Augustine makes a similar argument in *The Good of Marriage* (17.20) without citing this particular passage. Apparently the lascivious nature of the patriarchs was an old chestnut from Manichaean exegetical polemic.

13. Augustine, *On the Trinity*, 12.7. For fuller development of Augustine's argument see: Richard J. McGowan, "Augustine's Spiritual Equality: the Allegory of Man and Woman with Regard to *Imago Dei*," *Revue des Études Augustiniennes* 33 (1987), pp. 255–264. Also see: Mary Cline Horowitz, "The Image of God in Man—Is Woman Included?" *Harvard Theological Review* 72/3–4 (July–October, 1979), pp.175–206. Horowitz writes: "In context, Augustine was not referring to the two sexes literally but to the allegory which we have seen in Philo and Origen which identified the male with higher reason and the female with lower reason (*On the Trinity* 12.7.9)." (p. 202) Horowitz criticizes O'Faolain, Martines and Reuther for ignoring this allegorical aspect of Augustine and consequently making his biblical interpretation appear more sexist.

14. Augustine, *83 Diverse Questions*, trans. David Mosher in *The Fathers of the Church*, Vol. 70 (Washington: The Catholic University of America Press, 1977).

15. Jouette M. Bassler, "1 Corinthians," p. 327.

16. Ross Shepard Kraemer, *Her Share of the Blessings*, (Oxford: Oxford University Press, 1992), p. 149.

17. Augustine, *The Literal Meaning of Genesis*, Vol. 2, trans. John Hammond (New York: Newman Press, 1982).

18. Augustine, *Trinity*, trans. Stephen McKenna in *The Fathers of the Church*, Vol. 45 (Washington: The Catholic University of America Press, 1963).

19. See Richard J. McGowan, "Augustine's Spiritual Equality: the Allegory of Man and Woman with Regard to *Imago Dei*," *Revue des Études Augustiniennes* 33 (1987), pp. 255–264. See Mary Cline Horowitz, "The Image of God in Man—Is Woman Included?" *Harvard Theological Review* 72/3–4 (July–October, 1979), pp.175–206. Also see Kari Børresen, "Patristic 'Feminism': The Case of Augustine," *Augustinian Studies* 25 (1994), pp.139–152. All articles agree that Augustine argues that women are created in the image of God.

20. Sarah J. Tanzer, "Ephesians" in *Searching the Scriptures; A Feminist Commentary*, Vol. 2, ed. Elisabeth Schüssler Fiorenza (New York: Crossroad, 1994), pp. 334–335.

21. E. Elizabeth Johnson, "Ephesians" in *The Women's Bible Commentary*, ed. Carol A. Newsom and Sharon H. Ringe (London: SPCK, 1992), p. 340.

22. J. P. Migne, ed., *Patrologiae Cursus Completus Series Latina* 34 (Paris: J. P. Migne, 1861) pp. 819.

23. See Augustine, *Holy Virginity*, pp. 33–51. These 20 chapters are devoted to elaborating upon Christ as the incarnation of humility.

24. Augustine, *Continence*, trans. M. F. McDonald in *The Fathers of the Church*, Vol. 16 (New York: The Fathers of the Church, Inc., 1952).

25. Ibid.

26. Augustine, *Adulterous Marriage*, trans. C. T. Huegelmeyer in *The Fathers of the Church*, Vol. 15 (New York: Fathers of the Church, Inc., 1955).

27. Ibid.

28. J. P. Migne, ed., *Patrologiae Cursus Completus Series Latina* 42 (Paris: J. P. Migne, 1861) pp. 133–134.

29. Kathleen Corley, "1 Peter" in *Searching the Scriptures: A Feminist Commentary* Vol. 2, ed. Elisabeth Schüssler Fiorenza (New York: Crossroad, 1994), p. 356.

30. Sharyn Dowd, "1 Peter" in *The Women's Bible Commentary*, ed. Carol A. Newsom and Sharon H. Ringe (London: SPCK, 1992), p. 371. She writes: "The author of 1 Peter advocated this system not because God had revealed it as the divine will for Christian homes but because it was the only stable and respectable system anyone knew about. It was the best the culture had to offer."

31. All such discussions need to be read within the context of the general theological debate over the goodness of marriage between Jovinian, Augustine and Jerome.

32. Augustine, *Confessions* 9.9 for Augustine's description of his parents' marriage.

33. See Augustine, *Reply to Faustus the Manichaean*, Bk. 22.

34. Joanna Dewey, "1 Timothy" in *The Women's Bible Commentary*, ed. Carol A. Newsom and Sharon H. Ringe (London: SPCK, 1992), p. 353. According to Dewey it is precisely this concern for regulating the activity of women within the ecclesial sphere which betrays its second-century origins. Also see Linda M. Maloney "The Pastoral Epistles" in *Searching the Scriptures; A Feminist Commentary* Vol. 2, ed. Elisabeth Schüssler Fiorenza (New York: Crossroad, 1994), pp. 361–374. Maloney points out that the theology of the fall found in this passage occurs only one other time in scripture, Sir. 25:24. (p. 370).

35. Given the great influence exercised by his mother concerning his spiritual education it would seem out of character for Augustine to suggest that women could not teach men.

36. Gerda Lerner, *The Creation of Patriarchy*, (Oxford: Oxford University Press, 1986), p. 146.

37. The instances of this are almost too numerous to count. I include the following reference as an example. Augustine, *The Literal Meaning of Genesis*, 11.15.19–16.21.

38. Augustine, *City of God*, trans. Henry Bettenson (London: Penguin Books, 1984).

39. J. P. Migne, ed., *Patrologiae Cursus Completus Series Latina* 40 (Paris: J. P. Migne, 1861), p. 104.

40. Maloney, "The Pastoral Epistles," p. 370.

41. Augustine, *On the Trinity*, trans. Stephen McKenna in *The Fathers of the*

Church Vol. 45 (Washington: The Catholic University of America Press, 1963).

42. See *On Marriage and Concupiscence*, 1.9.10, *Two Books of Genesis Against the Manichees*, 2.11.15, *Continence*, 9.23.

43. Augustine, *Christian Doctrine*, 3.26.37, trans. J. F. Shaw in *Nicene and Post–Nicene Fathers*, Vol. 2 (Grand Rapids: WM. G. Eerdmans Publishing Company, 1956).

44. Ibid., 3.28.39.

20

Jesus Christ:
Source of Christian Humility

Centered as it is in the mystery of Christ, the hymn of the Epistle to the
Phillippians has profoundly influenced the thought and heart of Augustine. He found in Phil. 2:6–11 the strongest and most complete scriptural
basis for his christological reflection, his spiritual journey and his pastoral vocation.[1]

The frequency of both fragmentary and thoroughly analyzed references to Phil. 2:6–11 in Augustinian writing attests to the enormous interest attached to them by the scholar from Hippo. It had an impact
throughout his theology, his spirituality and his pastoral work.[2] Without
excluding the influence of other biblical texts, this Pauline pericope is
linked to the fundamental tenets of Augustine's christological doctrine. It
highlights the dignity of the divine Son of God (Phil.2:6) in his earthly
abasement as *forma servi* in the form of a servant (Phil. 2:7). It describes
the union of the two distinct yet not separate natures, and the normative,
salvific economy of Christ's kenosis "even to death upon the cross" (Phil.
2:8). Finally, it illustrates the excellence of Christ's exaltation "to the glory
of the God the Father" (Phil. 2:9–11) which had been anticipated by the
offering and sacrifice of his gift of love. Taken as a whole, these different
doctrinal themes highlight Augustine's originality. His christology is inspired by scripture and scripture provides the structure for his christology.
As early as 386, when Ponticianus arrived unexpectedly and discovered
to his great surprise, Paul's Epistles on Augustine's gaming table, Augustine revealed the great care he took in the reading of these scriptures.
Since that period, it would seem that Augustine's teaching sprang di-

rectly from scripture. As Anne–Marie la Bonnardière writes: "To the extent that one does not take into consideration this primordial fact, one is deprived of an insight, not only into a well attested scientific fact, but into the best key for understanding the work of Augustine."[3]

The work of Augustine is inseparable from his personal history and destiny. If the interpretation of Phil. 2:6–11 constituted for Augustine an enormous step forward in his exegetical, doctrinal, spiritual and pastoral thinking, it was also intimately linked to personal experience. In particular it echoes his second conversion where he discovered in the *via humilitatis* the path of privileged access to God. It was this conversion which demanded the renunciation of the soul's self–sufficient search for God since He was closed to all pretentious knowledge. God revealed himself in humbleness of heart. In Book 7 of the *Confessions* Augustine recalls that prior to mediating upon the scriptures and understanding the meaning of the Incarnation, he had discovered certain Neoplatonic writings. After igniting a veritable fire of enthusiasm in him, the reading of such works left him ill–equipped in his spiritual quest for Christ. He wrote: "It was because I was not humble enough to possess my God, the humble Jesus, and I did not know how to interpret His weakness."[4] Augustine recalled later that God Himself had permitted him to understand that His grace was given to those who embarked upon the *via humilitatis* which had been followed by the humiliated and destroyed Christ.[5]

In the twilight of his life, Augustine did not fail to insert into *Speculum Quis Ignorat*, an extraordinary biblical harvest of Phillipian texts which he compiled as an exegete. They were destined to prove normative for Christian ethical orientation and they surrounded the citation of the entire second chapter which had at its heart, the christological hymn (Phil. 2: 6–11).[6] In other words this hymn concerns not only theology and exegesis, but also the life of every Christian. Its theme is clear to Augustine. Christ in his annihilation provides us with the *forma servi*. This was the model and the secret for walking in the only path, the *via humilitatis*, which will lead to the Father.

The Way of Humility

In the work of Augustine, the normative and figurative value of Phil. 2.6–8 was principally deployed from the theme of humility.[7] Humility is the path by which God, in His Son, "abased himself in the form of a servant" and "was obedient unto death, death on the cross" so that sinful humanity could know and imitate it. The humbled Son was, for Augustine, the "model for humility" which defined Christian behavior.[8] The salvation of humanity, operative because of Christ's sacrifice, depended directly upon following the *via humilitatis*. Humanity's Savior had chosen this route and had accepted death in total obedience.[9] The relationship between the kenosis of Phil. 2:6-8 and the *via humilitatis* is incontestably the foundation for the behavior suggested by Augustine and the justification for the exigencies which he proposed to the faithful. It was the cornerstone for the entirety of his directives.

Framed by and supported by the theme of humility and driven by Phil. 2:6–8, Augustine's pastoral teaching finds its true meaning. Thus the healing of the original sin of human pride, is obtained by the those who follow the path of humility.[10] The believer's prayer being addressed to Christ in *forma dei* should mirror the attitude of humbleness and self–abasement adopted by Christ in *forma servi*. The prayer of the poor and the indigent and the humbled is most acceptable to God.[11] The movement from *forma dei* to *forma servi* is definitive of all human behavior as it submits to the will of God. Conformity[12] to divine will is an act of obedience which is lived in humility, patience and tenderness.[13] The gesture of humility, *in forma servi*, at the feet of those for whom he was going to die,[14] and Paul's call to "carry the load one for another" (Gal. 6:2) in light of the humility of the Son as presented in Phil. 2:6–8 demanded fraternal love[15] and acceptance of the law of love.[16] In this particular manner, making reference to Phil. 2:8 several times, Augustine anchors a series of attitudes, which are inspired by the humility and radical obedience of the Son. Justice has its source in Christ's mercy[17] and His gift of life promotes this justice.[18] Courage and steadfastness as seen in His death.[19] The spirit of detachment and perseverance in the following of Christ,[20] material poverty in the face of worldly goods,[21] modesty of heart in virginity,[22] fasting acting as a brake upon sensuality,[23] and finally patience in teaching catechetics or preaching.[24] The principal danger to losing the *via humilitatis* was the trap proffered by false doctrine which in one manner or another promoted pride and distance from God.[25]

From that global view about the imitation of the humble and humiliated Son found in Phil. 2:6–8, Augustine drew an important consequence. Conformity to the human Jesus, who was humble and obedient unto death on the cross, integrated humanity into the divine plan of mercy realized by the Christ Jesus. It placed humanity on the *via humilitatis* which was intended as the path of access to the Father. It worked to effect the reconciliation with God and fellow human beings, in the hope of its per-

303

fect accomplishment in the final vision of the *forma dei*.[26] In other words, the kenosis of Phil. 2:6–8 as interpreted by Augustine united three fundamental dimensions of the definitive worth of humanity which Christ had assumed. This humility was the antithesis of proud pretension. It was the inauguration of salvation. Furthermore, it was such an example for imitation that it gave humanity the possibility of participation in the work of redemption.

In terms of this brief overview which brings together the main Augustinian commentaries on humility and considers them in the light of Phil. 2:6–8, one question remains. How does the African bishop articulate the theological foundations of the mystery of humiliation?

The Foundations of the Humiliation of the Son

The last phase of the redemptive drama expressed by the Christ hymn: the exaltation of the humiliated Son in His death on the cross and in universal homage, is interpreted by Augustine as a consequence of the Christ's self–abasement. This does not operate in the sense of a moral test which could have motivated the humiliation inflicted by God, but rather as a revelation of the humility and obedience lived by the destroyed Son. God raised the one who had emptied himself, renounced himself, denied himself even to the point of the supreme sacrifice. Christian action and the imitation of the humiliated Christ find their roots and their true figurative meaning inscribed at the heart of this mystery of kenosis, and dynamized by the inner disposition of faith, hope and love.[27] More radically, one must return to the idea of divine mercy in order to establish the ultimate reason for Christ–like humility and consequently all Christian behavior. If the mystery of the Son's humiliation, which plays itself out in the supreme sacrifice on Golgotha, originates in the plan of divine mercy, then it becomes clear in Augustine's view that the voluntarily obedient being of Son must itself be considered as the ultimate foundation for this mystery. This is how it appears to Augustine. In effect, to the extent that the Word incarnate *in forma servi*, actualizes divine benevolence, it becomes the center and source of all humility.

1. God's Mercy

A.) THE ROLE OF MERCY

Augustine anchors the tripartite humility–obedience–death of Christ found in Phil. 2:8 in the mercy of God. This accords with God's

304

redemptive plan. Mercy forms the last horizon against which the mystery of the Son's annihilation plays itself out. It is mercy which begets the humility of the Son. Mercy fortifies humility. Mercy allows humility to accomplish itself in obedience unto death on the cross. This conviction is elaborated in Augustine's first writings. During 391–92[28] while discussing Psalm 20[29] which is applied to Christ, Augustine provides us with his explanation of Ps. 20:8a (Ps. 21:7):

> "Because the king puts his hope in the Lord." Because the king did not inflate himself but rather was humble of heart, he hoped in God. "And in the mercy of the Most High, he will not be shaken" (Ps. 20:8b). Thanks to the mercy of the Most High, he will not be shaken in his humility by an obedience (lived) "unto death on the cross" (Phil. 2:8).[30]

One will notice that the expression "to put his hope in the Lord" from verse Ps.20:8a introduces direct opposition between proud behavior and the attitude of humility. To begin with this opposition clarifies the meaning of humility in Phil. 2:8. Humility is moving out of oneself and opening oneself to the will of God. The humility of the crucified Jesus can only be conceived in relation to the Father's merciful plan. The redemptive death of the Son, which is the fruit of this humility, is viewed from the same perspective. Augustine specified this later in *Sermon 361*, 17 (17). It was due to mercy that Christ "was obedient unto death" (Phil. 2:8b). His death can, in no way, be considered a consequence of sin.[31]

The idea of mercy, introduced with Ps. 20:8b, allows Augustine to delineate the nature of the Son's humility, in such a way that strengthened by the all-seeing love of God, it can bear the heavy load of obedience up to the supreme sacrifice. In other words, the Son is not 'shaken' by an obedience which will lead to the cross, because he lives a humility hidden at the very heart of divine mercy. It is a humility fortified by divine love from which it surges, grows and blossoms.

The integration of kenosis into the loving work of the Father also appears in the prayer from Book 10 of the *Confessions*. This magnificent prayer, addressed to "the Father of Goodness," who, from abundant love delivers His Son "the faithless" (Rom. 5:6b), highlights the cause and effect relationship between "the victimized and victorious effect of Christ; (or) between His sacrificial and sacerdotal state."[32] This relationship originates in the mystery of kenosis which finds its depth in the acceptance of the Son, who "did not count equality with God a thing to be grasped and who became obedient unto death, even death on a cross" (Phil. 2:6b&c,

305

2:8).[33] At the heart of the impenetrable mercy of the Father lies the cross with salvation freely offered to humanity.

One should keep in mind Augustine's preciseness concerning this subject as found in *On the Merits and Remission of Sin* 1.26.39: "...it seems that the Lord Jesus Christ incarnated himself in the *forma servi* 'and made himself obedient unto death on the cross' (Phil. 2:7b, 2:8b) solely in order to allow all humanity into His plan of mercy."[34]

B.) THE PRIORITY OF MERCY

In fact, that the plan of mercy, as tied into the work of salvation, was the necessary preamble to the act of supreme kenosis, appears clearly in *Homily on John* 36.4. In light of the question of the final judgment, this priority of mercy is confirmed. In this passage, John 8:15b ("I judge no one"), seems, for Augustine, irreconcilable with the Catholic profession of faith. The profession explicitly affirms Christ's role as judge of the quick and the dead. This apparent contradiction is raised in two ways. The first refers to John 12:47b ("I have not come to condemn the world but to save it") where Christ does not deny his power of judgment but defers from using it. The second is based upon John 8:15 ("You judge according to the flesh"), where it is understood that Christ does not judge in this manner. In conclusion, Christ is certainly the supreme judge confessed by faith, but He wished rather to save the world. It is in function of the grace of salvation, that the exercise of mercy preceded the work of justice.[35] In order to explain that the exercise of this mercy is realized in the redemptive incarnation as voluntarily assumed "in obedience unto death on the cross" (Phil. 2:8bc) Augustine writes:

> Before all, what is mercy? The Maker of humanity condescended to make mankind, he became that which he had made so that, that which he had made would not perish. What can be added to this mercy? Even so he pushed it even further. It was little for him to become man, he wished to be condemned by men: It was little to be condemned, he wished to be dishonored; it was little to be dishonored, he wished to be killed; And that was still too little, he wished for "death by the cross" (Phil. 2:8c). Therefore, when the Apostle spoke of "his obedience unto death" (Phil. 2:8b), it was too little for him to say: "He made himself obedient unto death" (Phil. 2:8b); since it was not a death as such because he added: "and unto death on the cross" (Phil. 2:8c). Of all the ways of dying none is more horrible than that one.[36]

In conclusion, as the kenosis of Christ's act, from which the effectiveness of salvation spreads, finds its source in mercy, it seems that the plan of divine love should be understood as the ultimate foundation of the tripartite: "humility–obedience–death."

c.) MERCY AND JUSTICE

In *Sermon 144.3.4*, the bishop questions his listeners about John 16:10 "Concerning justice, because I go to the Father." Why does the Savior call the act of his return to the Father justice, rather than his coming? Would it be because it was mercy which brought him while it was justice which made him return to the Father?[37]

Augustine wanted his listeners to realize that the work of mercy is inseparable from the work of justice. He made them aware that they could not attain the perfection of justice if they ignored the works of mercy and love (according to Phil. 2:3–5). Far from being limited by each other, mercy and justice were called to harmoniously compliment one another in each heart. The prototype for such a synthesis was the Son himself. He had lived it and assumed it in his act of kenosis as described in Phil. 2:6–8.[38] The importance of this sequence was that mercy was the basis not only of Christ's kenosis, but also the entirety of human action surrounding justice in the imitation of the destroyed Son.

2. The Person and Doctrine of Christ

The mercy of the Father, the ultimate foundation of the supreme act of kenosis and the act itself as accomplished by the Son, are inseparable. In effect, the person and the doctrine of Christ are the unfolding of God's mercy not unlike a river which expands from its source. The Son, by his doctrine and his person, provides substance to, engenders and leads to fulfillment the whole act of humility and obedience unto death. This truth did not escape Augustine at the moment when he accepted to follow the life of the Master of Humility. He wrote: "And therefore you wished to show me how, you resist the proud but give grace to the humble" (Prov. 3:34; 1 Pet. 5:5b; James 4:6b) and with what mercy you showed men the path of humility, by the fact that your "Word was made flesh and dwelt among men."[39] Augustine continues by explaining how he knew of certain Platonic writings which partially agreed with the doctrine found in the prologue of John regarding the Word of God. However, these works did not teach that "the Word was made flesh and dwelt amongst us" (Jn. 1:14a). They did not teach that the Son "emptied himself, taking the form of a servant, etc." (Phil. 2:7–11). They did not teach that "at the appointed time he died for the ungodly" (Rom. 5:6b).[40] The author continues: "because these things you have hidden them from the wise and you have revealed them to the humble" (Mt. 11:25b), so that they will come to him when they "are sad and heavy laden" (Mt. 11:28 all) and he will comfort them, "for (he is) "gentle and humble of heart" (Mt. 11:29), he makes "the gentle walk with justice and teaches to the peaceful his paths" (Ps. 24:9), he who sees "our humility and pain and forgives all our sins," (Ps. 24:8)."[41] The *via humilitatis*, the dogma of the entirety of the incarnate Word, is presented by Augustine as "the dividing line between Neo–platonism and Christianity and the basis of the specific character of the latter."[42]

In certain texts, Augustine expressed very forcefully that humility and obedience unto the cross had their basis in the doctrine and person of Christ. *Sermon* 30.9, concerning humility and directed against the Pelagians, bears witness to the pastoral worries of the Bishop of Hippo. Augustine regrets the division and disputes engendered by heresy and invites his listeners to enroll in the school of Christ wherein the Son declares "Come unto me all who are heavy laden." (Mt. 11:28a)[43] In a fictitious dialogue between the Lord and the crowd, Augustine illustrates that it is not so much the knowledge of the creative work of "the Word from the beginning" (Jn. 1:13), nor the privilege of his "equality with God" (Phil. 2:6) which should inspire hearts but rather that which he became in "abandoning himself" (Phil. 2:8a) with a "gentle and humble heart" (Mt. 11:29b).[44] Humility was in this case the path by which God had made himself a man without sin so that sinful humanity could meet and imitate Him. In his old age, Augustine remained faithful to this call of Christ. In *Sermon* Mai 126.11–12, using an almost identical scriptural score (Mt. 11:28-29 and Phil. 2:6–8), Augustine invited his listeners to imitate the example of Him, who was the "model for humility."[45]

The radical obedience of Phil. 2:8bc is underlined clearly in *On the Trinity* 13.17.22 in the face of the proud who do not appreciate the lessons of the Incarnation. One such citation is the following: "It is only such a great descent on the part of God that was appropriate to confront and heal the pride of man, which was the greatest obstacle to his union with God. Man also learns how far removed he is from God and what force is given to him, in order to endure this cure which is pain; and to return to him by the intervention of such a mediator, who being God, comes to help men by his divinity, and being man, places himself to carry them by His weakness. And what is a greater model of obedience for we who have perished by disobedience than that of God the son, obedient to God the Father 'unto death on the cross?' (Phil. 2:8b) Where does the price of obedience appear in a more startling way than in the flesh of so great a mediator who has been rusticated to eternal life."[46]

There is the danger of wandering from the *via humilitatis* or the humility and obedience of the incarnated Word. Referring to Phil. 2:8, *Commentaries on the Psalms* 31.2.18 unmasks such temptation. For Augustine, the "mighty waters" of Ps. 31:6b (Ps. 32:6) as found in the following phrase, "meanwhile during the flood of mighty waters, they did not approach him..." represented the multiplicity of doctrines opposed to the doctrine of God. These false doctrines, written by strangers to the faith, such as the Epicureans, the Stoics, the Manicheans and the Platonists, all fell because of the same error. In all of them there was no doctrine of humility. On the contrary, they promoted pride and distance from God. Consequently for Augustine, the only doctrine, and the only water of salvation was the path of humility, since it originated in Christ's "humility unto the cross" (Phil.2:8). In addition all the teaching of Christ guaranteed its value. He had paid what he did not owe to erase man's debt to Him. He had received baptism even though he was without sin. He had died on the cross even though he was innocent. It was the whole person and teaching of Christ, who described Himself as "the Way, the Truth, and the Life"(Jn. 14:6a) which guaranteed the unfathomable value of this doctrine of humility.[47] Is this not what Augustine had discovered for himself in *Confessions* 7.9.14?

In descending from the heights of glory in the *forma servi* and by renouncing His enjoyment of the external glory from which He came, the annihilated Son pushed humility and obedience to the ignominious death of the cross. The Augustinian interpretation of Phil. 2:6–8 is marked by a sharp sense of the theological significance of the verses with respect to the mystery of humility. From the cross the Son effects the salvation of humanity and becomes the definitive norm for all Christian behavior. Originating simultaneously in the divine plan of mercy and in the voluntary obedient existence of the Son, Christian humility finds its ultimate foundation at the very heart of the mystery of kenosis.

According to Augustine, Jesus Christ is the center and the source of Christian humility since His actualization of the merciful plan of divine goodness, offers to humanity dual access to the mystery of humiliation. Christ offers the sacrament by which he confers to humanity the grace of divine salvation and the example by which He expects humanity to participate in His redemptive work. The kenosis of Christ was completed with his death. This is why such a death reveals the fullness of God's glory, which is precisely merciful humility as the power for self–sacrifice. Finally, Augustine seems to attribute humility, when he speaks of the humility of Christ which Christians are called to imitate, to the Word, to the divine person, hence to God and not to human nature assumed by God. In Augustine's mouth, the expression, "humility of God" should be taken, consequently, in all its rigorousness. This does not impede him from underlining, quite opportunely, the following: obviously only in His human form, His *forma servi*, could God humiliate himself and remain obedient unto the cross since in His divine form He is by nature immutable.[48] However, when speaking of God in general, the Bishop of Hippo never says that God is humble or that humility is God. He always describes the apparent humility of God in relation to the descent of the Word and His earthly life.

NOTES

1. The Augustinian interpretation of the christological hymns in Philippians (Phil. 2:5–11) was the object of study in my recently published work. See Verwilghen, "Christologie et spiritualité selon saint Augustin, L, Hymne aux Philippiens" *Théologie Historique*, 75 (Paris: Beauchesne, 1985), p. 556.

2. Ibid. pp. 61–69. In all of his works, Augustine cites the text 422 times and makes 563 allusions to the verses of the Christ hymn.

3. A.–M. la Bonnardière, *Recherches de Chronologie Augustinienne*, (Paris: 1965), p. 180.

4. *Confessions* 7.18.24, CSEL 33, p. 163.

5. *Confessions* 7.9.13, CSEL 33, p. 154.

6. *Speculum quis ignorat*, CSEL 12, pp. 235–236.

7. Concerning humility in Augustine, see P. Adnès, "L'humilité, vertu spécifiquement chrétienne d'après saint Augustin," *Revue d'Ascétique et de Mystique* 23, 1952, pp. 208–223. Also see F. Arsenault, *Le Christ, plénitude de la révélation selon saint Augustin*, Thèse de l'Université pontificale Grégorienne, Rome, 1965 and J.L. Azcona, *La doctrina augustiniana de la humilidad en los Tractatus in Iohannem*, Madrid, 1972, p. 146.

8. *Sermo Mai 126*, 11–12, MA 1, p. 365 and *Homilies on the Gospel of John* 51.3, CCL 36, p. 440.

9. *On Faith and the Creed* 5.11, CSEL 41, p. 14.

10. *On Faith and the Creed* 4.4, CSEL 41, pp. 268–272; *Against the Letter of Parmenianus* 3.2.5, CSEL 51, pp. 104–105; *Homilies on John* 29.8, CCL 36, p. 288; *Sermon 304.3.3*, PL 38, col. 1396.

11. *Commentaries on the Psalms* 85.2, CCL 39, p. 1177 and ibid. 120, I, p. 1785.

12. *Letter 140.28.68, CSEL* 44, p. 215–216.

13. *Sermon 157.2.2, PL* 38, col. 860.

14. *Homilies on the Gospel of John* 55.7, *CCL* 36, p. 466.

15. *83 Diverse Questions*, qu. 71.3, *PL* 40, col. 81–82 and *Against the Letter of Parmenianus* 3.2.5, *CSEL* 51, pp. 104–105.

16. *Sermon 144.3.4, PL* 38, col. 789

17. Ibid.

18. *On the Trinity* 17.14.18, *CCL* 50 a, p. 406.

19. *On Faith and the Creed* 5.11, *CSEL* 41, p. 14, and *Sermon 304.3.3, PL* 38, col. 1396.

20. *Letter 243.8, CSEL* 57, pp. 574–575.

21. *Commentaries on the Psalms* 126.5, *CCL* 40, pp. 1860–1861, and *Letter 140.27.66, CSEL* 44, pp. 212–213.

22. *Of Holy Virginity* 31.31–32.32, *CSEL* 41, pp. 268–272.

23. *Sermon 207.2, PL* 38, col. 1043.

24. *On the Catechizing of the Uninstructed* 10.15, *CCL* 46, p. 138.

25. *Commentaries on the Psalms* 31.2.18, *CCL* 38, p. 239.

26. A. Verwilghen, op.cit., pp. 321–331.

27. *Against Faustus* 13.8, *CSEL* 25, p. 388; *On the Trinity* 7.3.5, *CCL* 50, pp. 252–253; *Homilies on John* 40.2, *CCL* 36, pp. 350–351; ibid., 119.4, p. 660; *Commentaries on the Psalms* 10. 12–14, *CCL* 46, pp. 1611–1615; *Sermon 88,* 4.4, *PL* 38, col. 541; ibid., 194.3.3–4.4, col. 1016–1017; ibid., 288.5, col. 1307.

28. The *Commentary on Psalm 20* belongs to the series of first *Commentaries* which were dictated during the years 391–92.

29. Psalm 20 is very rarely cited by Augustine. Aside from the commentary on this Psalm found in the *Commentary on Psalm 20*, we have isolated only one other citation in his work (Ps.20:4) in *Against Two Letters of the Pelagians* 1.9.21, *CSEL* 60, p. 483.

30. *Commentaries on the Psalms* 20.8, *CCL* 38, p. 116.

31. *Sermon 361* 17.17, *PL* 38, col. 1609.

32. G. Rémy, *Le Christ médiateur dans l'oeuvre d' Augustin,* thesis presented to the Faculty of Theology, University of Strasbourg, April 22, 1977, Lille–Paris, 1979, T.I, p. 480.

33. *Confessions* 10.43.69, *CSEL* 33, pp. 278–279.

34. *On the Merits and Remission of Sin* 1.26.39, *CSEL* 60, p. 37.

35. *Homilies on John* 36.4, *CCL* 36, p. 325.

36. Ibid., pp. 325–326.

37. *Sermon 144.3.4, PL* 38, col. 789.

38. Ibid.

39. *Confessions* 7.9.13, *CSEL* 33, p. 154. See also *Commentaries on the Psalms* 18.2.15, *CCL* 38, pp. 112–113.

40. Ibid., 7.9.13–14, pp. 154–155. This text is constructed using its scriptural citations in an antithetical structure.

1st portion of antithesis	2nd portion of antithesis
Jn. 1:15, 7ab, 8b, 9, 10	Jn. 1:11–12
Jn. 1:13	Jn. 1:14a
Jn. 2:6	Phil. 2:7–12
Jn. 1:16 all.	Rom. 5:6b; 8:32a

41. Ibid. 7.9.14, pp. 155–156.
42. G. Madec, "Une lecture des *Confessions* 7, 8.13 – 21.27," (Critical Notes regarding the Thesis of R. J. O'Connel), *REAug* 16, 1970, p. 87.
43. *Sermon 30*.8, CCL 41, p. 387.
44. Ibid. 30.9, pp. 387–388.
45. *Sermo Mai* 126, 11–12, *MA* 1, p. 365.
46. *On the Trinity* 13.17.22, *CCL* 50 a., pp. 412–413.
47. *Commentaries on the Psalms* 31.2.18, *CCL* 38, p. 239.
48. *Sermon 124*.3.3, *PL* 38, col. 687–688.

21

Augustine, Sermon 43

On What is Written in Isaiah:
"Unless You Believe, You Shall Not Understand" (Is. 7:9 LXX)

Edmund Hill O.P., *The Works of Saint Augustine–A Translation for the 21st Century: Sermons II (20–50)* (New York Press, N.Y.: 1990, pages 238–239; 241–243).

—Date: 400

1. The starting point of a good life, whose due what's more is eternal life, is right faith. Now faith means believing what you don't yet see, and the reward of this faith is to see what you believe. So in the season of faith, which is like the season for sowing, let us not falter, and right to the end let us not falter but persevere instead, until we "reap what we have sown." When the human race, you see, had turned away from God and was lying weltering in its transgressions, we needed a savior in order to come to life again, just as we needed a creator in order to exist. God in his justice condemned humanity; God in his mercy sets humanity free. The God of Israel will himself give strength and courage to his people. Blessed be God (Ps 68:35). But it's those who believe that receive this gift; those who disdain him don't.

    2. Even about faith itself, however, we mustn't boast as though we could manage it on our own. Faith isn't a mere nothing, you know, it's something serious and important. If you possess it, then of course you have received it. For what do you possess that you did not receive? (1 Cor 4:7). Take note, dearly beloved, of what it is you give thanks for to the Lord God, in order not to be continuously ungrateful for any gift of his, and because you are ungrateful to lose what you have received. I cannot in any way at all unfold before you the priceless value of faith, but

any believer can reflect upon it. On the other hand, if in some respect you can reflect upon it as it deserves, is there anyone who can adequately reflect on how many gifts of God himself faith is to be preferred to? And if we are in duty bound to acknowledge God's lesser gifts to us, how much more should we acknowledge the one that so surpasses them?...

4. Someone says to me, "Let me understand, in order to believe." I answer, "Believe in order to understand." So when an argument of this sort somehow starts between us, so that he says to me, "Let me understand in order to believe," and I answer him, "On the contrary, believe in order to understand," let us go with this argument to a judge, don't let either of us presume to give judgment for his own side. What judge are we going to find? After considering all sorts of men, I don't know whether we can find a better judge than a man through whom God speaks. So in this matter, over this argument, don't let's go to secular literature, don't let us have a poet judge between us, but a prophet....

7. What were we arguing about? You were saying "Let me understand in order to believe"; I was saying "In order to understand, believe." An argument has arisen, let us put it before a judge, let a prophet judge, or rather let God judge through a prophet. Let's both of us keep silent. What we have each said has been heard: "Let me understand," you say, "in order to believe." "Believe," say I, "in order to understand." Let the prophet make his reply: *"Unless you believe, you shall not understand"* (Is 7:9).

8. Do you imagine, beloved, that the one who says "Let me understand, in order to believe" is really saying nothing very much? After all, what are we on about now, but getting people to believe—not those who don't believe at all, but those who do, though still not enough. If they didn't believe at all, they wouldn't be here. It's faith that brought them here, to listen. Faith brought them into the presence of the word of God, but this faith which has sprouted needs to be watered, nourished, strengthened. That's what we are concerned with right now. I, he said, planted, Apollo watered, but it is God who gave the increase. So neither the one who plants is anything, nor the one who waters, but God who gives the increase (1 Cor 3:6–7). By speaking, exhorting, teaching, persuading I can plant and water, but I cannot give the increase. That man he was talking to, who asked him to help his faith, which was budding and still tender and still weak and really very hesitant, but some sort of faith for all that and not no faith at all—he knew who it was to whom he said, I believe, Lord (Mk 9:23).

314

9. Just now when the gospel was being read, you heard If you can believe—the Lord Jesus said to the boy's father, If you can believe, all things are possible to one who believes (Mk 9:23) And the man took a look at himself, and standing in front of himself, not in a spirit of brash self–satisfaction but first examining his conscience, he saw that he did have some faith in him, and he also saw that it was tottering. He saw both things. He confessed he had one, and he begged for help for the other. I believe, Lord, he says. What was to follow, if not "Help my faith"? That's not what he said. "I believe, Lord. I can see this something in me, which I'm not lying about. I believe; I'm telling the truth. But I also see this other heaven knows what, and I don't like it. I want to stand, I'm still staggering. I'm standing and speaking, I haven't fallen, because I believe. But yet I'm still staggering: Help my unbelief" (Mk 9:24).

And so, beloved, that other man too whom I set up against myself, calling in the prophet as referee because of the argument that arose between us, he too isn't saying just nothing when he says "Let me understand, in order to believe." Of course, what I am now saying, I am saying to help those people believe who do not yet believe. And yet, unless they understand what I am saying, they cannot believe. So what this person says is partly true—"Let me understand, in order to believe"; and I on my side, when I say, just as the prophet says, "On the contrary, believe, in order to understand," am speaking the truth. Let's come to an agreement, then. So: understand, in order to believe; believe, in order to understand. I'll put it in a nutshell, how we can accept both without argument: Understand, in order to believe, my word; believe, in order to understand, the word of God.

Abbreviations

ACW	Ancient Christian Writers
BA	Bibliothèque Augustinienne
CCSL	Corpus Christianorum Series Latina
CSEL	Corpus Scriptorum Ecclesiasticorum Latinorum
NPNF	Nicene and Post Nicene Fathers
PL	Patrologia Latina
REAug	Revue des Etudes Augustiniennes, Paris
SC	Sources Chrétiennes

A Select Bibliography
(1945-1995)

CHARLES KANNENGIESSER

Based essentially on *Biblia Patristica* (Bonn), *Biblica/Elenchus Bibliographicus Biblicus* (Rome), *Ephemerides Theologicae Lovanienses* (Leuven) and *Revue d'Histoire Ecclésiastique* (Leuven), this bibliography, counting approximately 400 titles, illustrates the wealth and the diversity of the publications on Augustine produced since the end of World War II. Indeed the study of Augustine occupied a central position during those five golden decades of a Patristic renewal in the twentieth century.

The present selection witnesses also the limitations of that erudite legacy. To take but one example, the more than one hundred volumes of the prestigious series *Études Augustiniennes*, published during the past forty years, lack a single title that announces a thorough study of Augustine's biblical hermeneutics and exegesis. The surprising lacuna explains the fact that A.–M. la Bonnardière could appropriate the general title *Biblia Augustiniana* for her own publications in that series. She elaborated a set of monographs on the use of specific books of the Bible in Augustine's writings. Her highly refined analysis of biblical quotations and allusions represented an analytical undertaking in the pre–computer age which, though exceeding her individual capacity, demonstrated the exceptional richness of such painstaking inquiries. Her results, concerning Deuteronomy, the Historical Books (Joshua, Judges, Ruth, Samuel, Kings, Chronicles, Esdras, Tobit, Judith, Esther, Maccabees), Jeremiah, Proverbs, Wisdom, the Minor Prophets, Thessalonians, Titus and Philemon, were published in 1960–1975. They call for a study in depth of the bishop's use of the Bible, a study for which they claimed to provide only some preliminary materials. In her volume of "Bible de Tous les Temps," *Saint Augustin et la Bible* (1986), from which the present publication derives, la Bonnardière outlined such a study.

A final synthesis on Augustine and the Bible (if ever such a task could be achieved) would require a more extended survey of the work done in the field during the past five decades. Innumerable expositions of exegetical data spread over the general study of Augustine would lead the investigation far beyond the limits of the present choice of titles. The data presented here emphasize the major trends of scholarship on "Augustine and the Bible." With one or two exceptions, critical editions and modern translations have not been included among these data. They can be checked in the *Bulletin Augustinien* (Paris).

My special thanks to Phil Dunn, whose unexhaustible generosity and technical skills allowed the computerizing of the bibliography. For the selective categorization of titles I am solely responsible. The reader could add some cross–references by marking initials of various categories of titles next to the individual entrees. Obviously, some of these entries belong to several categories at once, hence my choices remain tentative and approximate.

The titles are distributed in alphabetic order of authors under the following rubrics:

A	Allegory
B	Bible
C	Christology
CR	Creation (*Genesis*)
E	Eschatology (*Revelation*)
ET	Ethics
F	Fall (Original sin, sin in general)
G	Gospels
H	Hermeneutics
HS	Holy Spirit
I	Incarnation (salvation, justification)
IS	Israel (Jews)
J	*John* (Johannine literature)
L	Liturgy

NT   New Testament

P   *Paul* (Pauline literature, except *Romans*)

PR   *Prophets* (Prophecy)

PS   *Psalms*

R   *Romans*

T   Trinity

W   *Wisdom* (Wisdom literature)

WO   Women

ALLEGORY

Altaner, B. "Augustinus u. Origenes." In *Kl. patrist. Schriften = TU 83*, 224-52, 1967.

Ayer, C. "Allegoria." *AugL* 1 (1986): 233-9.

Bastiaensen, A. "La *perdrix* animal méchant figure du diable; Augustin héritier d'une tradition exégétique." *AugLv* 40 (1990): 193-217.

Courcelle, P. "S. Augustin a-t-il lu Philon d'Alexandrie?" *RÉAnc* 63 (1961): 78-85.

Doignon, J. "Allégories du retour dans le *Contra Academicos* de S. Augustin." *Latomus* LII (1993): 860-67.

Evans, G.R. "*Absurditas* in Augustine's scriptural commentary." *DowR* 99 (1981): 109-18.

Ferrari, L.C. "The tree in the works of St. Augustine." *AugLv* 38 (1988): 37-53.

Marin, M. "Agostino e l'interpretazione antica di Gal 4:24; note sulla fortuna di *allegoria* in ambito latino." *VetChr* 24 (1987): 5-21.

Mayer, C. "Allegoria." In *Augustinus-Lexikon*, 233-39, 1986.

Mazzeo, J.A. "St. Augustine's Rhetoric of Silence (de typologia et allegoresi)." *JHistIdeas* 23: 175-96.

McGowan, R.J. "Augustine's spiritual quality; the allegory of man and woman with regard to *Imago Dei*." *RÉAug* 33 (1987): 255-64.

Pépin, J. "S. Augustin et la fonction protreptique de l'allégorie." *Rech. Aug.* 1 (1958): 245-86.

Shanzer, D. "Latent narrative patterns, allegorical choices, and literary unity in Augustine's Confessions." *VigChr* 46 (1992): 40-56.

BIBLE

Bavel, T. "Parallèles, vocabulaire et citations bibliques de la «Regula S. Augustini.» Contribution au problème de son authenticité." *Augustiniana* 9 (1959): 12-77.

Bonner, G. "Augustine as Biblical Scholar." In *Cambridge Hist. of the Bible*, edited by P.R.Ackroyd, 541-63, 597. London/New York, 1970.

Cantelmi, A. "La Sacra Scrittura nelle Lettere di Sant'Agostino." *Euresis. Notizie e scritti di varia indole del Liceo classico M. Tullio Cicerone di Sala Consilina* 6 (1990): 91-109. Salerno.

Cilleruelo, L. "S. Augustine intérprete de la S. Escritura." *Ciudad de Dios* 155 (1943): 455-89.

Cocchini, F. "Le Quaestiones di Agostino sull'Esodo; osservazioni storiche, esegetiche, dottrinali." *AnStoEseg* 5 (1988): 77-95.

Collins, R.F. "Augustine of Hippo precursor of modern biblical scholarship." *LvSt* 12 (1987): 131-51.

Coward, H.G. "Memory and Scripture in the conversion of Augustine." In *Grace, politics and desire; essays on Augustine*, edited by H.A. Meynell, 19-30. Calgary: Univ., 1990.

Dankbaar, W.P. "Schriftgezag en Kerkgezag bij Augustinus." *NedTTs* 11 (1956): 37-59.

Dassmann, E. "Schriftverständnis und religiöse Erkenntnis nach dem heiligen Augustinus." *TrierTZ* 87 (1978): 257-74.

Ferrari, L.C. "From Pagan Literature to the Pages of the Holy Scriptures. Augustine's Confessions as Exemplary Propaedeutic." In *Fs Andresen, C. Kerygma and Logos*, edited by A.M. Ritter, 173-82. Göttingen, 1979.

Fitzgerald, A. "Arise! A scriptural model for Augustine's conversion." *Angelicum* 64 (1987): 359-75.

Grill, S. "Der hl. Augustinus und das AT." *BiLit* 21 (1953): 312-20.

Hamman, A. G. "Saint Augustin, la Bible et la théologie spirituelle." *AugLv* 41 (1990): 773-82.

Hendriks, E. "Platonisches und biblisches Denken bei Augustinus." In *Augustinus Magister*, 285-92. Paris: Études Augustiniennes, 1955.

Isola, A. "L'esegesi biblica del Sermo 286 di Agostino." *VetChr* 23 (1986): 267-81.

Jouassard, G. "Réflexions sur la position de S. Augustin relativement aux Septante dans sa discussion avec S. Jérôme." *REAug* 2 (1956): 93-99.

Kienzler, K. "Der Aufbau der "Confessiones" des Augustinus im Spiegel der Bibelzitate." *RechAug* 24 (1989): 123-64.

Langa, P. "La autoridad de la Sagrada Escritura Contra Cresconium." *AugLv* 41 (1990): 691-721.

Loewen, H.J. "The use of Scripture in Augustine's theology." *ScotJT* 34 (1981): 201-24.

Luis Vizcaino, P. de. "La Sagrada Escritura como 'Testamento' de Dios en la obra antidonatista de S. Agustin." *EstAgust* 15 (1980): 3-38.

Manrique, A. "Interpretación y utilización de la Biblia en S. Agustin." *CiuDios* 182 (1969): 157-74.

Munier, C. "La tradition manuscrite de l'Abrégé d'Hippone et le canon des Écritures des Église africaines." *SacEr* 21 (1972): 43-55.

Niewiadomski, J. "Die Sorge um die ganze Bibel; Augustinus' Bemühung um den biblischen Gott des Zornes." *BLtg* 59 (1986): 238-44.

Obersteiner, J. *Augustinus Civ. Dei und die Geschichstheologie der Bibel.* Estudios sobre la Ciudad de Dios, vol. 167. Ciudad de Dios, 1954.

Pellegrino, M. "Appunti sull'uso della Bibbia nei Sermoni di S. Agostino." *RivB* 27 (1979): 7-39.

Penna, A. "Lo studio della Bibbia nella spiritualità di S. Agostino." In *S. Augustinus. Vitae Spiritualis Magister 1*, 147-68, 1959.

Polman, A.D.R. *De theologie van Augustinus. I: Het Woord Gods bij Augustinus.* Kampen: Kok., 1956.

_____. *The Word of God According to St. Augustine.* London: Hodder and Stoughton, 1962.

Pontet, M. "L'exégèse de S. Augustin, prédicateur." *AnT* 8 (1947): 331-36.

Recchia, V. "La memoria di Agostino

nell'esegesi biblica di Gregorio Magno." *AugR* 25 (1985): 405-34.

Ries, J. "La Bible chez S. Augustin et chez les manichéens." *RÉAug* 7/9 (1961/63): 231-43/201-15.

Román de la Immaculada. "La S. Escritura como fuente de vida espiritual según S. Agustin." *Rev. de Espiritualidad* (1955).

Rondet, H. "Thèmes bibliques: Exégèse augustinienne (résumé + discussion)." In *Augustinus Magister*, 231-46. Paris: Études Augustiniennes, 1955.

Salas, A. "La « koinônia » biblica y la « communitas » agustiniana." *CiuDeos* 182 (1969): 232-38.

Sampson, T.J.W. "The Scriptures in St. Augustine's Confessions." diss., Strasbourg, 1970.

Sasse, H. "Sacra Scriptura. Bemerkungen zur Inspirationslehre Augustins." In *Dornseiff-Fs*, 262-73.

Schultz, S.J. "Augustine and the OT Canon." *EvQ* 28 (1956): 93-100.

Smalley, B. "Prima Clavis Sapientiae. Augustin and Abelard." In *Fritz Saxl (1890-1948) Memorial Essays*, 93-100. Nelson, 1957.

Starnes, C. "Augustinian biblical exegesis and the origins of modern science." In *Collectanea Augustiniana*, edited by J.C. Schnaubelt-F.Van Fleteren, 345-55, 1990.

Stengers, J. "S. Augustin et l'inerrance biblique." In *Mémorial J. Préaux, Christianisme d'hier et d'aujoud'hui*, 27-39. Bruxelles: Univ. Libre, 1979.

Stransky, T.F. "St. Augustine's Use of Scripture." *AmER 143* (1960).

Tanner, R.G. "The use of the Old Testament in St. Augustine's De civitate dei." In *The Bible and european literature. History and hermeneutics. First conference,*

Melbourne, 15-18 May, 1987, edited by E. Osborn et al, 176-85. Melbourne: Academia Press, 1987.

Trapé, A. "La manducazione spirituale nella dottrina eucaristica di s. Agostino." *ParSpV* 7 (1983): 232-43.

Veer, A.C de. "« Revelare-Revelatio.» Éléments d'une étude sur l'emploi du mot et sur sa signification chez S. Augustin." *Recherches august.* II (1962): 331-57.

Veismann, F. "Biblia y vida monástica en San Agustin." *Stromata* 41 (1985): 87-96.

Verbraken, P. "L'édition critique des sermons de S. Augustin sur l'AT." *RBén* 72 (1962): 346-48.

Vogüé, A de. "Les plus anciens exégètes du Premier Livre des Rois (1 Sam); Origène, Augustin et leurs épigones." *SacrEr* 29 (1986): 5-12.

Wermelinger, O. "Le canon des Latins au temps de Jerôme et d'Augustin." In *Le canon de l'Ancien Testament; sa formation et son histoire*, edited by J.-D. Kaestli. Geneva: Labor et Fides, 1984.

Wohlmuth, J. "Theophanietexte in der Exegese des Augustinus. Ein systematisch orientiertes Gespräch zwischen Augustinus und der Phänomenologie." In *Stimuli, Fs.E.Dassmann*, edited by G. Schöllgen and Cl. Scholten, 512-25. Münster: Aschendorffsche V., 1996.

Zarb, S.M. "St. Augustine, the Biblical Scholar." *Scientia* 21: 129-44.

Zumkeller, A. "Biblische und altchristliche Leitbilder des klösterlichen Lebens im des hl. Augustinus." *AugLv* 18 (1968): 5-21.

CHRISTOLOGY

Arbesmann, R. "Christ the *medicus humilis* in St. Augustine." In

Augustinus Magister, 623-29. Paris: Études Augustiniennes, 1954.

De Bovis, A. "Le Christ et la prière, selon S. Augustin." *RAM* 25 (1949): 180-93.

Drobner, H.R. *Person-Exegese und Christologie bei Augustinus: zur Herkunft der Formel una persona.* Philosophia Patrum. Leiden: Brill, 1984/86.

_____. "Grammatical Exegesis and Christology in St. Augustine." In *St Patr XVIII, 4*, edited by E.A. Livingstone, 49-63. Kalamazoo, Mich.: Cistercian Publications, 1990.

Fontanier, J.-M. "Sur une image hiéronymienne; le visage sidéral de Jésus (Ep 65,8 on Ps 44: quiddam siderum)." *RSPT* 75 (1991): 251-6.

Geerlings, W. *Christus Exemplum. Studien zur Christologie und Christusverkündigung Augustins.* TübTSt, vol. 13. Mainz: Grünewald, 1977.

González, S. "La preocupación arriana en la predicación de San Agustin." diss., Rome: Inst. Patristicum Augustinianum, 1987.

Madec, G. *La Patrie et la Voie; le Christ dans la vie et la pensée de saint Augustin.* JJC, vol. 36. Paris: Desclée, 1989.

Marrevee, W.H. *The Ascension of Christ in the Works of St. Augustine.* Ottawa, 1967.

McGuckin, J.A. "Did Augustine's Christology depend on Theodore of Mopsuestia?" *RivStoSR* 25 (1989): 444-57.

Remy, G. "Le Christ médiateur dans l'oeuvre de saint Augustin." diss. Fac. Théol. Cath. Strasbourg, 1977.

Scholz, W. "Christus bei Augustin." diss., Kiel, 1955.

Welsch, P.J. "La foi au 'Verbe fait chair' dans le De Trinitate de saint Augustin." diss., Louvain, 1986.

CREATION

Alfeche, M. "Groaning creation in the theology of Augustine." *Augustiniana* 34 (1984): 5-52.

Álvarez Turienzo, S. *Regio media salutis; Imagen del hombre y su puesto en la creación, S. Agustín.* Bibl. Salm. Est. Salamanca: Univ. Pontificia, 1988.

Babcock, R.G. "Augustine's De Genesi ad litteram and Horace's Satire 1, 2." *RÉAug* 33 (1987): 265-8.

Bernardi, M.C. "« In principio fecit Deus caelum et terram » (Gen 1:1) in S. Agostino e le sue fonti." diss., Torino, 1959.

Carosio, L. "Ricerche sulle fonti all'esegesi agostiniana della Genesi." diss., Torino, 1951.

Cavalcanti, E. "Il significato dell'esegesi letterale in Basilio e in Agostino, Omelie sull'Esamerone e De Genesi ad litteram I-III." *AnStoEseg* 4 (1987): 119-42.

_____. "La Genesi alla lettera (Agostino) tra '800 e '900." *AnStoEseg* 5 (1988): 297-313.

Cizewski, W. "The meaning and the purpose of animals according to Augustine's Genesis commentaries." In *Collectanea Augustiniana. Augustinus. Presbyter factus sum*, edited by J.T. Lienhard, E.C. Muller, and R. Teske, 363-73. New York: P. Lang, 1993.

Costa Freitas, M.B. da. "À imagem e semelhança de Deus; um tema de antropologia Agostiniana." *Didaskalia* 19 (1987/89): 21-34.

Dolby Múgica, M. del, C. "El hombre como imagen de Dios en la especulación Agustiniana." *AugM* 34 (1989): 119-54.

Gallus, T. "Principia exegetica S. Augustini ad Gen 3:15 applicata." *VD* 32 (1954): 129-41.

Garcia de la Fuente, O. *Interpretación exegética del Génesis en la Ciudad de Dios*. Estudios sobre la Ciudad de Dios, vol. 167. Ciudad de Dios, 1954.

Goldschmidt, V. "Exégèse et axiomatique chez S. Augustin (de Gen 1-2)." In *Hommage à M. Guéroult*, 14-42. Paris, 1964.

Gorman, M. "The text of Saint Augustine's 'De Genesi ad litteram liber imperfectus'." *RechAug* 20 (1985): 65-86.

Gorman, M.M. "An unedited fragment of an Irish epitome of St. Augustine's *De Genesi ad Litteram*." *RÉAug* 28 (1982).

———. "A Carolingian epitome of St. Augustine's *De Genesi ad Litteram*." *RÉAug* 29 (1983): 137-44.

———. "The unstudied commentary on Genesis in Monte Cassino 29." *Manuscripta* 27 (1983): 8.

———. "Eugippus and the origins of the tradition of St. Augustine's 'De Genesi ad litteram'." *RBén* 93 (1983): 7-30.

———. "Marginalia in the oldest manuscripts of St. Augustine's *De Genesi ad Litteram*." *Scriptorium* 38 (1984): 71-77.

Gousmett, C. "Creation order and miracle according to Augustine." *EvQ* 60 (1988): 217-40.

Grotz, K. "Warum bringt Augustin in den letzen Büchern seiner 'Confessiones' eine Auslegung der Genesis?" diss., Tübingen, 1969/70.

Lamberigts, M. "Julian d'Éclane et Augustin d'Hippone; deux conceptions d'Adam." In *Collectanea Augustiniana*, edited by T. van Bavel, 373-410. Lv, 1990.

Lambot, C. "Une série pascale de sermons de S. Augustin sur les jours de la Création." In *Mél. C. Mohrmann*, 213-21, 1963.

Langa, P. "Análisis agustiniano de 'crescite et multiplicamini' (Gen 1:28)." *EstAgust* 18 (1983): 3-38, 147-76.

Lavallee, L. "Augustine on the Creation-days." *JEvTS* 32 (1989): 457-64.

Lehmann, H. "Espiritu de Dios sobre las aguas; fuentes de los commentarios de Basilio y Agustin sobre el Génesis 1, 2." In *San Agustin en Oxford = AugM 26, 103s (1981)*, edited by J. Oroz Rega, 127-39, 1979.

Maher, G.P. "St. Augustine's Defense of the Hexaemeron against the Manicheans." diss., Rome: Gregoriana, 1946.

Marin, M. "Nomen quasi notamen; una nota su Aug. Gen. litt. impf. 6, 26." *VetChr* 28 (1991): 267-75.

Messana, V. "L'esegesi tropologica presso i padri e le bibliche figure di Abele e di Caino in Ambrogio e Agostino." In *St Patr XV*, edited by E.A. Livingstone, 185-95. Oxford, 1975.

O'Meara, J.J. " 'Magnorum virorum quendam consensum velimus machinari' (804 D); Eriugena's use of Augustine's De Genesi ad litteram in the Periphyseon." In *Eriugena*, edited by W. Beierwaltes, 105-16, 1979/80.

———. *The creation of man in St. Augustine's "De Genesi ad Litteram."* Villanova: Univ., 1980.

Pagels, E. "The politics of Paradise; Augustine's exegesis of Genesis 1-3 versus that of John

Chrysostom." *HarvTR* 78 (1985): 67-99.

Pelland, G. "Augustin et le début de la Genèse. Cinq études sur les premiers versets de l'Écriture." diss., Rome: Pont. Univ. Gregorianae, 1969.

Peters, E. "What was God doing before he created the heavens and the earth?" *AugLv* 34 (1984): 53-74.

_____. "Aenigma Salomonis; Manichaean anti-Genesis polemic and the Vitium curiositatis in Confessions III, 6." *AugLv* 36 (1986): 48-64.

Pépin, J. "Le maniement des prépositions dans la théorie Augustinienne de la création." *RÉAug* 35 (1989): 251-74.

Pollastri, A. "Le quaestiones di Agostino su Genesi; struttura dell'opera e motivazioni storico-dottrinali." *AnStoEseg* 5 (1988): 57-76.

Rousseau, O. "La typologie augustinienne de l'Hexaéméron et la théologie du temps." *Festgabe J. Lortz* 2 (1958): 47-58.

Solignac, A. "La connaissance angélique et les jours de la création (Gen 1:3 dans le *De Gen. ad litteram* de S. Augustin)." *ÉcPratHÉt, RelAn* 69 (1971): 275-77.

Somers, H. "Image de Dieu. Les sources de l'exégèse augustinienne." *RÉAug* 7 (1961): 105-25.

Taylor, J.H. "S. Augustine De Genesi ad litteram liber duodecimus." Univ. St.-Louis, 1948.

TeSelle, E. "Nature and Grace in Augustine's Expositions of Gen 1:1-5." *Recherches Augustiniennes* 5 (1968): 95-137.

Teske, R.J. "*Homo spiritualis* in St. Augustine's De Genesi contra Manichaeos." *St Patr* X (1987): 351-55.

_____. "The image and likeness of God in St. Augustine's De Genesi ad litteram liber imperfectus." *AugR* 30 (1990): 441-51.

_____. "El Homo spiritualis en el De Genesi contra Manichaeos." *AugM* 36 (1991): 305-10.

_____. "St. Augustine's view of the original human condition in De Genesi contra Manichaeos." *AugSt* 22 (1991): 141-56.

_____. "Origen and St. Augustine's first Commentaries on Genesis." In *Origeniana Quinta*, edited by R.J. Daly, 179-85. Leuven, 1992.

Vannier, M.-A. "Le rôle de l'Hexaéméron dans l'interprétation augustinienne de la création." *RSPT* 71 (1987): 537-46.

_____. "Le rôle de l'hexaéméron dans l'interpretation augustinienne de la création." *St Patr* XXII (1989): 372-81.

_____. "Saint Augustin et la création." In *Collectanea Augustiniana*, edited by T. van Bavel, 349-71. Lv, 1990.

_____. "El papel del hexamerón en la interpretación agustiniana de la creación." *AugM* 36 (1991): 343-55.

_____. "Aspects de l'idée de création chez S. Augustin." *RevSR* 65 (1991): 213-25.

_____. "*Creatio*," "*conversio*," "*formatio*" chez saint Augustin. Paradosis, vol. 31. Freibourg/S: Univ., 1991.

Vásquez Gómez, J.J. "Interpretación patristica del Génesis 2:18-23; significado de la expressión 'mutuum adiutorium' hasta San Agustin." diss., Rome: Pont. Univ. Gregoriana, 1981.

Weisman, F.J. "Tipologia en el 'De Genesi adversus manichaeos' de San Agustín." *RelCult* 33 (1987): 247-58.

Weismann, F.J. "Teologia y simbolismo en 'De Genesi adversus Manichaeos' de S. Agustín." *Stromata* 42 (1986): 217-26.

Zacher, A. "De Gen. contra Manich. Ein Versuch Augustins, die ersten drei Kapitel von Genesis zu erklären und zu verteidigen." diss., Rome: Pont. Univ. Gregoriana, 1961/62.

Zimmerman, A. "Naked but not ashamed." *The Priest* 48, 9 (1992): 47-54.

ECCLESIOLOGY

Agterberg, M. "S. Augustin exégète de l'Ecclesia Virgo." *Augustiniana* 8 (1958): 237-66.

Berrouard, M.-F. "Deux peuples, un seul troupeau, un unique Pasteur; ecclésiologie de saint Augustin et citations de Jean 10:16." In *Collectanea Augustiniana*, edited by F. van Fleteren, 275-301. Villanova: Villanova Univ., 1986/90.

Eno, R.B. "Forma Petri - Petrus, figura Ecclesiae; the uses of Peter (in Augustine)." *AugLv* 41 (1990s): 659-76.

Giacobbi, A. *La Chiesa in S. Agostino I. Mistero di communione.* Rome: Città Nuova, 1982.

La Bonnardière, A.M. "La Chananéenne (Mt 15:21-28). Préfiguration de l'Église des Gentils d'après S. Augustin." *AugMadr* 12 (1967): 209-38.

Lécuyer, J. "L'oasis d'Élim et les ministères dans l'Église." In *Fs. C. Vagaggini Lex orandi lex credendi,* edited by G.J.Békés, 295-329. Rome: Anselmiana, 1980.

Luis, P. de. "De ministro donatista a ministro catôlico. A propósito de *Adnotationes in Iob xxxix,* 9-12 de S. Agustin." *RAg* XXXIII (1992): 397-431.

Oden, A.G. "Dominant images for the Church in Augustine's Enarrationes in Psalmos: a study in Augustine's ecclesiology." diss., Dallas, Tex.: Southern Methodist Univ., 1990.

Palmero Ramos, R. "« Ecclesia Mater » en S. Augustin. Teologia de la imagen en los escritos antidonatistas." diss., Rome: Pont. Univ. Gregorianae, 1967/68.

Rondet, M. "La typologie de l'Église dans le prédication et l'exégèse augustiniennes." diss., Rome: Gregoriana, 1960.

Sanchis, D. "Le symbolisme communitaire du Temple chez S. Augustin." *RAscMyst* 37 (1961): 3-30, 137-47.

_____. "Pauvreté monastique et charité fraternelle chez S. Augustin. Le comm. augustinien de Act 4:32-35 entre 393 et 403." *StMonast* 4 (1962): 7-33.

Simon, P. "Die Kirche als Braut des Hohenliedes nach dem hl. Augustinus." *Festgabe J. Kardinal Prings* (1960).

Verheijen, L. *Saint Augustine's Monasticism in the Light of Acts 4:32-35.* St. Augustine Lectures, 1975. Villanova, PA: Univ., 1979.

ESCHATOLOGY

Alfeche, M. "The basis of hope in the resurrection of the body according to Augustine." *AugLv* 36 (1986): 240-96.

_____. "The use of some verses of 1 Cor 15 in Augustine's theology of the Resurrection." *AugLv* 37 (1987): 122-86.

_____. "The rising of the dead in the works of Augustine (1 Cor 15:35-57)." *Augustiniana* 39 (1989): 54-98.

Bonner, G. "Augustine and millenarianism." In *Fs. H. Chadwick,* edited by R. Williams, 235-54. Cambridge, 1989.

Bright, P. "Augustine and the thousand year reign of saints." In *Collectanea Augustiniana. Augustinus. Presbyter factus sum,* edited by J.T. Lienhard, E.C. Muller and R. Teske, 447-53. New York: P. Lang, 1993.

Clarke, T.E. "The Eschatological Transformation of the Material World acc. to St. Augustine." diss., Rome: Gregoriana, 1956.

Folliet, G. "La typologie du sabbat chez S. Augustin. Son interprétation millénariste entre 389 et 400." *RÉAug* 2 (1956): 371-90.

Foubert, J. "Ad gloriam corporis; au-delà de Sagesse 9:15, 'corpus quod corrumpitur adgravat animam'." In *Fs. J. Pépin Sophias maietores,* edited by M.-O. Goulet-Cazé, 383-402. Paris, 1992.

Frahier, L.J. "L'interprétation du récit du jugement dernier (Mt 25:31-46) dans l'oeuvre d'Augustin." *RÉAug* 33 (1987): 70-84.

Fredriksen, P. "Apocalypse and redemption in early Christianity, from John of Patmos to Augustine of Hippo." *VigChr* 45 (1991): 151-83.

Koetting, B. "Endzeitprognosen zwischen Lactantius und Augustinus." *Hist.Jb.* 77 (1958): 125-39.

Lettieri, G. *Il senso della storia in Agostino d'Ippona; il "saeculum" e la gloria nel "De Civitate Dei": Cultura cristiana antica.* Rome: Borla, 1988.

Lohse, B. "Zur Eschatologie des älteren Augustin (De Civ. Dei 20, 9)." *VigChr* 21 (1967): 221-30.

Marin, M. "Note sulla fortuna dell'esegesi agostiniana di Mt 25:1-13." *VetChr* 18 (1981): 33-79.

_____. "Ricerche sull'esegesi Agostiniana della parabola delle dieci vergini (Mt 25:1-13)." *QuadVetChr* 16 (1981): 277-94.

Perrot, C. "La descente aux enfers et la prédication aux morts." In *Études sur la première lettre de Pierre (ACFÉB, 1979),* 231-46. Paris: Cerf, 1980.

Rondet, H. "Le symbolisme de la mer (cf. Apoc 21:1) chez S. Augustin." *Augustinus Magister* (1954).

ETHICS

Albertine, R. "Selected survey of the theme 'spiritual sacrifice' to Augustine." *EphLtg* 104 (1990): 35-50.

Bauer, J.B. "Dilige et fac quod vis." *Wiss. u. Weisheit* 20 (1957): 64s.

Becker, J.A. "Les béatitudes évangéliques dans la prédication populaire de S. Augustin, d'après les *En. in Pss. 118-133.*" diss., Strasbourg, 1965.

Benin, S.D. "Sacrifice as education in Augustine and Chrysostom." *ChH* 52 (1983): 7-20.

Berrouard, M.F. "L'enseignement de S. Augustin sur le mariage dans le Tract. 9, 2 in Joh. Ev." *AugMadr* 12 (1967): 83-96.

Canning, R. " 'Love your neighbour as yourself' (Mt 22:39); S. Augustine on the lineaments of the self to be loved." *Augustiana* 34 (1984): 145-97.

_____. "Augustine on the identity of the neighbour and the meaning of true love for him 'as ourselves' (Mt 23:24-30) and 'as Christ has loved us' (Jn 13:34)." *AugLv* 36 (1986): 161-239.

Chevalier, L., and H. Rondet. "L'idée de « vanité » dans l'oeuvre de S. Augustin." *RÉAug* 3 (1957): 221-34.

Demeulenaere, R. "Le sermon 84 de S. Augustin sur l'invitation de Jésus au jeune homme riche. Édition critique." In *Aevum inter utrumque. Fs. G. Sanders (Instr. Patr., 23)*, edited by M. Van Uytfanghe and R. Demeulenaere, 67-73. Steenbrugge (Belg.): La Haye, 1991.

Folliet, G. "Les trois catégories de chrétiens, à partir de Lc 17:34ss; Mt 24:40s; Ex 14:14." *Augustinus Magister* (1954).

Fontaine, J. "Augustin, Grégoire et Isidore; esquisse d'une recherche sur le style des Moralia in Iob." In *Grégoire le Grand*, 499-509. Paris: CNRS, 1986.

Hesberi, R. "S. Augustin et la virginité de la foi." *Augustinus Magister* (1954).

Lambot, C. "Le sermon de S. Augustin sur la femme forte (Prv 31)." *RBén* 65 (1955): 208-17.

————. "Le sermon 343 de S. Augustin: De Susanna et Joseph." *RBén* 66 (1956): 14-38.

Lenihan, D.A. "The just war theory in the work of Saint Augustine." *AugSt* 19 (1988): 37-70.

Locher, G.F.D. "Martha en Maria in de prediking van Augustinus." *Ned. Archief voor Kerkgeschiedenis* 46 (1964): 65-86.

Margerie, B. de. "*Preparatio cordis ad plura perferenda*. S. Augustin, *De Sermone Domini in Monte* I, xix, 59 et xx, 66 (Mt 5:39ss)." *Augustinianum* XXXII (1992): 145-60.

Menestrina, G. "L'epistola 167 de sententia Iacobi Apostoli (Giac. 2,10) di sant'Agostino." *BbbOr* 20 (1978): 43-49.

Mizzi, J. "The Latin Text of Mt 5ff in St. Augustine's De sermone Domini in monte." *Augustiniana* 4 (1954): 450-94.

Pizzolato, L.F. *Per foramen acus; il cristianesimo antico di fronte alla pericope evagelica del "giovane ricco."* In *Studia patristica mediolanensia 14*. Milan, 1986.

Scalabrella, S. "La Samaritana segno di riconciliazione; la lettura di Agostino." *StudiumR* 81 (1985): 789-97.

FALL

Beatrice, P.F. *Tradux peccati. Alle fonti della dottrina agostiniana del peccato originale.* Studia Patristica Mediolanensia, vol. 8. Milan: Vita e Pensiero, 1978.

Gross, J. *Entstehungsgeschichte des Erbsündendogmas. Von der Bibel bis Augustinus.* Mü/Ba: Reinhardt, 1961.

Harrison, C. "'Who is free from sin?' The figure of Job in the thought of St. Augustine." In *Letture cristiani dei Libre Sapienziali*, edited by F. Bolgiani, 483-8. Inst. Patr. Augustinianum, 1991/2.

Heaney-Hunter, J.A. "The links between sexuality and original sin in the writings of John Chrysostom and Augustine." diss., New York: Fordham, 1988.

Thonnard, F.J. "Sur le péché en S. Augustin." *RÉAug* 7 (1961): 250s.

Weber, H. "Die Sünde wider den Heiligen Geist nach der Auffassung des hl. Augustinus (Sermo 71)." *Salesianum* 22 (1960): 628-36.

GOSPELS

Baarda, T. "'A staff only, not a stick,' disharmony of the gospels and the harmony of Tatian (Mt 10:9f; Mk 6:8f; Lk 9:3, 10:4)." *Réception 86* (1989): 311-33 *The NT in early Christianity—La réception des Écrits néotestamentaires dans le christianisme primitif*, vol. 86, edited by J.-M. Sevrin. Bibl. ETL. Louvain: Peeters.

Coassolo, G.P. "« Panem nostrum quotidianum da nobis hodie » in S. Agostino." *Convivium Dominicum* (1962).

Cremer, F.G. *Der Beitrag Augustins zur Auslegung des Fastenstreitgesprächs (Mk 2:18-22 parr.) und der Einfluss seiner Exegese auf die mittelalterliche Theologie*. Études Augustiniennes. Paris, 1971.

Delforge, T. "Inferas - inducas: A propos de Mt 6:13 dans les oeuvres de S. Augustin." *RBén* 69 (1959): 348-54.

Deloffre, J. "L'enfant et le Royaume; recherche sur l'interprétation de Mt 18:3 à partir du Nouveau Testament et les oeuvres de Saint Augustin." diss., Paris: Inst. Cath., 1989.

Demeulenaere, R. "Le sermon LXXVI de S. Augustin sur la marche de Jésus et de Pierre sur les eaux." In *Instumenta Patristica*. Vol 24, *Fs. A. Bastiaensen Eulogia*, edited by G.J.M. Bartelink, 51-63. Steenbrugge, 1991.

Frot, Y. "Note sur l'utilisation de la parabole de l'Enfant Prodigue dans l'oeuvre de Saint Augustin." In *Fs. V. Saxer Memoriam Sanctorum venerantes.*, 443-8. Vatican: Pont. Ist. Arch. Cr., 1992.

Hebblethwaite, P. "St. Augustine's interpretation of Matthew 5:17." In *St Patr XVI*, edited by E.A. Livingstone, 511-16. Berlin: Akademie, 1985.

Holl, A. *Augustinus Bergpredigtexegese. Nach seinem Frühwerk De sermone Domine in monte libri duo*. Herder, 1960.

Jepson, J.J. "St. Augustine. The Lord's Sermon on the Mount." *VD* 27 (1949): 246.

Jonge, H.J. de. "Augustine on the interrelations of the Gospels." In *Fs. F. Neirynck The Four Gospels*, edited by F. van Seegbroeck, 2409-17. Lv: Univ./Peeters, 1992.

La Bonnardière, A.M. "Les commentaires simultanés de Mt 6:12 et Jo 1:8 dans l'oeuvre de S. Augustin." *REtAug* 15 (1955): 129-48.

_____. "*Tu es Petrus*. La péricope « Mt 16:13-23 » dans l'oeuvre de S. Augustin." *Irén* 34 (1961): 451-99.

Löfstedt, B. "Zu Augustins Schrift De sermone Domini in monte." *Orpheus* 9 (1988): 86-97.

Luis Vizcaino, P. de. "Exégesis, apologética y teologia; Poncio Pilato en la obra agustiniana." *EstAgust* 24 (1989): 353-90.

Mutzenbecher, A. "Über die Zuschreibung der von den Maurinern so benannten *Quaestiones XVII in Evangelium secundum Matthaeum* an Augustin." *SacErud* 23 (1978s): 95-122.

Ray, R.D. "Augustine's *De consensu Evangelistarum* and the historical education of the Venerable Bede." In *StPatrist XVI Oxford 1975*, edited by E.A. Livingstone, 557-63. Berlin: Akademie, 1985.

Scorza Barcellona, F. "La parabola della zizzania in Agostino; a proposito di Quaestiones in Matthaeum 11." *AnStoEseg* 5 (1988): 215-23.

Siniscalco, P. "'Intra in gaudium Domini tui'; nota su una citazione di

Matteo (25, 21 e 23) nelle Confessioni di Agostino; esperienza mistica e beatudine celeste." In *Fs. K. Albert, Probleme philosophischer Mystik*, edited by E. Jain, 187-96, 1991.

Solá, F. de, P. "La paternided de San José en San Agustin." *EstJos* 39 (1985): 11-24.

Straw, C.E. "Augustine as pastoral theologian; the exegesis of the parables of the field and threshing floor." *AugSt* 14 (1983): 129-51.

Thieme, K. "Augustinus und der ältere Bruder (Lk 15:25-32)." In *Universitas, Fs A. Stohr*, 79-85. Mainz, 1960.

Verbraken, P. "Le sermon LI de saint Augustin sur les généalogies du Christ selon Matthieu et selon Luc."*RBén* 91 (1981): 20-45.

―――――."Le sermon LXXXVIII de Saint Augustin sur la guérison des deux aveugles de Jéricho." *RBén* 94 (1984): 71-101.

―――――."Le sermon 53 de S. Augustin sur les béatitudes selon S. Matthieu." *RBén* CIV (1994): 19-33.

Verheijen, L. "The Straw, the Beam, the Tusculan Disputations and the Rule of St. Augustine—On a Surprising Augustinian Exegesis (of Mt 7:3-5)." *AugSt* 2 (1971): 17-36.

HERMENEUTICS

"Augustine De Doctrina Christiana." In *Oxford Early Christian Texts*, edited and translated by R.P.H. Green. Oxford: Clarendon, 1995.

Basevi, C. *San Agustin. La interpretación del NT. Criterios exegéticos propuestos por S. Agustin en el "De Doctrina Christiana," en el "Contra Faustum" y en el "De Consensu Evangelistarum."* Teológica, vol. 14. Pamplona: EUNSA, 1977.

Bernard, R.W. "The rhetoric of God in the figurative exegesis of Augustine." In *Fs. K. Froehlich Biblical hermeneutics in historical perspective*, edited by M.S. Burrows, 88-99. Grand Rapids: Eerdmans, 1991.

Brunner, P. "Charismatische und methodische Schriftauslegung nach Augustin's Prolog zu De doctrina christiana." *KerDo* 1 (1955): 59-69; 85-103.

Cantaloup, P. "Les rapports des deux Testaments dans le *Contra Faustum* de S. Augustin." diss., Institut Cath. de Toulouse, 1955.

De doctrina christiana. A Classic of Western Culture. Edited by D.W.H. Arnold and P. Bright. Notre Dame, Ind.: UND Press, 1995.

Della Terza, D. *Tradizione ed esegesi; semantica dell'innovazione da Agostino a De Sanctis.* Padova: Liviana, 1987.

Djuth, M. "The hermeneutics of *De libero arbitrio* III: are there two Augustines?" In *St Patr*, vol. XXVII, 281-89, 1993.

Dulaey, M. "La sixième Règle de Tyconius et son résumé dans le De doctrina christiana." *RÉAug* 35 (1989): 83-103.

Federico, C. "Principii di esegesi biblica nel *De doctrina christiana* di S. Agostino." diss., Rome: Pont. Univ. Lateranensis, 1965s.

Gaeta, G. "Le Regole per l'interpretazione della Scrittura da Ticonio ad Agostino." *AnStoEseg* 4 (1987): 109-18.

Grech, P. "I Principi ermeneutici di sant'Agostino, una valutazione." *Lateranum* 48 (1982): 200-23.

―――――. *Ermeneutica e teologia biblica.* Rome: Borla, 1986.

Hamilton, G.J. "Augustine's methods of biblical interpretation." In

Grace, politics and desire; essays on Augustine, edited by H.A. Meynell, 103-19. Calgary: Univ., 1990.

Holl, A. *Augustinus Bergpredigtexegese. Nach seinem Frühwerk De sermone Domine in monte libri duo*. Herder, 1960.

Istace, G. "Le livre 1er du « De Doctrina Christiana » de S. Augustin." *ETL* 32 (1956): 289-330.

Itterzon, G.P. van. *Augustinus en de H. Schrift.* 's-Gravenhage: Boekencentrum, s.d.

Jackson, B.D. "Semantics and Hermeneutics in St. Augustine's 'De doctrina christiana'." diss., New Haven: Yale, 1967.

Jacob, E. "À propos d'une ancienne formule sur l'unité des deux Testaments." In *Bulletin du Centre Protestant d'Études 36, 3s*, edited by R. Martin-Achard, 20-26, 1984.

Kannengiesser, C. "Local setting and motivation of De doctrina christiana." In *Collectanea Augustiniana. Augustinus. Presbyter factus sum*, edited by J.T. Lienhard, E.C. Muller and R. Teske, 331-39. New York: P. Lang, 1993.

Kato, T. "La voix chez Origène et saint Augustin." *AugLv* 40 (1990): 245-58*Fs. T. van Bavel Collectanea Augustiniana*, vol. 40, edited by B. Bruning.

Kevane, E. "Augustine's De doctrina christiana in world-historical perspective." *AugLv* 41 (1990s): 1011-31.

Luis Vizcaino, P. de. *Los hechos de Jesús en la predicación de san Agustín; la retórica clásica al servicio de la exégesis patrística*. Valladolid: EstAgust, 1983.

Marin, M. "Retorica ed esegesi in Sant'Agostino; note introduttive." *VetChr* 24 (1987): 253-68.

Mayer, C. "« Res per signa.» Der Grundgedanke des Prologs in Augustins Schrift *De doctrina christiana* und das Problem seiner Datierung." *RÉAug* 20 (1974): 100-12.

———. "Prinzipien der Hermeneutik Augustins und daraus sich ergebende Probleme." *ForKT* 1 (1985): 197-211.

———. "Herkunft und Normativität des Terminus regula bei Augustin." *Augustiniana* 40 (1990): 127-54.

McWilliam, J. *Augustine, from rhetor to theologian*. Waterloo: W. Laurier Univ., 1992.

Most, W.G. "The Scriptural Basis of St. Augustine's Arithmology." *CBQ* 13 (1951): 284-95.

O'Donovan, O. "*Usus* and *fruitio* in Augustine, De doctrina christiana I." *JTS* 33 (1981): 361-97.

Pizzolato, L.F. "Studi sull'esegesi agostiniana. I.S. Agostino 'emendator'." *RStorLettRel* 4 (1968): 338-57.

———. "Studi sull'esegesi agostiniana. II—S. Agostino « explanator »." *RStorLetRel* 4 (1968): 503-48.

Prete, B. "I principi esegetici di S. Agostino." *Sap* 8 (1955): 552-94.

Quacquarelli, A. "Il nesso 'sapientia-eloquentia' nel tratto esegetico di S. Agostino, De doctrina christiana IV." *AnStoEseg* 6 (1989): 189-202.

Riggi, C. "S. Agostino perenne maestro di ermeneutica." *Salesianum* 44 (1982): 71-101.

Ripanti, G. "Il problema della comprensione nell'ermeneutica agostiniana." *RÉAug* 20 (1974): 88-99.

———. *Agostino teorico dell'interpre-*

tazione: Filosofia della religione. TSt 3. Brescia: Paideia, 1980.

Robbins, J. *Prodigal son/elder brother; interpretation and alterity in Augustine, Petrarch, Kafka, Levinas.* Religion and Postmodernism. Chicago: Univ., 1991.

Schaeublin, C. "Augustin, De utilitate credendi, über das Verhältnis des Interpreten zum Text." *VigChr* 43 (1989): 53-68.

Schildenberger, J. "Gegenwartsbedeutung exegetischer Grundsätze des hl. Augustinus." *Augustinus Magister* (1954).

Schobinger, J.-P. "La portée historique des théories de la lecture (Réflexions à la lumière du *De doctrina christiana* de saint Augustin)." *RTPhil* 112 (1980): 43-56.

Schwoebel, B. "Augustine on Rhetoric and the Bible." *HomPastR* 72, 7 (1971s): 57-68.

Semple, W.H. "Some letters of S. Augustine (to Jerome, on exegetical questions)." *BJRylL* 33 (1950s): 111-30.

Sieben, H.J. "Die « res » der Bibel. Eine Analyse von Augustinus, *De doct. christ.* I-III." *RÉAug* 21 (1975): 72-90.

Simonetti, M. "L'ermeneutica biblica di Agostino." *Annali di storia dell'esegesi* XII (1995): 393-407.

Tabet Balady, M.A. "La hermenéutica biblica de san Agustin en la carta 82 a san Jerónimo." *Augustinus* 33 (1988): 181-93.

Trummer, P. "'Verstehst du auch, was du liest?' (Apg 8:30)." *Kairos* 22 (1980): 101-13.

Wenning, G. "Der Einfluss des Manichäismus und des Ambrosius auf die Hermeneutik Augustins." *RÉAug* 36 (1990): 80-90.

Westra, H.J. "Augustine and poetic exegesis." In *Grace, politics and desire; essays on Augustine,* edited by H.A. Meynell, 87-100. Calgary: Univ., 1990.

HOLY SPIRIT

Andreae, S. "Die Verheissung des Parakleten nach der Exegese des hl. Augustinus." Gregorianadiss. Rome, 1960.

Bentivegna, G. *Effusione dello Spirito Santo e doni carismatici; la testimonianza di S. Agostino.* Messina: Ignatianum, 1990.

_____. "Effusione dello Spirito Santo e doni carismatici; la testimonia di sant'Agostino." *AugM* 37 (1992): 396s.

Campelo, M.M. "Teologia de Pentecostés en san Agustín." *EstAgust* 22 (1987): 3-51.

Coyle, J.K. "Concordia; the Holy Spirit as bond of the two Testaments in Augustine." *AugR* 22 (1982): 427-56.

Roover, E. De. "Augustin d'Hippone et l'interprétation de Lc 1:35." *AnPraem* 45 (1969): 24-45, 149-69.

Santos Ferreira, J.M. dos. "Pneumatologia de Santo Agostinho." *Didaskalia* 13 (1983): 27-103.

INCARNATION

Bergauer, P. *Der Jakobusbrief bei Augustinus und die damit verbundenen Probleme der Rechtfertigungslehre.* Wien: Herder, 1962.

Bonner, G. "Augustine's conception of deification." *JTS* 37 (1986): 369-86.

_____. "The significance of Augustine's De gratia Novi Testamenti." *AugLv* 41 (1990s): 531-59.

La Bonnardière, A.M. "Quelques remarques sur les citations

scripturaires du *De gratia et lib. arb.*" *RÉAug* 9 (1963): 77-85.

Sage, A. "'Praeparatur voluntas a Domino'." *RÉtAug* 10 (1964): 1-20.

ISRAEL

Boyarin, D. "'This we know to be the carnal Israel' (Augustine on 1 Cor 10:18 in Adv. Jud.); circumcision and the erotic life of God and Israel." *Critical Inquiry* 18 (1992): 474-505.

Cohen, J. "The Jews as killers of Christ in the Latin tradition, from Augustine to the friars." *Traditio* 39 (1983): 1-27.

Dubois, M. "Jews, Judaism and Israel in the theology of Saint Augustine —how he links the Jewish people and the land of Zion." *Immanuel* 22s (1989): 162-214.

Springer, A. J. "Augustine's use of Scripture in his anti-Jewish polemic." diss., Southern Baptist Theol. Sem., 1989s.

Tkacz, C.B. "The Seven Maccabees, the Three Hebrews and a newly discovered sermon of St. Augustine (Mayence 50)." *RÉAug* XLI (1995): 59-78.

JOHN

Azcona, J. "Aspectos cristológicos de la humildad en los Trat. de S. Agustin sobre S. Juan." diss., Rome: Academiae Alphonsianae, 1965.

Bagur Jover, L. "La resurrección de Cristo en los 'Tractatus in Iohannis evangelium' de San Agustín." diss., Pamplona, 1989.

Berrouard, M.F. "Le Tractatus 80, 3 in Iohannis Euangelium de saint Augustin, la parole, le sacrement et la foi." *RÉAug* 33 (1987): 235-54.

————. "L'exégèse de saint Augustin prédicateur du

quatrième Évangile; le sens de l'unité des Écritures." *FreibZ* 34 (1987): 311-38.

Carleton, A.P. *John Shines Through Augustine.* Lutterworth Pr., 1960.

Clancy, F.G.J. "St. Augustine of Hippo on Christ, his Church, and the Holy Spirit; a study of the 'De Baptismo' and the 'Tractatus in Iohannis Evangelium'." diss. Oxford, 1992.

Cristiani, M. "Plus quam homo. Santità e umanità dell'Evangelista Giovanni fra Agostino e Giovanni Eriugena." In *Signum pietatis. Festgabe für Cornelius Petrus Mayer OSA zum 60. Geburtstag.*, vol. LXIV, edited by A. Zumkeller, 517-22. Würzburg: Augustinus, 1989.

Dassmann, E. "Überlegungen zu Augustinus Vorträgen über das Johannesevangelium." *TrierTZ* 78 (1969): 257-82.

Dideberg, D. "Esprit Saint et charité. L'exégèse augustinienne de 1 Jn 4, 8 et 16." *NRT* 97 (1975): 97-109, 229-50.

————. *S. Augustin et la Première Ép. de S. Jean. Une théologie de l'agapè.* Théol. Hist., vol. 34. Paris: Beauchesne, 1975.

Fernández Ramos, F. "Los signos en los Tractatus in Ioannem." *AugM* 33 (1988): 57-76.

Ferraro, G. "L'esegesi dei testi pneumatologici del Quarto Vangelo nell 'In Iohannis Evangelium tractatus' e nel 'De Trinitate' di Sant'Agostino." *Lateranum* 52 (1986): 83-214.

Folliet, G. "a) Problèmes scripturaires. b) Un passage de Tr. in Jo 44:2." *RÉAug* 5 (1959).

Gallay, J. "La conscience de la charité fraternelle d'après les Tractatus in

1 Jo de S. Augustin." *REtAug* 1 (1955): 1-20.

Grossi, V. "Il tema del 'sangue sparso' nel commento di S. Agostino al Vangelo di Giovanni." In *Atti della Settimana Sangue e antropologia biblica nella patristica*, edited by F. Vattioni, 481-93. Rome, 1982.

Hardy, R.P. *Actualité de la Révélation divine. Une étude des « Tractatus in Joh. Ev. » de S. Augustin.* Théol. Hist, vol. 28. Paris: Beauchesne, 1974.

Heintz, M. "The immateriality and eternity of the word in St. Augustine's Sermons on the Prologue of John's Gospel." In *Collectanea Augustiniana. Augustinus. Presbyter factus sum,* edited by J.T. Lienhard, E.C. Muller and R. Teske, 395-402. New York: P. Lang, 1993.

Hockey, F. "St. Augustine and John 1:3-4." *St Patr* XIV (1976): 443-45.

Le Landais, M. "La seconde partie de l'In Jo de S. Augustin et la date du commentaire." *RSR* 36 (1949): 517-41.

Mazzola, A. "Note sul commento agostiniano a Io. 13:26-27, la bucella e il traditore svelato." *VetChr* 25 (1988): 557-66.

Mosetto, F. "Esegesi agostiniana di Gv 9." *ParVi* 29 (1984): 473-80.

Nemeshegy, P. "Un passage du Tract. in Ev. Joh 15:10." *RÉAug* 34 (1988): 78s.

Noronha Galvão, H de. "Weisheitschristologie und Weisheitspneumatologie bei Augustinus; eine Untersuchung des Tractatus in Johannis Evangelium." In *Fs. J.Ratzinger, Weisheit Gottes—Weisheit der Welt,* edited by W. Baier, 651-66. St. Ottilian, 1987.

Norris, J.M. "The theological structure of Augustine's exegesis in the *Tractatus in Evangelium Iohannis.*" In *Collectanea Augustiniana. Augustinus. Presbyter factus sum,* edited by J.T. Lienhard, E.C. Muller and R. Teske, 385-94. New York: P. Lang, 1993.

Pellegrino, M. "Doppioni e varianti nel commento di S. Agostino a Giov. 21:15-19." *SMSR* 38 (1967): 403-19.

Poque, S. "Les lectures liturgiques de l'Octave Pascale à Hippone d'après les Traités de S. Augustin sur la première Épitre de S. Jean." *RBén* 74 (1964): 217-41.

Ruana de la Haza, P.-A. "El pan de vida en los 'Tractatus in Ionnem'." *AugM* 29 (1984): 95-147.

Smallbrugge, M.A. "Les notions d''enseignement' et de 'parole' dans le De magistro et l'In Ioannis Evang. Tr. 29." *AugR* 27 (1987): 523-38.

Spadafora, F. "S. Agostino esegeta e teologo nel commento al quarto Vangelo." *PalCl* 45 (1966): 321-26.

Stefano, F. "Lordship over weakness; Christ's graced humanity as locus of divine power in Augustine's tractates on the Gospel of John." *AugSt* 16 (1985): 1-19.

Studer, B. "I 'Tractatus in Ioannem' di Sant'Agostino." *Efeso* 1 (1990/1): 135-46.

————. "Spiritualitá giovannea in Agostino." In *Atti del II simposio di Efeso su S. Giovanni Apostolo,* edited by L. Padovese, 73-86. Rome, 1991/2.

Toribio, J.F. "El prólogo de san Juan en la obra de san Agustín; uso exegético y teológico." *Mayéutica* 12 (1986).

Trigueros, J.A. "El concepto de « vida » en los *Trat. sobre S. Juan* de S. Augustin." diss., Rome: Gregoriana, 1957.

Urgan, A. "Agustin de Hipona (s. IV-V, 354-430)." In *El origen divino del poder. Estudio filológico e historia de la interpretación de Jn 19:11a [Estudios de Filologia Neotestamentaria, 2]*, 105-25. Cordoba: El Almendro, 1989.

Weismann, F.J. "Introducción a la lectura e interpretación de los 'Tractatus in Iohannis Evangelium' de San Agustín." *Stromata* 42/43 (1986/7): 301-28/ 51-69.

Welch, P.-J. "Le Père et le Fils selon S. Augustin. Étude des Tractatus 1-54 sur l'Évangile de Jean." diss., Louvain-la Neuve, 1978.

Wright, D.F. "Tractatus 20-22 of St. Augustine's *in Joh.*" *JTS* 15 (1964): 317-30.

_____. "The manuscripts of the 'Tractatus in Johannem,' a supplementary list." *RechAug* 16 (1981): 59-100.

LITURGY

Dolbeau, F. "Le sermon 374 de S. Augustin sur l'Épiphanie. Édition du texte original." Philologia sacra, Fs. H.J. Frede- W.Thiele, vol. 2, edited by R. Gryson, 523-59. Vetus latina XXIV. Freiburg: Herder, 1993.

Drobner, H.R. "Die Osternachtspredigt Augustins *sermo* 221 (*Guelferbytanus 5*). Einleitung und Übersetzung." *Augustinus* XXXVIII (1993): 189-202.

Lambot, C. "Les sermons de S. Augustin sur les fêtes de Pâques (Exode)." *RScRel* 30 (1956): 230-40.

Schrama, M. "*Prima lectio quae recitata est*. The liturgical pericope in light of St. Augustine's Sermons." *Augustiniana* XLV (1995): 141-75.

NEW TESTAMENT

Altaner, B. "Augustinus und die neutestamentlichen Apokryphen, Sibyllinen und Sextusaussprüche." *AB* 67 (1949): 236-48.

_____. "Augustinus u. die neutest. Apokryphen, Sibillen und Sextussprüche." In *Kl. patrist. Schriften = TU 83*, 204-15, 1967.

Boyd, W.J.P. "Galilaea—a difference of opinion between Augustine and Jerome's 'Onomastica Sacra'." *St Patr* XV (1984): 136-9.

Petzer, J.H. "St. Augustine and the Latin version of Acts." *Neotestamentica* 25, 1 (1991): 33-50.

Willis, G.G. "St. Augustine's Text of the Acts of the Apostles." *Studia Ev.* 5 (1968): 222-25.

PAUL

Babcock, W.S. "Agustín y Ticonio; sobre la apropriación latina de Pablo." In *Congresso Oxford 1979 = AugM 26,103s 1981*, 17*-25*.

Bachmann, M. "Zum 'argumentum resurrectionis' 1 Kor 15:12ff nach Christoph Zimmer, Augustin und Paulus." *LingB* 67 (1992): 29-39.

Bammel, C.P. "Pauline exegesis, Manichaeism and philosophy in the early Augustine." In *Christian Faith and Greek Philosophy in late Antiquity. Fs. G.C. Stead (Vig Chr, Suppl. 19)*, edited by L.R. Wickham, C.P. Bammel and E.C.D. Hunter, 1-25. Leyden: Brill, 1993.

Benito y Durán, A. "S. Pablo en S. Augustin." *AugMadr* 9 (1964): 5-36.

Bochet, I. "'La lettre tue; l'Esprit vivifie,' l'exégèse augustinienne de 2 Co 3:6." *NRT* 114 (1992): 341-70.

Brandenburger, E. "Paulinische Schriftauslegung in der

Kontroverse um das Verheissungswort Gottes (Röm 9)." *ZTK* 82 (1985): 1-47.

Cole-Turner, R.S. "Anti-heretical issues in the debate over Galatians 2:11-14 in the letters of St. Augustine to Jerome." *Augustinian Studies* 11 (1980): 155-66.

Doignon, J. "La lecture de 1 Thessaloniciens 4:17 en Occident de Tertullien à Augustin." In *Mem. Stuiber A. JbAC Ergbd. 9*, 98-106. Münster, 1982.

_____. "L'exégèse latine ancienne de 1 Thessaloniciens 4:4-5 sur la possession de notre *uas*; schémas classiques et éclairages chrétiens." *BLitEc* 83 (1982): 163-77.

_____. "'Servi..facientes voluntatem Dei ex animo'(Eph 6:6), un éclatement de la notion de servitude chez Ambrose, Jerôme, Augustin." *RSPT* 68 (1984): 201-10.

Dolbeau, F. "Sermons inédits de S. Augustin prêchés en 397, 2/c, Sermo super verbis Apostoli ad Galatas." *RBén* 102 (1992): 44-63.

Doucet, L. "L'exégèse augustinienne de 1 Tm 2:4, 'Dieu veut que tous les hommes soient sauvés.'." *BFacCLyon* 73 (1984): 43-61.

Faul, D. "Ecclesia, Sponsa Christi. Origenes y Agustín ante la exégesis de Eph 5:27." *AugMd* 15 (1970): 262-80.

Ferrari, L.C. "Augustine's 'discovery' of Paul (Confessions 7.21.27)." *AugSt* 22 (1991): 37-61.

Fiestas Le-Ngoc, E. "El 'corpus paulinum' en las obras antimanqueas de San Agustin." diss. Pamplona, 1985.

Folliet, G. "Les citations de *Actes* 18:28 et *Tite* 1:12 chez Augustin." *RÉAug* 11 (1962): 293-95.

Fredricksen, P. "Augustine's Early Interpretation of Paul." diss., Princeton: Princeton, 1979.

Gerlin, A. "Comunidad y moralidad; prescripciones paulinas a los Corintios interpretadas en la Regla de san Agustín." *AugM* 36 (1991): 119-26.

Gilbride, T.V. "St. Augustine's Interpretation of the Pauline Antithesis between the Letter and the Spirit in his *De Spiritu et Littera*." diss., Cath. Univ. of America, 1968.

Gorday, P. *Principles of patristic exegesis; Romans 9-11 in Origen, John Chrysostom, and Augustine*. Studies in the Bible and Early Christianity, vol. 4, 1983.

Grasso, D. "Pietro e Paulo nella predicazione di S. Agostino." *Greg* 49 (1967): 97-112.

Hennings, R. "Der Briefwechsel zwischen Augustinus und Hieronymus und ihr Streit um den Kanon und die Auslegung von Gal 2:11-14." diss., Heidelberg, 1991s.

Journet, C. "Note sur l'Église sans tache ni ride. (Comm. Augustine in Eph 5:27)." *RThom* (1949).

La Bonnardière, A.M. "Le verset paulinien Rom 5:5 dans l'oeuvre de S. Augustin." *Augustinus Magister* (1954).

_____. "L'épître aux Hébreux dans l'oeuvre de S. Augustin." *RÉAug* 3 (1957): 137-62.

_____. "Ps 13:3 et l'interprétation de Rom 3:13-18 dans l'oeuvre de S. Augustin." *RechAug* 4 (1966): 49-65.

_____. "Recherches sur l'Ép. aux Galates dans l'oeuvre de S. Augustin." *ÉcPrat, RelAn* 80s (1971ss): 288-93.

Ladner, G.B. "St. Gregory of Nyssa and St. Augustine on the symbolism of the Cross (in luce Eph 3:18)." In *Late Class. and Mediaev. Studies,* edited by A.M. Friend, 88-95. Princeton, 1955.

Larrabe, J.-L. "El matrimonio 'en Cristo' y 'en la Iglesia' según san Agustín (Eph 5:22)." *CiuD* 200, 2 (1987).

Locher, G.F.D. "Het problem van het primaat van petrus bij Augustinus naar aanleiding van zijn uitleg van Galaten 2:11-14." *KerkT* 35 (1984): 288-304.

Lof, L. van der. "Die Autorität des Apostels Paulus nach Augustin." *AugLv* 30 (1980): 10-28.

Lyonnet, S. "Rom 5:13 chez S. Augustin." In *Mél. H. de Lubac,* 327-39. Théol. 56, 1963.

———. "A propos de Rom 5:12 dans l'oeuvre de S. Augustin. Note complémentaire." *Bib* 45 (1964): 541s.

Madec, G. "Connaissance de Dieu et action de grâces. Essai sur les citations de l'Ép. aux Rom 1:18-25 dans l'oeuvre de S. Augustin." *Recherches august.* 2 (1962): 273-309.

Mara, M.G. "Influssi polemici nella interpretazione Agostiniana di Gal 2:9." *CivClCr* 6 (1985): 391-7.

———. "Storia ed esegesi nella Expositio epistulae ad Galatas di Agostino." *AnStoEseg* 2 (1985): 93-102.

———. "Notas sobre el commentario de San Agustín a la Carta a los Romanos; exposición de algunas proposiciones de la Epist. ad Romanos." *AugM* 31 (1986): 185-94.

———. "Agostino e la polemica antimanichea. Il ruolo di Paolo e del suo epistolario." *Augustinianum* XXXII (1992): 119-43.

———. "L'interpretazione agostiniana del peccato contro lo Spirito santo nella *Epistulae ad Romanos inchoata expositio.*" In *Paideia cristiana. Fs. M. Naldini,* edited by G.A. Privitera, 235-46. Rome, 1994.

Martinetto, J. "Rom 8:28 nel « De moribus Ecclesiae catholicae » di S. Agostino." diss., Rome: Pont. Univ. Gregorianae, 1968.

McGrath, A.E. "(Rom 1:16s) 'The righteousness of God' from Augustine to Luther." *ST* 36 (1982): 63-78.

Miyatani, Y. "Spiritus und Littera bei Augustin. Eine historisch-hermeneutische Untersuchung zu 2 Kor 3:6b." diss., Heidelberg, 1972s.

Pollastri, A. "Osservazioni sulla presenza del corpus paolino nelle Quaestiones di Agostino su Deuteronomio, Giosuè e Giudici." *AnStoEseg* 9, 2 (1992): 425-66.

Quinot, B. "L'influence de l'Épître aux Hébreux dans les oeuvres principales de S. Augustin." diss., Rome: Pont. Univ. Gregoriana, 1959s.

Ries, J. *Le epistole paoline nei Manichei, i Donatisti e il primo Agostino.* Sussidi patristici, vol. 5. Rome: Augustinianum, 1989.

Stark, J.C. "The Pauline influence on Augustine's notion of the will." *VigChr* 43 (1989): 345-61.

Verwilghen, A. "L'hymne aux Philippiens dans l'oeuvre de saint Augustin." diss., P. Inst. cath., 1982.

———. *Christologie et spiritualité selon saint Augustin: l'hymne aux Philippiens.* THist, vol. 72. Paris: Beauchesne, 1985.

Prophets

Askowith, D. "Ezekiel and S. Augustine. A Comparative Study." *JBR* 15 (1947): 224-27.

Colunga, A. *S. Augustin expositor de las profecías en la Ciudad de Dios.* Estudios sobre la Ciudad de Dios, vol. 167. Ciudad de Dios, 1954.

Deléani, S. "Un emprunt d'Augustin à l'Écriture: 'Redite praevaricatores ad cor' (Isaïe 46:8b)." *RÉAug* 38 (1992): 39-49.

Ferrari, L.C. "Isaiah and the early Augustine." *AugLv* 41 (1990s): 739-56.

Geerlings, W. "Jesaia 7, 9b bei Augustinus: die Geschichte eines fruchtbaren Missverständnisses." *WissWeis* 50 (1987): 5-12.

Hermann, A. "Das steinharte Herz. Zur Geschichte einer Metapher." *JbAC* 4 (1961): 77-107.

La Bonnardière, A.M. "Les douze Petits Prophètes dans l'oeuvre de S. Augustin." *RÉAug* 3 (1957): 341-74.

Lof, L.J. van, der. "The 'prophet' Abraham in the writings of Irenaeus, Tertullian, Ambrose and Augustine." *Augustiniana* XLIV (1994): 17-29.

Mariafioti, D. *Sant'Agostino e la Nuova Alleanza. L'interpretazione agostiniana di Geremia xxxi, 31-34 nell'ambito dell'esegesi patristica. Brescia, Morcelliana.* Rome: Pontificia Università Gregoriana, 1995.

O'Connell, R.J. "Isaiah's mothering God in St. Augustine's *Confessions.*" *Thought* 58 (1983): 188-206.

Raveaux, T. *Augustinus, Contra adversarium legis et prophetarum; Analyse des Inhalts und Untersuchung des geistesgeschichtlichen Hintergrunds.* Cassiciacum, vol. 37. Wü.: Augustinus, 1984.

PSALMS

Anoz, J. "El salmo 50 en los escritos agustinianos." *AugM* 31 (1986): 293-342.

Brun, O. "'Qui me voit, voit le Père' (Jn 14:9). La place de ce verset dans la théologie d'Augustin dans les *En. in Pss.*" diss., Paris: Inst. Catholique de Paris, 1969.

Burns, P. "Augustine's distinctive use of the Psalms in the *Confessions.* The role of music and recitation." *Augustinian Studies* XXIV (1993): 133-46.

Capánaga, V. "La doctrina augustiniana de la gracia en los Salmos." *Augustinus* 5 (1960): 329-60.

_____. "La doctrina augustiniana de la gracia en los Salmos." *St Patr* VI (1962): 314-49.

_____. "El néctar de los salmos en san Agustín." *AugM* 29 (1984): 5-32.

Delamare, J. "Lorsque S. Augustin expliquait les Psaumes." *ViSpir* 82 (1950): 115-36.

Ferrari, L.C. "The peculiar appendage of Augustine's 'Enarratio in Psalmum LXI'." *AugLv* 28 (1978): 18-33.

Figueireido, F. "A teologia dos Salmos em S. Agostino." *REB* 44 (1984): 457-76.

Fischer, B. "Zur interpretatio christiana des Ps 51 in den Enarrationes in psalmos Augustins." *TrierTZ* 96 (1987): 199-206.

Folliet, G. "S. Augustin: « Enarratio in Ps 98:9.» La fortune de ce texte du Ve au XIVe siècle." In *Studi Card. M. Pellegrino,* 931-53. Turino, 1975.

Glorie, Fr. "Das 'zweite *Aenigma'* in Augustins *Opusculorum Indiculus* cap. X4, 1-4 'Tractatus Psalmorum'." In *Fs. E. Dekkers Corona Gratiarum I,* 289-309, 1975.

Grill, S. "Augustinus und die Psalmen." *Der Seelsorger* 25 (1955): 362-68.

Gruiec, P. "La catholicité de l'Église dans les « En. in Pss. » de S. Augustin." diss., Rome: Gregoriana, 1952s.

Humeau, G. *Les plus belles homélies de S. Augustin sur les Psaumes*. Paris: Beauchesne, 1947.

Imizcoz, J.M. *Cristo Rey y Sacerdote en las « En. Pss. » y « Tr. in Jo. Ev. » de S. Augustin*. Pamplona, 1959.

Jackson, M. "Formica Dei; Augustine's Enarratio in Psalmum 66:3." *VigChr* 40 (1986): 153-68.

Kannengiesser, C. "Enarratio in Ps 118: Science de la révélation et progrès spirituel." *Recherches August.* II (1962): 359-81.

Kirschner, R. "Two responses to epochal change; Augustine and the Rabbis on Ps 137 (136)." *VigChr* 44 (1990): 242-62.

Knauer, G.N. *Psalmenzitate in Augustins Konfessionen*. Vandenhoeck, 1955.

La Bonnardière, A.M. "Le Thème de la « terre » dans le Psautier d'après les « En. in Psalmos » de S. Augustin." *ÉcPratHÉt, RelAn* 78 (1970s): 293-96.

————. "Les *En. in Pss.* préchées par S. Augustin à l'occasion de fêtes de martyrs." *RechAug* 7 (1971): 73-104.

————. "Les trente-deux premières *En. in Pss.* dictées de Saint Augustin." *ÉcPratHÉt, RelAn* 79 (1971s): 281-84.

Lawless, G.P. "Psalm 132 and Augustine's monastic ideal." *Angelicum* 59 (1982): 526-39.

Lienhard, J.T. "'The glue itself is charity': Ps 62:9 in Augustine's thought." In *Collectanea Augustiniana Augustinus. Presbyter factus sum*, edited by J.T. Lienhard, E.C. Muller and R. Teske, 375-84. New York: P. Lang, 1993.

Mielgo, C. "Interpretación agustiniana de algunos salmos difficiles (149; 47; 2)." *EstAgust* 22 (1987): 261-81.

Miralles, A.J. "La Interpretación de los salmos en S. Agustin." *ScriptTPamp* 5 (1973): 789-829.

Occhialini, U. "De spe in *En. in Ps*. S. Augustini." diss., Rome: Pont. Univ. Lateranensis, 1964s.

Paciorek, P. "L'Écriture Sainte comme règle de foi et de moralité dans l'Église d'après les 'Enarrationes in Psalmos' de saint Augustin." diss., Lublin, 1991.

Perler, O. "Augustinus und die Psalmen." *Anima* 4 (1948): 289-93.

Pontet, M. "Recherches critiques sur les commentaires des Psaumes attribués à S. Jérôme et à S. Augustin. Thèse supplementaire." diss., Lyons, 1946.

Popescu, G. "Psalmii în predica Fer. (Beati) Augustin." *Studii Teol* 15 (1963): 155-72.

Poque, S. "L'alternative 'dictées ou prêchées' pour les *Enarrationes in Psalmos* de saint Augustin." *RBén* 88 (1978): 147-52.

Rondet, H. "Chronologie augustinienne. Le sermon sur le Ps 54." *HistB* 77 (1958): 403-7.

————. "Essai sur la chronologie des « En. in Pss. » de S. Augustin." *BLitE* 61 (1960): 258-86.

————. "Essais sur la chronologie des « Enarrationes in Psalmos » de S. Augustin (III) Sermons indépendants (sur les Ps 33-40)." *BLitE* 65 (1964): 110-36.

————. "S. Augustin et les « Psaumes des Montées »." *RAM* 41 (1965): 3-18.

————. "Petite introduction à la lecture des « En. in Pss »." *BFacCathLyon* 42, 89 (1967): 5-21.

Salas, A. "Una fórmula « chiástica » en S. Agustin (e.g. Mc 2:27; En in Ps 21:5; Zach 9:5; Gen 12:16)." In *Misc. Patrist. A.C. Vega*, 389-97. El Escorial, 1968.

Sanguinetti Montero, A. "Gratuidad y respuesta del hombre a Dios; estudio en las 'Enarrationes in Psalmos' de San Agustin." diss, Montevideo: Ist. Teólogica Soler, 1983.

Simonetti, M. "[Due note su testi di Agostino e] Arnobio il Giovane, Commentarii in Psalmos." *RFgIC* 119 (1991): 324-9.

Villegas, M.B. "Cuatro padres ante un psalmo. El Salmo 61 comentado por Hilario, Ambrosio, Jerónimo y Agustin." *TVida* 20 (1979): 63-75.

Vincent, M. "La prière selon saint Augustin d'après les 'Enarrationes in Psalmos'." *NRT* 110 (1988): 371-402.

_____. *Saint Augustin, maître de prière, d'après les Enarrationes in Psalmos*, 456 pp. ThH84. Paris: Beauchesne, 1990.

Weber, H. "Fluchpsalmen in augustinischer Sicht." *TGL* 48 (1958): 443-50.

_____. "Wesenszüge der Psalmenerklärung des hl. Augustinus." *TPQ* 109 (1961): 220-26.

Zarb, S. *Chronologia Enarrationum S. Augustini in Psalmos. Extractum ex « Angelicum » 12(1935) - 25(1948)*. La Valetta: St Dominic's Priory IV, 1948.

ROMANS

Anz, W. "Zur Exegese von Römer 7 bei Bultmann, Luther, Augustin." In *Fs. E. Dinkler. Theologia Crucis-Signum Crucis*, edited by C. Andresen, 1-15, 1976.

Babcock, W.S. "Augustine's Interpretation of Romans (AD 394-396)." *AugSt* 10 (1979): 55-74.

Basevi, C. "Cinco Sermones de san Agustin sobre Rom 7." *Augustinus* 35 (1990): 127-61.

_____. "Las citas de la Escritura, como recurso de estilo; estudio en los Sermones de san Agustín sobre Rom 8." *AugM* 37 (1992): 273-301.

Bonner, G. "Augustine on Rom 5:15." *Studia Ev.* 5 (1968): 242-47.

Burns, J.P. "The interpretation of Romans in the Pelagian controversy." *AugSt* 10 (1979): 43-54.

Châtillon, F. "Orchestration scripturaire (en S. Aug.—Rom 5:5)." *Rev. Moy. Âge Lat.* 10 (1954): 210-18.

González Montes, A. "La estructura teológico-fundamental de los *Sermones pascuales* de s. Agustin sobre la resurrección de Cristo." *Augustinus* XXXVIII (1993): 241-66.

Mara, M.G. "Note sul commento di Agostino alla lettera ai Romani." *AugR* 25 (1985): 95-104.

Pépin, J. "« Primitiae spiritus» (Rom 8:23). Remarques sur une citation paulinienne des Confessions de S. Augustine." *RHR* 140 (1951): 155-202.

Reid, M.I. "An analysis of Augustine's exegesis of Romans Five; a hermeneutical investigation into the contributions of Augustine's exegesis for contemporary interpretation." diss., SW Baptist Theol. Sem.

Ring, T.G. "Römer 7 in den Enarrationes in Psalmos." In *Signum pietatis. Festgabe für Cornelius Petrus Mayer OSA zum 60. Geburtstag.*, vol. LXIV, edited by A. Zumkeller, 383-407. Würzburg: Augustinus, 1989.

Veer, A. de. "Rom 14:23b dans l'oeuvre de S. Augustin (*Omne quod non est ex fide, peccatum est*)." *RechAug* 8 (1972): 149-85.

TRINITY

Bourassa, F. "Théologie trinitaire de S. Augustin." *Gregorianum* 58 (1977): 627-725.

Lof, L. van, der. "L'exégèse exacte et objective des théophanies de l'AT dans le « De Trin. »." *AugLv* 14 (1964): 485-99.

Smallbrugge, M. "Mt 3:13-17 chez Augustin, Sermon 52, vestiges de la Trinité; opposition de K. Barth." *RHPR* 69 (1989): 121-34.

Smid, F.L. "De adumbratione SS. Trinitatis in VT sec S. Augustine." *CleR* 34 (1950): 427s.

Stell, S.L. "Hermeneutics and the holy Spirit; Trinitarian insights into a hermeneutical impasse." diss., Princeton Theol. Sem., 1988.

WISDOM

Beierwaltes, W. "Augustins Interpretation von *Sap.* 11, 21." *RÉAug* 15 (1968): 51-61.

La Bonnardière, A.M. "Le Livre de la Sagesse dans l'oeuvre de S. Augustin." *RÉAug* 17 (1971): 171-75.

Marin, M. "I fideli 'chiamati alla sapienza' secondo Agostino." *VetChr* 28 (1991): 61-75.

Poque, S. "L'exégèse augustinienne de Prov 23:1-2." *RBén* 78 (1968): 117-27.

Studer, B. "Agostino d'Ippona e il Dio dei libri sapienziali." In *Letture cristiani dei Libre Sapienziali*, edited by F. Bolgiani, 115-25. Rome: Inst. Patr. Augustinianum, 1991/2.

Zocca, E. "Sapientia e libre sapienziali scritti agostiniani prima del 396." In *Letture cristiani dei Libre Sapientiaziali*, edited by F. Bolgiani, 97-114. Rome: Inst. Patr. Augustinianum, 1991/2.

WOMEN

Bavel, T.J. van. "Augustine's view of women." *AugLv* 39 (1989): 5-53.

_____. "Woman as the image of God in Augustine's *De Trinitate* XII." In *Fs C. Mayer Signum pietatis*, 267-88, 1989.

Bori, P.C. "Figure materne e Scrittura in Agostino." *AnStoEseg* 9, 2 (1992): 397-420.

Børresen, K.E. "L'anthropologie théologique d'Augustin et de Thomas d'Aquin; la typologie homme-femme dans la tradition et dans l'église d'aujour'hui." *RechSR* 69 (1981): 393-406.

_____. "L'antropologia teologica di Agostino e di Tommaso d'Aquino; sua influenza sui rapporti tra donne e uomini nella Chiesa d'oggi." In *La donna nella Chiesa oggi*, edited by A. Caprioli, 75-87; 88-105, 1981.

_____. *Subordination and equivalents. The nature and role of woman in Augustine and Thomas Aquinas.* Lanham, MD: Univ. Press of America, 1981.

_____. "In defense of Augustine; how *femina* is *homo*?" In *Collectanea Augustiniana*, edited by T. van Bavel, 411-28. Lv, 1990.

List of Contributors

MICHEL ALBARIC, O.P.

Centre national de la Recherche scientifique

Bibliothèque du Saulchoir, Paris

ANNE-MARIE LA BONNARDIÈRE

Centre national de la Recherche scientifique

Paris, Ecole Pratique des Hautes Etudes

GERALD BONNER

University of Durham, Durham

PAMELA BRIGHT

Concordia University, Montreal

MICHAEL CAMERON

Education Office, Archdiocese of Chicago

CHARLES KANNENGIESSER

Professor Emeritus of Theology, University of Notre Dame, In.

ROBERT A. KUGLER

Gonzaga University, Spokane

CONSTANCE E. MCLEESE

Université de Montréal, Montreal

ROLAND J. TESKE, S.J.

Marquette University, Milwaukee

ALBERT VERWILGHEN

Institut d'Etudes théologiques, Bruxelles

MARK VESSEY

University of British Columbia, Vancouver

JOSEPH WOLINSKI

Institut catholique, Paris

Index of Biblical References

COMPILED BY LÉON COUPAL AND GRACE ROSTIG